Visitors to Ancient America

ALSO BY WILLIAM F. MCNEIL
AND FROM MCFARLAND

*Gabby Hartnett: The Life and Times
of the Cubs' Greatest Catcher* (2004)

*The Single-Season Home Run Kings: Ruth, Maris,
McGwire, Sosa, and Bonds,* 2d ed. (2003)

*The California Winter League: America's First
Integrated Professional Baseball League* (2002)

*Cool Papas and Double Duties: The All-Time
Greats of the Negro Leagues* (2001)

*Baseball's Other All-Stars: The Greatest Players from
the Negro Leagues, the Japanese Leagues, the
Mexican League, and the Pre–1960 Winter Leagues in Cuba,
Puerto Rico and the Dominican Republic* (2000)

*Ruth, Maris, McGwire and Sosa: Baseball's Single
Season Home Run Champions* (1999)

*The King of Swat: An Analysis of Baseball's Home
Run Hitters from the Major, Minor,
Negro and Japanee Leagues* (1997)

# Visitors to Ancient America

*The Evidence for European and Asian Presence in America Prior to Columbus*

WILLIAM F. McNEIL

McFarland & Company, Inc., Publishers
*Jefferson, North Carolina, and London*

LIBRARY OF CONGRESS CATALOGUING-IN-PUBLICATION DATA

McNeil, William F.
  Visitors to ancient America: The evidence for European and Asian presence in America prior to Columbus / William F. McNeil.
    p.    cm.
  Includes bibliographical references and index.

  ISBN 0-7864-1917-2 (softcover : 50# alkaline paper)

  1. America — Discovery and exploration — Pre-Columbian.
  2. America — History — To 1810.   3. America — Antiquities.
  4. Europeans — America — History — To 1500.   5. Asians — America — History — To 1500.   6. Explorers — America — History — To 1500.   I. Title.
  E103.M45    2005
  970.01'1 — dc22                                          2004024773

British Library cataloguing data are available

©2005 William F. McNeil. All rights reserved

*No part of this book may be reproduced or transmitted in any form or by any means, electronic or mechanical, including photocopying or recording, or by any information storage and retrieval system, without permission in writing from the publisher.*

On the cover: Polynesian double-hulled canoe (oil painting by Herb Kawainui Kane)

Manufactured in the United States of America

*McFarland & Company, Inc., Publishers*
  *Box 611, Jefferson, North Carolina 28640*
    *www.mcfarlandpub.com*

To those courageous scientists who
continue to battle, against the odds,
to learn the truth about ancient America

# *Acknowledgments*

In the preparation of any manuscript, the author must rely on the assistance of many people and organizations if the work is to achieve its maximum potential.

I have been fortunate in receiving a tremendous amount of support from many directions. Frankly, I had not realized there were so many considerate people in the world, willing to go out of their way to help a stranger with a research project. Obviously, with such a response, I cannot thank everyone in these pages, but I am most appreciative for all the assistance I have received.

I would like to make a few grateful acknowledgments, however. First and foremost, I would like to thank my wife Janet for her constant support, for the many hours she spent typing the first draft (from illegible handwritten pages), and for just putting up with me throughout the project. I am also indebted to my son Michael for the long hours spent on drawings and maps, and to my daughter-in-law, Carol, for transferring many of the chapters from typed pages to a computer.

Other people who contributed significantly to my work either with their time, the use of their property, or their constant encouragement, include:

- The late David P. Barron, former president of the Gungywamp Society, who was kind enough to edit the manuscript for me, and who spent almost as much time editing the work as I did writing it.
- Earl E. Hill, Jr., of Annandale, Virginia, who did additional editing of the manuscript.
- The late James P. Whittall of the Early Sites Research Society, for permission to quote from their *Bulletin*.
- Gloria Farley, well known explorer, epigrapher and author, for permission to publish two of her photographs of ancient inscriptions.

- Mrs. Jessie Curtis, Mr. and Mrs. Garrett Hobart, and Mr. Walter Cyr, for permission to study their stone chambers.
- The Runestone Museum in Kensington, Minnesota, for the photograph of the Kensington Stone.
- J. Huston McCulloch, of Ohio State University, for permission to use his Newark Decalogue Stone and Keystone photos, as well as for his comments regarding many of the ancient America artifacts.
- Mr. Joseph Blaine and the Newport Historical Society, for their cooperation during my study of the Newport Tower.
- The National Geographic Society, for permission to quote from their magazine.
- Professor George Carter, of Texas A & M University, for his valuable information and constructive criticism.
- The Alaska State Museum in Juneau, for information pertaining to the Chinese coin discovery.
- Bord Failte, the Irish Tourist Board, and the Office Of Public Works, for the generous gift of numerous photographs of ancient Irish monuments.
- E. Grimstad, superintendent of the Viking Ship Museum in Roskilde, Denmark, for the photograph of the Viking Knorr.
- The Sherbrooke Seminary Museum, for information regarding the inscribed stones.
- Tom Mahoney of Argyle, New York, for information regarding the stone ruins in eastern New York.
- Salvatore M. Trento, for permission to quote from his book, *The Search for Lost America*.
- Malcolm D. Pearson for his excellent photographs of various stone structures and artifacts.
- Dr. Anne Ross of the University of Southampton, England, for her comments pertaining to the Vermont stone chambers, and the alleged Ogam inscriptions.
- The Yarmouth County Museum, Nova Scotia, for the photograph of the Yarmouth Stone, and for information about its discovery.
- The late Thor Heyerdahl, for permission to publish photographs of his oceangoing vessels.

- Herb Kawainui Kane, Hawaiian artist, for permission to use on the cover of this book (and on page 19) a photograph of his painting of a double hulled Polynesian canoe, and for his helpful comments on the chapter pertaining to the Polynesian explorations and settlement of the Pacific islands.

# Contents

*Acknowledgments* vii
*Introduction* 1

### PART I : THE INTERCONTINENTAL CONNECTIONS

1. The Sun Sets on American Archaeology — 7
2. Making the Impossible Possible — 15
3. Vikings: The People and the Legend — 41
4. Vikings: The American Evidence — 64
5. The Ancient Writers — 89
6. Legendary Travelers of the Ocean — 99
7. The Ancient Mariners — 115

*Interlude* 139

### PART II : EXPLORING ANCIENT AMERICA

8. America's Stonehenge at Mystery Hill — 145
9. The Great Stone Chamber Mystery — 159
10. Ancient Stone Monuments of America — 188
11. Inscriptions: Ancient Messages or Modern Frauds? — 202
12. Ancient Artifacts in North America — 236

13. Mound Builders and the American Indian: Where Do They Fit In? 246
14. The Secret of Ancient America 271

*Chapter Notes* 285
*Bibliography* 289
*Index* 297

# Introduction

Five hundred and twelve years ago, a daring young sea captain named Christopher Columbus sailed from the port of Palos, Spain, with three ships and 110 men, in search of a shorter route to the Indies, thought to be west across the Atlantic Ocean. On October 12, 1492, the intrepid explorer set foot on the island of San Salvador and was greeted by friendly inhabitants. He called them Indians, thinking he had reached his destination.

Over the next 200 years, the exploration and colonization of the Western Hemisphere proceeded slowly and deliberately, with Spain, France, and Great Britain all claiming specific parts of the continents. Spain established settlements in South America, Central America, and what would become Cuba, Mexico, California, and Florida. Great Britain explored the east coast of North America, while France, a late entry in the colonization stampede, claimed the future Louisiana and parts of Canada.

Explorations continued throughout the sixteenth and seventeenth centuries, with the Mississippi River being discovered by Hernando De Soto in 1533, followed by visits to the Kentucky and Ohio region by the French explorer LaSalle in 1669. The first settlement in Missouri dates to 1735. At first, life in the territories was a matter of survival, with no time for outside activities, but, once life became settled, people began to take note of the many strange artifacts that littered the landscape. Thousands of immense earthen mounds decorated the eastern part of the country, from as far north as Canada to as far south as the Gulf of Mexico. Many of the mounds were pyramid shaped and resembled the stone monuments erected by the pharaohs of Egypt over 4,000 years ago. The Indians claimed no knowledge of these mounds, and some of them, in fact, said they were built by a race of people who inhabited the country before their ancestors arrived.

Unusual stone constructions such as chambers, dolmens, and menhirs blanketed the northeast section of the country, and stones containing strange inscriptions were found everywhere. Historians had struck a bonanza, and they attacked with vigor. They scurried around the countryside excavating mounds, studying the strange artifacts, recording the mysterious inscriptions, and writing books detailing the discoveries and pondering their secrets. All clues seemed to lead to a single conclusion: that America had been visited by Europeans thousands of years ago.

The beginning of American archaeology can be traced back to the late seventeenth century when a Massachusetts clergyman named Cotton Mather found an inscribed stone in nearby Fall River, and sent a copy of the inscription to the Royal Academy in London. From that time, until the early twentieth century, there was considerable activity in the eastern half of the country as men strove to learn the secret of ancient America. At first it was an avocational pursuit, since survival was still a full-time job for American colonists. Later it became a profession, with universities training young men and women in many scientific fields including anthropology and archaeology. One of the first men to be called an archaeologist was a wealthy landowner and lawyer named Thomas Jefferson. The future president of the United States was fascinated by the many earthen mounds that existed in Virginia, and he proceeded to excavate one of the mounds, doing so in a scientific manner and keeping a detailed record of his work. He concluded, after studying the artifacts, as well as the cultures and languages of the Indians, that they had had contact with Europeans sometime in the distant past.

Caleb Atwater, called the father of American archaeology, spent a lifetime studying the ancient mounds in the Midwest, and publishing the first scientific study of pre–Columbian antiquities in America in 1820. Henry Rowe Schoolcraft, an ethnologist, explorer, and Indian agent, in the employ of the U.S. Congress after spending more than 40 years studying the Indians, published his findings in a multi-volume work titled *Historical and Statistical Information Respecting the History, Conditions, and Prospects, of the Indian Tribes of the United States* in 1857.

Ephraim George Squier, a newspaper editor, and Dr. E.H. Davis, a medical doctor, studied and surveyed hundreds of man-made earthworks in the Midwest, publishing their historical work titled *Ancient Monuments of the Mississippi Valley* in 1848. Their work is particularly important because many of the monuments they surveyed and diagrammed have since been destroyed by urban encroachment.

The Icelandic Sagas were being widely published during the middle of the nineteenth century, and they recounted in minute detail the stirring adventures of Viking seafarers along the coast of North America. Numerous studies of possible Viking intrusions into the United States were conducted by Scandinavian archaeologists as well as American scientists. One of the most intriguing artifacts was a round stone tower in

Newport, Rhode Island, that was alternately identified as an eleventh century Viking tower or a colonial windmill. Another interesting artifact was the inscribed stone first discovered by Cotton Mather.

During this same period, John Wesley Powell, a Civil War hero, explorer, and archaeologist, was appointed the first director of the Smithsonian Institution's Bureau of Ethnology, and he began a vigorous program to excavate the earthen mounds in eastern America. Cyrus Thomas, a botanist, was hired by Powell to supervise the excavations, and over a five year period between 1883 and 1888, his team excavated more than 2,000 mounds, carefully documenting the work, cataloging the artifacts, and shipping them back to the Smithsonian Institution in Washington, D.C. Thomas' report, *The 12th Annual Report of the Department of Ethnology to the Secretary of the Smithsonian Institution*, concluded that the mounds were the work of the ancestors of the Indians.

Archaeology was becoming a fascinating subject around the world in the nineteenth and twentieth centuries in countries like Mexico, Greece, Turkey, and Egypt. An Italian adventurer named Giovanni Battista Belzoni made the find of the millennium in 1817 when he uncovered the tomb of Seti I, in the Valley of the Kings. The tomb of that Egyptian pharaoh, who ruled from 1301 to 1290 BCE, was the most beautiful tomb ever discovered, and the find unleashed a stream of scientific activity in the region. In 1870, German archaeologist Heinrich Schliemann confirmed the Homeric legend of Troy when he discovered the ancient city on the Turkish coast. Six years later he conducted excavations at Mycenae in Greece. British archaeologist Howard Carter made a discovery in 1922 that dwarfed Belzoni's, when he found the tomb of Tutankhamen, one of the last pharaohs of the eighteenth dynasty, in the Valley of the Kings. King Tut's tomb contained more than 5,000 magnificent artifacts, far surpassing Seti I's tomb, which had been looted in antiquity.

The fascination with American archaeology continued into the twentieth century, when it suddenly ground to a halt. The focus of the archaeological community, with the exception of a few scientists who were working primarily in the Southwest, shifted to Egypt, Greece, Turkey, and Mexico. For more than 40 years, academic apathy regarding possible intrusions into ancient America by European mariners permeated the scientific community, with few studies being conducted, and a minimum of field work being done. Thor Heyerdahl, a Norwegian archaeologist, reawakened the interest in the early history of America in 1947 when he sailed an Inca-style seagoing raft, the Kon-Tiki, from Callao, Peru, to Papeete, Tahiti, across 4,300 miles of the hostile Pacific Ocean, proving that ocean travel in ancient times was possible.

Fourteen years later, one of the most important discoveries yet made in North America was credited to Helge Ingstad, a Norwegian lawyer, explorer and historian. After years of study and exploration, in 1961 he discovered a Viking settlement in L'Anse aux Meadows, Newfoundland, dating it to approximately 1000 CE.

A Viking coin from the period 1000 to 1075 CE was found in an Indian midden at the Goddard site on Naskeag Point in Brooklin, Maine, in 1957. The coin proved that there was at least contact between the aborigines in the United States and the Vikings, centuries before Columbus arrived.

In 1965, Betty Meggers, a research archaeologist at the Smithsonian Institution, reported on an exciting find she and her team made in Ecuador. At a site called Valdivia, she recovered fragments of pottery duplicating that made by the Jomon culture in Japan more than 5000 years ago. She theorized that there had been transpacific contact between Japan and Ecuador by 2500 BCE.

Other interesting discoveries made in caves, river beds, and mounds in the United States over the past 50 years include several skeletons and mummies of questionable race. Columbus' identification of the aborigines he met in San Salvador as "Indians" was an obvious misnomer. However, their new designation as "Native Americans" may also be a misnomer based on recent studies of ancient remains.

In 1940, a mummy was unearthed in Spirit Cave, near Fallon, Nevada. The male skeleton, dating to 7000 BCE, did not resemble either today's Indians or their Asian ancestors. Another skeleton, recovered from the Columbia River, near Kennewick, Washington, was dated to 9000 BCE and has Caucasoid features, not Asian.

The Twenty-first century promises to be an exciting time in the fields of American anthropology and archaeology, as the secrets of ancient America are finally revealed. Who were the first people to enter the country? Where did they come from? When did they arrive? How did they get here? These questions and more will be answered in the decades to come. As Dennis Stanford, the chairman of the anthropology department of the National Museum of Natural History, Smithsonian Institution, said, "We are rewriting the textbooks on the first Americans. The peopling of the Americas was never as simple as simple-minded paradigms said."[1]

# Part I

# The Intercontinental Connections

# 1

# *The Sun Sets on American Archaeology*

The history of early America is still being uncovered after more than 500 years of foreign occupation and settlement. Prior to the nineteenth century, there was only sporadic interest in the strange artifacts, stone monuments, and earthen structures that dot the American landscape. People of the seventeenth and eighteenth centuries were more interested in carving out an existence for themselves than in pondering the strange rock inscriptions that resembled alphabetic writing. Searching for food was more important than searching for ancient relics in the man-made mounds. Men who had curious minds, and the time to satisfy that curiosity, were few and far between. There were two such men, however, who deserve notice.

In 1689, a Puritan clergyman in Massachusetts noticed odd looking inscriptions on a rock located in the town of Dighton. The Reverend Cotton Mather meticulously recorded the inscription and mailed it to the Royal Academy in London. It created little or no interest in staid old England. The Academy did publish it in their periodical, but it was soon forgotten along with most things of a historical nature that were reported from the colonies. It is unfortunate that the England of 1700 ignored the goings-on in America, but there were more important things to discuss at home. The result of this indifference was that a significant amount of valuable information pertaining to the early history of this country was carelessly discarded in England, or filed away in musty old boxes and, perhaps, lost forever.

As the years passed, America gained her independence, and began to establish her own identity. The frontiers expanded, civilization grew, and all segments of society went through an evolutionary period of growth and refinement. The sciences also grew and developed in America during this period. In fact, in the late eighteenth century, Thomas Jefferson, one of the major architects of American independence, became interested in the early history of his new country and in the aborigines who possessed this land before the Europeans arrived. He studied the Indian cultures and languages in great detail, and was of the opinion that there had been contact between these people and the Europeans at some time in the distant past. His interest in the prehistoric natives of America led him to a study of the large earthen mounds that were prevalent in Virginia. He heard many stories identifying these mounds as mausoleums of a vanished race. His curiosity piqued, Jefferson decided to excavate one of the mounds in order to verify the stories. His method of excavation was scientifically sound, logical, and painstaking, as revealed in his notes. "I first dug superficially in several parts of it, and came to collections of human bones.... I proceeded then to make a perpendicular cut through the body of the barrow, that I might examine its internal structure. This passed about three feet from its centre, was opened to the former surface of the earth, and was wide enough for a man to walk through and examine its sides."[1]

Many of Jefferson's procedures were subsequently incorporated into the accepted practices of the archaeological profession, giving him the honor of being America's first archaeologist. Unfortunately for the scientific community, his work was interrupted by a call to duty. His country drafted him to be its third president in 1801. He served eight successful years in that office, and continued to be active in politics until his death in 1826, at the age of 83. He was never able to renew his Indian studies.

Except for Mather, Jefferson, and a few other isolated individuals, American archaeology languished until the beginning of the nineteenth century. Then Caleb Atwater appeared on the scene. In some circles, Atwater is considered to be the "Father of American Archaeology." It is a title he probably deserves, since he did publish the first preliminary scientific study of pre–Columbian antiquities in America. His work gave the necessary impetus to a burgeoning interest in our prehistory. Caleb Atwater was born in Ohio in 1778, and spent most of his life in that area. Like other men of his time, he was primarily self educated. His formal schooling was scant, amounting to a few years in the typical one-room schoolhouse. But he had a natural curiosity about people, and about his environment. From early boyhood he was interested in the earthen mounds that were widespread in his state, and he spent much of his free time studying them. When he became postmaster of Circleville, Ohio, he became even more fascinated with the ancient man-made works. Circleville had received its name from the two prehistoric earthen circles around which the town was built in 1806. It is unfortunate that all signs of these circles have been destroyed in the ensuing 192 years. They apparently had

## 1. The Sun Sets on American Archaeology

The Great Mound, Miamisburg, Ohio.

Earthworks, Hopeton, Ohio.

A sampling of the great variety of earthworks that greeted the first European pioneers to North America.

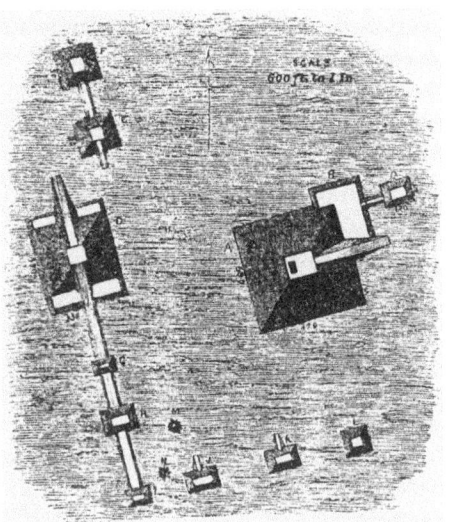

Earthworks, Washington County, Mississippi.

Ancient works at Marietta, Ohio.

significant religious meaning to the ancient natives of the area. Travel and study became Atwater's all-consuming avocation. He visited many structures in the Midwestern states, carefully studying each structure, recording all known facts. Finally, in 1820, he presented the results of his work in the publication *Archaeologia Americana*, in an article titled "Description of the Antiquities Discovered in the State of Ohio and Other Western States" (see illustration). Atwater concluded that the earthworks were not built by the Indians, but were built by a separate race entirely. No one in the scientific community even raised an eyebrow at such a conclusion in 1820. It seemed like a perfectly logical explanation at that time, based on the known facts. Atwater died in 1867 at the age of 89, but he left us his legacy: a curiosity to uncover the rich prehistory of our country.

Another gentleman who appeared on the scene during the first half of the nineteenth century was Henry Rowe Schoolcraft, perhaps the most important contributor to early American history to date. Schoolcraft was born in New York state in 1793, and graduated from Schenectady College, New York, after majoring in mineralogy. Following college and a tour of duty in the United States Army during the War of 1812, Schoolcraft immersed himself completely in his new career. He spent many years in the employ of the United States government as a mineralogist and geologist. His work carried him to all parts of the Midwest and stimulated his interest in the American Indian. At one time he held the position of Indian Agent for the government, living with the Indians in their natural habitat, beyond the encroachment of European culture. He respected the Indians as a people, and learned to appreciate their way of life. He even married an Indian woman.

Over a period of 40 years, Schoolcraft became America's foremost explorer and ethnologist. He carefully observed and studied the Indian society, recording their knowledge, their myths, and their traditions in minute detail. On one of his exploratory trips to northern Minnesota, he discovered one of the sources of the Mississippi River at Lake Itaska, a discovery that brought him considerable recognition within the scientific community. It also brought him a new appointment as superintendent of Indian affairs for the State of Michigan. Schoolcraft by that time was well established in his professional career, a respected explorer, archaeologist, and ethnologist. His reputation and influence spread around the world. In 1842, he and Albert Gallatin founded the American Ethnological Society. His crowning achievement followed several years later when he published his major work, *History, Condition, and Prospects of the Indian Tribes of the United States*, for the Ethnological Society. The work was published in six mammoth volumes, from 1851 to 1857. It is a major contribution to our knowledge of early America, covering the history, myths, and traditions of the Indians, as well as commenting on all known evidence of European visits to ancient America. It pointed out how little was known about the man-made mounds at that time.

Two residents of Ohio who were contemporaries of Schoolcraft also made a significant contribution to American archaeology during this same period. They were Ephraim George Squier and Dr. E.H. Davis. Squier was born in Bethlehem, New York, in 1821, and began his career as a journalist first in New York, then in Connecticut. After witnessing the demise of his newspaper in Hartford, Connecticut, Squier moved to Chillicothe,

Ohio, where he made his permanent residence. As the editor of the *Scioto Gazette*, he became an influential and respected member of the Ohio community. He soon made the acquaintance of Dr. E.H. Davis, a local physician, the two becoming fast friends. Both Squier and Davis had been intrigued by the man-made mounds that were frequent anomalies in middle America. Like Caleb Atwater before them, they were hypnotically drawn to these works time after time. Eventually they decided to conduct a systematic investigation of the mounds, hoping to identify the race of people who built them and to learn something about the Mound Builders' society and its ultimate fate. Their work was subsidized by the American Ethnological Society.

Over the next several years, Squier and Davis rigorously explored several hundred man-made earthworks. They became expert surveyors and made detailed measurements and drawings of the mounds and other earthen structures, carefully documenting all dimensions and other noteworthy data. They also made valuable contour maps of the areas under study. In addition to the survey, hundreds of controlled excavations were carried out, the interior of the mounds were meticulously mapped, and the artifacts found in the mounds were studied in great detail, being carefully catalogued and protected for future scientific research. Piece by piece, Squier and Davis worked their jigsaw puzzle, comparing one mound to another and one geographical area to another. When their study was completed, they concluded that the Mound Builders were a separate race from the Indians and superior to them , and had developed a civilized society, a society that originated in the north and spread south, constantly increasing its skills as it grew. It eventually reached its height in the great ancient civilizations in Mexico.

The results of Squier and Davis' work were published in 1848 under the title *Ancient Monuments of the Mississippi Valley*. The book was the first publication of the newly formed Smithsonian Institution's *Contributions of Knowledge* series. Interestingly, five of the first eight volumes of the Smithsonian publication dealt with the Mound Builders. Their work was warmly received by the scientific community and was regarded as the most complete compilation of ancient earthworks ever assembled. It became a valuable catalogue of the mounds and earthworks of the Mississippi Valley and was subsequently utilized by several generations of archaeologists. Many of the structures detailed in the book have since been destroyed by the relentless encroachment of civilization, but fortunately a permanent record of these relics has been saved for posterity.

Next on the scene was John Wesley Powell, who was born in New York State in 1834, the son of an immigrant minister from England. After several relocations, the family finally settled in Illinois. As a child, Powell was an excellent student, being proficient in the arts and sciences. He loved the classics, and was an avid naturalist. Like many of his predecessors, his attention was drawn to the ancient earthworks and, as a teenager, he began digging in the mounds. The artifacts he uncovered, such as arrowheads, stone implements, and glass beads, fueled his interest. During this period, he also came in contact with the Winnebago Indians, devouring and digesting as much information about the red man as he could gather from firsthand observation and conversation. He supplemented his information about the Mound Builders and the Indians by reading as many books as he could get his hands on, including the works of Caleb Atwater and Thomas Jefferson. This period in his life began a lifelong love affair with early American history, and he became one of the nation's foremost experts on the Mound Builders and the Indians.

As he continued to observe the Indians, Powell developed a sympathy for the problems they had incurred since the arrival of the white man. He gained an appreciation for their way of life and their philosophy. He also realized they were a highly intelligent people, not at all like the barbaric savages described in the documents emanating from the official government agencies in Washington, D.C. For about seven years, Powell increased the geographical area of his interest to include mounds not only in Illinois, but also in Missouri, Indiana, and Ohio. He continued to add to his collection of relics, which now included stone tools, shells, pottery, bone artwork, and copper ornaments. Initially, Powell believed that the Mound Builders were a separate race from the Indians, and very ancient. As the years passed, however, his beliefs changed, and he became convinced that the mounds were built after the white man began to colonize the country. The reason for his mistaken belief was the fact that European and Indian objects were found intermixed near the top of some mounds, indicating trade between modern European explorers and the Indians. What he failed to realize was that a mound was not built in its entirety at one specific time. A mound was usually built in stages and might cover a period of 1,000 years or more, from the first burial to the last layer of covering earth. There could be articles near the surface of the mound indicating a date of 1800 CE, while the base of the mound could date back to 800 CE, or even earlier.

The Civil War interrupted Powell's career, as it did with thousands of other young men in both the North and the South. Powell enlisted in the Union army at the outbreak of hostilities, was commissioned an officer, and was given command of an artillery battery. He distinguished himself in the service, fighting valiantly at Shiloh, where his right arm was shat-

## 1. The Sun Sets on American Archaeology

tered during the battle. Instead of returning home, Powell insisted on being reactivated following amputation of his arm, and he served gallantly for the remainder of the war, retiring from the army as a major in 1865. Returning to Illinois, he accepted a professorship at Illinois Wesleyan University, teaching geology. He also continued to explore the western wilderness during the summer months. In May 1869, he formed an expedition to navigate 900 miles of uncharted waters on the Colorado River. The trip was sponsored by the Smithsonian Institution and therefore received widespread publicity. Three men were killed by Indians during the trip, but Powell and the remainder of the party emerged successfully from Black River Canyon in late summer. John Wesley Powell was beginning to attract attention within the Smithsonian Institution hierarchy.

Most of his mound excavation work was now behind him, but his study of the Indians was on the increase, particularly those tribes in the western part of America. He studied many Indian vocabularies at the request of John Henry of the Smithsonian Institution, and published numerous volumes of the various tribal languages. Powell's enthusiasm for Indian studies and his influence with John Henry eventually paid dividends. The United States government appropriated funds that led to the creation of the Bureau of Ethnology of the Smithsonian Institution on March 3, 1879, and John Wesley Powell became its first director. The primary objective of the Bureau of Ethnology was to conduct extensive studies of the Indians.

Two years after the creation of the bureau of Ethnology, Cyrus Thomas joined the bureau. Thomas was born and raised in southern Illinois. Prior to joining the Bureau, he worked as a botanist for the Geological and Geographical Survey of the Territories. Now Powell needed him to resolve, once and for all, the identity of the American Mound Builders. Cyrus Thomas was given full responsibility for exploration of the mounds east of the Rocky Mountains, a budget of $5,000, three full-time assistants, and five part-time workers. There were 10,000 mounds east of the Rocky Mountains, quite a challenge for a group of nine people. Thomas attacked the mounds with a vigor unmatched in the field of archaeology. During the first year, his team excavated mounds in parts of eight states, including Georgia, Alabama, Arkansas, Tennessee, North Carolina, Illinois, Iowa, and Missouri. Thomas himself spent most of his time in Washington, D.C., directing activities from afar, while his three assistants ran amok in the field. The program proceeded at a frenetic pace, rapidly moving from one geographical locale to another, to take advantage of favorable weather conditions. Over a period of five years, the group explored over 2,000 mounds, an average of more than one mound per day.

The excavations were completed by 1888, and Cyrus Thomas set to work to compile the data in an organized form. This took several more years, during which time Powell and the Smithsonian hierarchy waited patiently. Finally in 1894, *The Twelfth Annual Report of the Bureau of Ethnology to the Secretary of the Smithsonian Institution* was published. It was over 700 pages long, and was devoted entirely to Cyrus Thomas' mound excavations. Thomas concluded that the Mound Builders were ancestors of the Indians.

Shortly after Cyrus Thomas' mound excavation report was issued, interest in early American archaeology waned. The conclusion that the ancient mounds and other monuments littering the landscape of the United States had been constructed by ancestors of the Indians and not by some unknown prehistoric race dulled the curiosity of the scientific community. In other parts of the world, monumental discoveries were being made. In Egypt, intensive excavations in the Nile Valley had uncovered many tombs of important pharaohs containing fabulous wealth in gold. Excavations in Ninevah, Pompeii, Mycenae, and Troy stirred the imaginations of American archaeologists and sent them scurrying to foreign lands, while ancient American history received little attention.

As the twentieth century got underway, archaeology in the United States descended into the scientific equivalent of the Dark Ages, and American scientists expended their resources on excavations in Mexico, Egypt, Turkey, and Greece. There were very few archaeological research programs being conducted in the United States, and essentially no excavations. The prehistoric mounds that littered the countryside were ignored completely, and exciting discoveries were brushed aside by the scientists. It would be more than 50 years before the sun would shine again on America's early history.

# 2

# *Making the Impossible Possible*

The previous chapter chronicled the demise of American archaeology. The format for the rest of this book will be somewhat different. Each chapter will begin with the conventional viewpoint of one particular phase of early American history, pertaining to the question of whether or not ancient European mariners visited America prior to the arrival of Christopher Columbus. The subject will then be studied in detail, presenting all the known facts, and the chapter will conclude with a summary of the findings and the author's conclusion based on the evidence presented.

## Conventional Thinking

Many people believed it was impossible for Europeans to visit ancient America because their flimsy vessels were not seaworthy enough to withstand the severe battering of a transoceanic voyage. They also believed the ancients had no sophisticated navigational instruments to guide them.

## Discussion

In grade school math class, students are taught that the whole is made up of the sum of its parts. So, too, in archaeology. In order to properly evaluate our theory, a number of important questions will have to be answered:

1. Was the distance required to travel from Europe to America short enough to allow a transatlantic crossing, while permitting the mariners to maintain adequate supplies, including proper rations of food and water?

2. Were the ocean currents and winds supportive of ocean voyages from Europe to America, and the required return voyage from America to Europe?
3. Is there any evidence that ancient voyages to America could have been accomplished in the type of ships that were utilized by the ancient European maritime nations?

The answer to the first question is simple enough. The narrowest point across the south Atlantic is from the west coast of Africa, north of the Gulf of Guinea, to Brazil on the east coast of South America. The distance is approximately 1,750 miles and, with the favorable current of the North Equatorial Stream, could be traversed in less than three weeks. This situation would certainly cause no problem with supplies, since large seagoing vessels were capable of storing enough food and water for several months.

A much more difficult task confronted the mariners from Asia who colonized the islands in the Pacific Ocean almost 2,000 years ago. Shortly after the discovery of America, the European pioneers gradually worked their way west across the continents of North and South America to the shores of the Pacific Ocean. Exploration of the Pacific islands followed, and much to their surprise, the explorers found most of the islands in the central Pacific already inhabited — and by the same race of people. The Europeans called the area Polynesia, meaning "Land of Many Islands." Some of the islands were separated by several thousand miles of open ocean. The fact that many islands were all inhabited by one race had profound implications. The ancestors of these people must have had a common origin, a common homeland, and they must have been transported across the ocean in some sort of oceangoing vessels at some time in the past. But when? And how?

Polynesia covers an immense area in the central Pacific Ocean, approximately 15 million square miles in size. Until 1500 BCE, none of these islands were inhabited. They were empty, desolate specks of land in the midst of a vast world of water. Yet, only 3,000 years later, when Europeans first explored these islands, they found them inhabited by a handsome, brown skinned, Caucasoid people, who claimed their ancestral home was somewhere in the far west.

Who were these people? Where did they come from? When did they settle in Polynesia? And how did they get there? Archaeologists believe they know the answers to all these questions, and more. J.E. Weckler, reporting for the Division of Ethnology of the U.S. National Museum, summed up the discovery and development of Polynesia for the United States government during World War II:

## 2. Making the Impossible Possible

> The Polynesians, who were the first human inhabitants of the far-flung mid–Pacific islands, were the most daring deep-sea voyagers and explorers the world has ever known. In the double-hulled ships they fashioned with stone tools, they sailed by stages across the widest part of the unknown Pacific, from Southeastern Asia, probably all the way to the coast of Peru. They did this centuries before Columbus ventured into the Atlantic, even before those great mariners, the Vikings, found their way by comparatively short island-to-island voyages, across the north Atlantic, to the New World. And the Polynesians found and populated every habitable island in the vast expanse between Hawaii on the north, New Zealand on the south, Easter Island on the east, and Tonga and Samoa on the west. What is more, they succeeded in bringing their domestic animals and their vegetable foods, some of which could be transported only as delicate young plants, to the isolated dots of land they found so widely scattered in the great reaches of the ocean world.
>
> These facts show, beyond doubt, that we must credit the Polynesians with purposeful exploration and settlement of the Pacific islands. If, as has sometimes been alleged, their long voyages had been accidental — a boat load of fishermen now and again blown before a storm — the castaways would not have had with them, the women to propagate the race, for women did not participate in deep-sea fishing. Neither would they have had the food plants and animals which they had spread throughout the islands, when the Europeans first encountered them. It is doubtlessly true that new islands were occasionally discovered by castaways who made their way back home, and later returned to settle. Polynesian legendary history gives us some such accounts. But that same history tells us of brave mariners who built exploring ships, stocked them like Polynesian arks, and set out in search of new homes upon the wide ocean.[1]

The study of Polynesia has been an ongoing project by the scientific community for over 60 years. Many diverse disciplines have probed the complex society of the central Pacific, including engineers, anthropologists, archaeologists, botanists, and linguists. They have crossed and recrossed the 15 million square miles, searching for answers. Answers have come, little by little. Eventually the scientists were able to trace the migration of the natives living on these islands from their previous homes in the western Pacific to their present homes, by combining their vast pool of technical and scientific information. A major clue was the discovery of a unique type of pottery as reported by Kenneth P. Emory.

> Beginning in 1909 in New Britain, archaeologists have found a type of prehistoric decorated pottery at various Melanesian sites. Edward W. Gifford, in 1947, excavated samples in Fiji, Melanesia's easternmost extension. Five years later, he and Dr. Richard Shutler, Jr., uncovered the same type at Lapita in New Caledonia. Now called Lapita-type pottery, these artifacts clearly trace the visits and attempted settlements of a maritime people moving along a Melanesian route toward Polynesia. Lapita pottery was excavated

by Dr. Jens Poulsen in Tonga in 1963–64, and has been recently found in Samoa as well — both in Western Polynesia.[2]

Ashes from ancient Polynesian fires have been radiocarbon-dated as far back as 1100 BCE, and reveal a continuing eastward movement with time. These ashes were found in conjunction with many stone tools and implements that were originally developed in Southeast Asia. Language was another clue to the Pacific adventure. Although the Polynesians had developed their own language over the centuries, the roots of their language indicate that it originated in Southeast Asia, probably Indonesia. According to the scientists, there is no evidence of human habitation in any of the central Pacific islands prior to colonization by the Polynesians.

The story of the Polynesians, as pieced together by world scientists, may have begun in the lower valley of the Ganges River in India, but if so, they had migrated to Indonesia thousands of years before the birth of Christ. Sea travel in this area had been common since early times. For example, Australia was discovered and colonized by people from the mainland, traveling across open water as long ago as 40,000 years. Similarly, mariners visited and settled New Guinea about 25,000 years ago. The first Polynesian migration took place about 1500 BCE, when a contingent of natives left their mainland home and settled in New Guinea. Among other things, these people were pottery makers, designing and constructing the distinctive Lapita pottery mentioned earlier. This pottery helped to trace their migration across the Pacific. In conjunction with radiocarbon dates from the ashes of ancient fires, scientists were able to plot the direction of the migration, island to island, and to determine the approximate date of settlement of each island.

The reason for the Polynesian migration is unknown, although one theory proposes that the people were forced to flee the mainland before an invading army of Mongoloids from the north. New Guinea was only a temporary home, however, and by 1300 BCE the migration had spread to the Fiji Islands, on the eastern fringe of Melanesia. Before long, Fiji was left behind, and the adventurers had moved into Western Polynesia, settling in Samoa and Tonga. Tonga was settled perhaps as early as 1100 BCE, and Samoa about the same time. The initial explorations were not very difficult because the islands in the western Pacific are mountain ranges of a submerged continent and, as such, lie close together and are visible for long distances. As travel proceeded beyond Fiji to the east, the islands became smaller, flatter, and farther apart, almost impossible to see in the endless ocean. Now the art of ship construction became of paramount importance, and required another leap forward in technology.

Polynesian mariners discovered that, if they ventured too far out into the ocean, the water became much rougher and the waves much higher, and occasionally swamped the boat. Oceangoing vessels had to be redesigned. They had to have more freeboard, that is, more distance from the surface of the water to the top of the gunwale, to prevent swamping. They also had to be larger and stronger in order to survive long ocean voyages. They needed to have sufficient room for colonists, animals and supplies. To solve this problem, the seafarers replaced the outrigger with a second canoe. Then they built a large platform between the two canoes to carry the supplies. The resulting configuration was the famous double-hulled canoe (see illustration). The Polynesians constructed exceptionally sturdy canoes. The hulls were made of a suitable wood found on the islands, and were held together by a rope made from coconut fiber. The hull was subsequently caulked with breadfruit sap to make it watertight. Plaited leaves made up the sail, and these were fastened to the mast with the same coconut fiber rope. These large oceangoing vessels "were commonly 60 to 80 feet long, and some were over 100 feet. In these big ships, the log that formed the entire hull of a small family canoe, and most of the hull of a

Polynesian double-hulled canoe from an oil painting by Herb Kawainui Kane (courtesy Herb Kawainui Kane).

deep sea fishing canoe, shrank in importance to little more than the keel section. Most of the hull was built of planking."[3] Although the canoes were equipped with sails, these mariners did not depend on the wind for propulsion. The primary method of propulsion was by paddling, and the larger canoes could have as many as 100 men available to handle this chore. This was such an important part of any exploration voyage that each man had his own paddle, intricately carved with a unique design. The Polynesian mariner gave his paddle a personal name, and treated it almost as if it were human.

The double-hulled vessels were exceptionally fast, and could cover up to 150 miles per day under favorable conditions. The size of the platform allowed the carrying of many passengers, as well as the provisions necessary to colonize a land. Animals such as dogs, fowl, and pigs were transported to each new island, as were the sources of a permanent food supply, including seeds, small plants, and rootstocks. Supplies for immediate consumption were also stored on the platform: coconuts, pandanus fruit, taros, bananas, dried fruits, dried fish, preserved foods, and gourds of fresh water. Fresh fish could be caught easily in the ocean, and were normally eaten raw, although provisions were made to cook food while at sea, if desired. These supplies were enough to support a voyage of about two months, or 6,000 miles. It is likely that the seafaring history of this adventurous people contributed to the sturdy race that exists today. It takes tremendous strength to paddle canoes of this size over a vast expanse of ocean, and often in a direction opposite to the prevailing current. Only the strong completed the voyage.

The art of Polynesian navigation boggles the mind of today's American archaeologists. The archaeologist argues that ancient Europeans could not have crossed the Atlantic Ocean because they had no adequate navigational aids, such as the compass. The Polynesians had no modern navigational aids either, but they had something even better: a basic intelligence, backed by 40,000 years of practical experience. Their navigational techniques included several that were also used by the ancient Europeans. They knew the position of the sun in the sky at any time of the day, and for any season of the year. They also used the constellations extensively, and made full use of the known currents in a particular area. Modern-day Polynesian navigators use the same techniques their ancestors used over 2,000 years ago. David Lewis, who discussed Polynesian navigational techniques in his National Geographic article "Wind, Wave, Star, and Bird," was extremely impressed with what he learned about the ancient mariners. "Devoid of written language or any instruments, guided solely by their senses, the early Polynesians ranged over an area bigger than all the Soviet Union and China combined."[4]

He subsequently had the good fortune to witness the expertise of their modern descendants firsthand.

> In 1965, armed with a knowledge gained from the writings of early European explorers and missionaries, I set out to follow the traditional (and archaeologically confirmed) migration route from the Tahitian archipelago to New Zealand, by way of Rarotonga. "Sail a little to the left of the setting sun in November," had been the legendary Kupe's command. In a catamaran called Rehu Moana—"Ocean Spray" in Maori—I followed his directions. Navigating entirely without instruments, steering toward stars setting in the southwest, and using the sun and swells as additional directional guides, as Kupe must have done, I reached New Zealand after 35 days at sea, with an error in latitude of only 26 miles.[5]

Another time, when discussing the method of nighttime navigation near a particular atoll, he was told by a local expert, "You head toward that star, and when it has moved too high and too far to the left, you follow the next to rise from the same point on the horizon. Then the next, and the next, and so on, until dawn. This we call kaveinga, the star path."[6]

In addition to these navigational tools, the Polynesians had several others that were less well known. Stationary clouds were used to direct them to land masses. Polynesian navigators became experts in differentiating between the various cloud formations. They knew that large, high, cumulus clouds might be held stationary by an island, while smaller, low-hanging clouds were blown away. They also were quick to notice green reflections from the bottom of the clouds, which might indicate an island lagoon directly beneath. Birds also assisted the navigator, particularly sea birds such as the frigate, booby, and gannet. Sea birds and their habits were well known to ancient mariners. Although these birds made their roosts on land, they were known to travel as far as 30 miles out to sea in search of food. They could be depended upon to point the mariner in the direction of land. If these birds were sighted late in the day, near dusk, their path could be confidently followed to land. Conversely, if they were sighted at dawn, they would be coming from their land roost. Ocean swells also provided clues as to a ship's location, as mentioned above. The pattern of the waves was well known to the Polynesian navigator. It was a learned skill that had been passed on from father to son for thousands of years. Small changes in the patterns might indicate an obstruction in the water, and would point the way to that obstruction; in most cases, a land mass. The Polynesians also played the odds. It has been reported that a migratory trip might include as many as 200 or 300 canoes. The canoes would spread out as far as possible across the ocean, while still maintaining visual contact with each other. This increased the odds that they would not miss a small island in their direction.

With their expertise in shipbuilding and navigation to sustain them, and an adventuresome and curious spirit to drive them, the Polynesians initiated one of the most exciting and unbelievable exploratory periods in world history. They made their first incursion into Western Polynesia around 1100 BCE, when they colonized Tonga. For some reason or other, contact with islands to their west apparently ceased shortly after this. As Emory has stated:

> To have developed the physical types, language, and culture that the Polynesians share in common, these Polynesian forebears must have been isolated for a time in a home group of islands. A chain of archaeological discoveries leads us to believe that this isolation started in the islands of Tonga and Samoa roughly 3,000 years ago.[7]

Sometime around 200 BCE, the eastern migration began again, moving outward from Tonga and Samoa, and by the time of Christ, they had reached more than 7,000 miles out into the Pacific, to Tahiti and the Marquesas Islands, locations that became the jumping-off points to the most exciting maritime voyages in the world between 300 CE and 1000 CE. The first of these voyages, between 300 CE and 500 CE, should quell the doubts of any skeptics as to the seafaring capabilities of ancient mariners. Polynesian voyagers, in their sturdy double-hulled canoes, using the navigational techniques they had developed over the ages, crossed 2,200 miles of open ocean to discover and colonize Hawaii. This feat was followed, in approximately 600 CE, by a voyage of 2,300 miles to colonize Easter Island. The period of exploration culminated between 750 CE and 1000 CE with the colonization of New Zealand, a trip of 2,400 miles (see illustration).

Some people have claimed these colonizations were the result of "drift voyages," that is, uncontrolled, one way trips following a prevailing current and requiring no navigational expertise. This possibility has received considerable attention from twentieth century scientists, but it has been discounted for numerous reasons, as noted earlier. It should also be noted that some of the migrations, such as the one from the Marquesas to Easter Island, were in the face of prevailing currents, not with them.

Once settled within Polynesia, and with routine contacts from one island to another, the culture developed rapidly. Language, art styles, and social customs became unique, unlike those of their ancestors in Southeast Asia. Genealogy became of prime importance to the colonists, and every family knew its genealogy, and could recite a complete list of its ancestors back into the distant past. As Buck reported, memorizing one's genealogy and reciting it regularly at family gatherings was an important part of the Polynesian educational system. For example, the inhabitants of

Rarotonga told Buck their ancestors lived in a land in the west until 92 generations previous. A realistic time frame for one generation is approximately 33 years; therefore 92 generations would place the first eastward migration from Southeast Asia at 3,036 years ago, or 1064 BCE. Earlier in this chapter, it was reported that ashes from ancient hearths on Tonga indicated that the first settlement in Western Polynesia had occurred in Tonga in 1100 BCE. Polynesian oral history was accurate in this case, and over a time frame of 3,000 years. The same technique of memorizing and reciting important information was also used in navigation. In this instance, it was a case of life and death. An incorrect star path, or an incorrect sun location, could result in a ship being lost at sea with all hands, instead of making safe port at a desired island.

It is apparent after studying the Polynesian migrations that the distance from Africa to America is not excessive for an ancient ocean voyage. It is, in fact, about 700 miles shorter than verified ancient voyages in the Pacific. And at normal speeds, the crossing would take only 17 days, compared to the estimated 50 days it took Polynesian mariners to travel from the Marquesas Islands to Hawaii. Peru is considered to have had contact with Polynesia, so South America can no longer be looked upon as having been completely cut off from outside influences. A Viking settlement has definitely been identified at L'Anse aux Meadows in Newfoundland, so Canada can no longer be considered to have been isolated from outside influences. Only the United States remains isolated.

The next question that needs to be answered is whether the currents and the winds were supportive of transoceanic voyages. To begin with, the situation was different in the Pacific Ocean than it was in the Atlantic Ocean. The currents were less important to Polynesian navigators than they were to mariners from Europe. The Polynesians did not have to depend on currents to take them where they wanted to go. They depended on paddle power, and they manned their boats with as many oars as they deemed necessary for a particular voyage. The Polynesians, however, were intelligent and skilled seamen and, given their choice, they would sail with the current whenever possible. They would also take full advantage of the changing wind patterns, knowing the currents remained relatively constant from season to season and from year to year. They were very careful in selecting a sailing date, often waiting months to take advantage of a favorable wind. Occasionally, on exploratory trips, they would intentionally venture forth into the wind and against the current. In that way, if an emergency occurred, the boat could return home more easily with favorable wind and current conditions. If a voyage were to be a round trip to a known distant island, the trip could take as long as a year or more while

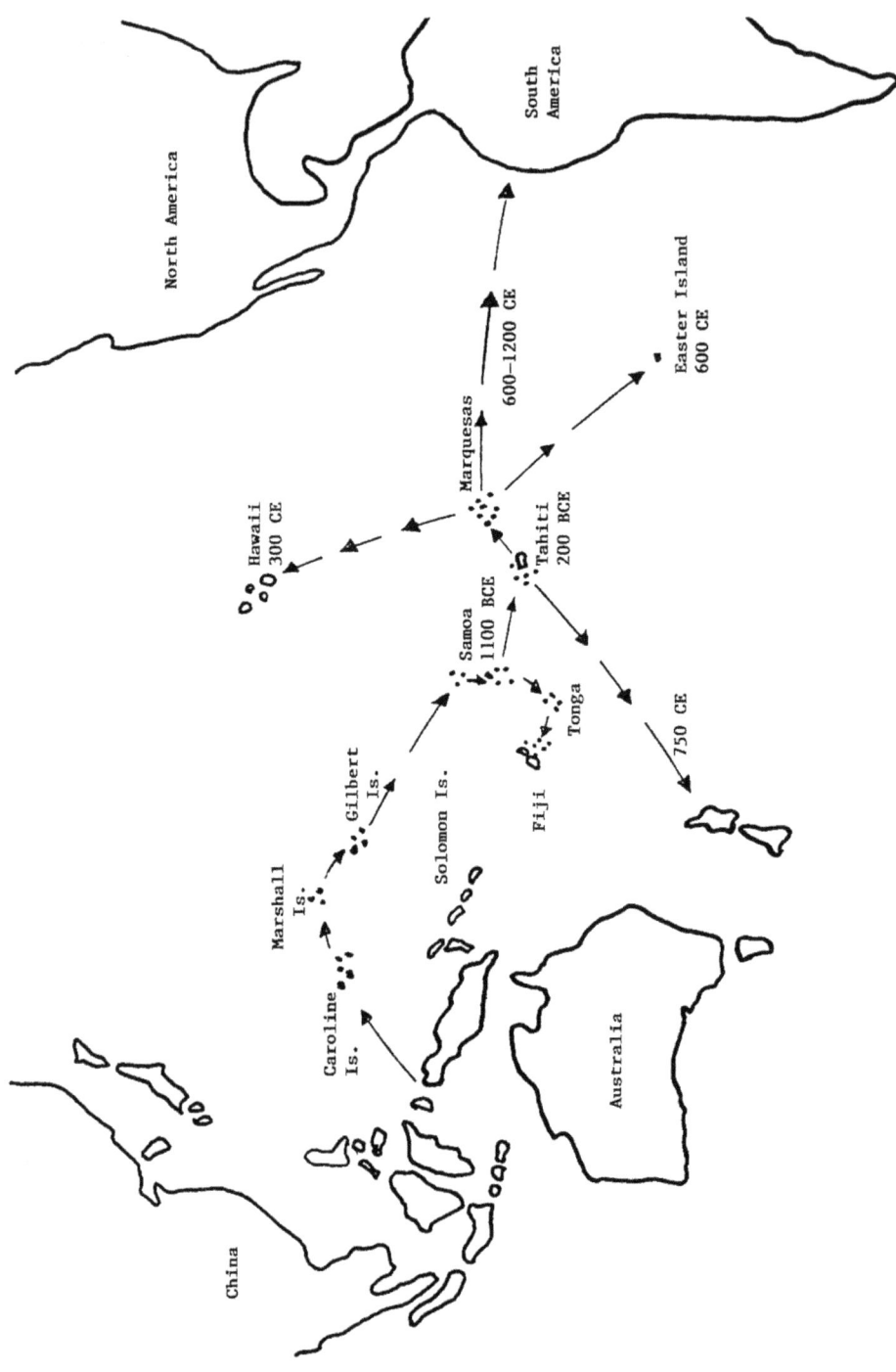

the crew waited for favorable wind conditions, first in one direction, then in the other. Time was of little importance in the central Pacific. The Polynesians never rushed anywhere. They lived a leisurely, slow-paced life, with none of today's pressures.

In the Atlantic, however, with the exception of the Vikings, sail power prevailed. Also, the purpose for crossing the Atlantic Ocean was different than the purpose for crossing the Pacific Ocean. The Pacific Ocean was crossed to discover and colonize new lands, essentially to find a permanent home for a displaced people. The Atlantic Ocean would have been crossed primarily for profit, to discover rich new lands with valuable minerals and raw materials, and plentiful fishing grounds. European cargo ships were designed to maximize available storage space. The more cargo a ship carried, the more profit could be made. Therefore, ships were built as large as possible without making them unstable. Next, the crew had to be kept to a minimum. Each person on board required space for sleeping and for food storage. The smaller the size of the crew, the less space was required for sleeping and for storing food, and the more space could be allocated to cargo storage. This situation necessitated relying on sail power. Sails took up no berths on the ship, and required no food or reimbursement. In an emergency, such as a becalmed ship, perhaps 20 oars could be put in the water. Other than that, the winds and currents controlled a ship's progress.

There were two basic routes from Europe to America, the northern route and the southern route (see illustration). The northern route is probably the easiest to use for a transatlantic crossing, and is the route most familiar to most people. It is the route the Vikings used, therefore it is a known entity. It requires the least time in the open ocean since it is primarily an island-hopping route. From the coast of the European continent, there are numerous stopping-off places across the north Atlantic, including England, Ireland, Scotland, the Orkneys, the Hebrides, the Faeroes, Iceland, and Greenland. The final leg of a trip to North America would follow the Labrador Current south from Greenland. This would require the longest open-sea voyage of the trip, a distance of 900 miles. It would eventually be assisted by a northeast wind from Nova Scotia requiring the mariners to sail as far south as southern New England or the Chesapeake Bay area before picking up a west wind for a return voyage to Europe. The Gulf Stream would provide the necessary east-moving current in this area, and would be the most logical return route to Europe regardless of whether

*Opposite*: Map showing Polynesian explorations between 1100 BCE and 1200 CE (courtesy Michael McNeil).

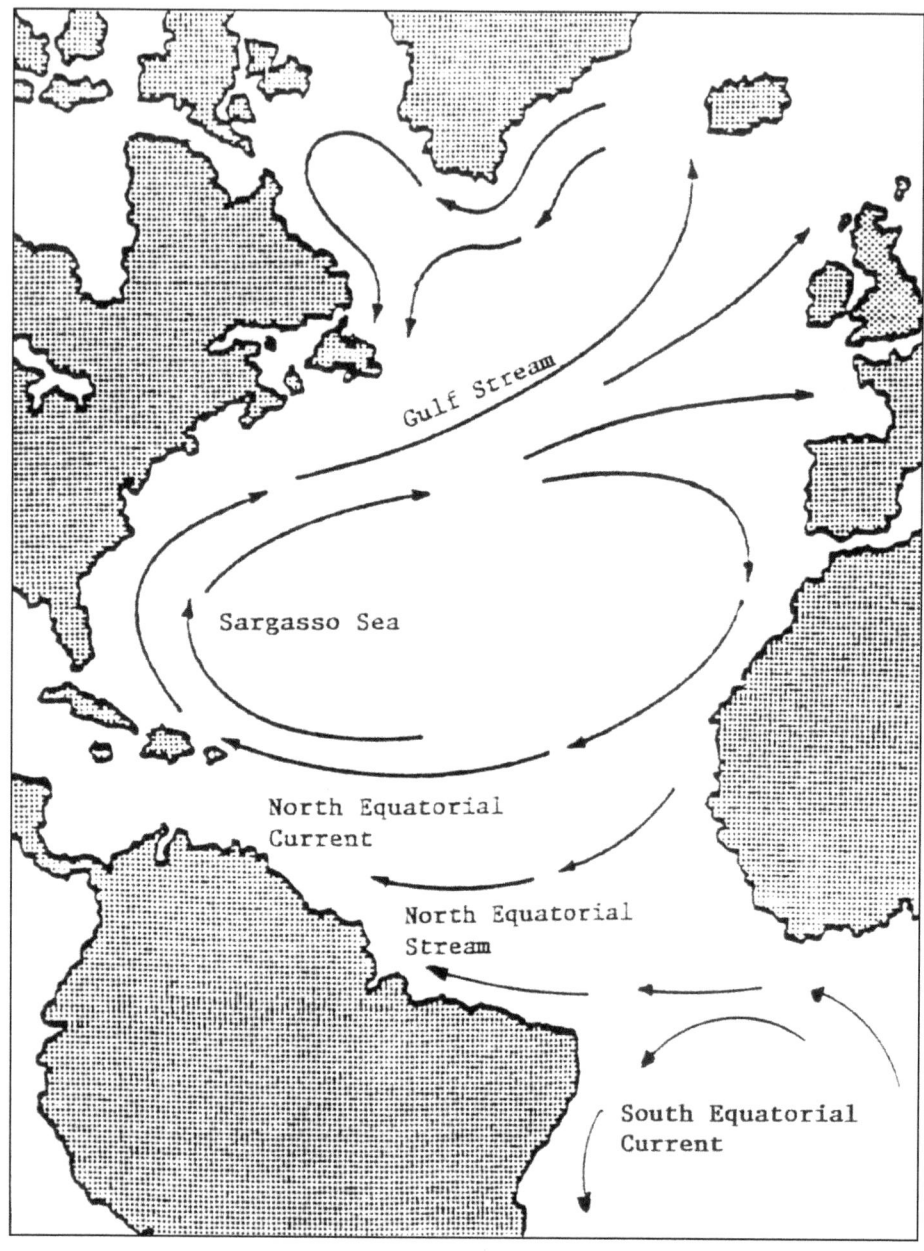

Prevailing ocean currents in the Atlantic Ocean showing the most common northern and southern routes from Europe to America, as well as the Gulf Stream return route to Europe (drawing by Michael McNeil, reproduced with permission).

the original voyage utilized the northern route to America or the southern route. The latitude of this return point of embarkation is 41 degrees north which, conveniently enough, is at the same latitude as Cadiz, Spain.

The southern route across the Atlantic from Europe to America could be initiated from Spain or Gibraltar. It would pass by the Canary Islands and be carried southwest by the Canary Current, eventually joining the North Equatorial Stream for a westward drive across the open Atlantic, assisted by the northeast trade winds. This course would take a ship near the Antilles, where Christopher Columbus first set foot on American soil. The Gulf Stream originates somewhere in the Caribbean Sea, and then proceeds in a northerly direction up the east coast of the United States. Mariners using this route would eventually reach the Chesapeake Bay area for the return trip home. There is another southern route that is not generally discussed, but may be the most important route of all in trying to determine if Europeans visited ancient America. This is the route that originates off the coast of Africa, just north of the Bay of Guinea. The South Equatorial Current sweeps north up the west coast of Africa until it reaches this area, at which point it breaks west until it contacts the continent of South America. Here it turns south, following the coast of South America to a latitude of about 45 degrees. The current then turns again, this time to the east, and joins the West Wind Drift, which travels an easterly route around the entire globe, passing, among other places, Cape Horn and the Cape of Good Hope.

The currents, it appears, would have been conducive to oceanic voyages across the Atlantic Ocean in both directions. Whether any ancient European mariner ever took advantage of these currents is still unknown, but one thing is certain. Some maritime nations, like the Phoenicians, understood the intricacies of seamanship and were expert navigators. The Phoenicians had explored their world from India in the east to the west coast of Africa in the west, and from Norway in the north to the Cape of Good Hope in the south. They knew the currents in the Atlantic Ocean, both outgoing and incoming. They knew the latitude of every city on the west coast of Europe and Africa and, if in fact they ever did reach America, they would not only have been confident about returning home, they would have been able to accurately predict the location of their European landfall. Better still, since they did know the Atlantic currents, they would have been able to select their own return route home, depending on their intended European destination. If they wanted to visit Scandinavia or England, perhaps for purposes of trade, they could have chosen the north Atlantic route past Greenland and Iceland. If, on the other hand, they intended to stop in Spain to ply their wares, they would have taken advantage of the Gulf Stream. And, if they wanted to return directly to their homeland in Phoenicia from the Southern Hemisphere, they would have followed the Southern Equatorial Current to the West Wind Drift, taking the route east past the Cape of Good Hope and into the Red Sea to Phoenicia. The Phoenicians were at home on the water.

The story of Pedro Alvares Cabral should be included in any study of the currents in the Atlantic Ocean. Pedro Alvares Cabral was born in Belmonte, Portugal, in 1460 CE, into a middle class family. Cabral was well educated in the private religious schools of his time, and became interested in commerce, and in the sea, as a young man. He spent over 30 years on the sea, and developed a well earned reputation as a maritime commander. He was also extremely knowledgeable in the art of commercial trading, and was familiar with all ports of call from Oslo to Suez. In the year 1500 CE, King Emmanuel I of Portugal was desirous of outfitting a large trading expedition to India to take advantage of Portugal's dominance of the oceans, and to exploit the magnificent riches of the East. He chose Cabral as commander of the expedition. Cabral assembled a fleet of 13 of Portugal's largest cargo ships, and a complement of over 1,000 men. He set sail for India on March 9, 1500 CE, on a course that would carry him down the west coast of Africa, around the Cape of Good Hope, and eastward to India. In order to escape the dangers of sailing too close to the African shoreline, Cabral chose a westerly course in the Atlantic Ocean. Unfortunately he was much too aggressive, and set his course too far to the west. Soon he was caught by the North Equatorial Stream, and violent northeast trade winds drove his ships further west, completely out of control. On April 22, 1500 CE, the Portuguese fleet sighted land and, within a few hours, Cabral became the first recorded European to set foot on the continent of South America. He had completed an involuntary non-stop voyage from Lisbon, Portugal, covering 4,600 miles, in 45 days. Cabral immediately named the country Island of the True Cross, and claimed possession of the land for Portugal. The Island of the True Cross later became the country we know as Brazil. The experience of Cabral is an important factor when one is evaluating the possibility of ancient mariners crossing the Atlantic Ocean. He had the sturdiest, most seaworthy ships of the fifteenth century at his disposal. He had the most detailed charts of the Atlantic Ocean then available, as well as the most sophisticated navigational aids, such as the compass and the sextant. His 13 ships were commandered by experienced officers, many of whom had traveled the African route many times before. Yet, in spite of all their experience, in spite of their superior ocean-going vessels, in spite of having the most modern navigational equipment in the world, the Portuguese fleet was completely helpless when battered by the savagery of the Atlantic elements. They were blown off course, blown further and further west at the mercy of the winds, until they encountered the coast of South America.

It is a fact that Phoenician ships sailed the eastern Atlantic Ocean for over a thousand years. They made innumerable voyages along the entire west coast of Europe and Africa. They had established hundreds of trading posts along the African coast as long ago as 450 BCE. Like Cabral, the Phoenicians shied away from traveling too close to the shore. They were well aware of the dangers of hugging the coastline. They knew only too well that ships traveling close to shore were often caught by sudden, strong, onshore winds and were driven on the rocks, with the loss of both ships and men. To avoid this possibility, the Phoenicians would set their course to the west, making a large circular arc in the Atlantic Ocean and approaching the coast only at the desired latitude. Over a period of 500 years or more, hundreds, perhaps thousands, of Phoenician vessels plied their trade along the African coast. Is it reasonable to assume that none of these ships was blown off course toward the western Atlantic? Is it possible that the Phoenicians, with their inferior ships, with primitive charts of the Atlantic Ocean, and with no navigational instruments to guide them, could have maneuvered in the Atlantic Ocean year after year, for 500 years, without a single miscalculation, while the commander of the world's greatest fifteenth century seapower was ignominiously blown across the Atlantic Ocean all the way from Africa to South America against his will?

Is there any evidence that ancient voyages to America could have been accomplished in the type of ships that were utilized by the ancient European maritime nations? Fortunately, that question can be answered with a fair degree of confidence, thanks to a daring group of modern adventurers who asked themselves the same question. Foremost among this group is Thor Heyerdahl, a Norwegian anthropologist who has spent more than 60 years studying the people and the cultures of the world. As a young man he attended the University of Oslo, majoring in zoology, but as his education progressed, his interest shifted from zoology to anthropology, particularly the Stone-Age society of Polynesia. He was determined to visit that area of the globe in order to study firsthand this primitive society. His curiosity was also aroused when he pondered the origins of the animals that populated the islands. Nineteen thirty-six was an important year in the life of Thor Heyerdahl. In rapid succession he graduated from college, married his college sweetheart, Liv, and departed for Fatu-Hiva in the Marquesas Islands, where he and Liv spent the next two years. Anthropology took a firm hold on Heyerdahl's life. For two years he roamed the Marquesas, studying the ruins of ancient temples, marveling at the immense stone statues that populated the islands, and absorbing the legends of ancient Polynesia as related by the islands' elders. Heyerdahl noted many similarities between Polynesia and ancient South America, especially Peru.

Peru has seen the rise and fall of numerous civilizations over the past 3,000 years, but one civilization in particular fascinated Heyerdahl. Before the Spanish conquered Peru, before the Incas built their great citadels of Cuzco and Machu Picchu, before the Chimu city of Chan-Chan existed, a great society rose from the dust of the Peruvian plain, flourished for a brief time, then returned to the earth from whence it came. The ruins of its temples, the remains of its great stepped pyramids, and the ragged splendor of its enormous stone statues lay overgrown with jungle brush, forgotten by twentieth century man.

The legends from both Polynesia and Peru seemed to coincide for Heyerdahl. Sometime in the distant past, according to Inca legend, a group of white men with long flowing beards arrived in Peru from the north. They were looked upon as gods by the aboriginal population. They taught the natives many things about the arts and sciences, agriculture and religion. They helped the natives build a great civilization, and themselves became the leaders of that civilization as earthly representatives of Kon, the sun god. Eventually, a jealous Indian chieftain attacked the white settlement near Lake Titicaca and massacred the inhabitants. A few survivors, including the reigning king, Kon-Tiki, "Son of the Sun," reached the coast, constructed a balsa raft, and disappeared west into the Pacific Ocean. At the same time, Polynesian tradition tells of Tiki, the great ancestor of the Polynesians, who arrived in the Marquesas Islands from a mountainous land in the east. Genealogy places the date of his arrival at about 500 CE.

Although this study is primarily interested in the events that took place in the Atlantic Ocean, two modern voyages that crossed the Pacific Ocean are pertinent to the overall understanding of ancient marine technology. One is a drift voyage on a balsa-wood raft, the *Kon-Tiki*, by Thor Heyerdahl. The other is a voyage of 2500 miles across open ocean in a double-hulled canoe by Ben R. Finney and Herb Kawainui Kane, to demonstrate ancient Polynesian navigational expertise. There have actually been many men who have sailed replicas of ancient craft across large expanses of water (see table). Heyerdahl has accomplished this feat, not once, but at least four times: once in the Pacific Ocean, twice in the Atlantic Ocean, and once in the Indian Ocean.

The story of the *Kon-Tiki* is an interesting one. Heyerdahl, after his years of study in Polynesia and South America, was convinced that Polynesian civilization originated in the jungles of Peru, not in Asia. He was

## 2. Making the Impossible Possible

### Comparison of Modern Exploratory Vessels: Estimated Dimensions and Voyage Data

|  | Viking | Kon-Tiki | Ra II | Hokule'a | Brendan | Tigris |
|---|---|---|---|---|---|---|
| Year | 1893 | 1947 | 1970 | 1976 | 1976 | 1977 |
| Length, Ft. | 60 | 40 | 40 | 60 | 36 | 60 |
| Beam, Ft. | 16 | 20 | 20 | 18 | 8 | 20 |
| Depth, Ft. | 3 | 2 | 5 | 2 | 3 | 8 |
| Nonstop Miles Traveled | 4,000 | 4,300 | 3,270 | 2,500 | 1,600 | 2,200 |
| Time of Voyage in Days | 28 | 101 | 57 | 33 | 47 | 49 |

also convinced that the initial settlers crossed the Pacific Ocean on balsa-wood rafts, which were familiar to Peruvians long before the Inca came to power. The Kon-Tiki voyage was intended to prove two points:

1. An ancient Peruvian balsa-wood raft could be constructed rugged enough, and seaworthy enough, to cross the Pacific Ocean.
2. The Humboldt Current and the South Equatorial Current would guide such a raft west in the Pacific Ocean, to the islands of Polynesia.

Heyerdahl assembled a crew of five other adventurers, including an experienced navigator and radioman. To supplement his supplies for the voyage, Heyerdahl approached the United States War Department. The department provided him with many experimental items, which he promised to evaluate during the open-ocean expedition. These included field rations, waterproof matches, stoves, and sunburn lotion. The next order of business was to assemble all goods and supplies in Peru, build the raft, and set sail toward the sunset.

The design of the raft was similar to that of ancient Incan rafts that were reported by sixteenth century Spaniards (see illustration). It was constructed of balsa wood, contained an open cabin, and was equipped with a large, square sail, a centerboard, and a large steering oar. The wood for the raft was cut on the coast of Ecuador and was transported by steamer to Callao, Peru, for assembly. Nine of the largest trees formed the main part of the raft, which was pointed in the center, both fore and aft. The raft was 45 feet long in the center and 30 feet long on the sides. The cabin, open on all sides, was about 10 feet square and 6 feet high at the point of the roof. As the raft neared completion, most experts predicted dire consequences if Heyerdahl should put to sea on such a flimsy vessel. There was a general fear that the men would be washed overboard sooner or later,

Oceangoing raft used by the Inca Indians of Peru (reproduced with permission from *History of the Indian Tribes*).

and that the raft would become waterlogged and would eventually be destroyed by the violent ocean gales and hurricanes. Heyerdahl, however, was confident of success. He knew the Incas sailed such rafts on deep sea fishing expeditions, using the morning offshore winds to transport them as far as 60 miles out to sea in search of dolphins and tunny, then utilizing the onshore winds to assist them back to port at night. Heyerdahl also believed the ancient legend of a fifteenth century Inca chief called Tupac Yupanqui. Yupanqui, it seems, had heard of inhabitable islands in the Pacific Ocean. He led a balsa raft expeditionary force of several thousand men into the Pacific Ocean in search of these islands. Although Yupanqui did discover islands, none were to his liking, and he returned home to Peru after a voyage of eight months.

The moment of truth, for Heyerdahl and his crew, arrived on April 28, 1947, when the *Kon-Tiki* was towed out of Callao harbor, and set free in the Humboldt Current (see illustration). According to Heyerdahl's calculations, the current should carry the *Kon-Tiki* north along the west coast of South America, then join the South Equatorial Current, subsequently veering west into the open expanse of the Pacific Ocean. He was right. The balsa logs absorbed some water as expected, then reached equilibrium, settling nicely in the water like a well designed vessel should. The currents directed the *Kon-Tiki* exactly as expected and, before long, had her moving west toward Polynesia. More than any other book about transoceanic voyages, Heyerdahl's book *Kon-Tiki* gives keen insight into the day-to-day

## 2. Making the Impossible Possible

The Kon-Tiki entering Polynesia after a voyage of more than 100 days across the Pacific Ocean (courtesy Thor Heyerdahl).

activities of a small vessel at sea, activities that most likely occupied ancient mariners as well as modern. From an operational standpoint, steering was by far the biggest problem. Controlling the 19-foot steering oar was a mammoth task, and was a constant strain on the muscles. The crew soon realized that steering was the most exhausting job on the raft. They quickly organized themselves into two-hour shifts, one shift during the day and one shift at night. The concern about *Kon-Tiki*'s ability to survive a storm was soon dispelled. High winds occasionally played havoc with her, once spinning her around in a complete circle. In general, she rode the waves like an angel, surprising everyone with her buoyancy and overall stability.

One important discovery made on the voyage was that food and water were not major problems. It was only necessary to have adequate fishing supplies and a lot of empty containers on board. Fish were constantly landing on the raft, particularly flying fish. The ocean supplied all the supplementary meals required. Dolphin were easy to catch, and tunny weighing up to 200 pounds were there for the taking. Fresh water was no problem either. The initial fresh water supply on the raft was consumed within 60 days, but it rained often, and the water was easily collected in the empty containers. One hundred and one days out of Callao, Peru, after a voyage of 4,300 miles, the battered but proud *Kon-Tiki* landed on Tuamotu Archipelago, in the Society Islands, not far from Tahiti. The voyage was an overwhelming success. Heyerdahl had proven that an ancient Peruvian balsa-wood raft could survive a one-way drift voyage from South America to Polynesia.

The voyage of *Hokule'a*, like the voyage of *Kon-Tiki*, took place in Polynesia. There the similarities end. *Kon-Tiki* was a raft, *Hokule'a* a double-hulled canoe. The *Kon-Tiki* voyage was a drift voyage undertaken to prove the raft was seaworthy and that the prevailing ocean currents could carry her from Peru to Tahiti. The *Hokule'a* voyage was designed to prove the seaworthiness of the canoe, and also to prove that ancient Polynesian navigational techniques could accurately guide the boat across 2,500 miles of open ocean to a predetermined destination. The initiators of this project were Ben R. Finney, professor of anthropology at the University of Hawaii, and Herb Kawainui Kane, Hawaiian artist and historian. Finney and Kane, along with Tommy Holmes, cofounded the Polynesian Voyaging Society, which planned the *Hokule'a* trip. Finney had long been interested in the Polynesian culture and was amazed by their successful colonization of such a large expanse of ocean area, using supposedly primitive vessels and apparently lacking navigational expertise. In 1973, he, Kane, and Holmes decided to build a large oceangoing canoe and sail it on a long ocean voyage in order to verify ancient Polynesian seamanship. The first problem they encountered was one of boat design. There were no remains of ancient oceangoing canoes to copy, and no drawings, paintings or carvings of such a vessel existed. What did these boats look like? Kane spearheaded the research effort to design the *Hokule'a* as close to an ancient Polynesian canoe as possible. He was familiar with modern canoe designs throughout Polynesia. He used this knowledge to conjecture what an ancient Polynesian oceangoing canoe might have looked like, comparing design features from one island to another. Features that were unique to a particular island were discarded as a local innovation. On the other hand, design features that were similar from island to island were assumed to have been inherited from the original Polynesian ancestors. Kane's final design provided the composite boat design shown in his painting earlier in this chapter.

The boat was built and launched in 1975. It was a large, oceangoing, double-hulled canoe, measuring 60 feet in overall length and weighing six tons. It was christened '*Hokule'a*', Polynesian for Arcturus, the bright star that appears over Hawaii. May 1, 1976, dawned hot and humid. It was the opportune time to initiate a round trip voyage from Hawaii to Tahiti, according to ancient tradition. The winter season had ended, and the prevailing northeast trade wind had returned to its normal pattern. The early spring departure also allowed for the return trip to be completed before the late summer storms arrived. Polynesian mariners avoided late summer excursions at all costs. Hurricanes and typhoons plagued the central Pacific during this time of the year, leaving death and destruction in their wake. Late summer was a time to stay home. Sailing was for a different season.

The *Hokule'a* left Maui on a Saturday with a crew of 17 men. The ship initially headed north for a day or so, then turned clockwise to achieve the correct direction and to be able to safely clear all the Hawaiian Islands. The navigator, who was a Micronesian from Satawal in the Caroline Islands, was an expert in the navigational techniques of his ancestors. He positioned himself on the port stern corner of the platform. At night, he watched the stars and the constellations. He made steering corrections based on the position of his guide stars. On overcast nights, the navigator directed the boat by the trade winds and ocean swells. The same winds and swells were used for daytime navigation, as was the position of the sun. One thousand miles out of Hawaii, the boat reached the doldrums, an area where the northeast and southeast trade winds meet. It is an area of calm, and ever changing wind directions. It slowed the voyage down considerably, and little progress could be made until the doldrums were left behind. Once out, the boat was well on its way to cover the last 1,500-mile leg of the journey. Nothing but open water and a strong following wind prevailed from there to Tahiti. There was one short period of hurricane-force winds and rough sea activity, but the *Hokule'a* weathered it well and came through unscathed. The rest of the voyage was uneventful. The Polynesian navigator guided the ship faultlessly. Thirty days out of Hawaii, terns were sighted. This sea bird was a sure sign that land was near. Two days later, the boat triumphantly arrived at Tahiti, demonstrating the accuracy of the ancient Polynesian navigational techniques. The total distance traveled was about 3,000 miles in 33 days, or an average of 91 miles per day.

The Atlantic Ocean had its share of "ancient" maritime activity going back to Magnus Anderson in 1893. Anderson, a Norwegian, built a boat fashioned after the recently discovered Gokstad ship, the first genuine Viking ship found intact. It was a type of ship known as a Karv, a ship smaller than the famous longships that are familiar to all Viking enthusiasts, but larger than the Viking cargo ships known as Knorrs. It was not as seaworthy as a Knorr, but it was still considered formidable enough to withstand a rugged journey across the north Atlantic. The ship, when finished, was about 60 feet long and had about three feet of freeboard.

Anderson was satisfied that it would do the job. On April 30, 1893, the newly christened *Viking* pulled out of Bergen harbor on its momentous voyage. The journey was not without its weather problems. Severe storms battered the ship for several days, but the *Viking* handled it well and survived the trials. When the winds were favorable, the *Viking* could do about 11 knots, but for most of the trip, she had to battle stiff headwinds. Still she averaged six knots for the journey and arrived in Newfoundland on May 27, 1893, covering almost 4,000 miles in 28 days. Magnus Anderson had made his point. His Viking ancestors were indeed capable of crossing the Atlantic Ocean in their sturdy craft. Another Viking ship crossed the Atlantic in 1932. A Captain Folgar built a replica of a small Knorr, 60 feet long, 16 feet in the beam, and with a three-foot draft. Folgar sailed the ship, the *Roald Amundsen*, to America, following one of Columbus' routes. He returned to Norway via the Newfoundland route, successfully completing a round trip voyage of over 6,000 miles with no major problems. The ship responded well to all ocean conditions, including the typical Atlantic storms and gales.

In the late 1960s, Thor Heyerdahl burst upon the scene once more. After his successful drift voyage in the Pacific, on the *Kon-Tiki*, Heyerdahl continued to study the civilizations of South America. He became intrigued with the apparent European influences in South America. He noted, "Numerous theories of voyagers drifting from Africa to Tropical America have been proposed to explain the sudden blossoming of high culture from Mexico to Peru. Like the ancient peoples of the Old World, natives of the Americas worshipped the sun, built pyramids and giant stone statues, married brother to sister in royal families, wrote in hieroglyphs, performed cranial surgery, and mummified the dead."[8] As his curiosity grew, Heyerdahl decided to investigate the possibility that an ancient ship could have crossed the Atlantic Ocean from the Old World to the New World, bringing with it revolutionary new technology. He decided to cross the Atlantic at the narrowest point, from the west coast of Africa and, since the American culture seemed to mirror that of Egypt in many ways, he would sail an Egyptian ship. He had noticed another similarity between the two worlds, and that was in their boat construction. Reed boats were a common mode of transportation in ancient Egypt, as recorded on tomb reliefs. Also, as he said, "In verses from the Bible, in scenes found in Nineveh, in writings of the Roman historian Pliny, the reed boat stands as one of man's most ancient vessels."[9] Reed boats are still in use today, on both sides of the Atlantic. They are used by fishermen on Lake Chad in Africa, and by Indians on Lake Titicaca in Peru.

So it would be a reed boat. Heyerdahl engaged the ship builders from

Lake Chad to construct a large papyrus reed boat capable of crossing the Atlantic. Unfortunately, the natives' expertise was in the construction of small fishing craft for lake use. This design was scaled up by assembling many small bundles of reeds such as would be used for small boats, then lashing them all together with ropes to make one large ship. When the ship was thus completed early in 1969, it was transported from Egypt to its point of embarkation in Safi, Morocco. The ship was christened *Ra I*, after the Egyptian sun god, setting sail on May 25, 1969, amid much fanfare. The voyage was doomed from the start. The rugged Atlantic took its toll on the flimsy craft immediately, the constant beating of the waves loosening the small reed bundles. The stern of the ship broke apart and collapsed soon after departure from Africa. The crew fought on, however, guiding *Ra I* south along the African coast, past the Canary Islands to Cape Blanc, then veering southwest past the Cape Verde Islands, and finally turning west toward America. But the odds were against them. As more and more of the ship disintegrated, it became obvious that *Ra I* would never hold together long enough to reach land. She had valiantly fought the Atlantic monster, but the fight was over. The crew had to abandon her in shark-filled waters on July 18, 1969. *Ra I* had covered 2,662 miles in 55 days, and came within 600 miles of the Antilles.

Heyerdahl went back to work. Realizing his mistake of trying to lash numerous small bundles of reeds together to make a single large unit, Heyerdahl approached the Indians of South America for help. Four Aymara Indians from the region around Lake Titicaca agreed to travel to Africa to assist with the project. An interpreter accompanied them. This time the boat was built at Safi itself, and was constructed differently than *Ra I*. Heyerdahl reported, "The hull consists of two main bundles, plus a small center one, all lashed together with a continuous spiralling rope. Thin bundles on each side form the gunwales. No metal, not a nail or screw, was used."[10] The unit construction method looked like it would be a success, and it more closely resembled the papyrus boats of ancient Egypt. The construction also included a high bow and a high stern to break up the waves, a small cabin amidship, and a large square sail supported by an A-frame mast. Upon completion, the 40-foot boat was transported to the harbor and launched on May 7, 1970. It was ceremoniously splashed with goats milk and christened *Ra II*.

*Ra II* was allowed to settle in the water for ten days; then, on May 17, the crew bid farewell to the crowd on shore and shoved off for America. Again it was south past the Canary Islands, then southwest toward the Antilles, this time passing far north of *Ra I*'s track. "Setting forth, the men dine well, but only on foods preserved in the manner of the ancients. In more than a hundred jars, goatskin bags, and baskets, *Ra II* carries water, dried and salted meat and fish, dates, figs, nuts, eggs, honey, flour, oil, dried vegetables, and Egyptian bread."[11] The voyage duplicated others that have been discussed previously. There were long periods of calm, when almost no progress was made. These were followed by periods of stiff trade wind support where *Ra II* could travel 70 miles a day. Storms buffeted the little ship, but she rode them out successfully, and survived, battered and bruised but not beaten. Fifty-seven days and 3,270 miles out of Safi, Morocco, *Ra II* reached her objective. An escort of four planes and 50 small boats welcomed her to Bridgetown, Barbados. The date was July 12, 1970. Heyerdahl remembered his thoughts at the completion of the journey: "The voyage had succeeded. But what had it proved? First we have demonstrated that a papyrus ship, properly built, can cross a major ocean. Secondly, we have shown that a craft of such ancient design coming from North Africa, a cradle of civilization—could have crossed the Atlantic Ocean with a crew, to bring cultural influences to the aboriginal population of the western hemisphere."[12]

There is one more ancient mariner who deserves recognition. He was Brendan the Navigator, a sixth century Irish Celtic monk who reportedly traveled from Ireland to America. Like Leif Erikson, and others, his adventures have been relegated to the land of "never was," a figment of someone's imagination, a cute Irish fairy story. Some years ago, in 1973 to be exact, a young adventurer named Timothy Severin was vacationing in Western Ireland with his wife Dorothy. As Severin recalls, "One evening, over tea at the kitchen table, Dorothy remarked, 'I don't see why Brendan couldn't have made it.' Nor did I, but that proved nothing. On the other hand, if modern sailors could cross the Atlantic using the same techniques and materials that Brendan had, the legend would gain some significance. At that moment, the idea of a Brendan voyage was born."[13]

It would be three years before the voyage would begin. Considerable research had to be done first, to study the route of Brendan's voyage and to determine the type of boat he might have utilized. The ancient story of the voyage, written in about 800 CE, described a boat built with a wood frame and covered with oxhide. The same type of boat, a curragh, is still used by Kerry fishermen in Southwest Ireland to this very day. Kerry fishermen, as a matter of fact, gave Severin his first taste of the open sea in a curragh, and assured him that it was a reliable ocean vessel, size notwithstanding. The 36-foot-long boat was finally designed as close to St. Brendan's as research and imagination could make it. "The Croggins Traditional Tannery cured all 49 hides in the way St. Brendan's tanners had, in a solution of oak bark."[14] Two square sails, one large and one small, both emblazoned with a Celtic cross, completed the outfitting of the *Brendan*. She was suitably blessed by Bishop Eamon Casey of Kerry, and was duly christened with the only acceptable fluid for such a vessel, a bottle of real Irish whiskey. It was another three months before the voyage actually began. First the crew had to be assembled, then the shake-down cruises completed, with the usual equipment debugging and personnel training. Finally, the route had to be mapped out, just as Brendan the Navigator had done 1,400 years previous.

The big day arrived on May 17, 1976, and the *Brendan*, with her crew of five, departed from Brandon Creek in Southwest Ireland, the same point of departure that, legend said, was used by St. Brendan and his monks. This voyage was unlike the other modern voyages that have been reported. It was not a drift voyage. It followed a predetermined route using modern instruments. It was not a direct voyage between two points either, but rather an island-hopping voyage, which took more than a year to complete. There were intermediate stops in the Hebrides and the Faeroes, and a ten-month layover in Iceland. Some of the notes from the voyage sound strangely like notes from the voyages of the *Kon-Tiki*, *Hokule'a*, and *Ra II*: "In these cramped quarters, each of us realized the need for strict self discipline, if we were to avoid those minor irritations that could erupt into quarrels, even hatreds." And, "It was a week of wild extremes, in which 'Brendan' was becalmed, swept backwards by headwinds, and finally lashed by storms and caught in the fierce tidal races surrounding the Faeroes."[15]

There were other occurrences which make one think of Polynesians. For example, the ten-month layover in Iceland was precipitated by adverse weather conditions: "For the next three weeks, steady southwest winds swept the island, barring 'Brendans' progress toward the New World. The autumn gale season was approaching, and there was pack ice off the east coast of Greenland to consider."[16] Patience was a virtue understood by all successful mariners, especially if they aspired to a long and fruitful life. The crew of the *Brendan* wisely waited until spring for favorable conditions. In early May, the final 1,600-mile leg of the journey to Newfoundland commenced. It was a tough leg. First there were severe north Atlantic seas to contend with; then the typical cold, damp, foggy weather that chilled the bones and numbed the senses. Finally, the dangerous and unforgiving ice floes threatened them with instant eradication. But the *Brendan* held fast and survived all. On June 26, 1977, she reached Peckford Island in Newfoundland, after 47 days at sea. As Severin noted, this successful crossing gave credence to the St. Brendan legend. The discovery of America by Irish monks could no longer be discounted on the basis of their small, fragile, inferior boats. The tiny curragh of Timothy Severin had withstood the trial by fire as well as any of her big sisters had, and now had to be considered a full-fledged oceangoing vessel.

## Summary

The following facts were uncovered during the investigation of ancient seamanship.
- The narrowest point across the south Atlantic Ocean is from the coast of Africa, just north of the Gulf of Guinea, to the coast of Brazil in South America. The distance is approximately 1,750 miles.
- Polynesian mariners penetrated more than 7,000 miles into the central Pacific Ocean from their home in Indonesia as early as 200 CE.
- Polynesian mariners, using ancient navigational techniques, also successfully sailed across 2,400 miles of open ocean and arrived precisely at a predetermined location, Hawaii.
- Prevailing ocean currents and wind patterns were of less importance to the Polynesians than to their European counterparts, since the Polynesians relied heavily on paddling their boats, while the Europeans relied almost exclusively on sail power. The Polynesians often traveled against the current.
- The prevailing ocean currents in the Atlantic Ocean would support at least three possible maritime routes from Europe to America, and a similar number of return routes.
- At least one medieval mariner, Pedro Alvares Cabral, was transported across the Atlantic Ocean against his will, by violent northeast trade winds. His involuntary voyage resulted in the discovery of Brazil in the year 1500 CE.
- Several modern adventurers constructed replicas of ancient vessels, and demonstrated their seaworthiness on both the Pacific Ocean and the Atlantic Ocean.

## Conclusions

Intentional, planned, round trip voyages between Europe and ancient America, were possible in the ships of the time, and with the navigational aids then in use.

# 3

# Vikings: The People and the Legend

## Conventional Thinking

- The Vikings did not visit North America.
- The Viking Sagas are not historical records. They are myths.

## Discussion

"Oh Lord, protect us from the fury of the Northmen." This prayerful cry echoed along the western coast of Europe as the ninth century dawned. The Northmen came from Scandinavia, the land of the midnight sun. They broke upon the great ocean from hundreds of fjords, rivers, and bays; their sinister dragon-headed boats gliding silently through the waters, their brilliant red and white striped sails billowing in the breeze (see illustration). These raucous seafaring marauders from the north were about to spread terror, death and destruction throughout the Western world. A tenth century poet described the Viking thusly: "Blond was his hair, and bright his cheeks. Grim as a snakes were his glowing eyes."[1] The Vikings' great dragon ships cruised the oceans and seas, pillaging and plundering from Turkey to England, from Frisia to North Africa. They even moved into the uncharted waters to the west, to the Faeroe Islands, and through the frigid waters of the north Atlantic to Iceland and Greenland. This we know from factual archaeological evidence. The questions that still existed in 1960 were:

1. Did the Vikings go even further west from Greenland, and visit the shores of North America?
2. If so, were they the first ancient visitors to North America?

The Viking longship (courtesy *The Indians and Antiquities of America*)

The Vikings were natives of Scandinavia: Norway, Sweden, and Denmark. The beginnings of their history are lost in antiquity, but we do know that the peninsula that bore them was inhabited back into the Stone Age. The population was obviously very sparse at that time, and Gjerset claimed there were fewer than 2,000 people in Norway itself. What people there were survived by farming, fishing, and hunting. They also built stone graves in which to bury their dead. Some of the graves were small, and contained only cinerary urns. Other graves, however, were mammoth structures containing single or multiple inhumations. One such grave, called a gallery grave, was 12 feet wide, 20 feet long, and six feet high, covered with a huge stone slab roof. A 20-foot entrance tunnel led to the main chamber. The size of the chamber and the type of construction is similar to that found in the stone chambers of modern New England.

As the Bronze Age arrived in Scandinavia, the population of Norway had increased to about 2,500 people. A trade network with other countries had already been developed, as witnessed by the many bronze items discovered throughout the peninsula, bronze being unobtainable in Scandinavia. Fishing and hunting were probably the major industries, and the most important trade items. Seaworthy oceangoing ships were probably used in Bronze Age Norway, Sweden and Denmark by 1500 BCE, to transport fish and furs to England and Southern Europe, and to return with a wealth of desirable bronze tools, weapons, and jewelry. Although their writing system was still some 2,000 years in the future, the Bronze Age people left us a record of their everyday activities on their numerous rock tracings, particularly in Sweden. A rock carving in Bohuslan, Sweden, gives some valuable insight into this prehistoric society. For instance, the natives apparently had large ships that could carry at least as many as 30 men. Battle scenes are common on the rock tracings, with men wielding shields, axes, and spears. Hunters with bows and arrows are evident, as are a variety of animals such as cows, horses, deer, and dogs. These drawings will be discussed again in a later chapter when similar rock carvings are investigated in Peterborough, Canada.

Civilization continued to expand in Norway through the Bronze Age and into the Iron Age. The population grew to 17,000 by the year 30 CE, the ships got larger, and trade with Western Europe expanded. The first Roman coins found in Norway date to this period. A discovery was made in 1863 that shows the advanced shipbuilding technology that had been attained by the second century CE. As Gjerset reported, "Two boats were unearthed in the Nydam Bog, near Sundeved in Schleswig, together with 106 swords, 552 spear points, seventy shield bosses, coins, toilet articles, and other objects."[2] And, "One of the boats is oak, the other pine. The oak boat is about 80 feet long, and eleven feet wide at the middle. It is made for 14 pairs of oars, and is riveted together with iron rivets. It has no mast."[3] It is obvious that Norway had very seaworthy boats at this time, being every bit as capable of crossing the Atlantic Ocean as were the Viking vessels of the ninth century. They apparently did not use sails, but rather relied on oar power. This gave them the advantage of being able to travel in any direction, not being at the mercy of the currents or the prevailing winds.

Although the history of Scandinavia during the early centuries of the Christian era is scanty, there are indications that these countries were already involved in significant maritime activity. Du Chaillu mentioned several references to the Scandinavians by early Roman and Greek writers. Tacitus (57–117 CE) was one of the first to describe them. "Hence the states of the Sueones, situated in the ocean itself, are not only powerful on land, but also have mighty fleets. The shape of their ships is different, in that, having a prow at each end, they are always ready for running onto the beach. They are not worked by sails, nor are the oars fastened to the sides in regular order, but left loose as in some rivers, so they can be shifted here or there as circumstances may require."[4] Du Chaillu believed the Sueones to be natives of Sweden.

He also associated the Scandinavians with the ancestors of the Franks and Saxons. He quoted the Roman emperor Julian as calling the Franks and Saxons "the most warlike of the tribes above the Rhine and the Western Sea."[5] After reviewing the mass of information recorded by the ancient historians, Du Chaillu concluded, "It would appear that these tribes must have come from a country further eastward than the Roman provinces, and that, as they came with ships, their home must have been on the shores of the Baltic, the Cattegat, and Norway; in fact, precisely the country which the numerous antiquities point to as inhabited by an extremely warlike and maritime race, which had great intercourse with the Greek and Roman world."[6]

Sometime during this same period, the art of writing was introduced into the north countries. It was called runic writing, a word derived from ryn, meaning a groove. As Slafter reported, "The runic characters were mostly made up of straight lines, cutting or meeting each other at certain angles, and were, for this reason, especially convenient for brief inscriptions on wood or stone, for which they were exclusively used. They were employed to fix dates, the ownership of property ... but were never used in writing books or extended documents of any sort."[7] It would be another 600 years or more before the Saga writers would reduce the history and explorations of their famous countrymen to book form. In the meantime, their recorded history continued to be at the mercy of the bitter and prejudiced historians of those European countries that had been pillaged and burned by them; that and the archaeological evidence the people left behind in the earth, such as the find at Nydam.

The population began to explode during the early centuries of the Christian era. Norway grew from 2,500 people in 1200 BCE to 17,000 people in 30 CE, then suddenly increased rapidly to 50,000 people by 400 CE, and to 100,000 people by 700 CE. It would reach almost a quarter of a million people by the year 1000. Something had to give. The country was rapidly becoming overcrowded. During its early history, society was primarily based on the family. Each family unit had a farmstead, and lived an essentially isolated life. They were self sufficient, and usually had little contact with their neighbors, except by boat. There was a social structure, however, with laws, governing units, and religious hierarchy. Chiefs were elected to govern and protect the people, but even they ruled from their farmsteads. Official meetings, court hearings, and even law-making sessions were held at the farmstead.

By the end of the eighth century, the population had grown so large that the country could no longer support the great numbers of people on farmsteads. When the population was small, there was enough farmland for all, but since only about 3 percent of the country was suitable for agriculture, farmland rapidly became very precious. Two things happened to relieve the pressure. First, Norway began to build towns so the people could live in more concentrated groups. Towns required new professions, so some people became carpenters, masons, blacksmiths, doctors, tavern owners, and civil servants. Agriculture provided much of the food and the economic support for the new society. Hunting did likewise, and so did fishing. But still it was not enough. The people needed and desired more commercial goods, not only to maintain their quality of life, but to improve it. It was at this point that the second event occurred to relieve the pressure on the society. The Viking Age began.

The sleek dragon ships ventured forth on excursions that would leave bloody pages in the history books of the world. Swedish mariners conducted foraging excursions to the east across the Baltic Sea into Russia, and south on the great rivers of Eastern Europe, the Dnieper and the Volga. The Danes and Norwegians, on the other hand, concentrated on expeditions along the western coast of Europe and the British Isles. The Norwegians alone ventured further west to Iceland, Greenland—and beyond. The first recorded Viking raid was on Lindisfarne, off the east coast of England. The year was 793 CE. It was duly noted by a contemporary chronicler: "The harrying of the heathen miserably destroyed Gods church in Lindisfarne by rapine and slaughter."[8] LaFay says, "The Vikings stepped into history with their attack on Lindisfarne. For these warriors, the ultimate aim of life was death in battle; only then could they enter Valhalla, the Hall of the Slain."[9]

The Viking Age lasted some 250 years, and affected every country in Europe. Ireland was first invaded around the year 797 CE, when the Vikings plundered the Isle of Raghlen, north of County Antrim, on the west coast of the country. They continued their harassment for over 200 years, sailing up the Shannon River, anchoring in the many lakes for which Ireland is famous, and generally holding the country at their mercy. They made numerous permanent occupations during this time, from Galway in the west to Cork in the south. The Vikings themselves built the town of Dublin around the year 842 CE. They held power until the Irish king Brian Boru defeated them at Clontarf in 1014 CE, destroying Viking authority once and for all.

The rest of the British Isles fared no better. England was battered mercilessly from coast to coast during the eighth, ninth, and tenth centuries. Many Viking lordships and domains were established in the country during this period, and the English peasantry worked almost as slaves to produce the tribute demanded by their new rulers. The Northmen remained a major force within England until William the Conqueror crossed the English Channel and defeated Harold at the Battle of Hastings in 1066 CE. The Viking menace disappeared in England after that.

With the Swedes controlling most of Eastern Europe, and the Danes occupying large segments of Western Europe, it was only natural for the Norwegians to venture further west, into the unknown ocean. To do this required two things: first, the ability to navigate in the open sea; and second, large, stable, seaworthy ships. There is no doubt the Vikings could navigate in the open sea, out of sight of land. This was proven many times in their voyages between Europe and Greenland. There are recorded nonstop trips from Norway to Greenland, covering a distance of 1,500 miles. The Vikings were known to have used the sun and the stars in navigating their ships. During the voyage of Bjarni Herjulfsson, when the fog lifted, he could use the sun to get his bearings during the day, and the stars at night. It is quite likely that these mariners, with over 2,500 years of recorded maritime history, used the sun and stars in the same manner as the Polynesians. They knew the position of the sun at different latitudes for every day of the year. They also knew the location of the stars and constellations throughout the year. From this, they could determine how far north or south they were from a given point. And they had enough knowledge of latitudes, currents, and prevailing winds to make voyages in the Atlantic Ocean in both directions.

A second key to the Scandinavians' success at maritime activity was their expertise at shipbuilding, an art they perfected sometime prior to the Christian era. The discovery of the Nydam boats brought to light the shipbuilding capabilities of second century artisans. One of the major ingredients in the construction of those boats was the development of clinkerbuilt hulls. The thin planks that made up the hull were overlapped and fastened together with iron rivets, giving much more strength than if they had been fastened to the frame individually. Almost all Viking boats were made in this manner. Although there are many different types of Viking boats, the two most important were the warship and the cargo ship. The warship, known as the longship, is the vessel that is commonly associated with the Vikings. It was built long and narrow, with a low freeboard, decorated with the famous dragon (actually serpent) figurehead, adorned with the imposing, large, red and white striped sail, and embellished with the overlapping design of the feared black and yellow shields along the sides. It was the perfect ship for marauding. It was fast and maneuverable. It could glide along the coast safely, dart into harbors or shallow rivers effortlessly, change direction quickly, and move with the prevailing wind or against it. It was a boat designed to operate on the rivers or along the coastline. It was not an ocean vessel.

The cargo ship, or Knorr, was designed for ocean voyages (see illustration). Knorrs were shorter and stubbier than their fighting sister-ships. Typical dimensions might be 70 feet long, 16 feet wide, and about 10 feet deep. Like the longships, the Knorrs were equipped with a large square sail, but they were not decorated as elaborately; no red and white striped sails, no gaudy painted hulls, and no shields lining the sides. Knorrs were primarily designed to haul cargo, not to impress or terrify a populace. They were also almost completely dependent on the wind for propulsion. In order to maximize space for cargo capacity, the crew was kept to a minimum, usually from six to 12 people; therefore, there was little manpower for rowing. The ships were equipped with partial decks fore and aft, and a hold in the center of the ship. The hold was used to store cargo, or in some cases carry passengers and livestock. The accommodations for passengers were not very comfortable. Sleeping space was crowded, and there were no provisions for cooking. The ship was extremely seaworthy, however, and with her light construction and flat bottom, she rode on top of the waves like a cork, with almost no roll. Two references to Knorrs in the Viking Sagas were reported by Du Chaillu: "King Olaf left behind in England, the longships, and went hence with two Knerrir, on which he had

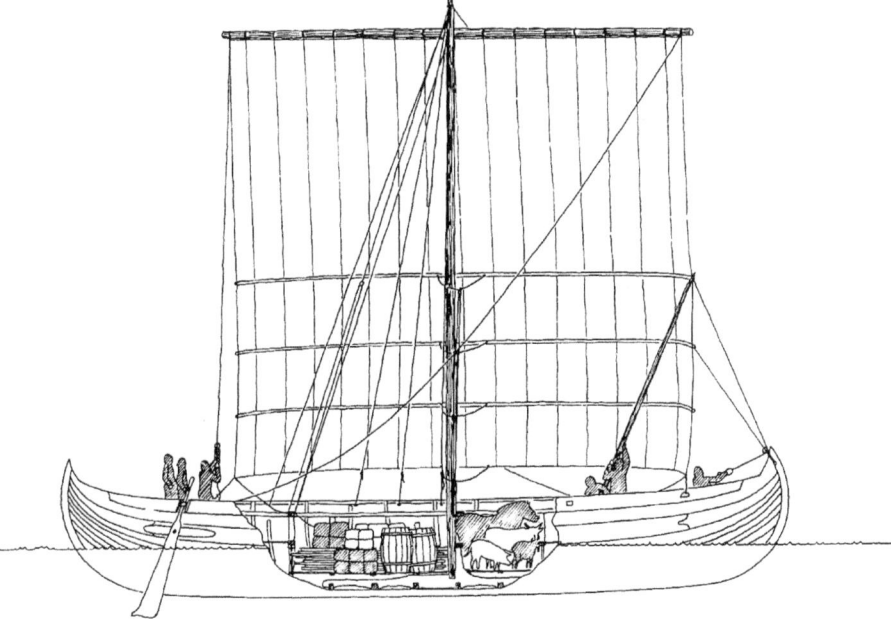

The Viking Knorr or cargo ship (courtesy the Viking Ship Museum, Roskilde, Denmark)

220 picked men, fully armed."[10] And, "Sigmund told Hakon Jarl that he wanted to leave off warfare and go to the Faeroes; he said he no longer wished to hear that he had not avenged his father and be upbraided for it; he asked the Jarl to aid him, and advise him how to manage it. Hakon answered that the sea to the islands was hard to cross, and the breakers strong; 'You cannot go on longships thither, but I will have two Knerrir made for you, and get a crew to man them.'"[11]

The history of Scandinavia confirms that the Vikings had a long and active maritime history, going back some 2,500 years before their voyages to Iceland and Greenland. Their ships were seaworthy and capable of long ocean voyages, and their navigational techniques were adequate to complete transatlantic crossings.

Next, the Viking Sagas have to be reviewed to determine their relevance to the study of ancient America, and to ascertain their historical accuracy. The Viking Sagas are actually an accumulation of many written sources, which include:

- *Íslendingabók*, by Ari Frode, written c. 1130 CE. This is the first history of Iceland and Greenland, containing the earliest mention of Vinland in Icelandic literature.
- *Landnámabók*, written c. 1100 CE. It is a history of Icelandic settlement, telling of the voyage of Ari Marson.
- *Kristni saga*, written c. 1300 CE. This saga discusses Christianity in Iceland.
- *Hauksbók*, written c. 1330 CE. It contains the Greenlander saga, the *Saga of Erik*, and relates Leif Erikson's discoverys of Vinland and the voyage of Bjarni Herjulfsson.

In addition to the Viking Sagas, there is a book written by Adam of Bremen about 1075 CE, *Ecclesiastical History of the North of Europe*, which contains the first known reference to Vinland.

The present work is not intended to dissect each of these sources in an attempt to locate the exact geographical location of Vinland. This has been done many times over the past hundred years, and has produced as many theories as it has theorists. Paul Chapman's *The Norse Discovery of America*, containing excellent navigational research, is the definitive book on the subject. The Saga stories themselves are of primary interest here. Do the Sagas corroborate other evidence of Viking intrusions into North America?

The Viking Sagas begin with the settlement of Iceland. The westward migration was probably caused by the War of Consolidation in Norway, in 872 CE. Harold Fairhair, who unified the country, undertook an expedition to the British Isles and surrounding islands, to punish those chiefs who opposed him during the war. Many Viking chiefs from the Faeroes, the Shetlands, the Orkneys, and the Hebrides fled before the avenging Harold and eventually found their way west to Iceland, beginning in the year 874 CE. The so-called settlement period covered the years from 874 to 930 CE. The Sagas relate that the population of Iceland at the end of the settlement period was about 20,000 people. When the census was taken in 1100 CE, there were 4,000 homesteads and a population of approximately 50,000 people. To the Vikings' surprise, when they arrived in Iceland, the country showed signs of previous occupation. "Before Iceland was colonized from Norway, men had been there whom the Northmen called Papas. They were Christians; for after them were found Irish books, bells, and croziers, and many other things from whence it could be seen that they were Christian men, and had come from the west over the sea. English books also show that, in that time, there was intercourse between the two countries."[12] The Papas "went afterwards away because they would not be here among heathens."[13] Irish history verifies this Icelandic account. The Irish historian Dicuil, a monk, records the flight of Irish monks before the pillaging Vikings in Ireland. The monks supposedly migrated to Iceland between 797 and 850 CE. They were aware of the existence of the island, having visited it in 795 CE.

Sometime around the year 950 CE, in the town of Jaeder, Norway, a man named Thorvold Erikson was dragged before the Thing, the high court of justice, accused of murder in a local brawl. He was found guilty and was permanently exiled. Erikson gathered up his belongings and, together with his son Erik, known to history as Erik the Red, sailed to Iceland. He settled down in the northern part of the country at Drauge on Hornstrand. Erik grew to manhood there, eventually married a local girl named Thorhild, and moved south to Erikstad near Vatshorn. In the year 980 CE, he was summoned before the Thing, accused of murdering Eyulf Soer and Rafn the duellist. He was found guilty and banished from the district. Two years later he killed a man named Thorgest in a dispute over the loan of a religious ornament. This time he was declared an outlaw, and was banished from Iceland for three years.

Erik, along with his family and friends, set sail from Iceland for the last time. Years past, he had heard stories of other lands to the west. A Viking named Gunnbjorn had been blown off course on a voyage from Norway to Iceland, and had sighted other unknown lands beyond Iceland in the great ocean. Following the directions given by Gunnbjorn, Erik sighted land after several days at sea. He approached the southeast coast of Greenland to find high, forbidding mountains of ice, land unfit for human habitation. He followed the coast around the southern tip of the country, and eventually wintered in a grassy area later known as the Eastern Settlement, located in the southwestern part of Greenland. In the spring, Erik moved to a more picturesque section of the settlement overlooking a fjord, and named it Eriksfjord. Here he built his chieftain's manor, called Brattahlid, from where he would rule his district. In addition to the Eastern Settlement, he founded the Western Settlement, somewhat further north on the west coast. In 985 CE, Erik was ready to recruit new settlers. He named the country Greenland, in order to entice people to leave Iceland and to emigrate to the new territory.

About 500 people were lured to Erik's project with visions of lush green pastures and fertile farmland. They engaged 25 ships and set sail for Greenland. At least some of the ships were Knorrs and carried many horses, cattle, and sheep, in addition to the passengers and supplies. It was not an easy voyage; 1,500 miles of treacherous north Atlantic gales and breakers. An untold number of ships were swamped by the high seas and were lost with all hands. Still other ships turned back before the fury of the storm. Fourteen ships arrived safely in Greenland. The colonists, perhaps 350 people in total, spread out between the Western and the Eastern Settlements and established their farmsteads. Everywhere they went, the new settlers found evidence of previous inhabitants: remains of dwellings, skin canoes, and iron implements. They resembled the remains discovered in Iceland, that had been attributed to Irish monks. It was reported that the monks fled Greenland when they observed the dreaded Viking ships exploring the shoreline between 982 and 985 CE.

The first Viking to set eyes on the North American continent, according to the Sagas, may have been Ari Marson in the year 982, the first year that Erik the Red was exploring Greenland. Ari Marson was born in Iceland about 940 CE. He rose to become an important citizen and a district chief by the year 982. Then, according to the *Landnámabók*, "He was driven by a tempest to White Man's Land, which some call Great Ireland; it lies to the west in the sea, near to Vinland The Good, and six days sailing west from Ireland. From thence could Ari not get away, and was there baptized."[14]

North America definitely entered the pages of history with the voyage of Bjarni Herjulfsson, in 986 CE. Bjarni was born in Iceland and grew to become a successful merchant. He owned his own ship, and carried on a flourishing trading business between Iceland, Ireland, and Norway. Every other year, Bjarni spent the winter with his father in Eyrar on the southwest coast of Iceland. During the winter of 985–986, Bjarni arrived in Iceland on a trading mission, and traveled to Eyrar to visit his father. He was

## 3. Vikings: The People and the Legend    51

shocked to discover that Herjulf had departed for Greenland several months before. Overcome with anxiety for his father's safety, Bjarni made ready to sail for Greenland, although he had never ventured forth upon the Greenland sea before. The story of that historic voyage was recorded in the *Flateyjarbók* or *Flatey Book*, a beautifully written and illuminated parchment manuscript discovered in a monastery on Flatey Island off the coast of Iceland. According to the *Flatey Book*:

> They put to sea so soon as they were ready, and sailed for three days, until the land was out of sight under the water; but then the fair wind fell, and there arose north winds and fogs, and they knew not where they were; and thus it continued for many days. After that they saw the sun again, and could discover the sky; they now made sail, and sailed for that day, before they saw land, and counseled with each other about what land that could be, and Bjarni said he thought it could not be Greenland. They asked whether he wished to sail to this land or not. "My advice is," said he, "to sail close to the land," and so they did. And soon saw that the land was without mountains, and covered with wood, and had small heights. Then they left the land on their larboardside, and let the stern turn from the land. Afterwards they sailed two days before they saw another land. They asked if Bjarni thought this was Greenland, but he said he as little believed this to be Greenland as the other; "because in Greenland are said to be very high ice hills." They soon approached the land, and saw that it was a flat land covered with wood. Then the fair wind fell, and the sailors said that it seemed to them most advisable to land there; but Bjarni was unwilling to do so. They pretended that they were in want of both wood and water. "Ye have no want of either of the two," said Bjarni; for this however, he met with some reproaches from the sailors. He bade them make sail, and so was done; they turned the prow from the land, and sailing out into the open sea for three days, with a southwest wind, saw then the third land; and this land was high, and covered with mountains and ice hills. Then asked they whether Bjarni would land there, but he said that he would not; "for to me this land appears little inviting." Therefore they did not lower the sails, but held on along this land, and saw that it was an island; again turned they the stern from the land, and sailed out into the sea with the same fair wind; but the breeze freshened, and Bjarni told them to shorten sail, and not sail faster than their ship and ships gear could hold out. They sailed now four days, when they saw the fourth land. Then asked they Bjarni whether he thought this was Greenland or not. Bjarni answered, "This is most like Greenland, according to what I have been told about it, and here we will steer for land." So did they, and landed in the evening under a ness, and just here lived Bjarni's father, and from him has the ness taken its name, and is since called Herjulfsness. Bjarni now repaired to his fathers, and gave up seafaring, and was with his father so long as Herjulf lived, and afterwards he dwelt there after his father."[15]

Bjarni's tale of new lands was not forgotten, and it was up to a young 24-year-old adventurer to complete the saga, to step ashore on these new lands, and to be hailed as the discoverer. His name was Leif Erikson. Leif was born in 979 CE, the son of Erik the Red, and the grandson of Thorvald. He had famous footsteps to walk in, and he more than filled them. When he was 22 years old, he heard the story of Bjarni Herjulfsson's sighting of strange new lands in the great ocean. His curiosity got the best of him, and he could not rest until he had personally searched out these new lands and explored them on foot. He immediately set to work organizing an expedition. He bought a ship plus all the necessary supplies, and assembled a crew of 35 experienced seamen. He then sought out Bjarni Herjulfsson to hear the story firsthand, and to memorize all the important navigational and geographical facts that Bjarni had accumulated. Returning once again to his ship, he checked all the last minute details, and set sail south on the Greenland Sea. The year was 1002 CE. The Sagas relate that historic voyage.

> Now prepared they their ship, and sailed out into the sea when they were ready, and then found that land first which Bjarni had found last. There sailed they to the land, and cast anchor, and put off boats, and went ashore, and saw there no grass. Great icebergs were over all up the country; but like a plain of flat stones was all from the sea to the mountains, and it appeared to them that this land had no good qualities. Then Leif said, "We have not done like Bjarni about this land, that we have not been upon it: now will I give the land a name, and call it Helluland." Then went they on board, and after that sailed out to sea, and found another land; they sailed again to the land, and cast anchor, then put off boats and went on shore. This land was flat, and covered with wood, and white sands were far around where they went, and the shore was low. Then said Leif, "This land shall be named after its qualities, and called Markland [Woodland]." Then they immediately returned to the ship. Now sailed they thence into the open sea with a north east wind, and were two days at sea before they saw land, and they sailed thither and came to an island which lay to the eastward of the land, and went up there, and looked round them in good weather and observed that there was dew upon the grass; and it so happened that they touched the dew with their hands, and raised the fingers to the mouth, and they thought they had never before tasted anything so sweet.
> After that they went to the ship, and sailed into a sound, which lay between the island and a ness [promontory], which ran out to the eastward of the land; and then steered westwards past the ness. It was very shallow at ebb tide, and their ship stood up, so that it was far to see from the ship to the water. But so much did they desire to land, that they did not give themselves time to wait until the water again rose under their ship, but ran at once on shore, at a place where a river flows out of a lake; but so soon as the waters rose under the ship, then took they boats, and rowed to the ship, and floated it up to the river, and thence into a lake, and there cast anchor, and brought up from the ship their skin cots, and made there booths. After this took they counsel, and formed the resolution of remaining there for the

winter, and built there large houses. There was no want of salmon either in the river or in the lake, and larger salmon than they had before seen. The nature of the country was, as they thought, so good, that cattle would not require house-feeding in winter, so there came no frost in winter, and little did the grass wither there. Day and night were more equal than in Greenland or Iceland, for on the shortest day the sun was above the horizon from half-past seven in the forenoon till half-past four in the afternoon. But when they had done with the house-building, Leif said to his comrades: "Now will I divide our men into two parts, and have the land explored; and the half of the men shall remain at home at the house, while the other half explore the land; but, however, not go further than they can come home in the evening, and they should not separate." Now they did so for a time, and Leif changed about, so that the one day he went with them, and the other remained at home in the house. Leif was a great and strong man, grave and well favored, therewith sensible and moderate in all things."[16]

One day a crew member named Tyrker wandered away from the group and was missing for several hours. Finally Leif became worried and organized a search party of 20 men to look for him. Before they could start, however, Tyrker appeared and explained his absence: "I have not been much further off, but still I have something new to tell of; I found vines and grapes." Leif gave the land a name after its qualities, and called it VINLAND."[17] Leif's exploration of Vinland lasted less than one year, but brought him everlasting fame. It also resulted in many questions, the most important question being, "Where is Vinland?" This subject has been discussed for over 100 years by dozens of experts, but to date there has been no definitive answer. There are many clues in the Sagas, including:

- The geography of the lands discovered
- The distances traveled between lands
- The comment of there being "no frost in winter"
- The discovery of grape vines
- The length of the day

Most experts agree that Vinland was located somewhere between Newfoundland and Cape Cod, Massachusetts. The length of the day limits the location to that general area. It is not critical to the study of ancient America that Vinland be identified as being within the borders of the United States. The great, adventuresome spirit of the Vikings, and their insatiable curiosity, is well known. Proof of that spirit lies in the discovery of a thirteenth century runestone over 1,000 miles north of Greenland's Western Settlement, in the frozen arctic region. Regardless of whether Vinland was on Cape Cod or in Newfoundland, it is almost certain that the inquisitive mariners would have explored America at least as far south as New York and the Hudson River. The physical evidence should still be there.

Shortly after Leif returned to Greenland, Erik the Red died at the age of 53, and Leif inherited the role of leader of the Greenland communities, which by this time had grown considerably. The Western Settlement had about 150 farms and 2,000 people, and the Eastern Settlement had 75 farms and 400 people. Modern archaeological research has identified the ruins of 300 farms, 17 churches, the bishop's residence, convents and monasteries. The maximum population was estimated to be 5,000 people. Further exploration of the New World by Leif was now out of the question. Civic administration became his full-time job. But brother Thorwald was ready to pick up the gauntlet and carry on the Erikson tradition of exploration.

In the summer of 1007 CE, Thorwald Erikson left Greenland on his Knorr with a crew of 30 men for a three-year expedition. They successfully located Leif's settlement in Vinland and spent the winter there. The following summer was spent in more expanded exploration, and the second winter was again spent in Leif's houses. Explorations continued again the following summer. A heavy storm at this time drove their ship on the beach, and separated the keel from the ship. Thorwald repaired it, leaving the broken keel on the sand, and naming the place Keelness. Putting to sea once more, they found land that was more suitable to them, and they built their own houses. It was at this time that Thorwald and his men came into contact with Indians for the first time. The Vikings foolishly decided to kill nine Indians they discovered sleeping under canoes, rather than to establish friendly relations with them. One Indian escaped, which proved to be the Viking's downfall. The Indians soon returned in force, and during the ensuing battle Thorwald was mortally wounded. At his request, Thorwald was buried on the land he settled. A cross was placed at his head, and also at his feet, and the land was called Krossaness. The survivors spent a third winter in Vinland, but in the spring they returned to Greenland with accounts of their explorations, and the sad news of Thorwald Erikson's death.

Another Erikson brother, Thorstein, decided to go to Vinland to bring his brother's body home. The voyage was a disaster. Sailing from the Eastern Settlement, the ship got lost, and wandered about the ocean for several months before finally returning to Greenland's Western Settlement. During the winter, a sickness swept the settlement, and Thorstein was overcome and died. The next Viking to explore Vinland was Thorfinn Karlsefni, a distinguished merchant and a very influential citizen in Iceland. During the summer of 1009 CE, Karlsefni made a trading expedition to Greenland with two ships, and he spent the winter at Brattahlid as a house guest of Leif Erikson. During the many jovial evenings in front of a roaring fire in the great hall, wondrous tales of Vinland were repeated over and over. Stories like this only served to whet the appetite of an ambitious merchant like Karlsefni. He soon decided to organize his own expedition to Vinland, to establish permanent trading posts. The spring of 1010 CE saw Thorfinn Karlsefni leave Greenland with 160 men in two ships to explore the Vinland paradise. They sailed south for two days and reached Leif's Helluland, an inhospitable land of flat stone. Another two-day voyage to the south and southeast brought them to a wooded country called Markland. Sailing further south they then discovered Thorwald Erikson's Keelness. The long, white sandy beaches in this area they named Furdurstrands, or wonder strands. Continuing south, they entered a sound they called Straumfjord, settling nearby for the winter. They built houses for themselves and shelter for the cattle they had brought with them. That winter a son, Snorri, was born to Thorfinn Karlsefni and his wife, Gudrid. Snorri was the first European baby known to have been born in North America.

In the summer, Karlsefni sent one boat northward to explore the land, while he went south. The northbound boat was caught by strong westerly winds and driven across the ocean to Ireland, where the crew was captured and enslaved. Karlsefni's southbound boat reached a river that flowed from a lake into the ocean. The river could only be navigated at high tide, so they called the place Hop, or landlocked bay. The boat was unloaded, including cattle, and shelters were constructed around the lake. Following another snowless winter, which permitted the cattle to graze in the open, many Indian canoes were sighted, and friendly relations were established with the Indians. These good relations did not last long, however, and within weeks hostilities broke out. Karlsefni decided that the unfriendly inhabitants made his people's position untenable, and he gathered his group together and returned to Straumfjord, where they spent the third winter.

When spring arrived the settlement was abandoned, and the ship headed north for Greenland. When they reached Markland, they saw five natives: one bearded male, two females, and two boys. They captured the boys, but the other three escaped. The boys, who appeared to speak Irish, called their mother Vathelldi and their father Uvaege. They said the people of their country did not live in houses, but in caves. They also said there was a country adjacent to theirs, where the people wore white robes, carried poles with banners, and made loud shouting noises. The Vikings thought this was White-Man's-Land or Great Ireland, the same country that was visited by Ari Marson. The voyagers reached Greenland with their cargo, and were heartily welcomed by Leif and the rest of the people. Karlsefni never returned to Vinland, but instead traveled to Norway where he and his family became prominent citizens, and lived happy and successful lives.

In the year 1029 CE, an Icelandic merchant named Gudlief Gudlaugson was on a trading expedition to Ireland. After completing his business in Dublin, he traveled up the west coast and veered to the west for Iceland. Before he could reach home, however, he was caught by the violent polar easterlies, and blown to a country in the west of the sea. After his ship entered a harbor and tied up on shore, the crew was surrounded by several hundred people who apparently spoke Irish. It seemed as if they were about to be killed, when suddenly the leader appeared and stopped the proceedings. The leader was an elderly, distinguished-looking man with long white hair. Much to their surprise, he spoke their language. He inquired about their voyage, about their country, and about specific people in Borgafjord and Breidafjord, Iceland, including a woman named Thurid. The leader intervened with the people on behalf of the captives, and succeeded in securing their freedom. He would not tell them his name, but gave Gudleif a gold ring, and asked him to present it to the lady Thurid on his return to Iceland. Gudleif and his crew put to sea and returned to Ireland, where they spent the winter. The following spring they continued on to Iceland, and Gudleif gave Thurid the ring as instructed. Thurid immediately recognized it as belonging to her lover, Bjorn Asbrandson, who had sailed from Iceland 30 years previous and had never been heard from again. Once again this land was thought to be Ireland the Great, because of the language the natives spoke, which was apparently Irish. It is important to note that these tales were reported by Vikings, who had no reason to fabricate stories about Irish lands in the western ocean. And although they could not speak the Irish language, they were familiar with it from having traded regularly at Irish ports.

The remaining history of Vinland is spotty and sometimes poorly documented. The first historical reference to Vinland was credited to Adam of Bremen in his book, *Ecclesiastical History of the North Of Europe*, published about 1075 CE. Adam related, "Sueno, King of Denmark, to whom I paid a visit, described to me in conversation on the northern countries, among many other islands, one which had been called Vinland because the vine would grow there without cultivation, and because it produced the best sort of wine. Plenty of fruits grow in this country without planting. This is not mere rumor. I have this news from very authentic and trustworthy relations of the Danes. Beyond this land however, no habitable country is found. On the contrary, everything to the north is covered with ice and eternal night."[18]

In 1112 CE, Henricus was appointed bishop of Greenland and the surrounding regions. He is mentioned as visiting Vinland between 1116 and 1121 CE.

In 1341 CE, the church in Norway lost touch with the Western Settlement. A priest named Ivar Bardson was sent to investigate and found the settlement recently deserted. There was no sign of violence, but the livestock was wandering wild and there were no people in the settlement.

In 1342 CE, a document recorded that the inhabitants of Greenland gave up the faith and joined their friends in Vinland.

In 1347 CE, the Eastern Settlement was harassed by Eskimos.

In the same year, a Greenland ship from a trading expedition to Markland arrived in Iceland after being lost at sea.

In 1354 CE, King Magnus Erikson of Norway appointed Paul Knutson to travel to Greenland to restore Christianity to the region. Knutson supposedly returned to Norway in 1364 CE (more about him later).

Vatican records report the destruction of churches in Greenland in 1418 CE.

There is no record of the Greenland settlements after 1500 CE.

This ends the historical record of Vinland. But what did the Sagas tell us?

In short, they chronicled the discovery of a new land that lay to the south of Greenland, in the Atlantic Ocean. This land was discovered by Leif Erikson and was named Vinland by him, because of the wild grapes growing there. There were at least four expeditionary voyages to Vinland, by Leif, Thorwald Erikson, Freydis Erikson, and Thorfin Karlsefni, and the people on these voyages explored the new land for a period of at least eight years.

Were the Sagas a factual account of Viking exploration in the eleventh century? The Vikings themselves can best answer that question. As Slafter reported, "At all public meetings, and particularly at the assembly of the Althing, the finest of the old traditions were recited ... the song of the skald and the narrative of the Sagaman when thus all eyes were fixed upon him, and all ears open to him, behooved not only to be artistical, lively and attractive, but true. If the recital ... contained falsehoods, the reciter was treated as a braggart and a liar."[19]

And the Sagas themselves tell us, "For it be the fashion with skalds to praise most those in whose presence they are standing, yet no one would dare to relate to a chief what he and all those who heard it knew to be false and imaginary — not a true account of his deeds; because that would be mockery, not praise."[20]

Assuming that the Sagas were geographically correct, what clues might identify the location of Vinland?

1. The distances traveled by the Vikings should be helpful, but the reports appear to be unreliable in some cases because of errors in translation, and for other miscellaneous reasons. For instance, it is well known that a sailing ship could travel between 75 and 150 miles per day. Yet the Sagas state that the trip from Norway to Iceland, a distance of 2,800 miles, took seven days; that Vinland was six days west of Ireland; and that Helluland was four days south of Greenland. This information obviously cannot be taken literally. In calculating sailing time, the Vikings included only the time when they were out of sight of land. As long as they could see land, they did not include that time in their estimates. Also, as Paul Chapman, noted historian and navigator, pointed out, the Vikings calculated sailing time as being time with a following wind. Time at sea with unfavorable wind conditions, or in a becalmed sea, was not counted. Chapman's calculations of Viking sailing times brought the entire adventure into focus. He identified the various Viking settlements in North America as being located between Northern Labrador and Newfoundland.
2. The length of the shortest day of the year in Vinland was recorded. The Sagas do not record the actual hours, but only periods of the day, leaving the result open to interpretation. Depending on the translation, the length of the day could be nine hours as in the translation used in this book, or it could be as short as eight hours as determined by Chapman. In either case, it does restrict the possible location of Vinland. An eight-hour day would put Vinland in Northern Newfoundland, while a nine-hour day would place Vinland near Cape Cod, Massachusetts.
3. There were at least two instances in the Sagas where ships were blown across the sea from Vinland to Ireland. Westerly winds prevail between 40 degrees and 60 degrees north latitude, making it possible for this to happen anywhere between Cape Cod and Newfoundland. In one instance, however, there was a description of the ship being bogged down in a massive sea of slimy green vegetation. The Sargasso Sea, located between 20 and 30 degrees north latitude, has a great accumulation of seaweed from the Gulf of Mexico, and is the only area in the Atlantic Ocean that fits that description. The ship that encountered the Sargasso Sea must have been on an exploratory mission to the southern part of the United States to have been driven out to sea at that location.
4. There was no frost during one winter in Vinland. This allowed cattle to graze outside. Cape Cod is bathed by the Gulf Stream, and it is not

uncommon to have mild, relatively snow free winters in this location. Further north, however, out of range of the Gulf Stream, winters are more severe, and a frost free winter in Newfoundland would be quite rare. It would have been unusual even in the milder climate that existed 1,000 years ago.

This evidence provided by the Sagas indicates that Vinland was located between Cape Cod and Newfoundland. The first piece of generally accepted hard evidence placing the Vikings in North America was discovered by a Scandinavian explorer named Helge Ingstad. Ingstad was born in Norway in 1899. Although he was educated as a lawyer, he gave up his law practice at an early age and turned to the field of anthropology. Over a period of 30 years, Ingstad studied the peoples of North America, the Indian and the Eskimo, in great detail. He also held several political positions in Greenland, developing an interest in the early Viking settlements in that country. Soon his interests spread to the Viking Sagas and to the reported voyages to the legendary land of Vinland, and he committed himself to locating, once and for all, the Viking settlement in the New World. His quest began in 1960, with an aerial search of the east coast of North America. The search began south of Newport, Rhode Island, but Ingstad felt it would be almost impossible to locate Viking ruins in the United States due to the tremendous growth of vegetation that would hide the ruins from aerial photographs, as well as the numerous population centers whose construction would have destroyed any ruins in their path. He was right.

The northern section of North America, with a paucity of people and retarded vegetation growth, held the key to Ingstad's search. In the northwest section of Newfoundland, in a place called L'Anse aux Meadows, he noticed the telltale signs of ancient foundations. Over the next six years, Ingstad and his team excavated the area in question. Eight house sites were uncovered, as well as a blacksmith shop with a smelting operation. Artifacts were almost nonexistent, but there were enough to positively identify the settlement as Viking. A bronze pin, used to fasten a cloak, and a Norse spindle whorl were two important discoveries. The spindle whorl is the oldest known European household article found in North America.

Ingstad, an amateur, had sparked a renewed interest in the early history of North America. After 100 years of archaeological dark ages, the first glimmer of light shone through, and a new day dawned in American archaeology. The Viking Sagas were true. The Vikings did visit North America 500 years before Christopher Columbus. Many qualified American archaeologists quickly jumped on the discovery, declaring the settlement to be

Vinland, but was it? Evidence indicates it was probably not the location of Leif's houses, but it may have been part of a larger geographical land mass commonly known as Vinland. The discovery of a spindle whorl points to a female presence in the settlement, but there were no women on Leif's voyage. The most important point, though, is that it was Viking, and it does establish the Viking intrusion into North America almost 1,000 years ago.

There are several arguments against Ingstad's site being Vinland. In addition to the female presence, there is the existence of a blacksmith shop with a smelting operation. As Chapman pointed out, this was not mentioned in the Sagas. According to all written evidence, Leif and his crew spent all their time cutting down trees and vines, and gathering grapes, to bring back to Greenland. They did not need a smelting operation. Also, there was no established settlement where Leif built his houses in Vinland (at least, he never mentioned any). Excavations at the L'Anse aux Meadows site finally eliminated the tiny settlement from any possible consideration as Leif Erikson's settlement. Charcoal samples taken from the eight houses gave radiocarbon dates as early as 580 CE, and indicate that L'Anse aux Meadows was finally deserted sometime after 1150 CE.

The location of L'Anse aux Meadows might better fit Markland than Vinland. There was a permanent trading settlement in Markland, and many women were living there. There are records of trading voyages between Greenland and Markland from 1000 CE right up to 1347 CE, a period of 350 years.

As Gary Jennings so aptly put it, "I found little to see there but the foundation outlines of their longhouses, ember pits, and saunas—and the dreary surrounding flatlands of cold and windswept muskeg. It made me wonder why, if the Norsemen had gumption enough to sail unknown seas all the way to this island, they were willing to settle down on the most appalling, inhospitable part of it."[21] The Vikings most likely would have maintained a permanent village there, as the nearest source of a much needed supply of wood for Greenland. But for more civilized living in a permanent settlement, their search would probably have continued further south.

Paul H. Chapman concluded a detailed study of the Viking presence in North America in 1981. Using his expertise in research and in navigation, Chapman examined the Viking Sagas in minute detail, particularly the geographical references, the length of the shortest day (as noted previously), and the distances between locations. His study resulted in some astounding conclusions:

1. Vinland was the entire island of Newfoundland
2. L'Anse aux Meadows was not Vinland, but was just one of several settlements in Vinland. The radiocarbon dates reported earlier prove that L'Anse aux Meadows was occupied by some unknown settlers several hundred years before Leif's party entered the area.
3. Leif's houses were located on the northernmost tip of Newfoundland, at Pistolet Bay.
4. Gander Lake, Newfoundland, was the settlement called Hop.
5. Southern Labrador was Markland.

There are other possible Viking settlements under study in the north country. One is on Ellesmere Island, northwest of Greenland and only 800 miles from the North Pole, in the Arctic Circle. This was a hunting camp. A second location, not far from L'Anse aux Meadows, is at Ungava Bay, just east of Hudson Bay in Canada. The site was discovered in 1957, although major archaeological digs have yet to be funded. The site includes the ruins of a large rectangular stone building, 85 feet long and 30 feet wide. There are at least three other large rectangular house ruins in the vicinity. The site also includes a number of cairns, which archaeologists believe are Norse. The settlement has been radiocarbon dated to 1050 CE, from hearth charcoal. Only time and an organized excavation will definitely determine the identity of the Ungava settlers.

One last piece of information should be noted. An Algonquian Indian legend refers to "foreigners" in their part of the country. The Indians supposedly drove the foreigners out of the New England area, and chased them north until the foreigners finally settled in Newfoundland. These people were reported to be light skinned with a wide range of hair colors. They spoke a language that was strange to the Indians.

# Summary

- Scandinavian civilization developed into a maritime culture during the Bronze Age (see illustration).
- The Scandinavian nations had oceangoing vessels by the time of Christ, perhaps earlier.
- Recitation of Viking history at social events was important for the prestige of the chieftains. Exaggeration and prevarication were unforgivable sins.
- Large oceangoing merchant vessels, called Knorrs, were utilized for transoceanic voyages, not the famous longships.

Simple ship design

Ship with crew of 13

Ship with animal figurehead

Ship with a sail ?

Ship with a steering oar

Double decked ship with animal figurehead, carrying a fowl

Ship carrying a horse

Ship with a sail ?

Ancient ships of Scandinavia as depicted on the rock carvings in Bohuslan, Sweden. Carvings dated to approximately 1800 BC. Drawings from Du Chaillu, *The Viking Age*.

- Helge Ingstad discovered a Viking settlement at L'Anse aux Meadows, Newfoundland.
- Paul Chapman's study of the Viking presence in North America identified the entire island of Newfoundland as Vinland.
- Another possible Viking habitation site exists at Ungava Bay in Canada. It needs further study.

## Conclusions

- The Viking presence in North America was established by the discovery of L'Anse aux Meadows in Newfoundland, by Helge Ingstad.
- The Viking Sagas can be considered to be true records of Viking visits to North America.
- The Viking Sagas pinpointed Leif Erikson's Vinland as being located somewhere between Cape Cod, Massachusetts, and L'Anse aux Meadows, Newfoundland.
- Paul Chapman's identification of the entire island of Newfoundland as Vinland is the result of a sound approach, and a scholarly research program. His study is the most scientific study conducted on the subject to date, and should be considered a valuable reference for future research.

# 4

# *Vikings: The American Evidence*

## Conventional Thinking (after 1967)

Recent discoveries proved the Vikings did establish a settlement at L'Anse aux Meadows, Newfoundland. But they never visited the (present-day) United States.

## Discussion

The Viking adventure in North America began with the popular studies initiated by the Royal Society of Northern Antiquities in Copenhagen, Denmark, in the year 1837. Professor Charles Christian Rafn was in charge of the section on voyages to America, and in that year published his *Antiquitates Americanae*. His study concluded that the Vikings did visit America, as far south as Newport, Rhode Island, in fact. As evidence of their visit, he identified the Newport Tower as a Viking structure and the famous Dighton Rock as a Viking inscription. Soon this popular theory exploded into Vikingmania of hysterical proportions. Every unidentified artifact was now of Viking origin. Every new discovery was classified as Viking. Scientists are still trying to separate fact from fiction more than 150 years later.

The first artifact of note is the Dighton Rock, which was discovered in 1680. This was the stone that the Reverend Cotton Mather reported to the Royal Academy in London. It is generally accepted that the pictographic inscription is genuine and very old, but who engraved it is still open to debate. At least some of it may have been inscribed by Indians. As Henry Schoolcraft stated in his history of the Indian tribes, "It is of purely Indian origin, and is executed in the peculiar symbolic character of the Kekeewin....

This Kekeewin is a rude ideographic mode of communicating thought, by which triumphs in war and hunting, deaths, and other subjects are commemorated by the Indians.[1]

Another purported great Viking discovery was the Fall River "Skeleton in Armor" that was subsequently immortalized in Henry Wadsworth Longfellow's poem of the same name. The skeleton was dislodged from its quiet repose in 1831 by a road building crew at the corner of Fifth and Hartly Streets in Fall River, Massachusetts. The unique feature of this particular skeleton was that it wore a metal breastplate thereby making it an apparent native of Europe. Further examination revealed the metal breastplate, and other ornaments were crude pieces of sheet copper, leading to the conclusion that seventeenth century man was an Indian.

There were many victims of the nineteenth century Viking hysteria, where every new discovery was identified as of Norse origin. One victim was a stone discovered near Aptuxcet on the western end of Cape Cod. This stone had been used as a doorstep outside an Indian meeting house, and had been considered by many generations of Indians to be a sacred stone. The nineteenth century scientific evaluation determined the stone to be a tenth century runestone of Viking origin. Even today that is the accepted identification by some scientists. The truth is that the stone, now called the Bourne Stone, may be ancient but not Viking. In fact, it may be much older than 1,000 years, but that will be discussed later in the book.

The fascinating Yarmouth Stone, a 400-pound rock, was discovered in a cove near Yarmouth Harbor in Nova Scotia. The stone first came to light in 1812, when Dr. Richard Fletcher stumbled upon it. Its strange carvings intrigued the populace. It seemed to be writing, but of a type unknown in America (see illustration).

In 1875 it was identified by the Numismatic and Antiquarian Society of Philadelphia as runic writing of the Viking Age. Many scholars over the past 100 years have failed to positively identify the script, or to offer a translation. The stone, which is probably not of Viking origin, will be discussed in more detail in the chapter on inscriptions. Today, the stone resides in the Yarmouth County Museum, on view to the public, a mysterious relic of an ancient visitor to North America.

The Grave Creek Stone, uncovered in an ancient mound in West Virginia in 1838, and the Braxton Stone, discovered near Triplett Creek in West Virginia in 1931, were also identified as runestones as recently as 1961, and were accepted as such by many well known historians. They have since been determined to be an entirely different language, as will be seen in the chapter on inscriptions.

Thus far, a handful of so-called Viking artifacts and inscriptions have

The Yarmouth Stone (Fred A. Hatfield).

been reviewed, only to discover that they were actually of Indian origin, ill defined, or misinterpreted. But the next artifact offers positive proof that the Vikings trod the soil of the United States almost 1,000 years ago. This much is known: About 40 years ago, a young man found a strange looking coin in an Indian shell midden on a beach at Brooklin, Maine. The coin was later identified as a Viking coin that had been minted in England during the period 1000 to 1080 CE. No other Viking artifacts or ruins were found in the vicinity. The discovery has been accepted by the scientific community as an authentic Viking coin found in situ.

The next reported visitor to North America left considerable information on four engraved stones he had buried for safe keeping. His name is not known for sure, but he did visit Spirit Pond on the southeast coast of Maine near the town of Bath, and he did leave clues as to his identity. His existence first came to light in late spring of 1971, thanks to Walter Elliott. Mr. Elliott, a history buff, enjoyed roaming the countryside searching for artifacts. He knew, as most history buffs do, that ancient people tended to build campsites on the shores of ponds and rivers. He also knew that significant topographical changes are constantly taking place all over the world and, as a result of these changes, some ancient shoreline campsites are now completely submerged, others become visible only at low tide, and still others are now several miles inland from a water source. An example of the latter is the ancient Greek city of Ephesus in Turkey, the "Queen of the World" 2,000 years ago. In her time she was a thriving seaport metropolis with a magnificent, bustling harbor. In 39 BCE, the legendary Egyptian queen Cleopatra once sailed into her harbor on a dazzling, gilded barge to meet the Roman triumvir Marc Antony. But times change, and now, 2,000 years later, the docks of Ephesus lie, broken and shattered, some five miles distant from the shoreline.

That day in 1971, Mr. Elliott was boating around the shoreline of Spirit Pond. A tidal pond, its level was always changing, and in the process the shoreline was slowly being washed away. Mr. Elliott's eyes were on this shoreline, searching for the slightest indication of primitive habitation. Suddenly he spied a stone protruding from the mud, then another, four stones in all. He carefully cleaned them of mud and grime, and noticed they were covered with strange markings. The curator of the Bath Marine Museum identified the markings as runic writing. Cyrus Gordon, one of America's most eminent philologists, examined the stones very carefully, and could find nothing to discredit them.

One of the stones was an amulet, or charm worn to protect the owner from evil and to bring good luck (see illustration). This particular artifact was reported by Mr. James P. Whittall II, the archaeological director of the Early Sites Research Society, in the March 1975 issue of the ESRS bulletin. The artifact was first reported to the ESRS in December 1974, but at that time Elliott had requested anonymity, since he did not want the location of the discovery made public for obvious reasons. Elliott did not mention the discovery of the other stones at that time, because he considered them to be Amerindian. According to the *Bulletin*:

> The amulet was discovered in a shell midden about thirty feet back from a tidal river. It is quite possible for a boat of some size to make a landing in that location. Though there is quite a tide change, the current is neither swift nor rough there. The shoreline generally alternates between sandy stretches, marshes and some rocky areas. The immediate area near the midden is a rocky beach; the area behind the midden is neglected farmland. The finder of the amulet considered it and the other stones he uncovered to be Indian until he read something of Nordic runic inscriptions. Even though the pendant was more or less cleaned by the finder, (he has worn the pendant off and on) small traces of charcoal remain in the grooves and pit-marks of the stone. The amulet is an oblong oval-shaped stone of diorite. At the narrow end is a well-worn hole. Presumably the artifact was made to wear about the neck. The stone is 69mm in length and 42mm at its widest point. Both sides are carved, the runic markings are about 5mm in height."[2]

**Viking amulet found on the coast of Maine (photograph by Malcolm Pearson, courtesy ESRS *Bulletin*).**

The obverse of the amulet contains three lines. Donal Buchanan of ESRS studied the amulet carefully, and in his opinion, the first line may be ogam, an ancient Irish script, the second line is runic for Vinland, and the symbols in line three represent the date 1010 CE. Paul Chapman, in his study of the Spirit Pond Stones for the Epigraphic Society, concurred with Buchanan's runic translation. He identified the first line as being Q in Irish ogam. Q may be an abbreviation for woman, and may identify the amulet as being a good luck charm from a woman to her husband or a male friend who was leaving on a dangerous journey. The reverse of the amulet shows a medieval Christian cross of a design common in eleventh century Western Europe. The specific date is of interest because 1010 CE was the date of Thorfin Karlsefni's voyage to Vinland. Since Karlsefni was an Icelander, and Iceland was Christianized in the last half of the tenth century, a cross on an eleventh century Viking pendant would not be unusual.

Whittall went on to say, "As far as the amulet itself, archaeological evidence has shown that Norsemen did wear stone or metal amulets as protection against evil. The weathering on the amulet seems to be consistent with the inscribed date and all indications are that both the thonghole and the inscription are contemporary to each other. The surface of the stone is very hard; therefore, the execution of the carving had to be difficult and time-consuming. The carver had difficulty in carving with a circular motion."[3]

One of the other three stones uncovered at Spirit Pond was a map runestone showing a shoreline with some offshore islands, and several lines of runic writing. Chapman deciphered the obverse to read "Hoop," "Vinland," and "1011." The writing to the right of the map, according to Chapman, gives the sailing instructions, "twelve day sail to Iceland." Chapman feels the stone was probably engraved by or for Thorfinn Karlsefni during his voyage to Vinland in 1011 CE. The reverse of the stone refers to the arable land found in Vinland, and the pictographs show the local natives, as well as the abundance of wild grapes, grains, fish and animals found there. Chapman noted that stone number three, the so-called Memorial Runestone, which contains a lengthy inscription both front and back, commemorated the death by drowning of 17 men, lost when their boat sank in the year 1010 CE. Stone number four is called the Christian marker. It asks God to look after lost loved ones. The Spirit Pond runestones are intriguing artifacts that may point to Viking visitations to the continental United States around 1000 CE. They appear genuine, they contain historical information that is verified in the Sagas, and they contain dates of Viking voyages that were not confirmed until *after* the discovery of the stones.

In addition to numerous inscribed stones and other evidence, many pieces of hardware relating to Viking incursions into North America have been discovered in the past 150 years. One of the more intriguing was the Beardmore find. Beardmore is a small town in Ontario, Canada, on the eastern end of Lake Nipigon, just north of Lake Superior. The hero of the story was James E. Dodd, an employee of the Canadian National Railway and an avid prospector. In his spare time Dodd searched for gold, and he was sure he had a promising vein near Lake Nipigon. One day in late spring in 1930, Dodd was feverishly working his claim and following a vein of white quartz, when his progress was stymied by a clump of trees. Instead of digging his way through, Dodd used his dynamite and blasted his way clear. The ensuing rubble contained a lot of stone, which he had to clear by hand. Suddenly he noticed an object embedded in a large stone. It was a sword, but when he tried to pry it free of the stone it broke in two. Eventually he recovered both pieces, and soon uncovered two other items: an axe, and a bar of metal that he could not identify. Believing them to be of Indian origin, Dodd took the pieces home and threw them in his junk pile, where they remained for several years.

One day a government game warden spotted the artifacts, recognizing them as possible Norse weapons. The Royal Ontario Museum in

Toronto was notified of the discovery and eventually purchased the relics for their own study and display. The items remain in their care to this day, although they hesitate to authenticate them, quoting conflicting testimony in their attempt to determine the facts relating to the discovery. On the other hand, the director and chief archaeologist of the Royal Museum of Denmark viewed the pieces in 1960 and confirmed the fact that they were genuine medieval Norse implements. Further research is needed to determine how the implements found their way to Lake Nipigon.

There is one artifact discovered on Cape Cod that is of particular interest: It is an axe that was unearthed at the John Howland house in Rocky Nook in 1939. The axe may be a battle-axe of Norse origin, but that is still open to question. At the present time, it is preserved at the reconstructed Howland House in Plymouth, which is open to the public daily. The axe has strange markings on the blade, which were originally determined to be runic writing. Barry Fell later identified the markings as tifinagh script, an ancient script used in Libya and Scandinavia. He translated it as an award to the widow of a man, probably a Viking, slain in battle.

About 400 miles to the northeast of Cape Cod lies the Canadian province of Nova Scotia, the discovery site of a similar Norse battle-axe. The axe was discovered at Cole Harbor, on the northeast coast of Nova Scotia, in the year 1880. An elderly farm woman was scouring the woods near her house for dry sticks to use as kindling in her fireplace, when she tripped over a hard object hidden by the brush. It was an axe, seemingly old and very rusted — and it contained the same kind of markings as the Rocky Nook axe. Howland reported that the axe was sent to Harvard University in 1939 for a metallurgical examination: the metallurgical structure was found to be consistent with an eleventh century weapon, matching the time frame of the Viking exploratory voyages.

Another recent discovery that has raised the eyebrows of American historians is the Vinland Map, a medieval cartographical representation of the island of Vinland, lying to the southwest of Greenland in the Atlantic Ocean. The story of its discovery began in October 1957, when Mr. Lawrence Witten, a rare book dealer in New Haven, Connecticut, purchased a medieval manuscript from a European collection. The book, which was in a nineteenth century binding, appeared to be much older and was separated into two distinct sections. One section dealt with Viking voyages to North America in the eleventh and twelfth centuries, and the other section dealt with the Friar Carpini expedition to the Mongols in the thirteenth century. As Witten examined the book he was intrigued by one of its maps, a map of the world, on which was shown an island in the western Atlantic Ocean identified as Vinland. Mr. Witten referred the book to Dr. Thomas E. Marston, curator of medieval and Renaissance literature in the Yale University Library. Quite independently, Dr. Marston had purchased a fifteenth century edition of Vincent of Beauvais' *Speculum historiale*, a popular history book of the period. In a clever piece of detective work, Mr. Witten determined that the Vinland-Mongol manuscript had originally been part of the Vincent manuscript. They apparently had become detached sometime during or prior to the nineteenth century and were subsequently bound independently of each other.

With the entire manuscript before them, a Yale University research team began an exhaustive study of the material to determine its authenticity, to establish the date of authorship, and to determine the geographical location of its preparation. The work was painstakingly slow and detailed. Tests had to be conducted on the vellum, the ink, and the bindings to establish the date of use of each material, and the compatibility of dates of all the materials. Historical facts had to be checked to determine their accuracy, and also to determine if the information was generally known in Europe during the time the manuscript was written. The entire process took eight long years. The completed work was considered by the authors to be a preliminary study only. Although there was considerable denunciation of the map in some academic circles initially, independent tests conducted by the University of California at Davis confirmed the authenticity of the map. In 1996, Wilcomb E. Washburn, director of the Smithsonian Institution's program in American studies, stated, "This is the first map showing the New World. Nobody doubted that the Norse were there. It's just the power of the picture."

The extensive research indicated that the works were genuine, and were possibly written in Basle, Switzerland, around the year 1440 CE. Without going further, this would make the Vinland Map the oldest known cartographical representation of Vinland, and the only known pre–Columbian map of North America — a-mind boggling discovery with obvious, far-reaching implications. The map, in its original form, is drawn on a piece of vellum 11 inches wide by 16 inches long, and folded in the middle. It depicts the entire known world in 1440 CE and contains numerous Latin legends. The legends of most interest are those near the island of Vinland. The short legend to the right of the island refers to its discovery by Leif and Bjarni. This is additional corroborative evidence of the historical accuracy of the Viking Sagas, although it does differ from the Sagas in that it states that Leif and Bjarni traveled together to Vinland. The Sagas credit the two explorers with separate voyages. The large legend on the top left-hand corner of the map also refers to Vinland voyages, two in particular.

The first is the voyage of discovery by Leif and Bjarni; the legend states that they traveled south from Greenland through numerous ice floes to discover the rich and fertile country of Vinland, which contained many vines. The second voyage referred to is that of Bishop Eric Knuppsen, bishop of "Greenland and neighboring regions." The legend states that Bishop Eric visited Vinland during the last year of the reign of Pope Pascal. He remained in Vinland for at least a year, then returned to Greenland and finally to Europe.

The map is important for many reasons in addition to verifying the Viking Sagas:

1. It indicates that Vinland was well known in the Vatican in the twelfth century, since Bishop Knuppsen was given the title of "Bishop of Greenland and neighboring regions." The only region neighboring Greenland is the continent of North America. It cannot refer to Iceland, since Iceland had its own Bishop.
2. The Vinland colony or colonies must have been of substantial size in the twelfth century to require Bishop Knuppsen to remain there for more than one year. The voyage from Greenland to Vinland was no more than eight days. A visit to a small colony of Christians could be completed easily within a month.
3. Bishop Knuppsen may well have made two separate voyages to Vinland. In addition to the voyage related in the legend, the Sagas report that Bishop Knuppsen visited Vinland in 1121 CE, where he died. Since a new bishop was ordained for Greenland in 1124 CE, Bishop Knuppsen must have died about 1123 CE, after staying in Vinland for two more years.
4. The Vinland map was known throughout Europe in 1440 CE. It is very probable, therefore, that Christopher Columbus was aware of the continent of North America long before his historic voyage.

Skeptics continue to challenge the authenticity of the Vinland Map, but without success. As recently as July 2002, a study in *Analytical Chemistry* claimed the ink used to draw the map was of modern manufacture. That claim was refuted by Thomas Cahill at the University of California at Davis, who noted that the chemicals whose presence in the ink initiated the argument put forth in *Analytical Chemistry* are, in fact, found in many medieval documents. The vellum itself has recently been carbon dated to 1434 CE, plus or minus 11 years, by scientists at the U.S. Department of Energy's Brookhaven Laboratory.

The Heavener runestone, a large rectangular slab of sandstone, is located on a mountain near Heavener, Oklahoma, a short distance from

# 4. Vikings: The American Evidence

## The Heavener Runestone

a tributary of the Arkansas River. It was originally discovered by a hunter in 1830, and was completely covered with lichen at the time. The stone was rediscovered by Gloria Farley, a well known field epigrapher, in 1951. It is approximately 12 feet high and 10 feet long. Cleaning revealed a total of eight deeply inscribed characters that may be Norse runes. They have been dated, by their style, to about 500 CE. No one has yet been able to translate the message (see illustration).

Another purported runestone sits quietly in Narragansett Bay, off the coast of Rhode Island (see illustration). It was first reported by members of the New England Antiquities Research Association in the 1980s, It is about eight feet long, and contains an easily discernible inscription. The large, barnacle covered boulder is visible only at low tide. The inscription, which appears to be Norse, was translated by Dr. Richard Nielsen in 1993 to read, "Victory of four men at this river."

The small town of Kensington, Minnesota, burst upon the "Viking" scene in 1898 CE. A written record of a Viking expeditionary force was

Narragansett Bay inscription (courtesy Malcolm Pearson)

discovered on a local farm during a field clearing project in that year (see illustration). The reverberations from that discovery continue to be heard throughout the archaeological world over 100 years later. The discovery occurred on the farm of Olaf Ohman, a Swedish immigrant who had settled in Minnesota many years before. Mr. Ohman was preparing a large parcel of land for agricultural purposes. This required the removal of many trees from the immediate terrain. Ohman, a strong, rawboned man, set about this task early one November morning in 1898, as he had been doing every morning for several months. He was assisted on this particular day by his son. The immediate task at hand was the uprooting of a large tree on the summit of a hill near the farmhouse. Ohman first cut the horizontal roots, then applied a lever beneath the tree as his son pushed against its side. The tree toppled to the ground, roots and all. As it fell, Ohman and his son noticed an object entangled in the roots. With some effort they pried a 200-pound slab of rock from the maze of roots that entangled it. The stone, about 16 inches wide and 31 inches long, seemed to contain a written text in the runic script of medieval Scandinavia. The notoriety of the discovery brought several Scandinavian scholars to Kensington to inspect the stone and to study the inscription.

The Kensington Runestone (courtesy Runestone Museum)

The scholars were able to detect the word Vinland in the text, but could not decipher the entire message. Eventually they declared the stone to be a forgery, probably written in the nineteenth century by its alleged discoverer. Ignoring the fact that Ohman was semi-illiterate, the experts expounded upon the fact that the language on the stone had a significant Swedish tinge to it, rather than the Norwegian language of the Greenland community. Mr. Ohman, humiliated and angered by the entire incident, threw the stone on the floor of his barn and buried himself in his work in an effort to forget. Nine years later, the Kensington Stone debate surfaced again. This time a Scandinavian scholar named Hjalmar Holand happened through Kensington as part of his research study on Scandinavian communities in America. He heard about the old runestone and promptly sought out Ohman to study the stone. He not only was able to study the stone, but he was given the artifact to keep. Ohman was glad to get rid of it. Mr. Holand's subsequent translation of the inscription on the stone created a new furor in academia. As Holand explained,

> The words in brackets are omitted in the inscription; those in parentheses are explanatory. Nine lines appear on the face of the stone as follows:
> 1. (we are) 8 Goths (Swedes) and 22 Norwegians on
> 2. (an) exploration-journey from
> 3. Vinland through (or across) the West (i.e. round about the West) We
> 4. had camp by (a lake with) 2 skerries one
> 5. days-journey north from this stone
> 6. We were (out) and fished one day After
> 7. we came home (we) found 10 (of our) men red
> 8. with blood and dead AV(e) M(aria)
> 9. Save (us) from evil
>
> The following three lines appear on the edge of the stone:
> 10. (We) have 10 of (our party) by the sea to look
> 11. after our ships (or ship) 14 days-journey
> 12. from this island (in the) year (of our Lord) 1362[4]

There were few converts in the scientific community. The general consensus was that the stone was a forgery. The reasons given were the same as before: the language was a mixture of Swedish and Norwegian, and the letters in the inscription were not consistent with other fourteenth century runestones. Over the years the battle continued; many reputable scholars became involved, including one of America's eminent philologists, Dr. Cyrus Gordon; and a world renowned cryptographic expert, the man who broke the Japanese code during World War II, Mr. Alf Monge. Slowly the pieces of the puzzle began to fall into place. The first clue was the date, 1362 CE. As discussed earlier, the Viking community in Greenland had become more and more isolated from the home country of Norway in the years following the Vinland voyages. The Greenlanders had continuing problems with the Eskimos, and after 1342 CE, only silence emanated from the western colony. King Magnus Erikson of Norway became greatly alarmed at the lack of news from the west. He did not want to lose his western colony and he certainly did not want to lose his Christian missionary outpost.

In the year 1354 the king decided to mount a religious expedition to Greenland and Vinland to renew the colonies and to restore Christianity to his subjects there. He charged one of his wealthy landowners, Paul Knutson, with responsibility for organizing and carrying out the expedition. Knutson was honored to be entrusted with such an important assignment. The crew were carefully selected by Knutson, and included many experienced Norwegian seamen as well as several members of the king's Swedish personal guard. Little more is known about the Knutson expedition. Apparently, it departed for Greenland and Vinland as intended. There was one additional notation in the annals, recording the fact that the survivors of the Knutson expedition returned to Norway in 1364.

Recent work by scientists at the Kensington Runestone Museum has strengthened the case for the authenticity of the stone. In 2002, Professor Henrik Williams of Uppsala and Dr. Richard Nielsen confirmed that the words on the stone are a fourteenth century language and not modern. And at least one of the Arabic numbers on the stone was unknown in 1898. Additionally, the weathering of the pyrite on the stone indicates an age much greater than 200 years.

The work of Holand, Gordon, Nielsen, and others has slowly eroded the critic's arguments. There are many points supporting the stone's authenticity:

- The tree in which the stone was entwined was estimated to be at least 70 years old based on type, size, and weather conditions. Since white settlers had been in the area for less than 50 years, the Kensington stone could not have been a nineteenth century forgery. It was engraved at least 20 years before the white man entered Minnesota.
- The mixture of Swedish and Norwegian dialects in the inscription is consistent with the mixed company on the Knutson expedition.
- The date of the Knutson expedition, found on documents in the Royal Library at Copenhagen, was not discovered until 1928, 30 years after the discovery of the Kensington Stone.
- The language on the Kensington Stone, and the letter styles on the stone, have been confirmed by other fourteenth century runic inscriptions that were discovered after the discovery of the Kensington Stone in 1898.
- The weathering of the pyrite on the stone indicates the stone was more than 200 years old when it was discovered by Olaf Ohman.
- Gordon and Monge found cryptographic evidence in the inscription that confirmed the authenticity.

Since the evidence heavily favors the authenticity of the Kensington Stone, it also supports the stone's confirmation of the Knutson expedition.

## 4. Vikings: The American Evidence

A review of that voyage might help to determine if there is a relationship between that voyage and any other Viking evidence in America. Knutson probably sailed from Bergen, Norway, sometime after to 1354 CE, traveling directly to Greenland's Eastern Settlement and then on to the Western Settlement. Finding both settlements empty, Knutson would have pushed off in search of Vinland. The rest of the story is conjecture but, based on the evidence, it could have happened. His next stop was the Viking settlement at Ungava Bay, in Canada. This settlement was also deserted. Knutson then entered Hudson Bay and proceeded southwest, eventually entering the Nelson River and following it to Lake Winnipeg, where he established a base camp on its southern shore.

His trip down the Nelson river was made in two small boats with about 20 men, with ten men left behind at Hudson Bay with the Knorr (the merchant ship was too large to navigate the inland river). Throughout this excursion, however, the Vinland settlement continued to elude Knutson, and in this strange country around Lake Winnipeg there were no signs of any European settlers. After a time, he moved his base camp further south, to Leech Lake, as his party continued to explore the surrounding terrain, moving deeper into the interior of Minnesota. One morning Knutson split the remaining group in half. Ten men stayed behind to protect the base camp and the other ten left camp on a fishing expedition. Returning the next day, Knutson found the base camp destroyed and the ten men savagely murdered. He and his group hurried back to the safety of the island they had spent the previous night on, at present-day Kensington. While they regrouped there for several days, one of the Swedish members of the crew engraved a memorial stone to their fallen comrades, and they held a Christian service over the standing gravestone.

Sometime later, the ten survivors headed east, away from the dangerous north country. They may have reached Lake Superior and, at its northern extremity, crossed over to Lake Nipigon. It is possible that another crew member died there, and was buried on the spot. It could have been his grave and armor that were discovered in 1930 — the so-called Beardmore find. The remainder of the group made their way back to the Knorr at the entrance to the Nelson River, and retraced the course back to Ungava Bay and eventually home to Norway. The expedition was, of course, a failure. The Vinland colony was never found, nor were there any traces of Greenlanders in any of the settlements. And the silence regarding the commander of the expedition, Paul Knutson, hints at the possibility that he lived his final days in North America.

So far, several impressive pieces of evidence have pointed to a Viking presence in Canada and the United States in the centuries before Columbus reached these shores. But perhaps the most remarkable testimony is a stone structure that stands silently on a hill overlooking the Atlantic Ocean, the famous Newport Tower (see illustration). Like the Kensington Stone, the Newport Tower has been the center of controversy for almost 150 years.

Prior to 1837, the Newport Tower (or Old Stone Mill as it is known to the locals), in Newport, Rhode Island, sat quietly in a park next to Mill Street, pretty much ignored by resident and tourist alike. Then Professor Rafn of the Royal Society in Denmark published his *Antiquitates Americanae* announcing the Viking visits to America. Subsequent to the publication of his book, he identified the Newport Tower as being the remains of a Christian church constructed in the twelfth century by Bishop Eric Knuppsen during his visit to Vinland. Immediately the battle lines were drawn. On one side were the so-called Arnoldists who contended that the tower was built by Governor Benedict Arnold of Rhode Island (an ancestor of the Benedict Arnold of American Revolutionary fame) between 1675 and 1677. The other side, the anti–Arnoldists, insisted the Vikings constructed the tower.

Before examining the different theories regarding the identity of the tower's architect, the construction of the building itself should be reviewed. The tower is circular in shape, approximately 30 feet high with an outside diameter of 25 feet. Apparently the tower was at least two feet higher when it was constructed, but the top is now missing. The building is made of small stones and mortar. Originally the entire structure was covered with a white plaster finish, but very little of that covering remains. The structure itself appears to be badly in need of repair. Much of the mortar has fallen out of the stonework leaving large crevices in the surface, and several large stones have also fallen from the building. The tower contains eight arches and eight columns of Romanesque design. The interior of the building at one time contained two floors above the ground level. A wooden ladder probably led from the ground level to the second floor, and a staircase connected the second and third floors. All woodwork has long since disappeared, but the sockets in the walls are visible remnants of the original design. The second floor contains a fireplace with a double flue arrangement exhausting from the building at the third floor level (see illustration). The second floor also contains a built-in shelf or table with a stone receptacle beneath. Several windows face from east to west along the southern half. There are no windows to the north. The third floor contains a similar arrangement of windows. The tower is presently open at the top, a silent reminder of a reported British attempt to blow it up during the Revolutionary War. Their ill-conceived plan only succeeded in blowing the roof off.

The Newport Tower

These views of the tower show a fireplace on the second floor, as well as a slot for a table, with a closet beneath.

Now to the theories. The Arnoldists claim the tower was built by the first governor of Rhode Island, Benedict Arnold. On December 24, 1677, Arnold wrote his last will and testament, and in it he requested to be buried in Newport near "his stone built wind mill." This statement is the primary evidence for colonial-period construction of the tower. The Arnold theory claims that Arnold was born in Chesterton, England, in 1615. During his youth he became enamored of a local stone windmill built in Chesterton in 1632. In 1635 Arnold sailed for the New World with his family. Thirty years later an opportunity arose in Newport, to build a windmill, and Governor Arnold, remembering with nostalgia the structure in England, built a similar stone edifice in Newport.

The anti–Arnoldists have refuted this theory over the years, and have successfully discredited the claim of Arnold's authorship of the mill. Philip Means, in his book *Newport Tower*, did a superb job in analyzing the theory and in determining the facts. First, Means discovered that Arnold was not born in Chesterton England, but in Ilchester, Somerset, 100 miles away. He probably never saw the Chesterton building during his residence in England; and even if he had visited Chesterton, he still would not have seen a windmill. The Chesterton structure was built in 1632 by the distinguished architect Inigo Jones for Sir Edward Payto, lord of the manor of Chesterton, as an observatory, not as a windmill. It was not converted into a windmill until after 1700.

Means also made a detailed study of colonial and medieval windmills and other structures throughout America, Canada, and Europe. He determined that, in general, mills were not built with arches and columns, because they were too flimsy to support the milling equipment; nor were they built with fireplaces, due to the danger of mill dust explosions. In those rare instances where fireplaces were incorporated into the structure they were located on the ground floor, away from the dust, not on the second floor as at Newport. Additionally, the design of the fireplace was pre-fifteenth century, as was the design of the windows. These designs were obsolete by the time the seventeenth century rolled around.

If the building was not a mill, what was it? Continued investigation by Means led him to the conclusion that the building was a medieval Christian church built between the eleventh and fourteenth centuries. The fireplace design and window design had already pointed to pre-fifteenth century construction. Means found that many European churches were constructed of a similar round design, particularly in Northern Europe. Means quoted from a previous study of the Newport Tower by Dr. F.J. Allen:

In most cases the Scandinavian churches have two upper floors, occasionally three, forming upper chambers the use of which is not certainly known. These chambers probably held the treasures of the church, — the silver, relics, documents, etc., — and afforded lodging for a priest or a custodian; but certain features in their structure make it probable that they were also used as places of refuge in times of danger from enemies. Similar habitable chambers existed in many, perhaps most, of the Anglo-Saxon towers of England; they may be seen in our own Anglo-Saxon tower of St. Benet's, also at Brixworth, Barnack, Barton-on-Humber, Deerhurst, and other churches; and they are occasionally met with in churches later than the Anglo-Saxon. In the tower of Irthlingborough Church, of the fourteenth century, the rooms were provided with fireplaces. I believe there is no record of the former presence or absence of upper chambers in English round churches: the four round churches still in use retain no evidence of such chambers.[5]

The Newport construction is consistent with a medieval round church. The tower would have been the central portion of the church, and would have been surrounded by a covered, circular aisle called an ambulatory, in this case made of wood. A church similar to the Newport Tower was built in North Bornholm, Denmark, between 1100 and 1250 CE. R.G. Hatfield, in his dissertation on the Newport Tower, compared it with an almost identical structure in Asti, Italy, which was built and used as a Christian church. Hatfield presented a visual comparison of the two structures, showing the Newport Tower with the roof restored and an ambulatory added. Although Hatfield took some liberties with the Newport Tower window design, there is no doubt that the similarity is striking. Lastly, it should be noted that the capstones above the columns on the outside of the tower protrude significantly, as if they were intended to support another structure.

A strong case already exists for pre–fifteenth century construction of the tower. Three other pieces of evidence will reinforce that argument. The first is the Plowden Paper, a colonial record that was uncovered by the Viking historian Frederick Pohl. Pohl learned that a British subject, Sir Edmund Plowden, had petitioned King Charles I for permission to establish a manufacturing colony on the eastern part of Manitie or Long Isle, today's Long Island. In his petition, Plowden listed 29 commodities, or assets, in the proposed land tract. One of these assets is of interest here. Paragraph 27 states "so that 30 idle men as souldiers or gent be resident in a round stone towre and by tornes to trade with the savages and to keep their ordinance and armes neate."[6] The petition was written in 1632, seven years before Newport was founded, yet here is positive evidence that the famous Newport Tower existed even then. There is no other stone tower on the adjacent mainland across from Long Island that would fit Plowden's description.

The Newport Tower appears to be precolonial. It may be of Viking construction, dating back to 1116 CE. However, James P. Whittall II, of the Early Sites Research Society, researched the possibility that the tower was built by Prince Henry Sinclair in 1398 CE. Whittall found many similarities between the tower and fourteenth century constructions in the north of Scotland. In 1993, a Danish team conducted radiocarbon dating tests on the mortar used in the construction of the Newport Tower. The team concluded that the tower was most likely built after 1492 but before Newport was settled, although their test procedures and results are considered suspect in some circles. Whittall stated that a date of 1398 still fell within the range of accuracy of the test.

The next piece of evidence comes from Giovanni Verrazano, the Italian adventurer who explored the east coast of America for the king of France. Verrazano cruised the shoreline in 1524 and included Newport in his many stops. A map of his exploratory voyage contains a notation at the location of Newport. It reads "Norman Villa." A Norman villa of medieval English design would resemble the Newport Tower from a distance. Detractors claim that his notes on the voyage do not mention the tower; therefore there must not have been a tower, and the map must refer to something else. Verrazano, however, would not have mentioned a Norman villa in his notes because he was in the employ of the French; he certainly would not have credited the English with an earlier exploration of the Rhode Island coast.

There is another visual representation of the Newport Tower, on an early colonial map, that supports Verrazano's description. It is a world map drawn by famous mapmaker Gerald Mercator in 1569 (see illustration). The map clearly shows a round stone tower at the location of Newport, Rhode Island — 70 years before William Coddington and a group of religious dissenters from the Massachusetts Bay Colony settled the area.

Frederick Pohl uncovered one additional, tantalizing piece of information. It seems that a young Englishman named William Wood lived in Lynn, Massachusetts, from 1629 to 1633. On his return to England in 1633 he authored a description of the Massachusetts-Rhode Island area, complete with a map. In the preface to his work Wood remarked, "To the reader I have layd downe the nature of the country, without any partiall respect unto it, as being my dwelling place where I have lived these four years, and intend God willing to returne shortly againe."[7] The most interesting feature of his book is the map. It is the earliest known topographical presentation of Rhode Island and Massachusetts. Wood identified the location of many of the settlements and towns that existed in the area in 1633. Many of the names are familiar to us today, such as New Plymouth,

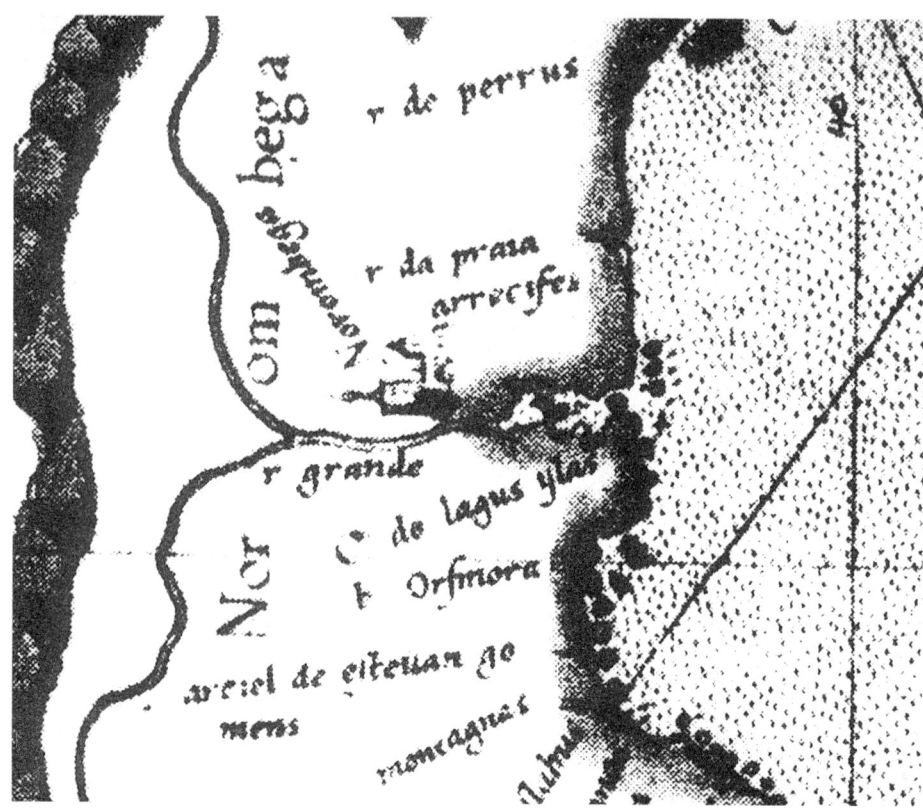

**Mercator map showing the Newport Tower in 1569 (courtesy Paul H. Chapman).**

Nahant Point, and Watertowne. But one name presents us with a mystery. On the southern coast of Rhode Island, near the mouth of Narragansett Bay, on the site of present day Newport, Wood located a settlement he called Old Plymouth. Remember, Newport wasn't settled until 1639, at least five years after Wood's map was drawn. And yet Wood believed that a settlement already existed on that site. What did he see that gave him the impression that an English settlement was thriving in southern Rhode Island in 1633? Could William Wood have seen the Newport Tower? Pohl claimed that the Wood map was subsequently verified by a Dutch map drawn prior to 1614. The Dutch map, now in the archives in the Hague, showed a settlement near the mouth of Narragansett Bay, which the Dutch identified as "New England."

One last piece of physical evidence seems to point to pre–Columbian construction. A 1740 painting by Gilbert Stuart shows the Tower as a roofless ruin, exactly as it appears today. If it had been built in the 1650 period as a windmill, it could not have deteriorated that much in just 90 years. The painting also discredits the reports that the British blew the roof off during the Revolutionary War.

Boland lamented the fact that all existing evidence was of a negative nature. The evidence helped to discredit the Benedict Arnold claim, but it did not give positive proof of Viking construction. Means was of the same opinion. He also felt that additional excavation was required to search for evidence of the ambulatory and to search for Viking artifacts. The only previous excavations were of limited degree and were tightly controlled by local officials. William Godfrey excavated under the tower in 1949, but his dig was limited to the area within the fence. He discovered a number of colonial artifacts, but nothing of a precolonial nature. Unfortunately, there were two things wrong with Godfrey's work. First, the area to which he was restricted did not include the potential locations of the footings for a medieval ambulatory. Second, the area under the tower had been previously excavated on several occasions, perhaps going back a hundred years or more. If there were any precolonial artifacts under the tower they had been discovered long ago, and squirreled away in a private collection somewhere. Means reduced his conclusions to probabilities. He felt that an excavation had a 35 percent chance of locating the ambulatory foundation, or a runic stone. As far as the identification of the structure was concerned, Means felt that it was Viking, but that some kind of positive evidence was required to support that contention.

A discovery made in 1946 may provide that kind of positive evidence. Two gentlemen from Scandinavia, Magnus Bjorndal and Peer Lovfald, were inspecting the tower one sunny day in 1946. Suddenly they spied an apparent inscribed stone on the outside of the tower, just above the southwest column. The stone, measuring approximately 5 by 12 inches was photographed for future research study. Subsequently it was scrutinized by Alf Monge, who determined it to be of runic script, and who translated it as "Henrikus," the first bishop of Greenland and Vinland. A cryptographic analysis of the runes by Monge gave a date of December 10, 1116 CE. His conclusion was that the Newport Tower was a Christian church constructed under the authority of Bishop Henrikus, also known as Bishop Eric Gnuppsen, bishop of Greenland and neighboring regions.

One June 9, 1984, the author traveled to Newport to inspect the tower personally. Mr. Joseph Blaine of the Newport Historical Society acted as a guide. He believes the tower to be of colonial construction. He also expressed a reservation about the authenticity of the runestone, due to the fact that the runes were slanted to the left instead of being perfectly vertical.

86　　　　　　　Part I : The Intercontinental Connections

Sunsequent research uncovered the fact that slanted runes are not unusual. In fact, they are so common that they are not even commented on in the literature. Two Etruscan inscriptions, taken from DuChaillu's work, are exhibited in the British Museum.

The first inscription is slanted to the right, while the second inscription is noticeably slanted to the left (see illustration). The Etruscan script is a predecessor of the runic script. A careful study of runes will quickly show that runes can go uphill or downhill, or slant to the right or the left. The explanation for this is that although runes made by professional scribes were correctly carved and properly vertical, many runes were not carved by professional scribes. Most people could not afford to pay a professional scribe to inscribe a gravestone, so amateurs or students were often used, with less than satisfactory results. Also, professional scribes were very seldom members of an expeditionary force. The need was for seamen, craftsmen, and warriors— not for scribes.

The radiocarbon dating conducted in 1993 with the authorization of the Newport City Council, as noted earlier, only tended to confuse the issue. Samples of the mortar taken by Jan Heinemeier and Hogne Jungner dated the construction of the tower to between 1635 and 1698. The subject didn't end there, however. Reportedly, a total of 30 samples were taken at the tower, but only ten were tested. And seven of the ten were discarded, because they varied too much from the norm. As a result, the final conclusions were based on just three tests. Many scientists from around the United States have subsequently questioned the validity of the Danish tests. Andre J. Bethune, emeritus professor at Boston College, was quoted as saying, "Thus the carbon-14 analysis of these three .2 fractions of gas gives us an indication that Newport Tower was standing in the years 1480–1440."[8] James P. Whittall, Jr., the former director of the Early Sites Research Society, stated that the radiocarbon tests did not preclude precolonial construction of the

Two Etruscan inscriptions, taken from DuChaillu's work, are exhibited in the British Museum.

tower, and he dated the structure to between 1150 and 1400 CE based on the design of such features as the arches, windows, niches, beam holes, keystones, mortar, and the orientation of the openings. J. Huston McCulloch, a graduate of Caltech, in an August 2001 article, also claimed that the Heinemeier study was inconclusive, and that it did not rule out an earlier date of construction. William Penhallow, a retired University of Rhode Island physics professor, insisted in October 2002 that the study was flawed. He dated the tower to about 1300 CE.

And so, the mystery remains. As with so many of these old structures and artifacts that decorate the American landscape, more work remains to be done. The town fathers need, once again, to try to resolve the origin of the Newport Tower, by authorizing one final, complete, and independent professional excavation of the area in and around the tower. They should also engage the assistance of two or three reputable runologists to make a determination relative to the identity of the inscribed stone, and to verify its inscription, if it is determined to be runic. And finally, the tower needs to be dated by a method that is accurate and irrefutable.

## Summary

There have been literally hundreds of alleged Viking artifacts unearthed in the United States over the past 150 years. Many of them are spurious. Some are undoubtedly family souvenirs that were lost. Some appear to be of Indian design. And still others appear to be ancient, but not of Viking provenance.

Once all these non–Viking artifacts have been eliminated however, many impressive pieces of evidence of Viking intrusion into the United States remain:

- The Vinland Map, an authenticated world map, drawn about 1440 CE, shows the island of Vinland located in the Atlantic Ocean to the west of Greenland.
- A map drawn by Gerald Mercator in 1569 CE shows a round tower in the location of Newport, Rhode Island. The map was drawn 70 years before Newport was settled.
- A map of Giovanni Verrazano, drawn in 1524 CE, describes a "Norman villa" in the location of Newport, Rhode Island.
- A map drawn by William Wood in 1634 CE notes a settlement called Old Plymouth, in the location of Newport, five years before Newport was settled.

- The Plowden Paper, a 1632 petition to King Charles I of Great Britain for permission to establish a colony on the eastern end of Long Island, mentions the use of an existing round stone tower.
- A Viking coin, dated to approximately 1050 CE, was found in an Indian midden in Brooklin, Maine.
- Four runestones, including a Viking amulet, or good luck charm, were discovered at Spirit Pond, Maine. They are dated to 1010–1011 CE.
- A runestone was discovered in Kensington, Minnesota. It records an expeditionary voyage of Vikings in 1362 CE.
- The Newport Tower remains a mystery. It contains a possible runestone dated cryptographically to 1116 CE. Radiocarbon dating indicates this structure could predate the colonial occupation of Newport.

## Conclusions

The evidence for Viking intrusion into the United States is impressive. Positive proof of a Viking presence in Newfoundland, Canada, and in Brooklin, Maine, has been established, just in the past 45 years. A strong case exists for Viking explorations along the Atlantic coast, as far south as Newport, Rhode Island, as well as for one expeditionary visit to the interior of North America, to Minnesota, but additional research is needed to confirm these possibilities.

# 5

## *The Ancient Writers*

## Conventional Thinking

There are no written records that indicate ancient Europeans knew of the existence of America.

## Discussion

The Atlantic Ocean was the end of the world as far as most ancient Europeans were concerned. For tens of thousands of years, Stone Age men on the west coast of Europe were terrified by the great expanse of water that loomed before them. The violent Atlantic storms, accompanied by torrential rains, spectacular bolts of lightning, and deafening claps of thunder sent these primitive people scurrying for the safety of their caves. Gale force winds that sent huge walls of water cascading against the rocks and shoreline intimidated the natives into keeping their distance from this unknown menace. It seemed like the end of the world, the land beyond the living, the land where great monsters lurked in the darkness waiting to pounce upon and devour the unsuspecting wanderer. Ancient man was wary of this threat to his life. He stayed on the land, where he felt secure and comfortable.

But slowly some peoples were drawn to the sea. On the Atlantic coast it was probably the Scandinavians who first gazed upon the great waters with curiosity rather than fear. As noted in chapter 3, the ancestors of the Vikings were in possession of oceangoing vessels as early as 2000 BCE. Their first boats left the fjords before 2000 BCE and made short, coast-hugging voyages south to Frisia and Gaul. Eventually they crossed the English channel and explored the land across the water, which by that time was being colonized by other primitive tribes from the continent, the architects of Stonehenge. The Scandinavians continued to explore their expanding world, becoming familiar with Ireland, the Orkneys, the Faeroes, and other islands in the north Atlantic, as well as the European continent as far south as Gibraltar. Over a period of 1,000 years they established a vast trading empire all along the Atlantic seaboard. Since these Northmen had no written language of their own, their knowledge of the great ocean and the lands beyond went unnoticed by the civilized nations of Europe.

About the year 1100 BCE, a new maritime power emerged in Western Europe. The Phoenicians, the master merchants of the eastern Mediterranean, passed through the Pillars of Heracles for the first time and founded the city of Gades on the coast of Spain. It was not long before the Phoenicians came in contact with the Scandinavians, and, since they had a common interest, a peaceful and profitable business enterprise may have been established between the two sea powers. The Phoenicians maintained the secret of the Atlantic enterprise as had the Scandinavians. In fact, they went the Scandinavians one better. Not only were they reticent about their business dealings outside the Pillars, but they spread horror stories about the beastlike creatures that roamed the world of darkness beyond the safety of the Mediterranean. Although the world's first alphabet was invented at the time of the Phoenicians, they probably did not utilize the written word to record historical facts, exploratory achievements, or the expansion of knowledge. To the Phoenician merchant, writing was only useful for maintaining business records and accounting procedures. In fact, most of what is known today regarding the Phoenicians, their life and times, comes from other European historians. Since these historians were from Greece, Rome, and Spain—countries that were often adversaries of the Phoenicians—the view is often biased and unfavorable.

In spite of all the precautions taken by the Scandinavians and the Phoenicians to protect their Atlantic ventures, some word was destined to leak out over the years. Perhaps a drunken sailor in a tavern somewhere was inclined to boast about his adventures at the end of the world. Or a young merchant desirous of impressing a customer might have related the story of where the trade goods had originated. Word of mouth is a great communicator, and over the centuries a wondrous story unfolded. The first written record of maritime activity in the great ocean was reported by the Greek historian Herodotus about 480 BCE. The story concerned the Egyptian pharaoh Necho, who lived in the sixth century BCE. Necho was involved in the construction of a large canal to connect the Mediterranean Sea with the Red Sea in order to facilitate trading expeditions to Southern Africa and India. Forced to interrupt that project for economic reasons, Necho decided to attempt a circumnavigation of Africa in order to locate new sources of raw materials. He commissioned a Phoenician fleet to make the voyage. Even at this time the Phoenicians were willing to do almost anything for money. The fleet embarked from the Red Sea port of Ezion Geber in the spring of 534 BCE and proceeded down the east coast of Africa, until autumn arrived. With the deterioration of the weather, the commanders beached their ships, planted crops and established a temporary winter settlement. The following spring the crops were harvested and the fleet put to sea once again, proceeding now around the Cape of Good Hope, and northerly up the west coast of the continent. The voyage was excruciatingly slow, as the fleet traveled close to the shoreline, sailing by day, and anchoring or tying the ships by night. After more than two years, the fleet turned east through the Pillars of Heracles and continued its journey back to Egypt. It was a memorable excursion, and the first recorded maritime activity to cover a wide area of the Atlantic Ocean.

In the year 427 BCE a baby was born on the Greek island of Aegina of wealthy Athenian parents. He was named Aristocles, but he is popularly known by his nickname, Plato, which means "broad shouldered." Plato was well educated in Athens, and like all well-to-do youths of his day, he studied music, philosophy, gymnastics, mathematics, and ethics. He also traveled a great deal and spent some time studying in Italy. His happiest days, however, were spent in Athens. Sitting in the shade of a large tree, young Plato whiled away many an idyllic afternoon listening to his beloved teacher, Socrates, expound on religion and morals. When Socrates was executed by the state for corrupting the youth of the country, Plato was shattered. He once again left Greece and traveled from one end of the Mediterranean to the other, visiting, among other places, Italy, Carthage, and Egypt. When he finally returned to Athens, he opened his own school, the Academy, and settled down to a life of teaching and writing. His method of teaching and of writing was by dialogue: questions and answers between student and teacher. Points of discussion were debated between the two. Plato was primarily concerned with defining the ultimate good for the individual and for the state, and what constituted the ideal society. His students included Aristotle and Demosthenes.

Although Plato's works focused on philosophical and ethical questions, some included historic or legendary tales that tantalize us today. In one of his famous works, *The Timaeus*, Plato wrote, "For in those days the sea there could be crossed, since it had an island before the mouth of the strait, which is called as ye say, the Pillars of Heracles. Now this island was greater than Libya and Asia together, and from there, was passage for the seafarers of those times to the other island, and from the islands to all the other continents which bound the ocean truly named. For these regions that lie within the strait aforesaid seem to be but a bay having a narrow entrance, but the other is ocean verily and the land surrounding it may with fullest truth and fitness be named a continent."[1]

The island referred to by Plato was Atlantis, an island situated somewhere in the Atlantic Ocean. Plato went on to relate: "Subsequently, through violent earthquakes and deluges which brought destruction in a single day and night, the whole of your warlike race was merged under the earth, and the Atlantic Island itself was plunged beneath the sea and entirely disappeared; when even now, the sea is neither navigable, nor to be traced out, being blocked up by the great depth of mud, which the subsiding Island produced."[2]

Plato told of a great island empire in the Atlantic Ocean, named Atlantis, and an enormous continent that was located to the west of Atlantis. Was Atlantis real? Did it actually sink beneath the Atlantic waves? Did Plato actually know of the American continent lying in the ocean where the sun sets? Unfortunately, it is pure conjecture to try to identify the lands described, or even to separate fact from fiction, which Plato mixed together in the quantities necessary to make a good story. Many scientists today believe the story of Atlantis was based on fact, but that Atlantis was actually located in the eastern Mediterranean Sea, not the Atlantic Ocean. One generally accepted theory is that Atlantis represented the Minoan civilization, which was centered on the island of Crete and which ruled the known world during the first half of the second millennium BCE. Sometime around 1500 BCE, a volcanic cataclysm enveloped the island of Thera located 90 miles to the north of Crete; a major portion of Thera disappeared beneath the sea, the ensuing tidal wave completely inundated the Cretan empire, destroying a once great culture.

Those are probably the facts. Whether Plato had heard stories of a great continent in the western Atlantic Ocean is not known, but it is possible. He traveled to many countries during his lifetime, including several that were under the authority of the Phoenicians. He certainly could have heard tales of Phoenician discoveries of new lands in the western sea, in a local tavern or at a private dinner party. Sailors who had been on such adventures were wont to thrill their audiences with firsthand accounts of their travels. It is known however, that Plato at least imagined there could be a continent on the other side of the ocean.

One of Plato's students provided the first substantial account of a newly discovered land in the Atlantic Ocean. His name was Aristotle, and he was born at Stagira, Greece, in 384 BCE. On reaching manhood, Aristotle was sent to the Academy in Athens where he studied under Plato. He soon earned a reputation for being the most intellectual student there. Aristotle's father, Nicomachus, had been the court physician to Amyntas II, king of Macedon and grandfather of Alexander the Great. When Alexander was old enough, Aristotle was invited to establish a school in Pellas, the Macedonian capital. Alexander and other boys of noble families attended the school to study the sciences, ethics, and philosophy under the master. Aristotle's teaching had a profound influence on Alexander, and molded his character in a way that allowed the future conqueror to establish the world's greatest empire, stretching from Greece to India, covering an area of 10 million square miles.

Aristotle has come down in history as one of the world's greatest thinkers, a man given to serious reflections, and not one to propose or repeat tales of fancy. His comments and observations are always made with careful consideration, and are among the most reliable of the ancient world. It is in this light that his comments regarding a continent in the Atlantic Ocean must be reviewed. Aristotle produced a work *On Marvellous Things Heard*, which described 178 wondrous things in the world. Wonder number 85 stated:

> In the sea outside the Pillars of Heracles they say that a desert island was found by the Carthaginians, having woods of all kinds and navigable rivers, remarkable for all other kinds of fruits, and a few days' voyage away; as the Carthaginians frequented it often owing to its prosperity, and some even lived there, the chief of the Carthaginians announced that they would punish with death any who proposed to sail there, and that they massacred all the inhabitants, that they might not tell the story, and that a crowd might not resort to the island, and get possession of it and take away the prosperity of the Carthaginians.[3]

The location of this land has been the subject of debate for many years. There are only two land areas that Aristotle could possibly be referring to in his description, the British Isles or North and South America. The Phoenicians are known to have frequented Britain in order to obtain tin from the mines at Cornwall. Britain, in fact, easily fits Aristotle's description, being several days sailing from ports on the Spanish seaboard, and having the geographical characteristics described above. The Phoenicians (including the Carthaginians) took careful precautions to prevent any vessels other than their own from passing the Pillars of Heracles, and venturing out into the Atlantic Ocean. Taken at face value, Aristotle's description would have to be assumed to be referring to the British Isles.

Three hundred years later, the area of the Atlantic Ocean came under scrutiny again, this time by the famous Greek geographer and historian, Strabo. Strabo was born in Amasia, Pontus, in what is now Turkey. In 64 BCE, when Strabo was born, Pontus was a Greek province under Roman rule. Like Plato, Strabo was well educated and well traveled. His early years brought him into contact with wide expanses of the Roman Empire, from Arabia to Thrace, and from Egypt to Rome. During his travels he kept detailed records of the geography of each area and the history of its people. He had a thirst for knowledge and information, and compiled volumes of material to be used in later years in his writings. When he eventually settled down to a more studious life, he began work on his geographical and historical endeavors. They were both mammoth productions. His histories comprised 47 books, most of which unfortunately have been lost over the years. His geographies totaled 17 books, and are regarded as his major achievement. Strabo's reputation as a reporter is of the highest caliber and can be relied upon for its accuracy. He was a careful, precise investigator, as his books attest.

There are several references to the Atlantic Ocean in his geography, which bear serious study. For instance: "Eratosthenes gives credence to many fables about the regions beyond the Pillars of Heracles mentioning an island named Cerne, and other countries which are nowhere pointed out today."[4] Cerne could be almost anywhere, but is generally considered to be one of the island groups off the coast of Africa. His last comment about "lands unknown today" is puzzling. Certainly all the lands that were previously discovered in the eastern and northern Atlantic, such as England, Iceland, the Azores, and others, were still known in Strabo's day. What countries that were once known could have been forgotten by 50 BCE? Could Strabo have been referring to America? If the Phoenicians had discovered America during their excursions into the Atlantic Ocean, they might have prevented other nations from learning the whereabouts of a such a wealthy country. And with their defeat by Rome in 146 BCE, all voyages to the New World would have ceased, and the knowledge of the existence of such a country would soon fade from memory. Another provocative comment in the *Geography* reads, "The ancients have made longer journeys by both land and sea than have men of a later time."[5] Journeys to where?

Returning to the Phoenicians, Strabo stated that they "explored regions beyond the Pillars of Heracles and founded cities both there and in the central part of the Libyan seaboard."[6] This is just a reaffirmation that the ancient discoveries in the Atlantic were still familiar to the people of Strabo's time.

There is one last reference to the Atlantic Ocean that is of interest: "The westerly parts of Britain lie opposite the headlands of the Pyrenees toward the north and in like manner the islands called Cassiterides [tin islands] situated in the open sea approximately in the latitude of Britain lie opposite to and north of the Artabrians."[7] The identification of the Cassiterides is still a point of conjecture, as is its direction from Britain. Many people feel it describes Sicily in the Mediterranean Sea. But if it is to the west of Britain the first land mass encountered is Labrador, Canada.

Probably the strongest piece of evidence suggesting ancient knowledge of America came from the pen of Diodorus of Sicily, who wrote during the first century BCE. Diodorus was born in Agyrium, Sicily, about the year 80 BCE. He subsequently spent some time in Rome, then traveled to Egypt where he resided for many years while researching the thousands of volumes in the famous library at Alexandria. While there, he wrote a 40-volume world history. Most of his information was derived from historians of earlier eras including Aristotle and the famous fifth century BCE historian, Hecataeus. The evidence that interests us begins in book 5, paragraph 19:

> But now that we have discussed what relates to the islands which lie within the Pillars of Heracles, we shall give an account of those which are in the ocean. For there lies out in the deep off Libya an island of considerable size, and situated as it is distant from Libya a voyage of a number of days to the west. Its land is fruitful, much of it being mountainous and not a little being a level plain of surpassing beauty. Through it flow navigable rivers which are used for irrigation, and the island contains many parks planted with trees of every variety.... The mountainous part of the island is covered with dense thickets of great extent, and with fruit trees of every variety, and, inviting men to life among the mountains, it has cozy glens and springs in great number. And, speaking generally, the climate of this island is so altogether mild that it produces in abundance the fruits of the trees and the other seasonal fruits for the larger part of the year, so that it would appear that the island, because of its exceptional felicity, were a dwelling-place of a race of gods and not of men.[8]

If this account is taken at face value, as was the account of Aristotle, there can be only one conclusion. Diodorus is referring to the continent of America, perhaps South America. He could not be referring to any other land. There is no country lying to the west of Libya (Africa) that has navigable rivers until the continent of North or South America is reached. The other geographical descriptions also fit easily into these continents.

In the next paragraph of Diodorus, there is a further reference to this land:

> In ancient times this island remained undiscovered because of its distance from the entire inhabited world, but it was discovered at a later period for the following reason. The Phoenicians, who from ancient times on made voyages continually for purposes of trade, planted many colonies throughout Libya and not a few as well in the western parts of Europe. The Phoenicians, then, while exploring the coast outside the Pillars for the reasons we have stated and while sailing along the shore of Libya, were driven by strong

winds a great distance out into the ocean. After being storm-tossed for many days they were carried ashore on the island we mentioned above, and when they had observed its felicity and nature they caused it to be known to all men. Consequently the Tyrrhenians, at the time when they were masters of the sea, purposed to dispatch a colony to it; but the Carthaginians prevented their doing so, partly out of concern lest many inhabitants of Carthage should remove there because of the excellence of the island, and partly in order to have ready in it a place in which to seek refuge against an incalculable turn of fortune, in case some total disaster should overtake Carthage. For it was their thought that, since they were masters of the sea, they would thus be able to move, households and all, to an island which was unknown to their conquerors.[9]

This evidence is such a strong argument for the ancient knowledge of America that it is difficult to dispute. To begin with, it is apparent that the settlement of the Iberian peninsula on the Atlantic seaboard was in the distant past, as was the discovery of Britain. Gadeira or Gades was settled about 1100 BCE, and Britain was discovered about 825 BCE. Yet Diodorus referred to the Phoenician exploration of the Libyan coast, which took place about 450 BCE. These dates therefore eliminate Britain from any consideration of being the mysterious land referred to by Diodorus. The description of ships being driven west across the Atlantic Ocean by a great storm is very familiar, since it was discussed in chapter 2; Pedro Alvares Cabral was blown across the ocean to Brazil, in a similar manner, in 1500 CE. Now there is strong evidence that the Phoenicians preceded Cabral by almost 2,000 years.

During the first century of the common era, in the year 46 CE to be exact, the future historian Plutarch was born in Boeotia, Greece. Plutarch, on attaining puberty, studied for many years in Athens. He subsequently traveled extensively throughout the Mediterranean world before settling down near Athens to teach and to write. He is best noted for his detailed biographies of famous Greeks and Romans including Alexander, Mark Antony and Julius Caesar. He did, however, contribute much valuable information concerning lands in the Atlantic Ocean in his famous work, *Morals*. During a dialogue in the book, one of the participants noted: "An isle Ogygia lies in Ocean's arms, distant about five days sail westward from Britain; and before it there are three others, of an equal distance from one another and also from that, bearing north-west, where the sun sets in summer. The adjacent sea, named the Saturnian, has his seat a little below. The continent, by which the great sea is circularly environed, is distant from Ogygia about five thousand stadia, but from the others not so far, men using to row thither in galleys."[10]

From the above description, Plutarch seemed to be aware of the existence of Iceland (Ogygia), which is approximately five days to the west of

Britain under favorable weather conditions. His reference to the continent that circles the great sea may reveal a knowledge of North America. In any case, Plutarch, like many other ancient writers, was of the opinion that the Atlantic Ocean was surrounded by land; Europe on the east and an unnamed continent on the west. Concerning the unnamed continent, Plutarch stated that a Greek colony inhabited a bay on the east coast. He further said that the original Greek colony had almost disappeared due to intermarriage with the natives. Evidently many years passed during which the original colony was isolated from the home country. The Greek language, laws, and manners had become almost nonexistent by the time a new expedition arrived. After a sojourn of 30 years the new colonists could elect to return to Greece, but as Plutarch noted: "Most of them choose rather to remain quietly there; some, because they are already accustomed to the place; others, because without any labor and trouble they have abundance of all things, as well for the offering of sacrifices and holding festival solemnities, as to support the ordinary expenses of those who are perpetually conversant in the study of learning and philosophy. For they affirm the nature of the island and the mildness of the air which environs it to be admirable."[11]

The identity of Plutarch's continent is unknown, but the evidence points strongly to North America. In addition to the above, there are two other ancient writers who supposedly made reference to America. One was Pausanias, a Greek geographer who published a description of Greece about 150 CE. Pausanias related a story about a mariner named Euphemus, a Carian, whose ship was blown through the Pillars of Heracles to a strange land in the outer ocean. According to such writers as Herman and Trento, the natives in this land were red skinned and had hair like a horse. It sounded like an obvious reference to the American Indian, but subsequent research uncovered a translation that disputed that identification. It described the natives thusly: "These islands, said he, are called by the seamen, the Isles of the Satyrs, and the dwellers on them are red haired, and have tails on their loins little less than the tails of horses."[12] The other writer was Rufus Festus Avienus, a Roman official of the fifth century CE and a geographer. Avienus had traveled throughout most of the Mediterranean area, eventually moving from Spain to Constantinople when the Vandals began to overrun the Iberian peninsula. His geography discussed the explorations of the Phoenician king Hanno along the western coast of Africa, but did not make any reference to continents in the western Atlantic Ocean.

## Summary

Several ancient writers referred to continents that existed to the west in the Atlantic Ocean. These include Plato, Aristotle, Strabo, Plutarch, and Diodorus Siculus. Diodorus' description closely matched that of North and South America.

## Conclusions

One ancient writer, Diodorus, accurately described the continent of North or South America. That suggests that ancient Europeans probably knew of the existence of America over 2,000 years ago.

Substantiating evidence exists in the works of Strabo, Plato, Plutarch and Aristotle. At the very least, the ancient scholars hypothesized that such a continent could be found in the western Atlantic Ocean.

# 6

# *Legendary Travelers of the Ocean*

## Conventional Thinking

There are no written records of factual voyages to North America prior to its discovery by Christopher Columbus.

## Discussion

There are numerous old documents that describe exploratory voyages to North America prior to its discovery by Christopher Columbus, even excluding the voyages of the Vikings, which have already been discussed in some detail. Among the more notable discoverers discussed in the literature are a fifth century Buddhist monk named Hoei Shin, a sixth century Irish monk named St. Brendan, a twelfth century Welch prince called Madoc, and the Zeno brothers of Italy who, in conjunction with Prince Henry Sinclair or Orkney, explored the western seas in the fourteenth century. There are written accounts of their exploits. But are they fact or fiction?

According to Chinese sources, Hoei Shin visited a country called Fu-sang in the year 499 CE. Some brief background information is required before delving into the meat of the story. Throughout most of its early history China was a closed society, content to isolate itself from the rest of the world and to develop its own resources independent of outside influences. This philosophy was obviously successful, since China acquired a high level of civilization several thousand years before Christ. They were world leaders in the arts and sciences. They have been credited with inventing the compass as early as 2300 BCE. They had metal money by 1200 BCE and began circulating true coins 600 years later. Paper was a Chinese invention and paper money was first issued in China as early as 200 CE. The list goes on and on. Suffice it to say that China was technologically equal to any country in the world throughout her early history.

This expertise carried over into the art of shipbuilding. China produced seaworthy vessels early in the common era. By the third century CE, China was entering an age of enlightenment, which not only increased her scientific and artistic achievements but also opened her doors to intercourse with other civilized nations. Soon trade agreements existed with such international powers as India, Persia, and Rome. Ships began to make routine voyages across the South China Sea and the Indian Ocean carrying cargoes of jade, silk, and spices to India, and returning to China with gold, silver and ivory.

Along with the ships went Buddhist monks, continually searching for new converts to the true religion. The Chinese Annals record one such expedition, carried out in the year 399 CE. A monk named Fa-Hsien along with 12 companions traveled overland from China to India, then booked passage on a boat from India to Ceylon. Two years later, after having established a small religious community on Ceylon, Fa-Hsien left his fellow monks and boarded a junk for home. The ship must have been of considerable size, since it carried a reported 200 passengers. Not only was it large, but it was obviously well designed and exceptionally stable. For once at sea, the ship encountered a fierce storm, and was battered mercilessly and incessantly for 13 continuous days. Miraculously, it survived the storm in good shape, and after a total of 105 days at sea, it made port in Java. After several months in drydock to repair the damage and to take on provisions, the ship again set sail, this time for Canton, in China. Luck once again failed the great ship, and she had to withstand another siege of violent weather. Gale force winds and high seas buffeted the vessel for days on end, but the return of good weather found her still afloat, and she entered Canton harbor undamaged, after a stormy passage of 82 days, a tribute to ancient Chinese shipbuilding techniques.[1]

Their missionary policy led to the first great Chinese Pacific adventure, the travels of a Buddhist monk to a faraway land in the eastern sea. The story of Hoei-shin is recorded in the Great Annals of China, a year-by-year record of Chinese historical achievements. A great civil war split China asunder in 420 CE and resulted in two empires, the Wei Empire in the north and the Sung Empire in the south. The ensuing turmoil unfortunately left a gap of almost 200 years in the Great Annals, a situation that was rectified shortly after 600 CE when Chinese scholars began to fill in the historical events of that period. The Hoei-Shin exploit was set down on paper during this time by the ancient historian Li-Yan-Chen, and was attributed to the year 499 CE. It was subsequently brought to the attention of Western scholars in 1761 by a French historian, M. de Guignes.

Hoei-Shin was reportedly a member of the college of priests at Cabul, a center of Buddhist activity and religious training. The Buddhist priests were divided into three categories:

1. Monastic monks who lived secluded lives in constant prayer and meditation.
2. Domestic monks who lived in parishes, or family groups.
3. Missionary monks who traveled continuously from one area to another, seeking converts to the faith.

Hoei-Shin fell into the latter category. He was forever searching out new lands in which to spread the word of Gautama Buddha, his spiritual leader. He had heard of a country a great distance to the east of China. The people there were barbarians who had never heard the holy word. Hoei-Shin considered it a great challenge and his holy responsibility to bring Buddhism to these people. Some time in the latter part of the fifth century he sailed from the coast of China and followed the Kuroshio current on a northeasterly route to a land called Ta-han, proceeding from there to the country of the barbarians, Fu-sang. In the year 499 CE he returned home, where the details of his missionary excursion were duly recorded by the government historian. A transcription of that record by Li-Yan-Chen was quoted by Edward Vining in his book, *An Inglorious Columbus*:

> In the first of the years Yuang-Yuan, of the reign of Fe-ti, of the dynasty of Ts'i, a shaman [or Buddhist priest], called Hoei-Shin, arrived from the country of Fu-sang at King-che. He related what follows: Fu-sang is twenty thousand li to the east of the country of Ta-han, and equally to the east of China. In this country there grow many trees called fu-sang, of which the leaves resemble those of the t'ung [Bignonia tomentosa], and the first shoots those of the bamboo. The people of the country eat them. The fruit is red and of the shape of a pear. The bark of the tree is prepared in the same way as that of hemp, and cloth and clothing are made of it. Flowered stuffs are also manufactured from it. Wooden planks are used for the construction of their houses, for in this country there are no cities and no walled habitations. The inhabitants have a species of writing, and make paper from the bark of the fu-sang. They have no weapons or armies, and do not make war. According to laws of the kingdom, there is a southern prison and a northern prison. Those who have committed crimes that are not very serious are sent to the southern prison, but great criminals are shut up in the northern one. Those who may receive pardon are sent to the first; those, on the contrary, to whom it can not be accorded, are confined in the northern prison. The men and

the women who are shut up in the latter are permitted to marry each other. The male children, born from their unions, are sold as slaves at the age of eight years; the girls at the age of nine years. The criminals who are confined there never come forth alive. When a man of high rank commits a crime, the people assemble in great numbers. They sit down face to face with the criminal, who is placed in a ditch, and regale themselves with a banquet, and take leave of him as of a dying man. Then he is surrounded by ashes. For an offense of little gravity the criminal alone is punished, but for a great crime, the culprit, his sons, and grandsons are punished; finally, for the greatest offenses his descendants to the seventh generation are included in the punishment. The name of the king of the country is Y-k'i (or Yit-k'i). The nobles of the first class are called Tui-lu; those of the second, little Tui-lu; and those of the third, Na-tu-cha. When the king goes forth he is accompanied by drums and horns. He changes the color of his garments at different epochs. In the years of the cycle kia and y, they are blue; in the years ping and ting, red; in the years ou and ki, yellow; in the years keng and sin, white; finally, in those which have the characters jin and kuei, they are black.

The cattle have long horns, upon which burdens are loaded which weigh as much, sometimes, as twenty ho (or one hundred and twenty Chinese pounds). In this country they made use of carts harnessed to cattle, horses, and deer. They rear deer there as they raise cattle in China, and make cheese from the milk of the females. A species of red pear is found there, which is preserved throughout the year. There are also many vines. Iron is lacking, but copper is found. Gold and silver are not esteemed. Commerce is free, and they do not haggle at all.

Their practices regarding marriage are as follows: He who desires to wed a girl establishes his cabin before her door; he sprinkles and sweeps the earth every morning and every night. When he has practiced this formality for a year, if the maid will not give her consent, he desists; but, if she is pleased with him, he marries her. The ceremonies of marriage are nearly the same as in China. At the death of father or mother they fast seven days. At that of a grandfather or grandmother they refrain from eating for five days; and only for three days at the death of brothers, sisters, uncles, aunts and other relatives. The images of spirits are placed upon a species of pedestal, and prayers are addressed to them morning and evening.

The king does not occupy himself with the affairs of government during the three years which follow his accession to the throne.

Formerly the religion of Buddha did not exist in this country, but in the fourth of the years ta-ming, of the reign of Hiao-wu- ti, of the dynasty of Sung [458 CE], five pi-k'ieu, or priests, of the country of Ki-pin [Cophene], came to Fu-sang, and there spread abroad the law of Buddha. They carried with them their books and sacred images and the ritual, and established monastic customs, and so changed the manners of the inhabitants."[2]

A multitude of scholars have studied the Hoei-shin story very carefully, many in the original Chinese. As W.C. Bryant et al. pointed out: "This alleged discovery has been the subject of a good deal of controversy. There is nothing incredible in the supposition that the Chinese may have sailed across the Pacific long before Europeans ventured over the Atlantic Ocean; for they were early navigators; knew in the second century of our era the use of the mariner's compass; and their junks, which have changed little in form since they were first known to Europeans, have been found wrecked upon the west coast of America, at different periods, from the time of the first Spanish voyages in the Pacific."[3]

One popular theory places Fu-sang in either California, Mexico or Central America during the Mayan period. There are many aspects of the story to support such a theory, particularly the Mayan version. The description of the trees and the fruit, the house construction, the lack of weapons, armies or walled cities, and the knowledge of writing, all fit comfortably into the Mayan culture. The only incongruous feature is the existence of carts harnessed to horses, cattle, and deer. The Maya had no wheeled vehicles (although they were familiar with the wheel), and they had no beasts of burden. Vining, however, deftly explains this sentence as being a mystical description of the journey a person must make to achieve nirvana, or the state of perfection. In the Buddhist religion, all living creatures make continuous journeys from one life to another through reincarnation, until nirvana is finally attained. It is a fact that many similarities exist between the Mayan culture and that of China; similarities in artwork, architecture, tools, metal money, and various other objects. Also, the reference to the monks who preceded Hoei-shin to Fu-sang in 458 CE is of interest historically. In China, in the year 458, there was a conspiracy to overthrow the government, and the conspirators included a number of Buddhist monks. It is possible that some monks fled China at that time, and sailed to the east to escape the government backlash of religious persecution that occurred as a result of the abortive plot.

All things considered, the visit of Hoei-shin to America still requires additional verification. But the possibility of some kind of Chinese incursion into the American continent has other evidence to support it. Chinese coins dating back to 1200 BCE were discovered in Victoria, Canada, in 1882; another batch of coins from about 680 CE were found in Alaska in 1927, in conjunction with a small ceremonial lamp.

In addition to the coin discoveries, there are other similarities between the two continents that indicate contact between East and West in ancient days.

- Many sculptures and paintings in Mayan, Olmec, and Aztec civilization have decidedly Asian features.
- There is a remarkable similarity between Mayan pyramids and those of Indochina.

- Alejandro von Wuthenau, the director of Humanitas Americana in San Angelo, Mexico, discovered a model of a boat with ten Asian faces (perhaps Japanese) in an Olmec tomb in Guerrero, Mexico, dating to 500 BCE.
- Japanese-style pottery, dating to the Jomon culture c. 3000 BCE, has been discovered in an ancient settlement in Ecuador.
- The peanut, which is indigenous to South America, reached China over 2,000 years ago.

It has already been proven that Polynesian mariners from Asia reached across the Pacific Ocean as far as Easter Island, and perhaps even to the coast of South America, by 500 CE. Although the voyage of Hoei-shin is still conjectural, the overall pattern that is developing suggests the possibility of Chinese contact with the west coast of America during the early common era. If the Polynesians crossed the Pacific Ocean, a Chinese monk could have too.

Not long after the Chinese explorer passed from the pages of history, another monk rose to prominence half a world away. He was Saint Brendan, born in Kerry on the west coast of Ireland in 484 CE. Being the first born in the family, Brendan was committed to a religious life, according to church law. And, since he was raised in Kerry, a fishing center from time immemorial, Brendan grew to manhood with a love of the sea and an expertise in seafaring. His education took place in the convent schools in Ireland, and after thorough training in languages, religion, history, and the sciences, Brendan was ready to bid farewell to the scholastic life and to don the habit of religious responsibility. Brendan, like Hoie-shin, was a true missionary and a great traveler; and being a Kerry man, he was equally at home on the water as he was on the land. An expert sailor, he has come down through history as Brendan the Navigator. His early life was one of constant motion, as he walked Ireland from one end to the other, then visited England, Scotland, and the surrounding islands.

He is most famous, however, for his voyages, of which there were supposedly three. The account of the voyages did not appear in written form until the eleventh century, some 500 years later. Until that time, the adventures of Saint Brendan the Navigator were an important part of Irish oral tradition and had been passed on by the bards for centuries. The Irish epic *The Voyage of Saint Brendan the Abbot* recounted the exploits of the famous navigator-priest, but the reliability of the account has been questioned in recent times. The problem lies in the fact that the Irish author embellished the story with many fanciful tales, such as Brendan's boat landing on the back of a whale, Brendan meeting Judas Iscariot, and Brendan visiting Saint Paul on an Atlantic island where Saint Paul had lived for 60 years. These diversions should not disturb anyone who is familiar with the "impossible" Irish, however. It is well known that the Irish love telling a good story, and that they are inclined to spice up the facts with colorful anecdotes. Certainly, their tendency toward poetic license should not detract from the facts.

Brendan's first voyage was the result of a conversation with a fellow monk named Fionn-Barr, who claimed he had sailed from Ireland some years previous in search of another monk named Mernoc. He found Mernoc on an island called the Delicious Isle, and together they sailed to a second island known as the Island of the Saints. This island was a very peaceful and enjoyable place to live; quiet, desolate, and blessed with an abundance of flowers, fruit, and sunshine. Brendan decided this would be an ideal place to establish a monastery, a place so pleasant and peaceful that monks could concentrate on their prayers and meditations. Brendan readied himself for a long voyage. First he had a large curragh built (a skin boat), made from wood and ox hide, and capable of withstanding the most violent Atlantic storm. Boats of this type have been reported that were large enough to carry 70 people. In the year 545 CE, Brendan set sail from Ireland with at least 14 fellow monks (some translations say 90) on a voyage that lasted five years. During that time, he visited many islands in the north Atlantic, and experienced many wondrous things, such as landing on the back of a whale. But he returned to Ireland without having discovered the Island of the Saints.

A second voyage was planned almost immediately. This time Brendan constructed a wooden-hulled vessel, probably similar to the familiar Roman cargo ships that frequently visited England. It was a large ship complete with a rudder, sails, and half deck. There was plenty of room for the 60 monks who accompanied Brendan on this historic venture. On March 22, 555 CE, the great ship left Kerry and headed north, then veered west across the Atlantic. This voyage was destined to blazon Saint Brendan's name across the pages of history forever, but with a dubious title, the "possible discoverer of America." For 40 days the ship sailed west, pushed by the brisk easterlies, her sails unfurled, and the large red cross that decorated the mainsail glistening in the afternoon sun. Suddenly the sun disappeared, and the vessel entered a sea that was blanketed by damp, cold fog. It was impossible to tell night from day. Brendan no longer could tell in which direction he was sailing. The crew could do nothing but pray and wait. Finally the sun reappeared, but another wondrous sight loomed before them: a giant mountain of frosty ice — floating on the water. They watched the iceberg, fascinated, for three days. They had never seen anything like it before. This was certainly an unusual world they were entering.

Scholars have dissected the Brendan voyage over and over again in order to determine his geographical locations. Many experts feel the description of the sea of mist and fog, and the encounter with the spring icebergs, place Brendan in the general area of Newfoundland, off the coast of Canada. The next clue also points to this area, perhaps even further south, near Nova Scotia. Still heading west, the lookout sighted land, and the ship prepared to drop anchor in a cozy harbor on the north side of the island. A visual inspection of the beach, however, revealed hundreds of monstrous animals basking in the sun on the warm sand. They were large fish-like creatures with hairy bodies and four flippers; and worst of all, they had heads like cats and huge elephant-like tusks. They looked ominous and dangerous. Discretion being the better part of valor, Brendan decided not to land. The magnificent ship weighed anchor and set course due south. The memory of those great ugly beasts however, lingered in the crew's minds for several days. What kind of animal had Brendan and his crew seen? Probably nothing more than a walrus. This animal is common on the northeast coast of North America, and can be seen lounging on the beaches as far south as Nova Scotia.

For many days, the southern journey continued. The icebergs were left far behind. The weather grew gradually warmer, and soon bright, sunny, comfortable days became the rule rather than the exception. Eventually another landfall came into view, and Brendan once more prepared to disembark. But this time hostile natives appeared on shore, and prevented the monks from landing. The ship sat at anchor for seven days observing the natives. When it became apparent that friendly intercourse was out of the question, the decision was made to move on.

Now the mariners turned to the west and steered straight for the setting sun. Eight days passed without sight of land, but time was no longer of the essence. The weather was ideal, the seas calm, and the fish abundant. When land appeared again, the monks were apprehensive, but this time they were welcomed ashore by a kindly old priest who was living there. He said his name was Festivius and he had come to this land of sunshine 30 years ago. Brendan and his crew explored the land for 40 days. They reached a river that was too wide to cross, and they met a young man who was able to speak their language, and who advised them to return to Ireland. Brendan took the young man's advice and departed for home as soon as the ship was properly provisioned. This ended the second voyage, and Brendan's American adventures. Many people believe that Brendan's first stop after leaving Nova Scotia was Bermuda, and his last stop, St.

Augustine, Florida. There are even those who believe that Brendan reached Mexico and became the Maya's great religious leader, the legendary Quetzalcoatl.

Brendan made one last voyage, his third, a voyage that lasted ten years. Brendan is reported to have traveled to many lands in the Mediterranean Sea and Europe on his last voyage, including Egypt and Palestine. He may have died on May 16, 577 CE.

In assessing Brendan's second voyage, it is necessary to strip away the fantasies and to evaluate the facts in an unbiased manner. Once this is done, it becomes apparent there are several pieces of evidence that strongly support the theory that Brendan did, in fact, visit North America. His description of the dreary, foggy sea, his encounter with an iceberg, and his confrontation with walrus are all consistent with the area around Newfoundland and Nova Scotia. And they were all things that were unknown in Ireland during Brendan's time. He could not have imagined them, and he could not have known about them unless he or someone else witnessed them firsthand.

Even without Brendan, there is reliable evidence that many Irish mariners visited America between the sixth and tenth centuries. A list of the total evidence is impressive:

- Brendan's second voyage, as noted above.
- The Viking Sagas. It is strange indeed, for bombastic warriors like the Vikings to admit the Irish had preceded them to various countries. But they did admit it, many times. It is not really difficult to understand, if you realize that the Vikings, although boastful, were not liars. They would boast of their conquests and discoveries, but they would never take credit for something they did not do. The Sagas relate that:
  1. Irish monks had lived in Iceland before the Vikings arrived.
  2. Irish monks had a settlement in Greenland before Eric The Red colonized the country.
  3. There was an Irish settlement, called Great Ireland, in North America, at least 30 years before Leif Erikson landed there.
- The Zeno brothers, who will be discussed shortly, testified in their letters, that Latin bibles existed in Newfoundland in the late 14th century, supposedly left by Irish missionaries.

There are two facts that are indisputable. The medieval Irish were great mariners; they were also world-renowned missionaries. Their ships controlled the seas to the west of Europe in the fourth and fifth centuries CE. O'Neill of the Nine Hostages constantly harassed the Romans in

England and on the continent around 400 CE, capturing St. Patrick during one foray into England. The Irish monks kept the intellectual and religious atmosphere of Western Europe alive during the dark ages, between the fifth and eleventh centuries. Their missionaries traveled across Europe from Germany to Greece, and then on to Palestine and Egypt. In a world of anarchy and despair, they were beacons of hope and promise.

The next possible American visitor, after Brendan, was a Welsh prince of the family of Gwynedd. He lived during the last half of the twelfth century and, like Brendan, his exploits became a popular folk tale, part of the oral tradition of Wales that was transmitted by bards from one end of the country to the other. Finally, sometime before 1270 CE, the story was recorded in the Register of Current Events that was maintained at the Abby of Conway, North Wales. A fifteenth century bard, Guttun Owen, copied the story from the register in 1480 CE and popularized it throughout the British Isles. Eventually it was claimed by several British historians, who published the story in an attempt to discredit Columbus and to gain prestige for England.

This is the story of Madoc, Prince of Wales, as recounted in Scribner's history, and based on the account of Gutton Owen:

> When Owen Gwynedd, Prince of North Wales, was gathered to his fathers, a strife arose among his sons as to who should reign in his stead. The eldest legitimate son, Edward, was put aside, or put himself aside, as unfit to govern, "because of a maime upon his face."— He was known as "Edward with the broken nose,"— and the government was seized by Howel, who was illegitimate, "a base son begotten of an Irish woman." But the next brother, David, refused allegiance to this Howel, and civil war followed. At length, the usurper was killed in battle, and the rightful heritage established, David holding the reins of government as regent till the son of Edward, the eldest brother, was of age. In this contention, Madoc took no part, but endeavored to escape from it; which inasmuch as it was a struggle for the lineal succession of his family, was not much to his credit. Leaving his brothers [about 1170 CE], to fight it out among them, he got together a fleet and put to sea in search of adventures. He sailed westward, leaving Ireland to the north which, it may be remarked, is nearly the only thing he could do, in sailing from Wales, unless he laid his course northward through the Irish Sea. But at length, he came to an unknown country, where the natives differed from any people he had ever seen before, and all things were strange and new. Seeing that this land was pleasant and fertile, he put on shore and left behind, most of those in his ships, and returned to Wales.
> 
> Coming among his friends again, after so eventful a voyage, he told them of the fair and extensive region he had found; there, he assured them all could live in peace and plenty, instead of cutting each other's throats for the possession of a rugged district of rocks and mountains. The advantages he offered were so obvious, or his eloquence so persuasive, that enough determined to go with him, to fill ten ships. They followed the manners of the land they came to, and used the language they found there.[4]

This is the complete story of Madoc as we know it. Unfortunately, there is no geographical evidence in the tale that would give it credence, such as is available in the story of Brendan. The strongest evidence for the Welsh colonization of America lies in the legend of the "white Indians," a tribe that existed in the U.S. for several hundred years. There are upwards of 100 eyewitness accounts and testimonials relating to meetings between European colonists and "white Indians," or Indians that spoke the Welsh language. A brief survey of three or four of these accounts is representative of the majority. The first account was found in a letter from the Reverend Morgan Jones to a Dr. Lloyd on March 10, 1686. According to Jones, he was serving as a chaplain in Virginia in the year 1660. During a journey through the wilderness in that year, Morgan and five companions were attacked and captured by Tuscarora Indians. The Tuscaroras intended to kill the six colonists, but when Morgan made a plea for mercy in the Welsh tongue, the Indians were astounded. They spoke the same language. Morgan's life was thus saved, and he and his friends were subsequently ransomed and allowed to return home.

The next testimony was reported by Bryant et al.:

> In 1785 was published a narration by Capt. Issac Stewart, to the effect that, having been taken prisoner by the Indians, with a Welshman named David, about the year 1767, they were carried seven hundred miles up the Red River, when they came to a "nation of Indians remarkably white, and whose hair was of a red color,—at least, mostly so." The Welshman found these people were of his own race. Their story was that their forefathers came from a foreign country and landed on the coast east of the Mississippi, which, from the description, must have been Florida. When afterwards the Spaniards took possession of Mexico, they fled west of the Mississippi, and up the Red River; and, as an evidence of the truth of this account, they showed to Capt. Stewart some rolls of parchment, covered with writing in blue ink, which they kept wrapped up in skins with great care. Unfortunately, neither Capt. Stewart nor his Welsh companion could read these precious documents.[5]

The governor of Tennessee, John Sevier, provided additional information on the "white Indians" in a letter to Major Amos Stoddard on October 9, 1810. Stoddard had requested any known facts regarding the existence of such Indians in the state of Tennessee. Governor Sevier recounted a meeting he had with an aged Cherokee Indian chief in the year 1782. Chief Oconostota, then about 90 years old, reviewed the history of the Indian nation for the governor. There were many ancient stone fortifications throughout the countryside that Chief Oconostota claimed were built by white people who had settled in Carolina. At some time in the past, a great war had developed between these whites and the Indians.

After much bloodshed on both sides, a truce was negotiated with the understanding that the whites would leave Cherokee country forever, and relocate a great distance away on the Missouri River. The Chief went on to say that over the years the white people intermarried with neighboring Indians, and now looked very much like any other Indians, having lost all physical characteristics of white people. Chief Oconostota dropped a final bombshell on the governor. According to him, he was told by his grandfather, sometime around 1700 CE, that the "white Indians" were Welsh and had entered this country near Mobile, Alabama, after crossing the great water in many ships.

George Catlin, the famous American historian and artist, had firsthand knowledge of the "white Indians." All previous evidence had indicated that they were a tribe called the Mandans. To learn the truth of this, Catlin searched out the Mandan tribe in 1832 and spent eight years living with them and studying them. If they had originally been white, the Mandans by this time were a well mixed race. Catlin painted many interesting portraits of Mandan men and women. He could not prove their Welsh heritage, but by the same token, he could not eliminate the possibility. The Indian portraits he painted revealed many European facial characteristics. His written accounts describe some Indians with blonde hair, others with red hair, and eye colors that ranged from hazel to gray to blue—certainly non–Indian attributes. Catlin himself would only say that the features of the Mandans were distinct from any other tribe. Unfortunately for posterity, a smallpox epidemic struck down the dignified Mandan nation in the middle of the nineteenth century, and obliterated them from the face of the earth forever.

Two hundred years after the specter of Madoc sailed the seas, another nebulous traveler emerged from the east. He was Henry Sinclair, Prince of Scotland and Earl of Orkney. The Sinclair account is the only pre–Columbian voyage that includes the testimony of an actual participant in the voyage; in this case, Antonio Zeno. The Sinclair discovery is based on a story by Nicolo Zeno written in the year 1558 CE. The Zeno narrative was drawn from actual correspondence by Zeno's ancestors, Nicolo and Antonio, who lived during the last half of the fourteenth century. As the story goes, Nicolo (the original) Zeno sailed from Italy in the year 1380 in search of adventure. Several mishaps brought him to Scotland, where he entered the service of Prince Henry Sinclair. Antonio followed Nicolo to Scotland the following year, and together they helped Sinclair unite his domain as a dependant state of Norway. Sinclair was a dedicated man of the sea, who constructed a fleet larger than that of Norway.

About this time, the Zenos heard of a new land in the western ocean. Supposedly a fisherman had accidentally stumbled on two great countries in the Atlantic Ocean, 26 years before. They were Estotiland and Drogea. According to Bryant:

> Four fisher-boats from Frisland were driven by a mighty tempest a thousand miles to the westward, when one of them was wrecked upon an island called Estotiland — supposed to be Newfoundland — and taken prisoners by the inhabitants. They were led to a "faire and populous city," and brought before the king who, learning who and what they were, through an interpreter — also, a shipwrecked sailor — who spoke latin, determined they should be retained in his service. Five years they lived there and found it to be a rich country, "with all the commodities of the world," with mines of all manner of metals, and especially abounding in gold. In the middle of it was a high mountain from which sprung four great rivers that went forth and watered all the land. The inhabitants they found to be a "witty people," having "all the arts and faculties" of civilized nations, speaking a language of their own, with letters and characters peculiar to themselves. Yet they had intercourse with other countries, for in the king's library there were latin books which, however, none could read, and they imported merchandise of various kinds from Engroneland.[6]

After many years, the fishermen were permitted to leave Estotiland and they sailed further south for an imposing country called Drogea.

> It was, he said, a very great country, as it were a new world; "but the people were very rude, very fierce and cruel, and voide of all goodness"; so savage that they all went naked; so wanting in intelligence that they had not even the wit to cover themselves with skins of the beasts they killed with their wooden spears and arrows, though they suffered from the cold. But farther to the southwest, the fishermen found a people of more "civility," as he found a more temperate climate, where they had cities and temples for their idols. To these idols they sacrificed men whom they afterward ate. They understood the use of gold and silver, whereas the more northern people knew nothing of metals.[7]

These accounts are not farfetched. The description of Estotiland compares favorably with Newfoundland. Similarly, the people who inhabited the northern part of Drogea are much like the North American Indian. And the people who lived further south "in the temperate climate, where they had cities, and temples for their idols," could be the Maya Indians living in the Yucatan peninsula of Mexico. Considering the vast amount of knowledge that has been developed in America in the past 30 years regarding the American mound builders, the story could also refer to a meeting between the fishermen and the mound builders of America.

Based on these accounts, Prince Henry Sinclair was determined to visit the new lands in search of valuable natural resources. Sinclair was not altogether unfamiliar with the western ocean, having previously sent a fleet to Greenland under the direction of Nicolo Zeno. Sadly, Nicolo died upon his return from Greenland, and it was with great difficulty that Prince Henry dissuaded Antonio from returning to his home in Italy.

The prince assembled a fleet of ships in the spring of 1398 CE, assembled the crews, took on adequate provisions, and reviewed the available maps one last time. In late May he disappeared into the fog surrounding the Scottish coastline. For eight days, the fleet was battered by violent north Atlantic gales; then the air became still and land was sighted dead ahead. Numerous attempts to go ashore were thwarted by the belligerent natives, and several crewmen were killed in the scuffles. Prince Henry realized it was futile to remain near this island (called Icaria), and he finally pulled up anchor and continued further west.

Nine more days passed before another land came into view. This time the country was hospitable. The Scottish expedition went ashore peacefully and immediately established a settlement near the coast. The land was more than they had hoped for. The weather was perfect, the soil was ideal for planting crops, several rivers flowed into the sea nearby, and wood was abundant. Satisfied that he had found a new home, the prince made plans to settle in for the winter. He directed Antonio Zeno to return home with the fleet, while he, Sinclair, would remain in the new land with those volunteers who chose to stay. Antonio sailed away for 20 days to the east, then five days southeast, before reaching Scotland. The narrative ends here, but Prince Henry Sinclair evidently returned to Scotland subsequently, for history records that the noble prince was struck down defending his beloved Orkneys from an invading English army in 1400 CE.

The evidence supporting the Sinclair discovery of America is all circumstantial now, but could increase in credibility in the near future. Frederick J. Pohl spent a considerable amount of time investigating the Sinclair legend, and he developed much of the evidence that presently exists. There are several geographical descriptions of Estotiland in the Zeno narratives, and Pohl dissected these descriptions very carefully in an effort to determine the territory in question. The most interesting account concerned a smoking hill that spewed pitch into the sea. As Pohl's investigation broadened, his geographical target gradually became narrower and narrower, until it was apparent that Nova Scotia was the bull's-eye. Prince Henry Sinclair had landed at Pictou, Nova Scotia. Pohl also concluded to his own satisfaction that the Micmac Indians who lived in the area were the natives who had welcomed Prince Henry to the new world. In fact, Pohl is convinced that the Micmac "Glooscap" legends actually refer to Prince Henry's voyage, and to his family as well.

There is an additional piece of silent testimony that may eventually prove the Sinclair theory, the effigy of a knight that is carved into the face of a cliff on Prospect Hill in Westford, Massachusetts, overlooking the Boston area and the Atlantic Ocean. The six foot long image, which is faint in some places and severely weatherbeaten, was actually made by hundreds of tiny punch marks. It was originally discovered back in the late 1930s, perhaps by amateur archaeologist William Goodwin. A description of the carving was published by Clay Perry in his 1939 book, *Underground New England*. Perry described the carving as being "a cross with a human face atop it."[8]

The effigy was rediscovered by Frank Glynn in 1954, using Goodwin's 1946 book, *The Ruins of Great Ireland in New England* as a reference. Glynn made a drawing of the image and sent a copy of it to Thomas Lethbridge at Cambridge University in England. Lethbridge identified the image as a fourteenth century knight. He also stated that the heraldry on his shield, consisting of a star, a crescent, a sailing ship, and a brooch, belonged to the Sinclair clan of Scotland. As mentioned earlier, James P. Whittall, Jr. of the Early Sites Research Society believed the Newport Tower may have been built by Sinclair. Research on that project is continuing.

For Sinclair enthusiasts, Pohl has deduced one last piece of interesting information: the exact date that Sinclair landed in Nova Scotia. The day that Prince Henry walked ashore at Pictou was Trinity Sunday, June 2, 1398.

# Summary

Four legendary travelers reportedly crossed the oceans to visit America between the years 499 CE and 1398 CE. They were:

- Hoei-shin, a Buddhist monk who crossed the Pacific Ocean in the fifth century CE, spent several years on the west coast of North America, possibly visited the Mayan Indians in Mexico and Central America, and returned to China in 499 CE. The written proof of the voyage is contained in official Chinese historical records. The trip is not in question, only the identity of the country he visited. Substantiating evidence of early Chinese visits to this hemisphere includes the discovery of an eighth century Chinese coin and an oil lamp in Alaska.

- St. Brendan, an Irish monk, is credited with a visit to a country in the western Atlantic Ocean in the year 545 CE. The narratives are questioned

due to the fantasies that were included in the story. The geographical descriptions accurately depict the area around Newfoundland and Nova Scotia, information that was unknown to Europeans of that time.
- The next voyager, Madoc, was a prince of Wales who may have reached America in the year 1170 CE. Like Brendan, the narrative of Madoc is not universally accepted. The principal evidence in support of the Madoc story lies in the legend of the "white Indians," supposedly the now extinct Mandan tribe. Nearly 100 firsthand accounts tell of the tribe of "white Indians" who spoke Welsh.
- The voyage of Prince Henry Sinclair of Scotland in 1398 is the only pre–Columbian voyage that is supported by written documentation by an actual participant of the voyage, in this case Antonio Zeno. Additional supporting evidence for this voyage consists of geographical descriptions, the Zeno map, and the Westford knight.

## Conclusions

- It is likely that America was explored by foreign visitors in ancient times, at least 1,000 years before Columbus.
- The Irish incursion into North America by Brendan the Navigator and others is well supported by geographical evidence unknown to the Europeans of the day, as well as by independent testimony from their long-time enemies, the Vikings. The exact locations described in the *Navagatio* and in the Viking Sagas remain to be defined.
- The voyage of Prince Henry Sinclair, too, is supported by previously unknown geographical evidence, as well as by the discovery of an effigy in Westford, Massachusetts, that portrays a fourteenth century knight in armor, carrying a shield bearing the heraldry of the Sinclair clan of Scotland.
- More hard evidence is required to verify those voyages, as well as the voyages of Hoei-shin and Madoc, to North America. The voyage of Madoc could possibly be confirmed by DNA analysis on Mandan remains and on the ancestors of Madoc.

# 7

# *The Ancient Mariners*

## Conventional Thinking

Ancient maritime nations with access to the eastern Atlantic did not possess enough knowledge of the Atlantic Ocean to make transoceanic voyages to America. They knew nothing of either the wind patterns or the prevailing currents in the great ocean. Additionally, they had neither the opportunity nor the incentive to attempt such a crossing.

## Discussion

It was previously shown that the currents and winds in the Atlantic Ocean were conducive to round trip transoceanic voyages between Europe and North or South America. It was also shown that the ancients possessed vessels capable of ocean travel. This was verified in the twentieth century by Thor Heyerdahl and other enterprising adventurers, who built replicas of ancient ships and sailed them across the ocean. It is now accepted in most scientific circles that the Vikings explored North America sometime around 1000 CE. And finally, a review of the ancient writers revealed that, if they did not know of the American continent, they at least surmised there might be a large land mass on the western side of the Atlantic Ocean. The plausibility of Viking visits to ancient America having been demonstrated, it only remains to determine if there were any maritime nations who had sufficient knowledge of the vagaries of the Atlantic Ocean, who had the necessary incentive, and who had the opportunity to successfully navigate that most unpredictable of all oceans.

The modern voyages of Heyerdahl and others indicate that many nations might have been capable of ocean travel. These included the Sumerians, the Minoans, the Egyptians, the Libyans, the Iberian Celts, and the Romans. Ancient cargo ships came in a variety of sizes and designs.

Phoenician cargo ships generally approached 100 feet in length, as did the ships of Greece. Roman ships, on the other hand, sometimes grew to gargantuan proportions, with ships of 130 to 150 feet in length not uncommon. Viking ships, and the ships of Christopher Columbus, were dwarfed alongside the vessels used in the ancient world. While the Santa Maria was capable of carrying up to 75 tons of precious cargo (or "burden") back to Spain, the merchant ships of Greece and Rome could store up to 250 tons of merchandise and treasure comfortably in their holds, a much more lucrative situation for their owners (see table).

### Comparison of History's Famous Cargo Ships

|  | Egypt 1500 BCE | Phoenicia 700 BCE | Greece 500 BCE | Rome 100 CE | Viking 1000 CE | Spain 1492 CE |
|---|---|---|---|---|---|---|
| Length, Ft. | 100 | 100 | 150 | 130 | 60 | 59 |
| Beam, Ft. | 20 | 14 | 20 | 20 | 20 | 20 |
| Depth, Ft. | 4 | 10 | 8 | 10 | 7.5 | 9 |
| Burden, Tons | 75 | 120 | 240 | 250 | 75 | 75 |

It is apparent that any substantial eastern Atlantic nation was capable of obtaining the necessary transportation to support a transatlantic expedition, for exploration, colonization, or profit. All wealthy countries had access to reliable oceangoing vessels. They could build their own ships if they so chose, or they could charter a ship, or a fleet of ships, from any one of a number of wealthy shipping magnates. Perhaps a study of these countries will ascertain which of them, if any, might have been America's first visitor.

## The Sumerians

Thor Heyerdahl successfully navigated a replica of an ancient Sumerian reed boat, the *Tigris*, from the confluence of the Tigris and Euphrates Rivers to the east coast of Africa, a journey of over 4,000 miles, thereby demonstrating the naval capabilities of Sumerian vessels. But did the Sumerians travel to America?

Civilization began in Mesopotamia, the land of the Sumerians, over 6,000 years ago. The first cities arose from the fertile valleys along the Tigris and Euphrates Rivers, in the country that is now Iraq. Cities like Ur, Uruk, Lagash, and Babylon soon became famous centers of commerce throughout the ancient world. Religion and business flourished. Beer became the people's drink and, sometime around 3000 BCE, writing was invented as a means of maintaining adequate business and accounting records.

Artifacts, art objects, and seals found in Sumerian graves have established the fact that oceangoing vessels were used in Mesopotamia over 4,000 years ago, and that a vast trade network already existed at that time, one bustling with activity. There were ivory carvings and cotton textiles from the Harappan civilization in Pakistan, linen, faience, and papyrus from Egypt, spices and ostrich feathers from the east coast of Africa, and cedar wood from Phoenicia. Sumerian reed boats routinely cruised the Tigris and Euphrates Rivers, north and south, trading with the cities along the way. They also ventured into the Persian Gulf, stopping first to trade at the island of Bahrain, then proceeding through the Arabian Sea to the Indus River to visit the Harappan metropolises of Harappa and Mohenjo Daro. Other ocean journeys may well have carried them through the Indian Ocean and the Red Sea to the land of the pharaohs. But, as far as is known, this was the extent of the Sumerians' world. In fact, this area did cover most of the civilized western world during the third millennium BCE. The rest of Europe and Africa was still struggling to free itself from the Stone Age.

## The Minoans

Simultaneous with the rise of the Sumerian civilization was the development of a magnificent culture in the eastern Mediterranean Sea, the mysterious Minoan empire. Unlike the, autonomous cities of Mesopotamia, the Minoan cities were ruled by an autocratic king who governed his people from the great citadel of Knossus on the island of Crete. During the third millennium BCE, the influences of the Minoan empire spread throughout the Mediterranean world. Spurred on initially by the need for copper and tin to manufacture tools and weapons, the Minoans built a sizeable merchant fleet. They initiated trading voyages to Egypt, where copper was plentiful. The Minoans not only obtained copper and other necessities, but also began to acquire luxuries like ivory, gold, perfume, and incense. Before long, commerce was established with other countries, including Greece, Syria, and Sumeria. As trade items began to flow back into Crete, the people quickly developed an appetite for ornate and frivolous trappings. The Minoan merchant fleet expanded rapidly. It soon became necessary to construct a large fleet of war galleys in order to protect the merchant ships from pirates. By 1800 BCE, the Minoan kings ruled the entire Mediterranean. Their maritime activities spread further and further west in search of new wealth, such as amber and tin. They visited Libya in North Africa and also reached the coast of Spain. Had fate smiled upon them, the Minoans may well have ventured out into the

Atlantic Ocean. They had all the ingredients necessary to achieve great feats in the field of exploration. They had the expertise in shipbuilding, the wealth required to support ambitious projects, and the curiosity to discover what lay beyond the horizon. But fate was not kind to the Minoans. As noted in a previous chapter, a monstrous catastrophe destroyed their civilization in one day and night. The explosion on Thera, and the resulting tidal wave, inundated the great cities of Knossus, Phaistos, and Mallia, leaving the magnificent island of Crete desolate and lifeless. The Minoan empire was gone, leaving only ruins.

# The Egyptians

There was yet another powerful empire in the Mediterranean world in the third millennium BCE: Egypt, the land of the pyramids and the Sphinx. Egypt's development began around 3000 BCE, and like other flourishing cultures, she quickly acquired a taste for the luxuries that were available around the world. An inscribed rock near the tomb of the pharaoh Snofru attests to the fact that Egypt was a leader in maritime activity as early as 2720 BCE. The inscription describes the construction of a large vessel made of strong cedar wood and covering the length of 150 feet. It also describes the arrival of 40 cargo ships traveling from Phoenicia to Egypt, laden with cedar logs. The annals of Egyptian history are filled with descriptions of sea voyages to faraway lands. In 1470 BCE, Queen Hatshepsut sent a fleet of ships to Punt in search of gold, incense, and antimony. The location of ancient Punt is still open to conjecture, but the general opinion is that it was on the coast of Africa, some 4,000 miles distant from Egypt. In those days, a single expedition could take as long as 18 months.

Another reported Egyptian voyage was made to India during the reign of Ramses II, in the thirteenth century BCE. This time, the voyage was made at the request of the king of Bakhtan, whose sister-in-law was gravely ill and in need of expert medical attention. Since Egypt at that time was famous for her knowledge of medicine, the royal Egyptian physicians were in demand around the world. The voyage to India was reported to have covered 3,000 miles in 17 months—an average of less than 180 miles per month. How was it possible that a large seagoing vessel sailed an average of only six miles a day? The answer is that Egyptian ships were not seagoing vessels. They always sailed in sight of land. They stayed close to the shore, sailing only during daylight hours, and beaching their boats at night. They stayed on shore during stormy weather, and they did not attempt to sail at all during the winter season.

In those rare instances when Egypt desired to venture forth onto the ocean, she would call upon the maritime experts for assistance. More often than not, she would commission a fleet from a reliable Phoenician shipowner, such as the pharaoh Necho II did when he wished to attempt a circumnavigation of Africa. It is obvious that Egypt was never a maritime nation. Her ships sailed primarily up and down the Nile River, with occasional voyages down the east coast of Africa. Her penetration into the Mediterranean Sea was a rare occurrence and was restricted to coastline journeys to Phoenicia for wood. It is not likely that Egypt could have supported a transatlantic voyage using her own ships. She had neither the expertise nor the desire.

## The Libyans

Ancient Libya was Egypt's neighbor to the west. From early times, the Libyans had a reputation for being expert navigators and superior mariners. But most of Libya's ancient history comprised prolonged periods of servitude to other nations, such as Egypt, Persia, Greece, Macedon, and Phoenicia. Libyan mercenaries served in the Egyptian army for centuries. One time, the mercenaries revolted, usurping the Egyptian throne, and founding the twenty-second dynasty, the so-called Libyan dynasty. This dynasty lasted from 940 BCE to 630 BCE. After 630 BCE, the Greeks settled in Eastern Libya and spread their influence throughout Northern Africa. Darius the Great, of Persia, followed swiftly on the heels of the Greeks, and subjugated Libya sometime around 490 BCE. Alexander the Great regained control of the country for Greece around 330 BCE and, following his death, Ptolemy I annexed Libya to his new Egyptian empire. In 96 BCE, Libya fell again, this time to the Romans. So it went, continuing to this very day.

The western part of the country fell under the influence of the Carthaginians during the seventh century BCE, and continued to be an ally of Carthage until the Roman legions sacked Carthage and burned it to the ground in 146 BCE. All in all, it is a black picture of constant subservience, rather than one of independent nationhood. It would appear that, if the Libyans did in fact voyage to America, it was probably in the service of a foreign king.

## The Greeks

Greece is the first bonafide maritime nation to come under our scrutiny. While Sumeria, Egypt, and Crete were basking in their own magnificence, Greece was just beginning to escape from the Stone Age and establish her identity. By the time the Minoan empire sank into oblivion, Greece was ready to emerge as the world's newest power. Fresh from a victory over Troy, the Mycenaean kings of Greece burst upon the stage as the new rulers of the maritime world. Survivors of the Minoan tragedy reportedly found their way to Greece, and contributed significantly to her naval expertise. The Greeks became proficient mariners, honing their skills over the next millennium. They explored the Mediterranean world extensively, searching for new sources of raw materials and for desirable trade goods. Greek settlements sprang up on every continent. In Africa, they established colonies along the northern coast, including Cyrene in Libya. The wealth of the great continent began to flow back to Greece: animals of all kinds, leopard and zebra skins, ivory, precious stones and metals—and slaves. The search for material goods continued along the European shore. From Italian colonies came amber and marble. From Southern Spain came silver, copper, iron, and tin. And from France came minerals and the finest of wines.

About 650 BCE, Greeks ships passed through the Pillars of Heracles, and gazed upon the waters of the Atlantic Ocean for the first time. They sailed north along the Iberian coast as far as Tartessus, in search of tin. Unfortunately, the Greek association with the Atlantic seaboard was short lived. By 600 BCE, the Carthaginians had exerted their influence in the western Mediterranean area, and had successfully sealed off the Pillars of Heracles to maritime traffic. From that time until the defeat of Carthage by the Romans, no ships were allowed to pass through the Pillars and enter the Atlantic Ocean without the permission of the Carthaginians. And the Carthaginians didn't give anyone permission.

Occasionally, however, a vessel would slip past the Carthaginian sentries and enter the great ocean. One such expedition was recorded by ancient historians and is well documented. It concerns one Pytheas, a resident of the Greek city of Massalia in Southern Gaul, and took place around 306 BCE. Pytheas was a respected scientist, proficient in geography, geology, and astronomy. He was recruited by the town fathers to lead a naval expedition along the Atlantic coast to Northern Europe. The Massalian vessel set sail in the spring of the year, hugged the coastline until it reached the Pillars of Heracles, then somehow avoided the Carthaginian patrol boats, quietly entering the Atlantic Ocean. The Greek ship was a sturdy seagoing vessel, capable of surviving the fierce north Atlantic storms. She sailed north along the coast of Spain, crossed the English Channel to Britain, then proceeded to circumnavigate England, Ireland, and Scotland. The great ship stopped frequently to explore the surrounding countryside, but she always did so at locations that were safely distant from the Carthaginian's sphere of influence. She could not afford to be discovered, since it would mean certain confiscation of the ship, and death or slavery for the crew.

On leaving the British Isles, Pytheas and his compatriots encountered one of the common north Atlantic storms. Gale winds, driving rains, and 50-foot-high waves battered the ship for days, but she withstood the assault with no significant damage. Pytheas then apparently visited Iceland, which he called Ultima Thule, an island lying six days north of England. From Iceland the great expedition headed east, passed Denmark, and sailed through the Baltic Sea as far as the Vistula River in Poland. Whether or not the purposes of this voyage was purely scientific is not known, but we do know that Pytheas made many revolutionary astronomical observations during the trip and significantly advanced the scientific knowledge of his time. For instance, he was the first scientist to note the moon's influence on tides.

Pytheas' voyage is notable because it demonstrates the ability of ancient European mariners to successfully cross open expanses of the wild Atlantic Ocean in seagoing vessels of the period. The voyage covered a total distance of as much as 16,000 miles, and took as long as six months (see table). According to the histories, Pytheas and his crew returned safely home to Massalia at the completion of the expedition, somehow evading Carthaginian patrols once more.

## Reported Ocean Voyages

| Voyage | Date | Miles Traveled One Way | Comments |
|---|---|---|---|
| Phoenicians circumnavigate Africa | 534 BCE | 14,000 | Exploratory voyage |
| Hanno, west coast of Africa | 450 BCE | 4,000 | Colonization |
| Himilco to west coast of Europe | 450 BCE | 4,000 | Exploration |
| Pytheas to west coast of Europe | 306 BCE | 8,000 | Exploration |
| Hoei-shin to west coast of America | 499 CE | 7,000 | Missionary voyage |
| St. Brendan to east coast of America | 550 CE | 4,000 | Search for Peaceful Isle |
| Unknown mariner to Hawaii | 600 CE | 2,300 | Polynesian colonization |
| Leif Erikson to east coast of N. America | 1003 CE | 1,000 | Exploration |
| Prince Madoc to North America | 1170 CE | 1,600 | Colonization |
| Prince Henry Sinclair to N. America | 1398 CE | 1,800 | Exploration |
| Christopher Columbus to America | 1492 CE | 3,600 | Find route to Indies |
| Pedro Alvares Cabral to Brazil | 1500 CE | 1,750 | Blown across ocean |

Based on the available evidence, the Greeks were capable of transoceanic voyages and could have reached America under the right conditions, but like the Minoans before them, they were victims of their fate. Their maritime evolution was stopped by the Carthaginians in 600 BCE. Except for unusual occurrences, such as the voyage of Pytheas, the Greeks were prisoners of their Mediterranean world, finally falling to the Roman war machine in the second century BCE.

## The Celts

Most people do not regard the Celts as a maritime people, but certain Celtic tribes developed exceptional naval expertise as a result of their geographical location. The Celts presumably originated in central Europe. Sometime during the second millennium BCE, they began to spill out of Southern Germany, dispersing throughout the known world, south, east, and west. Some tribes traveled west to Gaul, to the Iberian peninsula, and to the British Isles. It is these tribes, the Celts that populated the western frontier of Europe, that are of interest to this study. The Celts of Ireland, Gaul, and Spain quickly organized a maritime commercial confederacy amongst themselves, and they also included the pre–Viking mariners of Scandinavia. About 1100 BCE, the Phoenicians emerged from their Mediterranean lair and penetrated the unknown world of the Outer Ocean. They were eventually admitted into the trade network, but they were sworn to secrecy regarding the riches of the Atlantic coast and the adjacent islands. For their part, the Phoenicians, then operating out of Carthage, agreed to blockade the Pillars of Heracles, to prevent other European countries from destroying the monopoly.

Eventually it became necessary for the Celts to protect their interests militarily. The Romans began to develop a power structure in Italy during the fourth century BCE, and it grew incessantly during the next 300 years. Unlike the nations of the Atlantic alliance — the Scandinavians, the Celts, and the Carthaginians— the Romans were bent on conquest. They were not averse to maritime commerce, but their real goal was to rule the world. It was only a matter of time before the maritime merchants were forced to confront the Roman war machine. Being a Mediterranean nation, the Phoenicians of Carthage were the first to do it. Carthage and Rome fought three major wars over a period of 118 years. The first two wars were inconclusive. Carthage was totally destroyed after the third war. The first war was fought from 264 to 241 BCE. Carthage's naval power was annihilated during this war, and her commercial ventures ceased to be significant thereafter. She attempted to regain her lost power through a land war beginning in 218 BCE, but again she was defeated, and was forced to vacate her European colonies. In 149 BCE, Rome brought the war to the Carthaginian homeland, invading North Africa, and eventually forcing the Carthaginian people into an unconditional surrender. Carthage was burned to the ground in 146 BCE, and salt was poured on the ruins, a gesture to prevent her ever coming back to life.

During this 200-year period, it became evident to the Celts of Gaul and Iberia that they would be forced to confront the Romans sooner or later. They prepared well. Their army grew tough and disciplined, and their naval fleet became one of the largest and strongest in the ancient world. The man who brought the situation to a head was the great Roman general, Gaius Julius Caesar, who invaded Gaul in 58 BCE. Caesar's war experiences are well documented in his autobiographical account of the Gallic Wars. It was Caesar himself who informed the world of the naval expertise of the Celtic sailor. As Caesar advanced through Gaul, he had an unbroken string of successes against the Celtic armies, but not without great difficulty. The Celts were brave and ferocious warriors and, as a result, Roman losses in manpower and equipment were staggering. Subduing the coastal fortifications was an even more formidable task. Caesar encountered problems he never anticipated. The Celts fought stubbornly to protect their coastal towns, and when the situation became hopeless, they brought hundreds of shallow-bottomed boats into the harbors, to evacuate the defenders and remove them to more strategic positions.

Caesar was surprised by the immense sea power of these barbarian tribes. Little did he know that he was witnessing the culmination of 1,000 years of naval research and development. Caesar's admiral of the fleet had considerable difficulty in maneuvering the cumbersome Roman galleys in the unpredictable Atlantic waters. The Roman ships were much faster than the Celtic vessels, but they were much more difficult to turn, less stable in the violent ocean swells, and useless in shallow water conditions. The Celtic ships, on the other hand, could maneuver in any kind of weather. The high prows, sterns, and freeboard protected the vessels in gale winds and high seas, and their relatively flat bottoms allowed the ships to move in and out of shallow water quite easily. When the weather was foul, a frequent condition on the Atlantic coast, the Roman ships remained at anchor in protected harbors, but the Celtic ships carried on with business as usual.

Caesar became increasingly frustrated by the superior Celtic ships. Rome was not used to losing; they were not even used to being detained for very long. Caesar's military tacticians studied these new ships in detail. They were too well constructed to be rammed, and they were too high to be boarded under the dynamic conditions of a sea chase. Eventually however, the Roman strategists saw a weakness. The Romans constructed very large missiles that could be used to destroy the immense sails on the Celtic craft, rendering the ships helpless in the water. Without the ability to maneuver, the Celtic vessels were at the mercy of Roman boarding parties, and the great Atlantic sea war soon came to an end. With it, so did Caesar's Gallic Wars. Mopping-up operations were completed in short order, and Gaul became a Roman province. With the conclusion of the campaign, Celtic sea power along the Atlantic coast of Europe ceased to exist.

There is archaeological evidence that Celtic voyages reached as far west as Iceland prior to the Roman invasion. Whether or not they visited North America is still a mystery. But they had the expertise. It is possible that the Atlantic alliance, comprised of the Phoenicians, the Celts, and the Scandinavians, used its combined forces on transatlantic voyages.

## The Romans

Rome quietly entered the pages of history in 510 BCE, when she drove the last of the Etruscan kings from her city and established the first republic. She developed her government and her society over a period of 200 years. Then, as the third century BCE dawned, Rome initiated her relentless drive for world domination. For the first 50 years, she concerned herself with the Italian peninsula. Having subdued all the local Greek colonies, Rome was confronted by the seemingly endless waters of the Mediterranean Sea, and the specter of Carthaginian naval superiority. But Rome was undaunted. Having subdued the Etruscans early in the fourth century BCE, Rome had inherited the Etruscan naval expertise, which was extensive. So, when she was confronted by the Carthaginian naval forces, she did not have to start from scratch to build a navy. And, as she did so many times throughout her history, Rome proved herself to be adaptable and resourceful, particularly in military matters. She built a formidable fleet of war galleys and, when she felt the time was right, she challenged Carthage for undisputed control of the Mediterranean waters. The time was right in 241 BCE. The encounter was known as the First Punic War, and Rome, as a result of a great naval victory off the Aegadian Islands, emerged victorious and assumed the position of masters of the sea. She maintained control of the European sea lanes for over 700 years, well into the Byzantine era.

Roman merchant ships evolved from those of the Phoenicians and the Greeks, and resembled them in size and design. As Rome developed, however, her ship design became innovative, and some of her cargo vessels grew to immense size. There is a report that the Roman emperor Caligula built one cargo ship large enough to hold 1,300 tons burden in order to convey a large obelisk from Egypt to Rome. Other reports tell of Roman ships carrying 1,000 passengers. The nucleus of the Roman merchant fleet was the proud "round ship," the staple of not only Rome but of Greece and Phoenicia before her. That Rome had ships capable of navigating the open sea is a foregone conclusion.

Beginning with the formation of the empire and the ascendancy of Caesar Augustus, Roman maritime activity increased. Her ships were frequent visitors to the tin mines in England and to the silver mines along the west coast of the European continent. It is possible that Roman cargo vessels also frequented ports as far north as Scandinavia and the Baltic Sea, in search of furs, fish, and amber. Voyages along the west coast of Africa would have provided animals, animal skins, ivory, and gold for the Roman gentry. Hamilton Child, writing in 1884, quoted the Roman emperor Honorius, the son of Theodosius the Great, as affirming that "at or about the time of the Christian era, voyages from Africa and Spain into the Atlantic Ocean, were both frequent and celebrated."[1]

Rome did not confine her maritime activities to the western Mediterranean Sea and the Atlantic coast. The Roman merchant ships were familiar visitors to Phoenicia, Israel, Egypt, and even beyond. The round ships found their way into the Red Sea and the Indian Ocean to visit ports along the Arabian Peninsula and the west coast of India, voyages that far exceed the distance from Europe to America. But there's a catch. Regardless of whether the Roman merchant fleet departed on a journey of a few hundred miles or an 18-month expedition to India, the ships could travel to all destinations without ever venturing out of sight of land. But it is likely that, once the Romans became familiar with a trade route, such as across the Mediterranean Sea or across the Indian Ocean, they would gradually begin to take shortcuts. They would slowly venture out of sight of land for a period of time, and as they gained confidence in their ability to navigate the seas accurately, they would increase their "out of sight" time until they had optimized the sea route to achieve the shortest sailing time possible between ports of call.

But the Romans were not expert navigators and mariners to the extent the Phoenicians were. Like their predecessors, the Egyptians, if the Romans decided on a difficult ocean expedition requiring precise knowledge of navigation and seamanship, they would call on the Phoenicians. There is no substitute for 1,500 years of practical experience. It is not known if Roman ships ever reached America, but it is known that Roman experience in ocean travel out of sight of land was severely limited. And the

Romans were not adventurers. They did not take the risks the great Phoenician mariners took. The Romans were very cautious and calculating people. If they did reach America, it was probably due to either an accidental drift voyage, or a joint venture with Phoenician entrepreneurs. Child suggested that, when he wrote "there is a strong possibility that the Romans and Carthaginians, even 300 years BCE, were well acquainted with the existence of this country."[2]

# The Phoenicians

The Phoenicians were the ancient world's premier merchants and seamen. They were the ultimate businessmen, surviving more than a dozen foreign occupations over a period of 2,600 years, beginning with the Babylonians and ending with the Muslim Arabs. Since their interests were mainly business oriented, they always assumed the image of their conquerors. Diplomacy was their forte, and they always made invading armies feel right at home. As soon as the military atmosphere subsided, the Phoenician merchant would gather his fleet together and get on with business as usual. A most unusual and enterprising people, the Phoenicians. As one of the most likely candidates for ancient America's first visitors, it is necessary to learn more about their origins, their history, their maritime adventures, and their experiences in the Atlantic Ocean to determine the probability that Phoenician vessels preceded Christopher Columbus to the North American shores by 2,000 years.

Ancient Phoenicia occupied a slip of land on the eastern shore of the Mediterranean Sea, in what is roughly today's Lebanon. It was bordered on the north by Syria and on the south by Israel. Diplomacy came early to the Phoenicians. It had to, in order to maintain peace with these two hostile neighbors. The inhabitants of the country referred to themselves as Canaanites. They were known for a purple cloth that they manufactured by a secret dyeing process. It made the country so famous throughout the world that the Greeks began referring to the inhabitants as Phonikes, the "purple people." The name "Phonikes" stuck, and the country has come down through the pages of history as the "land of the purple people."

At the dawn of civilization, when the cities of Ur and Lagash began to bustle with activity, Phoenicia was an empty and barren country. There was an ancient agricultural community located at Jericho, several hundred miles to the south, but that was the nearest habitation. Sometime around the beginning of the third millennium BCE, there was a stirring of Bedouin tribes in the eastern section of the Arabian peninsula, near the Persian

Gulf. For some unknown reason, some tribes began to leave the peninsula and migrate toward the north. One of these tribes eventually worked its way west, over or around the Lebanon Mountains, until the people reached the coast of the Mediterranean Sea. Here they made their home. Their early Bedouin heritage had been one of barter, so it was natural for the settlers—who would become the Phoenicians—to continue in their old ways. A business relationship was gradually established with Egypt, a country that was embarking on a semi-maritime strategy and required strong, hard wood to use in the construction of her ships. She also needed wood to build palaces and temples, since the land of Egypt was essentially treeless. Phoenicia, on the other hand, had cedar wood in abundance. By 2700 BCE, Egyptian boats were making routine round trip voyages to Phoenician ports, like Byblos and Sidon, to purchase the precious wood. In return, Phoenicia received many raw materials and manufactured goods from Egypt: metals, such as gold and copper, and commodities including papyrus, linen cloth and decorative glassware.

During the early years of their history, the Phoenicians had noticed that their coastline was cluttered with thousands and thousands of shellfish. Legend has it, that one day a dog bit into one of the shellfish, releasing a stream of purple liquid, to the surprise of the dog's owner. Not being the type of people to waste anything, the industrious Phoenicians began experimenting with the shellfish in hopes of producing something that could be converted into a marketable product. Their perseverance eventually paid handsome dividends. Two families of shellfish, the Murex and the Purpura, were found to produce the purple liquid, which could subsequently be extracted and distilled into a viable dye, ranging in color from blue to a deep crimson. Cloth goods dyed with it exhibited brilliant and long lasting colors. The vibrant purple cloth proved particularly desirable. The dye, which became known as Tyrian purple after the port city where the large manufacturing operations were located, made the Phoenicians both famous and wealthy. Tyrian purple was soon in great demand all over the Mediterranean world. And, since the dye was necessarily obtained in small amounts, and the preparation and dyeing process itself was very complicated, the cost of Phoenician purple cloth was very high; so expensive, in fact, that only the rich could afford it. Zvi Herman stated that a ten-pound ream of purple silk cost the equivalent of $30,000 in the year 300 CE. Even today, purple is considered to be the color of royalty. Twentieth century babies, born into a royal family, are still said to be "born to the purple." And Roman Catholic bishops who are elevated to the post of cardinal, are "promoted to the purple."

With a surplus of cedar wood and purple dye, Phoenicia began to establish her merchant empire shortly after 2000 BCE. Being a naturally industrious and enterprising people, the Phoenicians soon realized that overland caravans were too slow to allow them to realize their ultimate ambitions. They needed a fleet of merchant ships in order to reach all the countries surrounding the Mediterranean Sea in the shortest possible time. It was not necessary for the Phoenicians to develop their maritime expertise from scratch however. They were already well educated in matters relating to the sea, having by necessity been fishermen from their early days on the Persian Gulf. Ships were second nature to them, and they were well versed in the art of seamanship as well as techniques of navigation.

The last half of the second millennium BCE was an exciting time for the Phoenicians. Their technology developed rapidly and their business acumen was honed to a fine edge, until they were widely recognized and admired as being the world leaders in business and seamanship. The key to their success was the development of the round ship, the backbone of the Phoenician merchant fleet, the world's first authentic oceangoing vessel. Their technical advances in the art of ship construction set the standard for centuries to come. Merchant vessels were no longer tiny, unstable, flat-bottomed river boats. The new breed of merchant ship was large, rugged, and dynamically stable. These ships were capable of traveling anywhere in the world. This accomplishment required a complete redesign of their traditional ship construction. The Phoenicians had to convert the ship from a coast-hugging river boat to a rugged, deep sea, oceangoing vessel. The depth of the vessel had to be increased significantly for ocean travel. Instead of a depth of three or four feet, such as was common on existing ships, the new Phoenician ships had a depth of 10, 15, and even 20 feet. This design gave the ships a strange tubby look, hence the name "round ship."

The Phoenicians also developed the keel, the bottommost structural member of the hull running fore and aft. The keel supported the planking of the hull, and gave the boat increased structural strength, in addition to providing stability and better steering capabilities. The Phoenicians then redesigned the sails to provide superior maneuverability in the open ocean, thus eliminating most of the oarsmen and their benches, and increasing the ship's cargo-carrying capacity. As a final step, the ships were constructed with decks fore and aft, while the center hold area was left open, similar to the Viking Knorr in chapter 3. To set off the entire design, the Phoenicians dyed their large, square sails with the expensive purple dye as an advertisement of their wares. Everyone knew when a Phoenician merchant ship entered the harbor.

This new ship design revolutionized the ancient maritime world. Soon more than a thousand Phoenician merchant ships were criss-crossing the Mediterranean Sea on trading expeditions. In addition, the enterprising ship owners offered ships for hire to anyone who could pay the price. One of their first customers was King Solomon of neighboring Israel. Israel and Phoenicia were allies during the eleventh and tenth centuries BCE, and King Hiram of Phoenicia participated in many joint ventures with Israel during the period from 970 to 940 BCE.

Hiram, also known as Hiram the Great, sent hundreds of craftsmen and a fleet of ships laden with cedar wood to Israel, to assist Solomon in constructing his magnificent temple in Jerusalem. He also entered into an agreement with Solomon to conduct trading expeditions to the Red Sea, the Indian Ocean, and the Persian Gulf. As part of the arrangement, Phoenician ships were allowed to use the port of Ezion Geber freely. Ezion Geber was located on the Gulf of Aqaba, an arm of the Red Sea, and it gave the Phoenicians a strategic point of departure for excursions to India and South Africa. Phoenicia, for her part, supplied ships and crews for Solomon's expeditions to distant lands. The most popular port of call on the Israeli-Phoenician voyages was Ophir, which was visited every three years for gold, silver, sandalwood, ivory, and precious stones. Ophir is another of those ancient countries whose location is unknown today. Guesses as to its site include the east coast of Africa, Southern Arabia, and India. In any case, it is very likely that Phoenician ships were very familiar with the entire coast of Arabia, and probably even the west coast of India.

Another instance of Phoenicia's service to another country occurred in 534 BCE, when Necho II, pharaoh of Egypt, contracted with Phoenician merchants to dispatch a fleet of ships on a three-year circumnavigation of Africa, a feat which incidentally provided the Phoenicians with a wealth of information about the ocean currents and prevailing wind patterns in the southern hemisphere of the Atlantic Ocean, information that would be invaluable to mariners traveling to and from South America. It is safe to assume that countless unrecorded sea journeys were made by Phoenician ships in the service of foreign flags or individuals. Voyages around Africa, and excursions to India, are mind boggling enough; a trip to America would not be much more surprising than what has already been recorded.

Additional information regarding the navigational expertise of the Phoenician mariners was provided by Rawlinson:

> At first they sailed, we may be sure, only in the daytime, casting anchor at night, or else dragging their ships up upon the beach, and so awaiting the dawn. But after a time, they grew more bold. The sea became familiar to them, the positions of coasts and islands relatively one to another better

known, the character of the seasons, the signs of unsettled weather, the conduct to pursue in an emergency, better apprehended. They soon began to shape the course of their vessels from headland to headland, instead of always creeping along the shore, and it was not perhaps very long before they would venture out of sight of land, if the wind might be trusted to continue steady, and if they were well assured of the direction of the land that they wished to make. They took courage, moreover, to sail in the night, no less than in the daytime, when the weather was clear, guiding themselves by the stars, and particularly by the Polar Star, which they discovered to be the star most nearly marking the true north.[3]

Using the North Star to navigate by was probably another innovation of the Phoenicians. The Greeks gave them credit for discovering its value, referring to it as the Phoenician star.

As Phoenician maritime expertise increased, their desire to locate new business enterprises also grew. A royal decree declared that Phoenicia would launch a program of exploration and colonization to the far reaches of the Inner Sea. One of the first colonies to be established by the merchants of Tyre was on the nearby island of Cyprus, sometime around 1400 BCE. Cyprus was a beautiful island, green and lush, and abounding with grapes from which a full, rich wine was produced. Even more important, Cyprus was rich in valuable metals, including gold, silver, iron, and particularly copper. Cyprus was noted for her copper mines and, in fact, the name of the metal is derived from the name of the island, originally being called cyperium. For 600 years, the tentacles of the "sea kings" reached inexorably westward. Trading posts were built on the islands of Rhodes and Malta and, in 1100 BCE, the city of Utica was founded in North Africa. The round ships visited the coast of Italy, explored Sardinia, and founded the settlement of Palermo in Sicily. They reached and passed through the Pillars of Heracles to establish a colony at Gades, on the Atlantic coast of Spain. But they didn't stop there. They eventually crossed the English Channel to exploit the tin supply in Cornwall, England. Their ships also sailed south along the west coast of Africa, and even west into the Atlantic Ocean to the Canary Islands, where they discovered a new source of purple dye. Vast new resources were made available to the eastern civilization as a result of these bold excursions into a hitherto unknown world. In addition to the tin of England and the purple dye of the Canaries, silver, gold, and wool were obtained in Spain, and ivory, apes, and slaves were purchased in Africa. Exotic birds provided feathers with a dazzling variety of colors for the markets in Alexandria and Baghdad, with leopard skins and zebra skins being popular items in Athens and Mycenae. In return, the western colonies were the recipient of the rich exports of the east, such as brilliant purple silk, perfumes, frankincense, rare jewels, and papyrus.

Rawlinson summarized the Phoenician theory of colonization:

> The colonization was not so continuous as the Greek, nor was it so extensive in one direction, but on the whole it was wider, and it was far bolder and more adventurous. The Greeks, as a general rule, made their advances by slow degrees, stealing on from point to point, and having always friendly cities close at hand, like an army that rests on its supports. The Phoenicians left long intervals of space between one settlement and another, boldly planted them on barbarous shores, where they had nothing to rely on but themselves, and carried them into regions where the natives were in a state of almost savagery. The commercial motive was predominant with them, and gave them the courage to plunge into wild seas and venture themselves among even wilder men.[4]

In the year 825 BCE, an event occurred that would have a profound and lasting effect on the history of the Phoenician people: The city of Carthage was founded on the north shore of Africa, near modern day Tunis. The city rapidly grew in size and in influence, until it rivaled Tyre itself as the seat of Phoenician power. In the year 574 BCE, Carthage assumed complete leadership of the Phoenician empire. The great Babylonian king Nebuchadnezzar had invaded Phoenicia in 587 BCE and had subdued all the cities along the Levantine coast. Only Tyre resisted. After a siege of 13 years, the mainland city was completely destroyed, and refugees from the island fled before the marauding Babylonians. Hundreds of ships rescued the residents before the last onslaught, and delivered them to the new capital in North Africa. Phoenicia, as a dominant political entity in the east, ceased to exist after this date.

The Carthaginians continued the Phoenician policy of exploration and colonization, and extended it deeper into the Atlantic Ocean. Only two of these excursions were documented for posterity, the voyages of Himilco and Hanno, but these provide us with important insight into the capabilities and accomplishments of this great maritime nation. Himilco, a Carthaginian navigator, was directed to explore the west coast of Europe around 480 BCE. His exploit is duly recorded by the Roman geographer Avienus in the fifth century CE, but the account is very brief and disturbingly vague. The objective of this particular voyage was not chronicled, but one popular theory is that Himilco was searching for a new source of tin. He sailed along the Iberian peninsula, explored Brittany, then veered west across the English Channel to Great Britain. He subsequently circumnavigated the British Isles, stopping as necessary to explore and evaluate the terrain. Himilco may have traveled as far north as Scandinavia during his four-month absence from Carthage; at least, the description of a frozen sea in the narrative hints at such a possibility. On his return voyage,

Himilco's ship was reported to have been becalmed for an extended period of time, and subsequently became entangled in a sea of weeds. If that statement is correct, Himilco must have strayed too far south en route back to Carthage and inadvertently sailed into the doldrums, the band of still air that separates the north and south trade winds. Such a location would have placed him between 10 degrees north latitude and 10 degrees south latitude. If he then proceeded to the Sargasso Sea, as indicated by the description of the sea of weeds, he would have been roughly at 25 degrees north latitude, and halfway across the Atlantic Ocean.

The account of Hanno's expedition along the African coast, although concise, is much more informative regarding the intentions of the Carthginians. Hanno's accomplishment was recorded permanently on a bronze plaque that was prominently displayed in the Temple of Baal in Carthage. As translated by Rawlinson, it began: "It was decreed by the Carthaginians that Hanno should undertake a voyage beyond the Pillars of Heracles, and there found Liby-Phoenician cities. He sailed accordingly with sixty ships of fifty oars each, and a body of men and women, to the number of thirty thousand, and provisions, and other necessaries."[5] Hanno's voyage therefore must have been one of colonization, a typical Phoenician strategy, designed to increase their already burgeoning business empire. Hanno's journey took place in approximately 450 BCE and lasted for a period of several months. The account of his expedition included many vivid descriptions of unique geographical features, which made it possible to identify some of the areas he visited and explored. In addition, Hanno provided details of the people he met en route and the many species of wild animals that inhabited the countryside. All these clues helped to pinpoint the territories where the colonists disembarked.

If Hanno's report is studied carefully, it would appear that he traveled as far south as Guinea before terminating the journey. His fleet was at sea a total of at least 40 days, according to the narrative. Considering the time required to explore the terrain, and to select sites for new colonies, the entire voyage would have had to encompass the better part of six months. If, in fact, his fleet did proceed to Guinea before turning back, it would have put Hanno at the closest point of approach to South America. In this area, the force of the trade winds and the strength of the westward flowing North Equatorial Stream constantly attempt to push sailing vessels toward the Brazilian coast. This scenario is very likely to have happened, if not to Hanno, then to one of his countrymen, who frequented those waters.

By Hanno's account, some of the localities on the west African coast were already known by name in 450 BCE, indicating they were familiar to the Carthaginians from previous voyages. Hanno's objective, therefore, would have been to colonize territory that had already been discovered by the Phoenicians. What courageous mariner had preceded Hanno and first discovered these lands is unknown, and how many men and ships were lost in the process will forever remain a mystery. It is conceivable that many ships were dashed against the rocks and destroyed as they cruised too close to the unknown and treacherous shoreline. Many other ships were probably caught up in the ferocious Atlantic hurricanes and sent to the bottom with all hands. And, perhaps a few were even separated from the fleet and carried to strange new lands in the distant west.

Subsequent reports of Carthaginian expeditions along the African coast were documented by Roman and Greek historians over a period of more than 600 years. One prime candidate for an accidental voyage to America was a Phoenician mariner named Eudoxus, whose experiences were set to paper by Strabo. Eudoxus, who lived from approximately 300 to 250 BCE, had made two voyages to India at the request of Ptolemy II, king of Egypt. His experiences with the Egyptian hierarchy were unpleasant ones, however. His cargo was confiscated by Egyptian customs officials at the completion of both expeditions, and he received no remuneration for his endeavors. To prevent this situation from occurring a third time, Eudoxus decided to launch his next voyage from Gades, Spain. In Gades, he outfitted his ship, signed on a crew, and made all the preparations necessary for an extended sea journey. In the spring of the year, when the weather improved, Eudoxus put to sea on the waters of the Atlantic and set out for India. His intention was to sail south past the Pillars of Heracles, to circumnavigate Africa in a counterclockwise direction, and to proceed through the Indian Ocean unencumbered by Egyptian interference. Several days after departing from Spain, Eudoxus was observed by Phoenician colonists, his ship struggling south along the African coast, toward the Gulf of Guinea. His ship was being buffeted by the northeast trade winds and was slowly cutting its way through the North Equatorial Current, which was attempting to alter the ship's course from south to west. Eventually the ship passed out of sight of the colonists and disappeared over the horizon. With that last view, Eudoxus disappeared from the pages of history forever. He was never seen again—at least not on the European side of the Atlantic. Strangely enough, the route of Eudoxus was precisely the route taken by Cabral on his journey to India—and it's common knowledge where he ended up.

There is one additional Phoenician explorer that should be mentioned here. His name was Hippalos, and he commanded a fleet of merchant ships on regular trading expeditions between ports on the Red Sea and on the west coast of India, supposedly during the reign of Tiberius Caesar (14–37

CE). Like all other commanders on the India run, Hippalos followed the shoreline around Arabia, Iran, and Baluchistan, to India, a voyage of 2,500 miles. Hippalos, however, was unusually observant, and he soon realized from the direction of his voyages that he could significantly reduce the sea time if he were able to sail in a northeasterly direction out of sight of land, instead of following a circular path around the coastline. He also noticed that the monsoon breezes blew in different directions at different times of the year. After a lengthy period of observation and data collection, Hippalos determined that he could safely travel from the Gulf of Aden, across the Arabian Sea to Bombay, India, with a following monsoon breeze during one particular season of the year. After due preparation, Hippalos sailed out of the Gulf of Aden, and set his course east-northeast in hopes of reaching India. Less than three weeks later, his fleet entered the harbor of Bombay, successfully completing the first recorded open sea voyage by a European, a voyage of 1,500 miles. Soon, other Arabian Sea mariners followed suit, and within a few years, most of the maritime trade in the area was directly across the sea, from one continent to another, with routes being determined between any two ports of call. That took place almost 2,000 years ago. It is possible that similar events took place even earlier in the Atlantic Ocean, since the heaviest Phoenician and Carthaginian activity occurred in the west.

The Phoenicians, of all the European, African, and Middle Eastern nations, were the most likely people to visit America. Their maritime expertise coupled with their ability to survive as a nation provided them with the opportunity to practice their naval skills over a period of 2,500 years, a feat unmatched by any other country with access to the eastern Atlantic. Rawlinson summed it up succinctly:

> Tyre and Sidon were great commercial centers down to the time of the Crusades, and quite as rich, quite as important, quite as flourishing, commercially, as in the old days of Hiram and Ithobal. Mela speaks of Sidon in the second century after Christ as "still opulent." Ulpian, himself a Tyrian by descent, calls Tyre, in the reign of Septimius Severus, "a most splendid colony." A writer of the Age of Constantine, says of it: "The Prosperity of Tyre is extraordinary. There is no state in the whole of the East which excels it in the amount of it's business. Its merchants are persons of great wealth, and there is no port where they do not exercise considerable influence."[6]

# Summary

- A number of ancient European, African, and Middle Eastern countries were studied to determine their capability of crossing the Atlantic Ocean and visiting America over 2,000 years ago.

- Sumeria and Egypt had limited maritime expertise and essentially no oceangoing vessels. Their world was confined to the eastern Mediterranean Sea and the Persian Gulf.
- The Minoans met all the requirements for transoceanic travel, but their culture was destroyed by a natural catastrophe before they reached their full potential.
- The Greeks had acceptable navigational expertise and reliable vessels, but they were restricted to the Mediterranean Sea by the Carthaginian naval blockade at the Pillars of Heracles.
- The Libyans were expert seamen who practiced their craft primarily in the service of foreign kings, being a subjugated nation for most of their history.
- The Iberian Celts were capable of transoceanic voyages, having over 500 years' experience navigating along the Atlantic coastline of Western Europe.
- The Romans were capable of transoceanic voyages, but they were primarily a land power bent on conquest. They lacked the incentive for ventures of this nature, and they were too cautious to challenge the unknown waters of the Atlantic.
- The Phoenicians were the ancient world's ultimate mariners and merchants. They developed and maintained a vast trading empire, stretching from the west coast of Africa all the way to India, over a period of 2,000 years. Their shipbuilding techniques and their navigational expertise were second to none, and they were willing to take major risks in order to discover new lands or to locate untapped sources of raw materials.

## Conclusions

- It is probable that at least one of these nations, Phoenicia, was aware of the continent of North America more than 2,000 years ago.
- Phoenician mariners may well have visited the eastern seaboard of America for hundreds of years, ending sometime in the early Christian era. They may even have established colonies there.
- There may have been other voyages to ancient America by European mariners, such as the Iberian Celts and the Romans, but hard evidence is lacking.
- A more vigorous research effort on the part of the scientific community will be required to identify the ancient American visitors, and to locate their settlements.

# Interlude

# *Interlude*

Our search for ancient America began with the distant past, and will proceed to the present day. But before we examine the American evidence, let us briefly review the results of our search so far.

The journey through the pages of history, in countries such as China, Norway, Egypt, and Phoenicia, produced many revelations regarding the capabilities of the ancient peoples to traverse the oceans of the world. The written information was supplemented by the oral traditions of people like the Polynesians, which were found to be extremely accurate.

Part I produced the following facts:

- The Polynesians colonized the Pacific Ocean from Tonga to Hawaii over a period of more than 1,500 years, beginning in 1100 BCE. They colonized dozens of islands in the Pacific over that period, sailing and rowing their double-hulled canoes with and against the prevailing current and winds.
- Ben Finney and Herb Kawainui Kane successfully sailed a replica of a Polynesian sailing canoe from Hawaii to Tahiti in 1976, confirming the ancient methods of navigation, which utilized the stars, the wind, and the ocean currents.
- Other modern mariners, such as Tim Severin and Thor Heyerdahl, crossed the Atlantic Ocean in replicas of ancient boats, proving the seaworthiness of the oceangoing vessels of St. Brendan the Navigator and the ancient Egyptians. Heyerdahl also successfully crossed the Pacific Ocean from Peru to Tahiti on a replica of an Incan raft.
- A study of the ocean currents and the prevailing winds in the Atlantic Ocean verified the practicality of water crossings from Europe and Africa to North and South America. The shortest crossing, from the Gulf of Guinea to South America, entails a distance of only 1,750 miles, and could have been traversed in about two weeks. One medieval sailor, Pedro Alavares Cabral of Portugal, was blown across the Atlantic Ocean against his will in 1500 CE, landing on the coast of Brazil.

- Helge Ingstad, an amateur archaeologist, discovered a Viking settlement at L' Anse aux Meadows, Newfoundland, confirming the Viking Sagas and proving that the Vikings did visit North America around the year 1000 CE.
- Paul H. Chapman, a well known navigator and historian, meticulously analyzed the Viking Sagas. He identified the entire island of Newfoundland as being Vinland, and Pistolet Bay as being the location of Leif Erikson's first settlement.
- A Viking coin discovered on the coast of Maine was dated to approximately 1050 CE. Its discovery established a Viking presence in the United States during that period.
- The Phoenicians, who had over 2,000 years' experience sailing the oceans from India to the west coast of Africa, were identified as the most likely candidates for being America's first visitors. Their experience included more than 500 years of traversing the wild Atlantic Ocean, up and down the African and European coasts.
- An analysis of the works of the ancient writers indicated that many of them, particularly Diodorus Siculus and Aristotle, may have been aware of the existence of North or South America. At least they hypothesized that such a continent might exist in the western Atlantic Ocean.
- The adventures of the alleged ancient travelers to North America, including Hoei-shin, St. Brendan the Navigator, Madoc, and Prince Henry Sinclair, were analyzed to determine their reliability. Two of the explorers, St. Brendan and Prince Henry Sinclair, presented geographical information in the stories of their visits to this continent, information that was not known in Europe at the time of their voyages. Additionally, Prince Henry's excursion is supported by written documentation by participant on the trip, Antonio Zeno.

Part II will examine the American evidence of ancient intrusions into the continent to determine if this evidence is strong enough to confirm visitations to the United States by legendary mariners such as Vikings like Leif Erikson, Thorfinn Karlsefni, and Paul Knutson; Prince Henry Sinclair; St. Brendan the Navigator and other Irish mariners; or Phoenicians, Iberians, Romans, Chinese, and Japanese.

The study of the evidence of ancient visitations to the United States will include a significant amount of photographic support. This author has been deceived many times in the past by books that were written about similar subjects, the author stating that certain American structures or artifacts were identical to structures or artifacts found in the Old World.

At a later date, however, when a visual representation of the Old World evidence was located, it in no way resembled the reported American evidence. This book will endeavor to eliminate that problem by presenting side by side comparisons of the strongest evidence.

Part II will visit two of America's most intriguing lithic settlements, America's Stonehenge in North Salem, New Hampshire, and the Gungywamp complex in Groton, Connecticut. It will also visit and examine many stone chambers from Vermont to New York State, including the fascinating beehive hut in Upton, Massachusetts, and the imposing slab roofed chamber in south Woodstock, Vermont.

Many supposedly ancient stone monuments will be studied, including dolmens, menhirs, cairns, and stone circles. The 90-ton dolmen in North Salem, New York, will be compared with similar dolmens found in Ireland.

The United States has thousands of inscribed stones cluttering the landscape, from the Atlantic coast to the Pacific coast, and from Canada to Mexico. Many inscriptions are alleged to be in such scripts as Libyan, Phoenician, Iberian Celt, Irish ogam, Norse runes, Latin, Egyptian, and Hebrew. Some of the inscriptions are carved into small stones, no larger than a person's hand, while others are cut into large boulders weighing many tons. Some even decorate the sides of cliffs and cave walls. These inscriptions will be analyzed for evidence that will identify their owners, whether ancient or modern.

In addition to the stone structures and stone monuments, other American evidence to be studied includes ancient coins, amphoras, oil lamps, and metal and stone weapons.

The famous American Mound Builders will also be visited, to determine if they are a part of the mystery of ancient America, and to determine their relationship, if any, to the European or Asian inhabitants of precolonial times.

Part II will be a journey back in time, to the America of two thousand years ago. It will present evidence of stone monuments, standing stones, and carefully assembled stone piles that were painstakingly constructed by a mysterious, and as yet unknown, people sometime in the distant past.

# Part II

# Exploring Ancient America

# 8

# America's Stonehenge at Mystery Hill

## Conventional Thinking

America's Stonehenge (formerly known as Mystery Hill), is a colonial construction erected in the nineteenth century to store root crops and farm implements, and to house sheep.

## Discussion

America's Stonehenge is a small complex of stone structures situated on a hilltop overlooking North Salem, New Hampshire (25 miles west of the Atlantic Ocean and 45 miles northwest of Boston). The Merrimac River passes south of North Salem, and is navigable from the ocean to a point about ten miles south of the complex. The site itself consists of a large grouping of stone chambers surrounded by a network of stone walls, and a number of menhirs. An old Indian trail passes within two miles. The size of the entire site is estimated to be 20 acres or more, much of it still unexplored. The building complex covers an area of about one acre, and has been fenced in to protect the structures from vandalism. There are about 20 small stone chambers, of various sizes and styles. Some of them are in good condition, some have been reconstructed, and some still lie in ruins. There are several beehive huts just large enough to comfortably hold one or two persons. Other huts resemble ancient European dolmens. Some of these are large enough to hold one or more people seated, while others are even smaller. The most imposing structure on the site is the so-called Oracle Chamber.

The Oracle Chamber is a T-shaped building. The upper arm of the "T" is a corridor 27 feet long, 6 feet high, and 4 feet wide, with the entrance to the chamber at one end of the arm, and a fireplace at the opposite end (see illustration). The fireplace hearth is one foot above bedrock, and the walls all about have been blackened by ancient fires. There is an intricate chimney design above the fireplace and, until recently, it was equipped with two movable stone louvres, presumably designed to control the draft. A horizontal air vent is located near the top of the chimney. Outside the Oracle Chamber, across from the top of the stem, is a large stone table. It weighs approximately four tons, and measures 14 feet long by 12 feet wide. There is a grooved trough around the top edge of the table, with what looks like a drain leg at one end. The table presently sits on three legs, with one corner being supported by the chamber wall. It has been dubbed the Sacrificial Table because of its resemblance to similar pagan altars used for human sacrifice. One unusual aspect of this structure is an open conduit that originates in the chamber and exits underneath the Sacrificial Table. Since this arrangement was common in ancient pagan temples to allow the oracle to be heard as if by magic, the entire edifice inherited the name Oracle Chamber. Next to, and on the same wall as the speaking tube, is a hidden, hollow area just large enough to hold a body; perhaps a hiding place for the oracle.

**Main corridor in the Oracle Chamber**

The "stem" corridor of the T-shape measures 18 feet long, 6 feet high, and 3 feet wide. A seat has been carved out of the stone at the head of the corridor. Across from the seat is a deep closet also carved out of the stone. A number of stone shelves and an altar decorate this corridor. There is an exit from the structure at the far end of the corridor, but it may be of modern construction. An elaborate covered floor drain is located at the foot of the corridor and travels over 40 feet downhill, away from the chamber. One last interesting item to note in this chamber is a petroglyph resembling a running deer, carved into the wall.

The building complex appears to be laid out with the stone chambers surrounding a main, open plaza. A wide street enters the plaza from the northwest. In addition to the drain in the Oracle Chamber, there are several other drains strategically located in the village, guaranteeing that all the chambers remain dry in any kind of weather. As Clay Perry noted, "Grooves in the stone floors of the huts indicate painstaking carving of the rock to carry off such water as might seep in, to the main drains."[1] America's Stonehenge was little known until the 1930s, and was generally ignored by the few people who were aware of its existence. Apparently they all assumed the structures were built by the first colonial inhabitants, or by Indians. For a long time, the chambers were popularly called Pattee's Caves after the nineteenth century owner of the site, Jonathon Pattee, a resident of North Salem who had run afoul of the law in the year 1826. To avoid arrest, Pattee fled to the hills, taking up residence amongst the stone ruins. He eventually built a house nearby and raised a large family. According to his grandson, Pattee's house was actually located over a mile from the ruins. His grandfather, he said, did not build the huts, only improved them. It is obvious from the nineteenth century artifacts that were found on the surface of the ground that the chambers had been used for various storage purposes during Pattee's occupation. Pattee died in 1848 and the site remained unoccupied after that date. Unprotected, the site became vulnerable to an archeological calamity.

The mid–nineteenth century was a period of hectic construction in northeastern Massachusetts, particularly around Haverhill and Lawrence. Because of the construction craze, there was a desperate need for stone, for street paving and curbings. Someone who was familiar with the abandoned stone houses in North Salem, brought them to the attention of the owner of a construction company. Soon a small army of laborers descended on the site and began to demolish the village. The ancient ruins were turned into one gigantic stone quarry. Stone chambers were destroyed, walls were torn apart, and ox-drawn sleds removed numerous huge stone slabs from their mountain resting place and transported them 15 miles overland to Lawrence. Piece by piece, large sections of the site disappeared, possibly destroying much of the evidence of prehistoric habitation. It has been estimated that the construction company removed up to 50 percent of the stone ruins before their job in Lawrence was completed, ending a shameful episode in American history.

The first recorded reference to the site appeared in a local publication, *The History of Salem*, printed in 1907. The Haverhill *Evening Gazette* published the first detailed description of the site on August 15, 1934. It said in part,

> Subterranean caves and passages, of mysterious origin and purpose, possibly used in the underground railway system to smuggle slaves into Canada to escape bondage, years before the Civil War, are located on a hill in a remote section of North Salem, N.H., where they have gone unobserved for years by all but a comparatively small number of persons living in the vicinity or a few others who have happened to come upon the spot by chance while roaming through the woods. Covering an area of about 100 square feet, the main section of the underground caves is almost hidden from sight by trees that have grown up among them, and appear at a glance to be more like the ruins of some large structure or breastworks built by the early settlers as a protection against attacking Indians. Upon closer observation, openings which make one think immediately of the entrance to a sepulchre, are found to lead into underground caves and chambers, giving credence to the opinion that the underground construction was once used as some kind of temporary hideout.[2]

Another reference to the site appeared in the *Boston Globe* on October 24, 1935. It reported:

> Indian's cave or robber's den? Many of the residents of this town have engaged in lively arguments as to the origin of a series of caves and passageways that are burrowed into the side of a hill here in North Salem. The caves, which are connected together by a series of tunnels, have attracted the attention of many people, but none have found the solution to the origin. Old inhabitants claim that the caves were built by a band of nomadic Indians who arrived here early in the spring and stayed late until fall. It is said that the council fires could be seen for miles along the Merrimac Valley.[3]

So, from the very beginning, mystery and intrigue were associated with the lithic complex located in the small New Hampshire town. Romantic stories of Indians and robbers, and runaway slaves, were continuously bandied about whenever the topic of conversation swung around to Pattee's Caves. In 1936, the property was purchased by William Goodwin, a retired insurance executive from Hartford, Connecticut, and a longtime amateur archaeologist, who was now able to devote his full time to his first love. The romantic stories surrounding the site continued, but now the stories were of a more distant time and a more ancient people. Goodwin believed the architects of the ancient village were eighth century Irish Culdee monks. The first thing Goodwin did on acquiring the site was to construct a chain link fence around the main ruins to prevent further damage from vandals who had already done serious damage to the site. Next, he studied the site in minute detail; then began the long tedious job of excavation. When he first visited the area, it was overgrown with brush and trees, as mentioned earlier. It was also littered with years of refuse, since it had become a favorite local dump in the late nineteenth century.

Slowly, the weeds and debris were cleaned from the hillside to expose the remains of small stone chambers. Some of the chambers were intact, but most of them were in various stages of disrepair. A layer of silt had accumulated to a depth of 15 feet in some places. Silt deposits are a clue to the age of a site, since silt accumulates in abandoned areas at a more or less constant rate. According to an article printed in the *Hartford Courant* on June 19, 1938:

> No average picnicker would pay any attention to silt. He wouldn't know there are three kinds, or that silt consisting of decayed grass vegetation will tell its age fairly accurately. United States authorities declare this type of silt gathers to an average depth of 18 inches in 300 years. Yet when silt (various types mingled) was removed from the streets of Stone Village this spring, it was found in some places to be 15 feet deep above bedrock. Experts estimate it had been gathering there for 2000 years. Even inside the small entrances of the stone huts, silt had drifted nearly four feet deep.[4]

According to government figures, 15 feet of silt would indicate an age of 3,000 years, placing the habitation as far back as 1000 BCE. It became evident to Goodwin that he was dealing with a site of great antiquity. As the silt and refuse were removed from the ruins, each bucketful was carefully sifted in search of artifacts. Many colonial artifacts were found, as well as arrowheads and tools that were subsequently identified as belonging to the Woodland Indians. But very little was found that would indicate a foreign origin. There were three artifacts, however, that pointed toward ancient European habitation. A stone mace, discovered in the ruins, was tentatively identified as a European Bronze Age implement. A piece of metal from the refuse was analyzed and declared to be from Swedish iron ore similar to a pre–1260 CE battle-axe. And finally, a pottery shard found on the site was of prehistoric origin, and resembled pottery made in Europe around 100 CE. None of these suggestions of ancient European origin is conclusive, however. More evidence is required.

Goodwin continued to dig and search, but the elusive incontrovertible artifact eluded his grasp. The ground yielded no definite proof of ancient European origin. Still the site continued to reveal evidence of antiquity. Lichen growths on some of the stone slabs indicated those structures had been built more than 1,000 years ago. As Goodwin's work progressed, he restored a number of chambers that had collapsed with age. This brought him into immediate conflict with the professional community, whose leaders accused him of destroying the site. From this time on, the professionals declared the site to be essentially useless because of the destruction of evidence by inept excavators. Yet reconstruction of sites is an accepted archaeological practice worldwide, from Uxmal, Mexico, to Mohenjo Daro, Pakistan. Certainly Goodwin was at least as competent as the excavators who worked for Cyrus Thomas and the Smithsonian Institution in the late nineteenth century.

The first salvo was fired in 1939 when Goodwin, in an attempt to give the ruins credibility, invited Hugh Hencken to visit America's Stonehenge (then called Mystery Hill) and to give his comments as to the site's historic importance. Hencken was the curator of European archaeology for the Peabody Museum at Harvard University. Unfortunately, he made only a token appearance at the site, and ignored the totality of the evidence. The site has to be evaluated as a whole in order to properly identify its origin. Hencken chose instead to pick and choose his evidence, and to comment only on select artifacts. Much to the chagrin of Goodwin, Hencken concluded that the site was built by Jonathon Pattee in the mid–nineteenth century. He was forced, however, to make one concession. It revolved around the stump of a large tree that had grown on the site. The roots of the tree had forced their way into the wall of one of the chambers, indicating that the chamber had been built before the tree began to grow. Since the tree was estimated to be anywhere from 162 to 300 years old, the chamber obviously could not have been built by Pattee in 1826. This situation did not disturb Hencken, who deftly concluded that at least one structure was of pre–Pattee vintage, and had been built by white colonials subsequent to the Mayflower landing. As Hencken stated it: "Though it is difficult to accept the view that Pattee's Caves are the work of an early Irish colony, the site deserves more than a merely negative conclusion. Though the writer is ill equipped to make a positive statement, a few suggestions may be put forward. In the first place, the site no more resembles the Norse remains of the Viking Age in Scandinavia, Iceland, and Greenland, than it does the early Irish monasteries. It is also most unlikely to be the work of local Indians. It must therefore, date from after the white settlement of New England in the early 17th century."[5]

After Goodwin had recovered from this attack, he invited Dr. Junius Bird, an archaeologist from the New York Museum of Natural History, to visit the site and to conduct an archaeological survey. It was then 1945. Dr. Bird spent five days in North Salem, excavating and studying the ruins. In the end, Dr. Bird could not substantiate Goodwin's theories. As he said: "I can only point out that the results of our brief examination are only contradictory. There is the suggestion of age anti-dating colonial times from the charcoal distribution in the soil in the hill slopes. The critical locations examined inside the 'Y' cavern were inconclusive."[6] He did note the possible antiquity of the site. And he also favored the continuing archaeological evaluation of the site when he declared, "No structure could have been so thoroughly cleared or disturbed in recent times as to completely obliterate the evidence of several centuries abandonment if they were constructed in pre-colonial times. Even if builders left no artifacts, there should be evidence of occupation, at least charcoal, which should be separated from subsequent material by sterile dirt."[7]

The next archaeologist to pass through the stone village was Gary Viscelius, a Yale University graduate student. After a six week sojourn in New Hampshire, Viscelius had found only a handful of postcolonial artifacts and, like Hencken, ignoring the evidence of the total complex, proclaimed the village to be the fantasy of an eccentric nineteenth century farmer. It seems that the archaeology at America's Stonehenge is to take one step forward and two steps backward. Many people were upset with Viscelius' apparently slipshod study. One in particular was Frank Glynn, a Connecticut archaeologist and a director of the Early Sites Foundation, an organization formed to specifically study the stone ruins. It was Early Sites who had sponsored the Viscelius program. Now Glynn decided to become actively involved himself. From 1955 until 1967, Glynn concentrated his archaeological efforts on America's Stonehenge, carefully studying the territory, centimeter by centimeter. In Jim Whittall's review of the stone chambers, he noted: "In 1967, Frank Glynn turned his attention to the pine tree stump outside structure XI B. The stump was no longer there, but it's roots were still intertwined about the wall of structure XI B. Samples of the roots were submitted for carbon 14 dating. The results gave a date of 260 +/- 90 BP (Before the Present), or about 1707 CE. This indicated that structure XI B was constructed before Pattee arrived at the site. Furthermore, the date was earlier than any known colonial settlement in the area (1743)."[8]

Frank Glynn's final conclusion prior to his untimely death was that America's Stonehenge was a Bronze Age community of European origin. But the final proof again eluded the investigator. He had, however, contributed strong evidence in the form of radiocarbon dating results, proving that America's Stonehenge was in fact, of precolonial construction.

Radiocarbon dating, at this time, was beginning to be a major tool of archaeologists for dating ancient sites around the world, often sites that had been previously categorized as of unknown origin. It has been used more frequently at the North Salem site since Frank Glynn introduced it in 1967. Whittall, the archaeological director for the New England Antiquities Research Association, was a prime mover in the studies conducted at the stone village in the late 1960s, and he utilized the radiocarbon dating technique to the fullest.

In 1967, Whittall conducted an archaeological study of the Oracle Chamber. At one point, he excavated the ground above a short section of drain pipe to uncover the capstone above the drain. He then removed significant amounts of dirt from the drain, and discovered bits of charcoal mixed in with the dirt. The charcoal was separated from the dirt by accepted laboratory techniques, and was analyzed by an independent laboratory using the carbon-14 dating method. As Whittall reported, "The results seem to indicate an age of greater that 520 CE for the Oracle Chamber."[9] A scientific date of 520 CE for the Oracle Chamber not only predates Columbus, it also retreats well back before the Viking Age. After completing his study of the Oracle Chamber, Whittall moved to the stone chamber identified as structure XI B, and proceeded to excavate in and around this building. In the wall of structure XI B, Whittall uncovered a layer of charcoal which subsequently carbon dated to 2995 BP +/- 180 years. Working backward from the date of the find in 1969 gives a radiocarbon date of 1026 BCE, back into the Bronze Age. Whittall repeated the study in 1970, and came up with a date of 1505 BCE +/- 210 years. To date, this represents the oldest occupation level at the site. But did these early inhabitants construct the lithic complex that exists today? The answer to that question is not clear.

Another interesting piece of evidence was gleaned from the rubble. It also came from structure XI B. In 1967, Whittall recovered an inscribed stone from the interior surface of the structure. Eight years later, the stone was "brought to the attention of Dr. Barry Fell, President of the Epigraphic Society and an astute scholar in ancient languages. Though the markings were badly worn, he recognized them as an Iberic inscription. He suggested the following translation dating to approximately 800 BCE. 'To Bel, they the Canaanites set it up — May he have mercy on us.'"[10] Although the mystery of America's Stonehenge has not yet been solved, there is mounting evidence that the site was occupied as far back as 1500 BCE, and that at least some of the structures were built during the period from 385 CE to 655 CE. If that is correct, it would present only two possibilities as far as the architects were concerned: ancient people from another continent or early American Indians.

# 8. America's Stonehenge at Mystery Hill

Perhaps the most fascinating feature of the complex is located outside the central building area; this feature only came to light as recently as 1970 and gave the complex its current name, America's Stonehenge. Robert E. Stone, who purchased Mystery Hill in 1957, was clearing the land surrounding the main site when he noticed that the stone wall network around the perimeter contained a number of menhirs, or standing stones. Some of the menhirs were still upright, while others had fallen down. An intensive research study of these stones determined they were part of a large astronomical calendar (see illustration). The stones are strategically located so that, when viewed from a central platform in the complex, the sun would rise or set over specific stones at different times of the year, such as on the winter or summer solstice. Such a calendar is of prime importance to an agricultural people who rely on the land for their sustenance. They must know when the seasons change so they can plant and reap their crops at the opportune time. The scientists who studied the calendar concluded that the stones were aligned to the position of the sun around 1500 BCE.

A study of stone alignments in Europe revealed a number of similarities. In Brittany, for instance, a menhir complex was determined to be an astronomical calendar as long ago as 1923. Charles Buxton Going, who reported on the calendar, noted: "These alignments correspond generally

**Janet McNeil at the Equinox Stone**

with the following dates: November 8, February 4, May 6, August 8, which are simply the mean dates of the principal agricultural seasons. The beginning of November is the time for seeding the crop, which will sprout in February. Blossoming begins in May, and harvest in the first days of August. Thus the neolithic calendar might regulate the work in the fields and we know that these Asiatic invaders were agriculturalists."[11] Going also determined that the site in Brittany was constructed about the same time as the North Salem calendar:

> The orientation, be it understood, is not exact at the present date. Calculations made independently by two astronomers reached the same result — that it was correct at a period about 1600 years before the beginning of the Christian Era. This curious testimony to the age of the monuments agrees with the conclusions reached on other grounds by M. Le Rouzic, placing only the earliest of the megalithic structures prior to 2000 BCE; the greatest development of dolmen-building and the erection of the alignments and cromlechs between 2000 BCE and 400 BCE, and the latest work, expressed by small galleries and stone coffers, in the first century before the Christian Era.[12]

Finally, Going contributed one last piece of information that could help solve the riddle of America's Stonehenge. In referring to the purpose of the menhirs distributed along the coast of Brittany, Going observed, "Isolated menhirs have yielded little or nothing indicative of use as monuments for individual tombs. They seem to have been generally commemorative, indicators of roads and territorial boundaries, and symbolic of an immortal God. The alignments, on the other hand, appear to have been designed as open-air temples. Each group (with its cromlech placed always at the western end of the lines) having been erected on a single comprehensive plan and at one time. They are the remains of huge religious monuments."[13] And thus it may be with America's Stonehenge. This may be a religious or ceremonial center for an early Bronze Age agricultural society.

In searching for similar sites around the world, one is continually drawn to Western Europe, particularly to Scandinavia, the Iberian Peninsula, Brittany, and the British Isles. It is known from previous studies that cultural contact between all those European locations existed as far back as 2000 BCE. The construction methods at America's Stonehenge find their counterparts in the colony of Skara Brae in Scotland, where the walls and built-in shelves could have been the work of the same hands. The pre–Roman ruins at Chrysanter, England, and the earth houses in pagan Scotland both exhibit features found in the Oracle Chamber. There are a couple of pieces of photographic evidence that are intriguing. First there is the Sacrificial Table located next to the Oracle Chamber (see illustration).

# 8. America's Stonehenge at Mystery Hill

**The Sacrificial Table outside the Oracle Chamber**

Almost identical tables were utilized in pre–Viking Scandinavia (see illustration). The exact age of the Scandinavian tables is unknown, but they go back some time prior to 800 CE. The Northmen used their tables in religious ceremonies, frequently to placate their gods through the offering of a human sacrifice. Obviously, the North Salem example is of the right size and the proper design for such a purpose. To the west of the Sacrificial Table lies the East-West Chamber, commonly referred to as the Tomb of Lost Souls. Similar chambers in Ireland and Brittany date back to the period from 2000 BCE to 400 BCE. Some European chambers were constructed as tombs, and it is possible that this chamber served the same purpose (see illustration).

America's Stonehenge has a number of beehive huts, which are of similar construction to the beehive hut in Slea Head, County Kerry, Ireland, though of a much smaller size. Another small chamber at the New Hampshire complex is similar to a chamber discovered in Norway. The Norwegian chamber dates back to the Bronze Age. When discovered, it contained a burial urn complete with partially burnt bones. Roman coins of the emperor Marcus Aurelius were also found in the chamber, giving a date of approximately 162 CE.

Comparison of the America's Stonehenge chambers with those in

A sacrificial table at Viala, Sweden, from the Viking Age, 800 to 1100 CE (reproduced with permission *The Viking Age*).

Western Europe could easily lead to the conclusion that the American site was an ancient necropolis, complete with a religious temple, the Oracle Chamber. It does fit the mold. With the exception of the Oracle Chamber, the 20 or so other structures seem to be too small to have served any other useful purpose than burial vaults. None of the chambers are large enough for a person to stand upright in. Perhaps as many as six chambers could provide a person with refuge from the elements, and could serve as cramped sleeping quarters. But most of the chambers appear to be suitable for nothing more than inhumation. Certainly it is difficult to reconcile the design of the complex with the theory of colonial construction for the purpose of root storage, or for use as sheep pens. The physical effort involved in building such a complex had to have been enormous. To have expended so much time and energy on a project in order to provide shelter for 20 or 30 sheep, or to store small amounts of rootstocks, would have been folly indeed. And regardless of what some people have said, history does not categorize Jonathon Pattee as being an eccentric. That was the invention of people trying to give a simple explanation for a mysterious site that was unexplainable.

# Summary

- A lithic complex covering 20 acres exists in North Salem, New Hampshire. The ruins include almost two dozen small stone chambers, a network of stone walls, and numerous menhirs.
- The menhirs appear to be the remains of an ancient astronomical calendar constructed about 1600 BCE. A similar calendar, dated to the same period, exists in Brittany.

**East-West Chamber**

- The chambers bear a resemblance to ancient Bronze Age chambers located in Western Europe. Carbon dating of charcoal found on the site indicates human habitation as early as 1500 BCE.
- A large grooved stone table, located outside the Oracle Chamber, is almost identical with a sacrificial table found in Scandinavia and dated to sometime before 800 CE.
- An inscribed stone found in the Oracle Chamber was said by Dr. Barry Fell to contain Iberic writing, dating to 800 BCE.

## Conclusions

- America's Stonehenge was occupied as far back as 1600 BCE either by ancient transatlantic colonists or early American aborigines who worked in stone.
- The early society depended on agriculture for survival, and utilized a large stone astronomical calendar to help select the proper planting seasons. The calendar, as well as an inscribed stone found in the Oracle Chamber, both have their counterparts along the southwest coast of

Europe, from Brittany to the Iberian Peninsula. The first inhabitants of America's Stonehenge could have come from that location.

- Some of the stone structures were built between 385 to 655 CE, possibly indicating a second wave of users of the complex.
- The site may have been a religious center, complete with a temple, a large altar on which to offer sacrifices to the gods, and small stone tombs in which to house the remains of the dead.

# 9

# *The Great Stone Chamber Mystery*

## Conventional Thinking

The hundreds of strange stone chambers that are widespread in New York and New England are either colonial root cellars or postcolonial structures.

## Discussion

The state of Vermont may well be the most beautiful state in the union, though admittedly it does not have the scenic grandeur of the western part of the United States. The Green Mountains, which run north and south through the state, reach a maximum height of 4,393 feet at the summit of Mt. Mansfield, quite small by Western standards. But there is more to this land than meets the eye. For hidden away near the top of these hills, and lying innocuously beneath the underbrush of the peaceful valleys, stand mysterious stone structures of unknown origin. No one knows who built the strange edifices, nor how long they have been gracing the landscape. Several years ago, there was some hope that the state of Vermont might be able to identify the architects of these strange buildings. The Vermont state archaeologist was commissioned to conduct an official study of the stone chambers in order to determine their origin. The archaeologist concluded that the structures were root cellars, some of which were constructed during the colonial period, others as late as 1930. This amazing conclusion was based almost exclusively on hearsay evidence from a handful of local residents, none of whom were born much before 1900. She referred to this hearsay as oral tradition. Oral tradition, however, is defined as organized teachings of historical, religious, or sociological significance, passed on in a structured format from one generation to another within a culture. The hazy recollections of local senior citizens cannot be construed to be oral tradition by any stretch of the imagination.

## *The Stone Chambers: Their Design and Location*

The stone chambers of east America generally fall into two categories: corbeled and flat roof. All the structures are of a dry wall construction. The corbeled type are further divided into beehive structures, which are normally round huts resembling the Eskimo igloo, and long, barrowed chambers that are quasi-rectangular in shape, and not unlike the more geometrically designed slab roofed buildings. There are hundreds of these stone chambers decorating the hills and valleys of east America. The heaviest concentration seems to be in the New England states and a section of New York state east of the Hudson River and north of New York City. Trento estimated that about 50 slab roofed chambers were grouped together in one small area of southeastern New York and southwestern Connecticut, an area of about 300 square miles. Most chambers are within a short distance of a navigable waterway. In addition to the structures in the vicinity of the Hudson River, there are clusters of chambers all along the Connecticut River valley, from Long Island Sound to central Vermont. Other buildings lie scattered about the watershed of the Merrimac River between Massachusetts and New Hampshire.

Both the "ancient Europe" advocates and the "colonial root cellar" backers have explanations for this phenomenon. The "Europeans" are convinced the chamber locations are the result of normal explorations along the large river bodies by seagoing vessels from across the Atlantic Ocean. The "colonials," on the other hand, claim the chambers were built by colonial farmers as storage areas for root crops that were needed to feed their livestock, particularly sheep, during the winter months. These two theories will be tested against the weight of evidence in the next few sections.

There are a wide variety of designs encountered in the American stone chambers, as well as significant differences in construction technique and overall construction quality. These differences apparently resulted from two things: the use for which the chamber was intended, and the locality where the chamber was built. Some ancient European chambers served as tombs, others as religious temples, and still others as places of habitation, food storage or refuge. Each end use had its own specific design.

It is not possible to review all the chamber designs that are found in east America, but a description of the four most popular designs should suffice. There are two chambers in particular that are impressive both in design and in construction quality. One is a beehive chamber, the other a slab roofed

9. *The Great Stone Chamber Mystery* 161

*Top*: The entrance to the beehive chamber in Upton, Massachusetts. *Bottom*: Janet McNeil inspects the construction of the interior of the chamber.

chamber. The beehive chamber is located in the small Massachusetts town of Upton, about 50 miles west of Boston, and is probably the best example of this type of construction to be found in the entire United States (see illustration). The chamber is on private property to the rear of a two-family dwelling and is not open to the general public. The entrance to the chamber faces away from the house and is directed toward the northwest. On first glance the site appears to be nothing more than a small earthen mound, but an opening, about 3 feet wide and 4.5 feet in height, is located on the northwest side and leads into a long tunnel. The construction of the tunnel is the dry wall type common to all these chambers. There is no evidence that mortar was ever used in building this chamber, nor is there any evidence that the entranceway was ever secured with a door. Large granite boulders, some weighing several hundred pounds, were used to construct the passageway. These boulders were so intricately fitted together that they settled into a single cohesive unit that has withstood the rigors of time and has safely supported the stone and earth covering for untold centuries. The roof of the tunnel was formed by many small flat stones laid side by side and extending from one wall to the other. Stone wedges were utilized between wall and roof to solidify the structure. The chamber is approximately 10 feet in diameter, and rises to a height of 12 feet, the roof being covered with a single, large capstone. It is impressive in stature and exudes an aura of extreme antiquity.

South Woodstock, Vermont, harbors another stone structure of immense proportions, this one a large rectangular, slab roofed structure (see illustration). The chamber is perched atop a small hill overlooking a vast expanse of rich, fertile farmland. At one time it was surrounded by a large farmstead, including a house, a barn, and several outbuildings. Today nothing remains of the buildings except foundation holes. The stone chamber, on the other hand, looks as if it had just been built. There is an entrance on the uncovered side of the chamber, 5 feet wide and 5.5 feet high, opening into a large, rectangular room, measuring nine feet wide, 18 feet long, and 9.5 feet high. The magnitude of the physical effort that went into the construction of the building is overwhelming. Unlike the Upton chamber, this one required the monumental task of moving tremendous slabs of flat stone, some weighing upwards of three or four tons, over long distances, and then placing them very precisely side by side over the top of the walls. There is no evidence that a door ever adorned the entrance. A small air vent or chimney is located in the roof at the far end of the chamber. Its dimensions are approximately 32 inches long by 15 inches wide. Dry wall construction again predominates. The roof slabs are easily the most imposing aspect of the chamber, averaging 3.5 feet wide and 10 feet long, a silent tribute to an indomitable and as yet unknown people.

# 9. The Great Stone Chamber Mystery

The entrance to the slab roofed chamber in South Woodstock, Vermont.

The author examines the large roof slabs.

Close by Woodstock, perhaps 20 miles north, in the town of South Royalton lies another unusual chamber. In fact, this entire area of Vermont bordering the Connecticut River, from South Royalton in the north to Putney in the south, is a treasurehouse of strange, unexplained stoneworks, including the chambers as well as menhirs, possible inscribed stones, and curious wandering stone wall complexes. South Royalton itself contains numerous examples of each of the above types of artifact. The chamber of interest here is within a short distance of Dairy Hill Road near the Joseph Smith memorial. It too is covered by an earthen mound. The mound has an enormous tree growing on it, 5 feet in diameter. An examination of the soil shows that the chamber was built before the tree began to grow. This particular chamber is of quasi-beehive design. The entrance is quite small and difficult to get through, measuring only 3 feet in height and barely 1.5 feet in width. Until 1975 this entrance was filled with dirt, and the only way into the chamber prior to that was through a small hole punched in the top of the hut. The hole was made when the chamber was accidentally discovered by a farmer over 100 years ago, and was not part of the original design. The original front entrance was only recently discovered. The chamber dimensions are 10 feet in diameter and 6 feet high. Like the South Woodstock chamber, it opens toward the southeast. The quality of construction found in the previous two chambers is lacking in this one. The reason for the more slipshod construction is unknown. It does, however, have a flagstone floor, a feature that Trento says is common in this particular design. The chamber also has several apparently man-made carvings.

A stone chamber in the town of Webster, Massachusetts, not far from Upton, will complete the review. Just east of the town, near Route 16, were once located a cluster of small stone huts. Several of them were destroyed by the owner about 25 years ago to discourage curiosity seekers from trespassing on his property. All the chambers were originally of a beehive design, somewhat similar to Upton, yet different in overall concept. The chamber visited is next to a small brook. It has an entrance 3 feet wide and 4.5 feet high, requiring a person to stoop over to enter. An 8-foot tunnel leads to the main chamber, although the outside entrance indicates that the tunnel might originally have been longer. The chamber itself is of an asymmetrical design, with one straight side and one oval side. According to Dix, there are more than 300 such chambers in the area bounded by New York City, the Hudson River, the Canadian border, and the Atlantic Ocean.

## Stone Chambers: The Root Cellar Theory

The stone chambers of New England are the remnants of ancient temples constructed by European mariners, many of them Celts from the Iberian peninsula. So said the "Ancient Europe" advocates.

The Vermont stone chambers are root cellars, constructed in the nineteenth century by local farmers. So said Vermont state archaeologist Giovanna Neudorfer.

The battle lines were drawn. The root cellar theory will be examined first. The bulk of the evidence supporting this theory was gathered by Neudorfer as part of a study financed by the Vermont Division for Historic Preservation and carried out by Neudorfer and two assistants. The study was initiated in response to Fell's claim that the chambers were ancient European religious centers, and was intended to conclusively determine the origin of the chambers. Neudorfer began her study in the summer of 1977, completing it 18 months later. During that time, her team identified 52 stone chambers in Vermont and collected extensive data on 36 of them. Additionally, they spent numerous hours researching the literature, seeking historical evidence for the construction of the chambers. Lastly, they conducted personal interviews with many elder citizens in locales where the chambers stood. As a preliminary study of the stone chamber mystery, Neudorfer's work was valuable in cataloguing the chamber dimensions, construction materials, astronomical alignments, and geographical concentration, as well as providing some background information about root cellars and sheep raising from the literature, and recording the recollections of some of Vermont's senior citizens. Had the study stopped there, it would have served its purpose, as an introduction to a more definitive study to determine the origin of the chambers. Unfortunately, the author forced the issue, and drew conclusions based on the scant evidence at her disposal, primarily hearsay testimony. A search of the literature by the research team failed to locate any written historical documentation supporting colonial construction of the chambers. And the statistics on the chambers themselves only weakened her case.

Her book stated that 52 chambers were identified in five Vermont counties, four of them in the eastern part of the state, along the Connecticut River valley. Of the 52 chambers, 14 were incorporated into the foundation of a farmhouse or barn and were apparently modern. Seven others contained mortar, and were not the dry wall construction that is typical of the chambers in question. They may be modern also. Next there were 16 chambers that were not visited. And finally, there were seven chambers that were not equipped with the air vents so necessary in a well designed root cellar. Only eight chambers remained, plus the oral evidence. And even those could not be reconciled with each other. The verbal testimony identified eight chambers as having been built during the historic period expressly as root cellars. But they were not the same eight chambers that remained in the sample. Only two of the identified root cellars were equipped with the critical air vent; only two of 52 chambers could match proper design with oral testimony in support of the colonial root cellar theory.

A brief review of root cellars in general, and a few facts about the sheep industry in Vermont, are in order. In historic times, cellars were an important part of American homes, being used to store root crops such as onions, radishes, and turnips for winter consumption. Cellars were also used to store meats, dairy products, and salt. Normally cellars were built under the house and were incorporated into the foundation. In those instances where the house had no foundation, such as in a log cabin, the cellar was located close to the house, always under the ground. Alfred Hopkins, in his book *Modern Farm Buildings*, noted, "For the isolated root cellar, the only satisfactory one is found by going into the side of a bank and constructing a chamber whose top as well as sides, are completely covered by the earth."[1] He goes on to say, "Ventilation for the root cellar is as important in preventing undesirable conditions as ventilation for the cow barn or horse stable. Roots mold and spoil very quickly if deprived of a circulation of air."[2] Mr. Hopkins, a recognized expert on farm buildings, continued with his description of the ideal root cellar: "The ground above the top should be at least three feet deep, the entrance — the one side exposed to the air — had best face south, tho its exposure may incline to the east or west but never to the north."[3] Mr. Hopkins' final design, with dimensions of 21 by 31, by 9 feet, is surprisingly close to the size of the South Woodstock chamber. But Mr. Hopkins was apparently not familiar with the Woodstock chamber, or with any existent root cellar of similar design. He arrived at his design through experimentation. Two last facts that should be kept in mind relative to root cellars are that the temperature of the cellar must be kept above freezing to protect the produce, and the cellar must be kept dry at all times. Many of the stone chambers in New England, including the two at Upton and Webster, are wet during much of the year.

If the stone chambers were constructed as root cellars, one of their intended purposes was supposedly to store root crops to feed sheep during the winter. Sheep raising came to Vermont in the early 1800s, increased to a large scale business by 1820, peaked about 1840, and then rapidly declined. At its peak, it is estimated that 1.7 million sheep grazed on the

Vermont highlands. Certainly they had to be fed during the winter. But were they fed root crops? And if so, were the root crops stored in stone chambers built for that purpose? That is not so clear. Many of the chambers, in fact, have been dated at least as far back as the eighteenth century, which was prior to the time that sheep raising was introduced into Vermont; so they couldn't have been originally constructed as root cellars for sheep feed.

It is reasonable to assume that at least some of the stone chambers, even if they were of ancient construction, would have been used as root cellars, just because they were there. It is also reasonable to assume that, if ancient stone structures did exist in the Vermont hills, the farmers would have been intelligent enough to appreciate their value, and would not only have used the ones they found, but might have constructed others just like them, as needed. There were many Welsh and Irish immigrants in Vermont during the nineteenth century, and dry wall construction was a heritage with them, going back to the time of their Celtic forebears more than 2,000 years ago. But is there evidence of such construction? The literature does not support that theory.

- Neudorfer's study included extensive research into the literature of the time including local histories, land deeds, and maps. Her team found absolutely no proof of stone chambers, of the type under study, being constructed in Vermont during the historical period.
- Eric Sloane, the farm building expert, in his book *An Age of Barns*, noted that eighteenth century root cellars were built into the side of a hill and were covered with earth. An entrance wide enough for a wheelbarrow to pass through was built into one wall, and the entire structure was carefully mortared to keep the frost out; not dry wall. The entrances to many of the stone chambers in east America were much too narrow for a wheelbarrow to get through, making it unlikely that they were built to store root stocks.

Several of the Vermont chambers were examined in March 1988, including those in South Woodstock and South Royalton. The unmortared chambers were all very wet, as melting snow oozed through the earthen mounds and dripped incessantly from the stone walls. The floors too were puddled, and melted ground water continued to flow through the entranceways. If roots had been stored in these chambers they would have rotted in short order.

- Thomas Jefferson in his *Notes on Virginia* mentioned that stone was used extensively for foundations, walls, and chimneys, but that all the buildings were constructed of wood.

- Ulysses Prentiss Hedrick, discussing the history of agriculture in the state of New York, said, "Outside against the black background of the forest wall there might be a shack or two for the farm animals."[4] And again, "Whatever the condition of the dwelling house, farm outbuildings were usually of cheap construction, small and mean."[5]
- H.P. Smith wrote *The History of Addison County Vermont* in 1886. Addison County is one of the four eastern Vermont counties with a heavy concentration of stone chambers. In discussing the sheep raising industry, Smith noted that the sheep were "mostly fed in winter in yards beside the barn or at stocks, sheep sheltering barns at that time being unknown (1828–1832)."[6]
- Zadock Thompson wrote *History of Vermont* in 1842. In it, he pinpointed the arrival of Merino sheep in Vermont as taking place in 1823. Thompson said that the sheep "should be yarded in winter from the last of November to the latter part of April, but never crammed into tight enclosures."[7] The food allowance per head of sheep in winter was reported to be "three pounds hay, or two pounds hay plus half a pint of oatmeal or other food equivalent."[8] In tracing the history of Woodstock, Thompson reported that "in the early days there was no population to the north or west, and settlers were subjected to frequent alarms of Indian raids, and they also suffered the ravages of wild beasts. In order to preserve their young cattle and sheep from the bears and wolves, they were compelled to guard them during the night or shut them up in yards or buildings prepared for that purpose."[9]
- Henry Vail, in writing a history of Pomfret, Vermont, declared that "in the early days all sorts of things were made of wood — wood was only too abundant, and almost every other material was scarce."[10]
- Windsor County was another large center of stone chamber construction, as mentioned before. The local history of Windsor County reported an Indian raid in the town of Royalton in 1780. "Twenty one dwelling houses and sixteen good new barns, well filled with hay and grain, the hard earnings of industrious young farmers were laid in ashes by the impious crew. Hogs in their pens, and cattle tied in their stalls were burned alive."[11]
- The Vermont Historical Society published a history of the town of Peacham in 1948. There was no indication in that book that the early settlers of Peacham ever built or used stone chambers. Many types of buildings were mentioned but they were apparently all constructed of wood, including the barns and outbuildings. Most buildings were

reported to be connected to the main house so the settlers did not have to go outside in the winter.

- The history of Litchfield, Connecticut, reported that the first barns were constructed of hewn timber, which lasted for years. They were built mainly for the storage of grain and fodder rather than the comfortable housing of cattle. Another note of interest included the fact that sheep were stabled in wooden barns.
- The Connecticut State Historical Society, in an 1859 report, stated that houses of rough-hewn logs were built with cellars under them.

The history books are full of references to colonial house construction, to barn construction, and to the construction of any number of outbuildings. But to date there has been no positive evidence of stone chamber construction discovered in the literature. There are numerous reports on the raising of sheep and cattle, on the agriculture of the area over the centuries, and on the need for proper storage of grain and fodder. But there is no mention of dry walled stone chambers ever being built or used, either for animal pens or for produce storage in the seventeenth, eighteenth, or early nineteenth centuries.

At this time, the evidence for the root cellar theory is very thin, almost to the point of being nonexistent. It consists entirely of the unreliable oral testimony of a handful of people; interesting as a conversation piece, but nothing more. It cannot be used to prove the origin of the mysterious chambers one way or another.

## Stone Chambers: The Ancient Europe Theory

Conjecture about visits to ancient America by European mariners goes back more than 300 years. Thomas Jefferson, the third president of the United States, after a detailed study of American Indian cultures and languages concluded that the aborigines had been in contact with Europeans in ancient times. Many other prominent men have had the same opinion, including Cotton Mather, Benjamin Franklin, and Henry R. Schoolcraft. Interest in this theory has ebbed and flowed over the centuries. The mid–nineteenth century was particularly hectic as the Viking Sagas were published in Scandinavia and were circulated around the world. Periods of intense historical and archaeological activity designed to prove European intrusion into the continent have been followed by periods of disinterest and inactivity, but each flurry of activity has contributed a little more evidence toward the final proof of the theory.

In 1962 Helge Ingstad provided the hard evidence that demonstrated once and for all that Viking adventurers had indeed established a settlement in North America. Other pieces of evidence continue to accumulate, documenting Viking explorations along the east coast of the United States, and evidence of even more ancient visits to these shores. There is a feeling in some scientific circles that hard evidence will be discovered in the near future that will confirm these theories.

The stone chamber mystery is the latest area of speculation. These structures came to light as a possible example of ancient architecture only as recently as 1975, when Barry Fell began his study of the stoneworks and claimed he found inscribed stones in and around the buildings, stones that had writing on them in ancient Ogam and Iberian-Punic scripts, from languages that existed before the time of Christ. Many people have become embroiled in the new dispute since that time. The meager evidence of the "root cellar" supporters has been examined. Now the evidence that has been uncovered by the "ancient Europe" enthusiasts will be examined, as well as any additional information from the literature that might support such a theory.

- Eaton's *History of Rockland and South Thomaston* (towns in Maine) reported that early settlers in the town of Cushing on the Georges River had discovered a precolonial cellar.
- Nash Hope wrote the history of Royalton, Vermont, for the Royalton Historical Society in 1975. Royalton is a hotbed of mysterious stoneworks, including numerous chambers. Yet Hope stated that the chambers were in existence when the first white men moved into the area. The colonists were aware of their existence, but did not consider them unusual, nor did they know who built them.
- Salvatore Trento and his 200 dedicated volunteers scoured the northeast section of the United States in 1976 and 1977 studying the phenomenon of the stoneworks for his newly created research organization, the Middletown Archaeological Research Center (MARC). They received firsthand testimony from a number of Vermont farmers "who told of horses falling into 'field caves' and 'stone-lined' pits."[12]
- Other testimony uncovered by Trento was second- or third-hand, interesting but less reliable: "They recounted stories of their great-grandfather's plows uncovering stone huts that looked like they'd always been there."[13]
- A pamphlet published in 1895 documented the discovery of slab roofed chambers near Norfolk, Massachusetts. The author, Cornelia Horsford, invited two scientists from the Canadian Institute in Toronto to inspect

the sites. These men, experts in ethnology and anthropology, were unfamiliar with the particular type of stonework, but did note that they were not of Indian construction. Had the structures been of colonial construction these eminent scientists should certainly have recognized them.

More impressive was the visit to the sites of Gerard Fowke and W.J. McGee of the Smithsonian Institution Bureau of Ethnology. After five weeks of intensive study the two men stated that "collectively and with but one or two exceptions individually these works differed more or less, but always distinctly, from anything they had previously studied, and that they could not be classed with the works of any race known to them."[14] This statement is a powerful testimonial by representatives of the Smithsonian Institution Bureau of Ethnology in favor of outside influences on early American cultures.

- John Winthrop, Jr., was one of the early settlers in Connecticut, founding the town of New London in 1645 and becoming one of the area's most influential citizens. On November 30, 1645, John Pynchon of Springfield, Massachusetts, wrote to Winthrop, making the following inquiry: "Sir I heare a report of a stonewall and strong fort in it, made all of stone, which is newly discovered at or neare Pequot. I should be glad to know the truth of it from your selfe, here being many strange reports about it."[15] There is a stone wall complex, complete with slab roofed chambers, located near Groton, Connecticut. It is known as the Gungywamp site. This could possibly be the fort to which John Pynchon was referring, but if so, the architects have never been identified. The site is still under constant study, as scientists endeavor to learn the origin of the strange construction.

- Daniel Fiske wrote an article for the Milford *Journal* on April 26, 1893, relating his lifelong familiarity with the Upton chamber. His attempts to identify the builders of the structure were unsuccessful. "From our youth we have occasionally sought information of our oldest citizens whose ancestors lived on this road from 150 to 200 years ago and they were as ignorant of its origin as we of today."[16]

- James P. Whittall, Jr., of the Early Sites Research Society and John Williams of the Epigraphic Society surveyed a large drywall corbelled stone chamber in North Salem, New York, in 1976. The chamber was on property that had been owned by the same family since the area was first settled in 1685. According to information passed down through the family, the stone structure had been there 20 years before the barn was built in 1710, and at that time no one knew who had constructed it. At one point the current owner tried to store ground crops in the chamber over the winter. He was thwarted in this attempt, as his crops rotted within a few months."[17]

- Whittall was actively involved in the archaeological study and excavation of other sites containing slab roofed chambers for many years. He probably contributed the most significant evidence to date regarding the great antiquity of these sites. He provided radiocarbon dating on a number of chambers. As mentioned in chapter 7, Whittall obtained radiocarbon dates of 520 CE, 1045 BCE, and 1525 BCE from several chambers at America's Stonehenge. In 1978, Whittall's Early Sites team excavated a section of drystone chamber in Putney, Windham County, Vermont. A sample of charcoal from the original ground level gave a construction date of 545 CE.

- The New England Antiquities Research Association excavated a stone chamber in Newton, New Hampshire, in 1968, and a charcoal sample obtained from that structure was dated to 1100 CE. A shelf built into the rear wall of the chamber resembled the shelving in the Oracle Chamber at Mystery Hill only ten miles away.

- E.B. O'Callaghan in his *Documentary History of the State of New York*, quoted from a missionary journey of the Reverend John Taylor to an area north of Syracuse in 1802. "This town, and apparently all this country, has been, in some ancient period, thickly inhabited. In many places there are evident marks of houses having stood as thick as to join each other. The remains of old fireplaces built of stones — wells evidently dug and stoned, to a considerable depth: and the remains of old forts and entrenchments, — are all evidences of this fact." And, "Last summer a man digging a cellar, found a foot under the surface, that he had fallen upon an old colepit."[18]

The evidence, although far from complete, continues to mount in favor of precolonial and perhaps ancient construction of the great stone chambers of east America. Perhaps a review of the stone structures in Western Europe will support one of the theories.

## Stone Chambers: Their European Counterparts

European megalithic chambers are widespread along the European coast of the Atlantic. They are found in Scandinavia, Brittany, the Iberian Peninsula, Ireland, Wales, Scotland, and the Scottish Isles. They are the remains of a culture that extends back in time 5,000 years or more. The

## 9. The Great Stone Chamber Mystery

chambers are built exclusively of dry wall construction. There are mammoth rectangular slab roofed chambers covered by stones weighing in excess of three tons. Some of the chambers are free standing; others are covered by a mound of earth. There are oval beehive huts built with corbelled walls and covered by a single capstone. These huts are sometimes built above ground and at other times are subterranean. And there are the passage graves, which are also located under stone or earthen mounds. In a passage grave, a long passageway leads from the opening in the outer extremity of the mound to the burial vault located in the center of the mound. The mound itself is usually round or oval shaped, while the chamber can be oval, round, or even rectangular. A description of a few of the chamber designs will suffice to demonstrate their construction techniques as well as their universal popularity.

- A passage grave in Guarda, Portugal, bears an eerie resemblance to the Upton chamber. The Guarda grave consists of a long slab roofed passageway culminating in a large burial chamber. Another passage grave in Locmariaquer, Brittany, is of a similar design. Skeletons were found in this grave as well as many stone implements such as arrowheads, spear points and celts.
- A Scandinavian passage grave within a large tumulus was discussed in chapter 3. A typical chamber of that type might measure 10 feet wide by 23 feet long and 4.5 feet high.
- There is a passage grave in a tumulus at Newgrange, Ireland, that dates to 3000 BCE. The walls are constructed of boulders weighing upwards of several tons and the ceiling is 20 feet high. The opening faces the southeast towards the position of winter solstice sun, indicating that the builders may have been interested in astronomical alignments.
- Other Irish passage graves are located in Knowth and Dowth, all on the east coast of the country. The grave at Knowth, although constructed in 3000 BCE, was utilized as a habitation site around 400 BCE, at which time a number of souterrains were added to the complex. Dr. George Eogan, a professor at University College, Dublin, who is excavating this site, feels that the builders originally came to Ireland from the Iberian Peninsula.
- At Antequera, Portugal, a tumulus 250 feet in diameter houses a passage grave with a beehive vault at the end. The slab roofed passageway is 25 feet long and the beehive chamber is 15 feet in diameter and 12 feet high, almost a duplicate of Upton.
- Macalister reported an underground structure at Carrabeg, County Mayo, Ireland. The main chamber measured 14 feet long, 6 feet wide,

and 7 feet high. The sides were constructed of large stones rising in a corbelled fashion to the large, flat flagstone slabs that formed the roof. A passage entered the chamber from the east side. Two skulls and a rusty spearhead were found in the chamber. It is believed that this chamber was used as a tomb during the Iron Age.

Slab roofed chambers of a rectangular design are also common in Western Europe as demonstrated by the following examples.

- A large slab roofed chamber is situated in Bagneux, Brittany. This particular chamber, of Bronze Age construction, was thought to be either a religious shrine or a tomb.
- There is a slab roofed chamber located in Gouveias, Portugal. It measures 10 feet wide by 21 feet long and 8 feet high. Archaeologists feel that this chamber was built as a tomb during the Iron Age.

Beehive structures are found all over Ireland, on Skellig Michael, on the Aran Islands, in County Kerry, and elsewhere. They have also been found in France, Portugal, Scotland, the Shetland Islands, and in America. How could so many people in so many countries all develop the same architectural designs at approximately the same time? The answer is that an amalgamation of peoples and a diffusion of cultures were responsible for the widespread building of the megalithic monuments that dominated the west coast of Europe during the Bronze Age. In some of these areas, particularly Brittany and the Iberian Peninsula, it is not possible to isolate one culture and assign the huge lithic complexes to them. One culture after another made their way into Southwestern Europe during the late Stone Age and through the Bronze Age, "constantly striving westward to find the resting place of their God, the sun, but ever baffled by the impassable ocean, and forced northward until the effort died out in Scandinavia."[19] According to Going, "each superimposed culture seized upon and adopted, or adapted, some parts at least of the pre-existing beliefs and institutions of the land, especially its holy places."[20]

One of the first significant migrations toward this geographical area occurred in the dawn of history, over 6,000 years ago. It apparently began near Mesopotamia, in the melting pot of Asia, and it proceeded in a westerly direction, slowly but inexorably across the northern coast of Africa until it reached the Atlantic Ocean, then veering northward into the Iberian Peninsula and Brittany. Here the people settled down on the land and established a permanent society, one dominated by a need to measure and anticipate the changing seasons, and by a strong belief in a deity who would escort deceased members of the society to a renewed afterlife in the west. As part of this agrarian culture, the people of Brittany constructed huge astronomical calendars to help them determine when the seeds should be sown and when the crops should be reaped. A similar calendar is located in America's Stonehenge, in New Hampshire. Both calendars have been dated to 1600 BCE. The settlers in Europe also built gigantic stone chambers during this same period, with most of the activity occurring between 3000 BCE and 400 BCE. The chambers bear a strong resemblance to chambers in America, as was mentioned previously.

Modern research continues to uncover new facts about ancient Europe. The migration from Africa into the Iberian Peninsula was only one of many migrations that would change the face of Europe over the next 4,000 years. The megalithic people of Spain and Portugal may have transmitted their knowledge of stone construction to the peoples of Scandinavia and Ireland around 3000 BCE. Scandinavia had barely been populated from central Europe when the Iberian influence set in. And it was only another thousand years before the battle-axe people from the Russian steppes moved into Denmark and Sweden, bringing their knowledge and their technical innovations with them. The Scandinavians learned about bronze and its many uses. They saw their first oxcarts and horse-drawn chariots as well. The north country was becoming more civilized thanks to migrations from the south. Until 30 years ago, historians believed that the great megalithic monuments of Western Europe had originally been developed by Stone Age people on the islands of Crete and Malta, and the knowledge was subsequently carried to Spain and Brittany by the more advanced cultures of the eastern Mediterranean. It has now been established that the Stone Age structures in Brittany are in fact the oldest known stone structures in the world. If there was cultural contact between Spain and Crete, the knowledge of the great stone builders was transmitted from west to east, rather than vice versa.

It has also been learned quite recently that Western Europeans had oceangoing vessels as early as 2000 BCE. Rock tracings in Bohuslan, Sweden, dating to 1800 BCE, depict large ships with crews of 30 or more, as shown in chapter 3. Even as far back as 3000 BCE, hardy adventurers from Brittany and the Iberian Peninsula had somehow traversed the English Channel to settle in Ireland, as witnessed by the megalithic monuments at Knowth and Newgrange on the east coast.

T.C. Lethbridge reported that people from the Iberian Peninsula were scooting to and fro on the Atlantic Ocean in large, flat-bottomed vessels about 2000 BCE. The boats, which were devoid of sails or rudder, exceeded 50 feet in length and carried a crew of 40. The Irish nautical expertise can be traced back to an ancient grave discovery in Broighter, Ireland. The grave, dating to 100 BCE, was discovered in a plowed field in County Derry in 1896. It contained, among other things, the model of an oceangoing vessel. The magnificent golden boat contained eight seats and 14 large oars, plus a steering oar located aft on the port side. The mast and yards indicated that the vessel, which would have been about 50 feet long, was square rigged.

It was only natural that, once these countries had developed capable ships, significant intercourse would be initiated from one land to another. This intercourse was established by 2000 BCE, and has continued uninterrupted for 4,000 years. Ancient grave finds have verified these contacts. For instance, Irish objects of gold and bronze, from the period 2000 BCE to 1200 BCE, have been unearthed in Denmark, a location that would have required mariners to cross the treacherous waters of the North Sea out of sight of land for several days. Evidently the Irish were familiar with ocean travel, and with adequate navigational techniques, even at this early date. An ancient grave in England produced Egyptian faience beads and Baltic amber dated to 1400 BCE. Pottery drinking cups discovered in Scotland were manufactured in Spain around 1800 BCE. These cups belonged to the Beaker people, an ambitious mercantile people who actively plied their wares and established a network of trading posts from England to the Rhine River during the middle of the second millennium BCE. Honey colored amber from the Baltic Sea area was traded in Greece. Shimmering black jet, a semiprecious stone found in Yorkshire, England, was in great demand in Egypt. And bolts of Phoenician woven cloth, dyed in the expensive royal purple, were made into robes for the kings of Brittany and Sweden. The Beaker people may have been Phoenician, or they may have learned their trade from the Phoenicians. Whatever the case, they were Western Europe's most proficient merchants.

Coin finds also have been important in tracing man's trade routes around the world. As mentioned previously, Carthaginian coins from the fourth century BCE were discovered in the Azores. Roman coins from 162 CE were part of a grave find in Scandinavia. And Roman coins covering the reigns from Probus to Diocletian (270–300 CE) have been unearthed in Hamarsfjord in Southeastern Iceland.

Completing the cycle of European travel, it is a matter of historic record that Irish monks became the pioneers of the Middle Ages, keeping the flame of Christianity burning brightly throughout the western world while Europe strove to free itself from the barbaric yoke imposed upon it by Attila the Hun and his savage descendants. The Irish historian Dicuil recorded the exploits of these devoted servants of God for posterity in his monumental work, *Extent of the Terrestrial Globe*, written about 825 CE. It is well known that Irish monks made countless missionary journeys throughout Western Europe from 500 CE to 1250 CE, as well as completing a number of pilgrimages to the Holy Land. One such pilgrimage by a monk named Fidelis was recorded by Dicuil. Fidelis visited the Holy Land from 750 to 760 CE. What makes this journey of particular interest is that he sailed there by a very curious route. He circumnavigated Africa and sailed up the Nile River to the Red Sea. Yet twentieth century historians insist the Irish could not have visited America because they didn't have the nautical expertise or seaworthy boats. Dicuil also detailed the Irish voyage to Iceland in 795 CE, a voyage that was subsequently substantiated by the Viking Sagas. The Sagas, as you recall, took the story one step further, reporting an Irish settlement in Greenland in 982 CE, not to mention the several references to the colony of Great Ireland that existed near Vinland during the same period. Completing the adventures of Irish mariners to Iceland, Gjerset had this to say: "Adamnan, Abbot of Iona from 679 to 704, mentions in his 'Vita S. Columbae' a prophecy of the saint regarding a man named Kormac who in Columba's days (521–597), made three voyages from Ireland in search for the 'Desert in the Ocean,'"[21] a land that Gjerset identified as Iceland.

This review of Western Europe has digressed somewhat, but it does add further evidence that not only was ancient man capable of crossing large bodies of water, out of sight of land, in oceangoing vessels, but that he made these crossings as long ago as 2000 BCE, as proved by recent grave finds. It also proves that Irish monks had a long history of open sea voyaging to distant lands during the Middle Ages.

The first unknown immigrants to Western Europe between 4000 BCE and 2000 BCE were the great stone builders. Subsequent invaders, such as the Celts, just used what was already there, and continued to construct similar monuments to the end of the Iron Age and beyond. One building design that was popular in ancient Europe was the beehive hut. Irish beehive huts are identical to the hut at Upton, Massachusetts. When they were built underground they had a hidden entrance and were used to store valuables or to hide in during enemy attacks. There are also examples of aboveground beehives stretching from Brittany to Ireland. These spanned the centuries from 400 BCE to 800 CE, and were built without the entrance tunnel. They served as places of habitation, as sweat houses, as out buildings, and in later years as monastic cells. According to W.G. Wood-Martin,

> Tacitus in his "Germania (XVI)," states that, besides their ordinary habitations, the Germans possessed a number of subterranean caves dug out and carefully covered over with soil. In these they found shelter from the rigors

of the seasons, and in times of foreign invasion their efforts were safely concealed. [This description sounds very similar to the Viking description of the Skraelings disappearing into the ground in Greater Ireland, in the Sagas.] Numerous allusions to forays by bands of Northmen occur in the Irish Annals of a later period. In the year 866, the provinces of Leinster and Munster were plundered by the Danes, "and they left not a cave there underground that they did not explore."[22]

Since the Celts occupied much of the territory on the west coast of Europe between 400 BCE and 50 BCE, they may have played a major role in the American stone chamber mystery. Their preference in building materials therefore should be reviewed. Celtic houses in Ireland were normally made of wood, not stone, although there are some exceptions. As Macalister observed, "Only the less important buildings have been preserved. Timber was plentiful and easily worked. Undoubtedly, all the large houses of the men of wealth were wooden erections. The only domestic buildings that have remained are poor huts of dry stone erected in poverty stricken, stony districts. There is a record of the erection of a church at Lindisfarne 'not of stone, but of hewn oaks, after the manner of the Scots (Irish). Tirechan tells us of St. Patrick building a church of earth 'because there was no wood hard by.'"[23]

Richard Holt Brash, in his discussion of Irish churches, reported that "St. Keenan built a church of stone. Before this time, the churches of Ireland were built of wattles and boards."[24] St. Keenan died about 490 CE.

Going back to pagan times, the priestly sect of Irish society, the Druids, normally practiced their religious rites in open groves deep in the forest. Roman historians such as Pliny and Tacitus noted that the Druids preferred outside locations for their services. The Druids, however, were influenced by their contact with the Greeks and Romans, and in many instances did construct temples of stone. One such temple that has remained intact is in Ullastreet in the Eastern Iberian Peninsula. It is a large, rectangular Hellenistic-style temple of dry wall construction measuring 20 by 22 feet. The construction date is estimated to lie between 600 BCE and 270 CE. The houses of this particular tribe were also made of mortarless stone, one such house being 20 feet wide and 33 feet long.

Another stone structure built by the Celts is located on the island of Eilean-na-Naoimh, in Scotland. It was a church dating back to the early Christian era, approximately 500 CE. Dowden described the chamber:

> Here we find a small church, twenty one feet in length, dry-built of undressed stones. It has in the east end one small, square-headed window, widely splayed both inside and outside, and a square-headed doorway in the west end, the jambs of the door being inclined so that the entrance is

narrower at the top than at the bottom. Close to the shore is a beehive cell, the roof of which has fallen in.... Close by the great cliff of the promontory of Deerness in Orkney, is a little island on which are the ruins of a group of eighteen cells of uncemented stone, together with a little church, of dimensions similar to those described above.[25]

It is obvious that the Celts used whatever building materials were available in the area, and that they used the designs of settlers who preceded them. The question still remains. Could the giant stone chambers of east America have been constructed by visitors from ancient Europe? A comparison of some of the European chambers with their American counterparts would go a long way toward proving that the American structures were of European design. The chamber just described on Eilean-na-naoimh seems very similar to the chamber in South Woodstock, Vermont. Both are rectangular, flat-roofed chambers with one doorless entrance. The chamber in Scotland is 21 feet long, while the South Woodstock chamber is 18 feet long.

Two other interesting chambers are located in Gouveias, Portugal, and Kent Cliffs, New York. On first glance the two chambers appear to be dissimilar. The Gouveias chamber is constructed of large, oblong stones, while the Kent Cliffs chamber is made up of small boulders. Also, the Gouveias chamber includes a large stone door jamb which is absent in its American neighbor. Barring these differences, however, there are a number of similarities. To begin with, the basic design is identical. Both chambers are earth covered. Both chambers are of dry wall construction. Both chambers have large slab stone roofs. Both chambers are rectangular in shape and have a single opening at one end of the chamber. There are no windows, no air vents, and no doors. The Gouveias chamber was dated to about 500 CE.

The floor plan of the Gouveias chamber has an identical floor plan to another chamber in New York, this one at North Salem. Both chambers are divided into two rooms, and the manner in which they are divided is similar. According to David Barron, there is another similar chamber located in Ledyard, Connecticut.

Although the Gouveias chamber has an entranceway that is different than the New York chambers, many European chambers have entrances that are identical to the American chambers. For instance, the entrance to Staigue Fort in County Kerry, Ireland, built between 500 BCE and 1000 CE, mirrors the entrances to the American chambers; the dry wall construction, the small flat stones used, and the trapezoidal shape of the entrance with the opening being wider at the bottom than at the top. The South Woodstock chamber encompasses the same design. Yet another stone struc-

Notice the similarity in the construction of the entrances to the stone structures in Ireland and America. This is the entrance to Staigue Fort in County Kerry, Ireland, which was built between 500 BCE and 1000 CE.

The entrance to Dunbeg Fort on the Dingle Peninsula, Ireland.

The entrance to the slab roofed chamber in South Woodstock, Vermont.

ture, this one Dunbeg Fort on Dingle Peninsula, also resembles the other two. It is dated to between 500 BCE and 1000 CE (see illustration).

Two beehive chambers, one on the Ring of Kerry in Ireland, the other in Webster, Massachusetts, are shown in the next illustration. Again, notice the overall design of the room. Even the stones used in the two chambers

## 9. The Great Stone Chamber Mystery

The chamber on the left is in Webster, Massachusetts. The chamber on the right is in County Kerry, Ireland. Both huts are a beehive design, and both demonstrate the same type of corbelling construction (Webster photograph courtesy Malcolm Pearson).

are similar. Both chambers use a corbeling technique in the wall design, and both chambers are covered by a single, large capstone. The two photographs almost appear to be of the same chamber. Other chambers having similar designs are located in Kermaric, Brittany, and Dowth South, Ireland.

A distinctive feature of some of the European and American chambers is their shelving. The shelves from an old house in Slievemore Village on Achill Island off County Mayo, Ireland, are identical to the shelves in the Oracle Chamber in America's Stonehenge. The age of the house is uncertain. It might only be 200 years old. On the other hand, it could go back a thousand years or more. The Oracle Chamber was radiocarbon dated to 520 CE by Whittall.

One last point of comparison can be made between the stone structures of Europe and America. A subterranean rectangular chamber in South Royalton, Vermont, is remarkably similar to the description of the Iron Age burial chamber located in Carrabeg, County Mayo, Ireland. Although no photograph of the Carrabeg chamber is available, a drawing based on Macallister's description of the chamber could easily be mistaken for the South Royalton structure.

A study of the various stone structures on both sides of the Atlantic Ocean indicates that the stone chambers of east America could easily have been constructed by colonists from ancient Europe. If they were, the period of construction would appear to be during the first thousand years of the Common Era, based on the age of the European structures. This time period agrees with the radiocarbon dates obtained from some American chambers, which ranged from 355 CE to 1240 CE.

There are two other contributors to the great chamber study who need to be recognized. Byron E. Dix and James W. Mavor, Jr. were actively involved in the study of the American chambers from the mid-1970s on. Their approach was somewhat different than most, however. They were archaeoastronomers. They knew that the early megalithic cultures of Western Europe were based on an agricultural economy, and therefore had to have exact knowledge of the seasons. Dix and Mavor operated on the assumption that the stone chambers of east America had very specific and identifiable astronomical alignments. One of their studies was of the Upton Chamber. Their astronomical evidence indicated that the Upton Chamber was built in 710 CE. The date was confirmed by four separate alignments. The Upton Chamber faces the northwest, in the general direction of the summer solstice sunset. Now, however, the sun sets 23.6 degrees further south on June 21 than it should set to be accurately aligned to the passageway of the Upton Chamber. Since the sun is always moving slowly to the south, at the rate of .017 degrees every hundred years, the sun would have been properly aligned with the chamber in 670 CE +/- 300 years, a very rough measurement. Three other astronomical measurements subsequently pinpointed the construction date more accurately, to 710 CE. Some of these alignments only occur every 26,000 years, so there can't be any confusion in the dates. As a result of their study, Dix and Mavor concluded that "the date of 710 CE narrows the field of speculation about the builders of the Upton Chamber and lends support to the theory that they might have been Irish travelers to America from the Boyne Valley before the Norse incursion into Ireland. The fact of specific and unique architectural similarity between Upton and Boyne tombs and the fact that residents of the Boyne Valley knew of the interior of the megalithic tombs at the date of Upton is supportive of an Irish connection."[26]

## Miscellaneous Stonework

In addition to the stone chambers, there are other stone enclosures that are often associated with the megalithic people of Western Europe.

## 9. The Great Stone Chamber Mystery

These stoneworks include souterrains and cashels. Wood-Martin described a souterrain in his book *Pagan Ireland*, a definitive study of the prehistoric people of the Emerald Isle: "In the interior of many earthen forts and stone cashels there are often chambers and subterranean passages, which vary in length as well as in breadth and height. These passages are built of uncemented stones, and are covered with flagstones, the extremities of which rest on parallel walls; and whilst some are too low to stand erect in, and the explorer has to proceed on hands and knees, others are upwards of six feet in height, and of corresponding breadth. They were constructed not only for habitation, but also for defensive purposes. The entrances to these retreats appear to have been concealed with great care."[27]

Macalister adds that "the simplest form of souterrain is a small single chamber 6–8 feet long and 3–4 feet wide. A hole, usually at or about the middle of the enclosed area gives admission to the souterrain."[28]

The construction techniques used in the passageway at the Webster, Massachusetts, chamber compare favorably with those found in the Knowth, Ireland tunnel (see illustration). The photographs speak for themselves. The two passageways are of similar design and similar method of construction. Again, dry walling is used exclusively, the walls are constructed of relatively small stones, and the entire channel is covered with

A comparison of souterrains in Europe and America. *Left*: The souterrain passage in America leads into the beehive chamber in Webster, Massachusetts. *Right*: The souterrain passage in Ireland is located beneath a medieval hut in Knowth.

large, flat stone slabs. The Knowth souterrain belongs to the Iron Age and probably dates between 100 and 400 CE. The Webster tunnel was built for an unknown purpose at an unknown date. It is approximately 3 feet wide by 4.5 feet high and 8 feet long. It has a small asymmetrical chamber at the end of the tunnel. The Knowth souterrain is about the same height, but is wider and longer.

Two other souterrains are located in New England. One is located in Vermont, the other in Massachusetts. The Vermont souterrain is located in Putney, Windham County, and is situated 1000 feet above sea level on the north side of a mountain near the Connecticut River. The mounded chamber can be entered through an opening in the top, near the center of the chamber. This souterrain is a single-chamber type, consisting of a room measuring 8 feet in diameter and 6 feet high. A charcoal sample obtained from the original floor level inside the chamber was radiocarbon dated to 545 CE +/- 190 years. It is not known for what purpose the souterrain was constructed. What is obvious, however, is how closely the Windham chamber resembles the description of the Irish souterrain put forth by Macalister. And the Windham chamber was apparently built at the same time that souterrains were being built in Ireland. The Massachusetts structure is located in the small town of Goshen in the western part of the state, and is of a completely different design. It is located on the ridge of a hill overlooking a cemetery. The entrance to the souterrain exposes a vertical shaft 3.5 feet in diameter and 14 feet deep. Three and a half feet above the bottom of the shaft, a horizontal tunnel travels 15 feet in a northerly direction. The tunnel is 2.5 feet high and 2.5 feet wide. At the very bottom of the shaft another horizontal tunnel measuring 3 feet wide by 3 feet high extends for 60 feet in a southerly direction. Several surveys of the tunnels have been conducted by qualified scientists to determine if hidden chambers exist at the extremities of the tunnels. No chambers were found. At one time, a back hoe was actually brought in to excavate the exterior soil down to the level of one of the tunnels, again in search of a chamber. Again the search was fruitless. There was no chamber. Perhaps the scientists should study the ground beneath the flagstone floor of the tunnels. The Irish always hid the chambers very carefully in this type of souterrain since they were used as places of refuge in case of attack. And one of their favorite hiding places was beneath the floor.

A cashel (hill with ruins of cathedral and castle) was an ancient Irish stone fort. The most imposing feature of the cashel was a large defensive stone wall that completely circled the village. Some cashels had enormous walls, up to 15 feet high with a thickness of 20 feet at the base. The walls were usually of a trapezoidal shape. Some cashel walls were circular, some oval, and some appeared to follow the contour of the land. In some locations, the cashel was built at the top of a cliff, with one side of the enclosure protected by the cliff walls. The settlement inside the walls consisted of houses (often beehive huts), churches, altars, menhirs with ogam inscriptions, and the ever present souterrain. During times of strife, if the enemy succeeded in storming the walls, the populace would quietly melt away into the maze of subterranean passages that criss-crossed beneath the cashel courtyard. Some cashels even had to be entered through souterrains that passed beneath the walls.

The cashel and buildings on the island of Innishmurray can be traced back to a monastic site founded by St. Columcille about 563 CE. It is not known if St. Columcille actually constructed the cashel or if he just used an existing structure. Wood-Martin again had the last word. "The grand barbaric fortresses, styled cashels, raised in ages when might was right, were built on sites selected for the wide range of country which they dominated, and they were deemed most eligible, when nearly inaccessible. Provided it was accompanied by defensive characteristics—a high precipice, and overhanging crag, the brink of a sea-washed cliff, the brow of a bleak mountain, an isolated rock, or a promontory, was chosen—sites so suitable that on many of them were afterward raised the turreted keep of the Anglo Norman baron."[29]

Northeast America has numerous cashel-like complexes. One of these complexes is located in Putnam Valley, New York, the same area that contains over 50 slab roofed chambers. The Putnam Valley ruins were discovered by volunteers of MARC under the direction of Salvatore Trento in 1976. The site consists of a mammoth stone wall complex enclosing an area of about 500 square yards, according to Trento. The walls rise to a height of 16 feet in some areas. Within this fortification are located two collapsed slab roofed chambers and several stone lined pits. Like other stone ruins of east America, the identity of the architects of the Putnam Valley complex remains a mystery, as does the intended use of the site.

Another mysterious American cashel, known as the Gungywamp, is located near Groton, Connecticut. The site was mentioned previously, in the letter written to John Winthrop, Jr., by John Pynchon in the year 1654, inquiring about "a stonewall and stone fort in it." The derivation of the name, Gungywamp, is unknown. It may be an Indian name, or it could be an early colonial name. In any case, it goes back at least as far as the mid–seventeenth century. The Gungywamp was first brought to light by John Dodge, a member of the New England Antiquities Research Association (NEARA), who spent several years surveying the site during the 1960s and '70s. According to David P. Barron and Sharon Mason, "Located in a forested region of hills, cliffs, and swamps, the Greater Gungywamp Complex covers nearly three hundred acres. Surrounded on two-thirds by swamps and bogs, and protected on the other third by 65 foot cliffs, the location seems to lend itself naturally to a place of defense. Whether or not this was ever its use is debatable."[30] Whittall studied the site during the mid 1970s. At that time, he believed the site might have been built by Celtiberians during the Iron Age.

The Gungywamp Society was formed in 1979 to try to identify the builders of the complex. David Barron, the president of the organization, was the prime mover and the group's most enthusiastic archaeologist. The site consists of a number of low meandering stone wall systems that appear to be of a defensive nature, five or more stone chambers or ruins thereof, standing stones, a double ring of stones, and several Chi-Rho symbols carved into rocks. The Chi-Rho monogram is a Christian abbreviation for Christ, dating back to early Roman times. The Chi-Rho symbols that were cut into several of the rock faces in the Gungywamp are a transitional style that was in use in Europe between 400 and 600 CE. One of the stone chambers is about 18 feet long, 6 feet wide, and 6 feet high. It contains a small room near the right front of the entrance. This room, which measures about 3 by 3 by 3, will hold about two people in a crouching position. Two other smaller chambers are typical dry wall chambers with large capstones. The most intriguing feature of the site is the double ring of stones, resembling a tan bark mill. Tanning, a process for converting animal hides into leather, is an age-old process, used around the world for at least 1,400 years. According to Barron, "The so-called tan bark mill has given up one C14 test result, placing its construction somewhere around 560 CE."[31] The Gungywamp complex is truly a fascinating archaeological puzzle. David Barron's successors believe the site is of great antiquity. They continue to hope that one day soon they will uncover the key artifact that will identify the builders of the stone enclosure.

## Summary

- There are over 300 recorded stone chambers in east America. These primarily fall into two categories: slab roofed chambers and corbeled chambers.
- There is a significant difference of opinion as to the provenance of these chambers. One group claims the chambers were ancient religious temples constructed by colonists from the Iberian Peninsula. Many in the scientific community believe the chambers were colonial root cellars.

- The root cellar advocates point to a study by Giovanna Neudorfer, the Vermont State Archaeologist, as proof that the stone structures fall into the historic period. The Neudorfer study presented no hard facts to substantiate that theory.
- The ancient Europe theory appears to have more support, based on existing evidence. Some of the local histories of New England towns mentioned the first settlers discovering "stone cellars" already there. The histories record that no one knew who built them or why.
- The most positive evidence in support of the great age of the stone chambers rests in radiocarbon dates obtained from charcoal recovered from the original ground surface within the chambers. Carbon dates have ranged from 1525 BCE to 1100 CE, at different sites.
- A study of authenticated ancient European chambers revealed many similarities between those chambers and their American counterparts.
- In addition to chambers, both Ireland and America showed similarities in other structures, such as souterrains and cashels.

## Conclusions

- The majority of the great stone chambers of east America were not constructed as root cellars by colonial farmers.
- Many of the stone chambers seem to be of ancient construction as confirmed by radiocarbon dating techniques.
- The evidence indicates that a number of them may have been built between 355 CE and 1240 CE, possibly by Irish mariners, but supporting evidence is required before that theory can be proven.
- Other chambers appear to be of an even earlier date, falling back into the Bronze Age. They may have been constructed by visitors from either Scandinavia or the Iberian Peninsula, but again, supporting evidence is necessary to substantiate the theory.

# 10

# Ancient Stone Monuments of America

## Conventional Thinking

Many unusual stone structures are located throughout Northeast America, including dolmens, menhirs, and cairns. Some of these formations are the result of natural phenomena, including the processes of the last glacial period. The man-made structures are either the products of colonial field-clearing or modern fantasies.

## Discussion

There are many mysterious stone structures adorning the landscape of Northeast America in addition to the stone chambers already discussed, but before an attempt is made to determine the origin of these relics, it is necessary to return to ancient Europe to learn more about the beliefs and traditions of the early Europeans. The ancient inhabitants of Western Europe were among the world's first great architects, erecting gigantic stone structures in Brittany as long ago as 4000 BCE. Over the centuries, the art of building with stone spread out from this center on the Atlantic coast of France to cover most of the world's surface. Menhirs, dolmens, and other megalithic monuments became commonplace in such diverse areas of the globe as India, Persia, Algeria, Norway, and Ireland.

Ancient man began life as a nomad who roamed the forests and plains in search of food. For tens of thousands of years the annual cycles were repeated. He was primarily a hunter-gatherer and a fisherman, and he patiently tracked the herds of auroch, red deer, and wild boar from one grazing area to another. There were no permanent settlements in the predawn of history, only temporary shelters that required no time-consuming construction and could be broken down quickly whenever it was time to move on. This usually occurred when the herds left for greener pastures, the wild cereal grains had been harvested, or the seasons changed.

About 10,000 years ago, man began to forsake the nomadic existence and settle permanently in one location. The domestication of sheep, goats, cattle, and pigs, and the agricultural control of cereal grasses, such as wheat and barley, made this transition possible. The settlement of Jericho in ancient Palestine, founded in 8000 BCE, was one of the world's first known permanent communities. As civilization developed, it quickly spread from one area to another. The community of Çatal Hüyük, in the Konya plain of Anatolia in present day Turkey, flourished about 7000 BCE, with over 1,000 permanent dwellings. By this time, farmers were already cultivating many different types of food plants, and local craftsmen were producing woven cloth and jewelry made from pure gold and copper. Irrigation became a science, and crop rotation was practiced to protect the vitality of the soil.

Two thousand years later, travelers from Northern Africa crossed over to the European continent at Gibraltar, and made their way north as far as Brittany, where they too settled down and established a permanent society. Civilization was becoming the normal way of life in Stone Age Europe, and with it came the most powerful force known to man — religion. In Macalister's study of ancient religion, he noted, "An important element in their religion would be the cult of the dead, who have entered a mysterious supernatural state in which they have much capability for good or for ill."[1] So, from the very beginning, death and religion were closely united. As a result, burial customs were followed most reverently. At first, simple inhumation was practiced, where the body was placed in a fresh hole and covered with earth. But soon, cists came into vogue as a means of isolating the body from the surrounding ground. A cist, or stone coffin, consisted of a stone floor, four stone sides, and a stone cover. It normally measured about five feet long and three feet wide, and was built beneath the surface of the ground, much like today's burials. Ancient man gradually developed the "conviction that death is not the end of all things, but the door to another life."[2] This belief in a future life is evidenced by the deposits that were left in the graves of the dead. Mourning relatives and friends supplied the deceased with food, weapons, war paint, domestic implements, and ornaments. In the case of royalty, the dead person's wife, servants, and horses were often slaughtered around his tomb. As worship of the dead increased, so too did the pomp and circumstance surrounding the funeral ceremony. Tombs gradually grew in size, culminating in the great passage graves of Locmariaquer in Brittany, and Newgrange in Ireland. These massive stone depositories were covered by large, earthen mounds called tumuli, that stretched skyward 50 feet or more. Man frequently crowned these tumuli with towering, vertical memorial stones. These stones belong to a class of monuments known as menhirs.

The societies of Neolithic man were primarily agricultural in nature, and the people of 4000 BCE, in addition to being fascinated with death, were mystified by the capriciousness of the land. They depended on the land for their sustenance, but, then as now, they were at the mercy of the elements. The sun gave birth to the grain, and the rain nourished the roots. The crops grew, and life was good. But life was not always good. Plagues of insects periodically destroyed the crops. Adverse weather, such as hail, snow, wind, and freezing rain, frequently ruined the food supply. Nature was a force to be studied, to be feared, to be revered. Man developed many objects of worship during the formative years of civilization, and these, quite naturally, included "the great incarnate powers and forces of nature — the wind, the rain, the sun, the storm, the thunder, givers now of life and now of death."[3]

And the greatest of these was the sun. The sun moved across the sky from east to west every day, and traveled from north to south, then from south to north, during the year, on a never-ending journey of warmth and cold, light and dark. The priests of the community noted these passings year after year with keen interest, keeping detailed records of the solar cycle. It was critical to the society that the farmer know the precise time to plant his crops and to reap his harvest. After many years of scientific observation, an unknown priest in a forgotten sanctuary on the coast of Brittany developed the world's first astronomical calendar to assist the farmer in predicting the changing seasons. As noted in chapter 8, a series of vertical standing stones were placed in a circle containing a central viewing platform. The winter solstice, the summer solstice, and the other seasonal changes could be witnessed by standing on the platform and watching the sun rise or set over specific menhirs. The changing seasons eventually became a time for festive ceremonies where man could welcome the spring planting season or celebrate the fall harvest. "Of the worship of the powers of nature, the agricultural and pastoral deities, we have the clearest evidence in the periodical assemblies. They took place, as a rule, at or near cemeteries, and thus were bound up with the cult of the dead: but the fact of their incidence on the critical days of the year proves that they were also connected with the annual phenomena of seasonal change."[4]

In Ireland, these assemblies were held in different sections of the country during the year, and were arranged to coincide with the calendrical changes. "The assembly of Uisnech celebrated Beltane, the first of

May, the beginning of summer. The assembly of Tailltiu celebrated Lughnasadh, the first of August, the beginning of autumn. The assembly of Tlachtgha and that of Teamhair, celebrated Samhain, the first of November, the beginning of winter — the season of the death of the corn-spirit.... There is evidence ... that the rebirth of the corn-spirit was also celebrated at Teamhair, with a feast at or about 25th March."[5]

Eventually specific areas of each community were designated as religious centers, and were held sacred. All burials were conducted within this sanctuary. Temples, astronomical calendars, and religious monuments of various types were all erected within the carefully defined sacred ground. Carnac, in Brittany, was one such sanctuary, according to Going: "This region, it appears, was a sort of Mecca, or peculiarly holy ground, to which the remains of heroes and leaders were brought for entombment, to which the faithful flocked in pilgrimages, and in which the great religious ceremonies were held."[6] Carnac, in fact, is the greatest example of megalithic accomplishment in the world. Stone monuments abound, and on a scale unmatched anywhere else in the world. Within a radius of seven miles, there are over 300 monuments, not counting alignments. Although the first great megalithic society was born in Brittany, it did not remain isolated in that one area for very long. Over a period of several thousand years, the stone structures spread across the face of Western Europe, into all the areas that border the Atlantic Ocean.

Chapter 9 observed the migrations of races across the face of Western Europe, as well as the diffusion of cultures from one country to another. This transmission of ideas was responsible for the widespread use of megalithic structures all the way from the coast of tropical Africa in the south to the snows of Scandinavia in the north. Brittany maintained close contact with her neighbors to the south along the Iberian Peninsula, even during the Stone Age. It was only natural that stone chambers and other stone monuments should find their way into the Iberian religion. Around 3000 BCE, colonists from Brittany settled on the northeast coast of Ireland, bringing with them the tradition of the huge communal passage graves located deep within enormous tumuli. These same people settled in Northern Scotland. The religion of the megalith builders found its way into Scandinavia some 500 years later, either from Brittany or from the Iberian Peninsula, and the Scandinavians accepted some of these philosophies and combined them with their own beliefs of god, life, and death, to develop their own unique religion. Denmark, Norway, and Sweden were not as well equipped as their neighbors to the south for constructing large earthen tumuli, so they utilized the cairn mode of burial, whereby the body was buried in a cist and then covered by a mound of small stones. The people of the northland were skilled stonemasons in their own right, and made widespread use of cairns, stone circles, and menhirs.

Ireland received more than one wave of colonists from the mainland, and with each new wave came additional ideas of social behavior and religion. From Brittany came the magnificent stone chambers and tumuli. Brittany also contributed the concept of the dolmen to the Irish culture, and Ireland began to construct dolmens by the hundreds around 2500 BCE. The idea of communal burial chambers became less popular over the years, and individual burials gained in acceptance, with the deceased placed beneath a dolmen and the entire grave then covered with a small tumuli. Other monuments, such as menhirs, cairns, and circles, were adopted from the practices of visiting Scandinavians who invaded Ireland between 2000 BCE and 1500 BCE. The Iberians, under King Milesius, made their contribution to the Irish culture around 1000 BCE, and the Celts entered the picture between 800 BCE and 400 BCE. In spite of all these intrusions by their European neighbors, Ireland was still able to develop her own individual personality. Being on the edge of the civilized world, she managed to remain isolated from the influence of the early Greek world and also from the spread of the Roman Empire. In fact, Ireland was one of the few countries that escaped the Roman influence. As a result, she was able to grow and to develop as a unique culture.

England and Scotland also received outside influences from the megalith builders, and each of them accepted those practices they found desirable and rejected the ideas that were abhorrent to them. Both countries became renowned centers of circle worship, the remains of which can still be seen today in Callernish, Stennis, Avebury, and Stonehenge, to name a few of their ancient sanctuaries. Other tombs and monuments are also found in great numbers in the British Isles, but circles are by far the most prevalent.

Megalithic communities therefore could be found all over the western seaboard of Europe from the Stone Age on, communities that utilized such religious monuments as menhirs, cists, cairns, dolmens, circles, tumuli, and alignments. Menhirs were not only used as astronomical calendars, however. They were also used for gravestones, boundary markers, and as memorial stones to commemorate a celebrated historical event or a famous person. The menhirs of Brittany were gargantuan sculptures of mind-boggling dimensions, the majestic menhir of Locmariaquer measuring 70 feet high and weighing 375 tons. For all intents and purposes however, all menhirs appear to have had religious significance. According to Macalister, "Even when the stone was ... a mere landmark, it was necessarily a sacred stone.... The 'Stone of Adoration,' set up to mark the boundary of a property was likewise watchful over the interests of the property owner."[7]

The use of multiple menhirs produced two other types of monuments, one known as an alignment, the other as a circle. The alignment consisted of a number of menhirs erected in a straight line, or in several parallel lines over distances anywhere from several feet to many miles. The purpose of alignments is still unknown, although Going speculated that some alignments in Brittany were avenues along which the faithful marched during religious services, the avenues terminating at a temple area. In Carnac, "there are traces of these alignments of stones extending for a total length of nearly five miles. There are 10, 11, or 13 parallel lines, spreading over a width of 330 to 450 feet. Many of the stones have fallen and been removed by the natives for building use, but nearly 3000 remain."[8]

The avenue theory is not unique to Going. Anderson noted similar uses in Scotland: "At Callernish, in the island of Lewis, there is a very remarkable stone circle, with lines of standing stones proceeding from its circumference."[9] That circle constituted yet another type of monument. As with other monuments, circles had many uses. Occasionally they surrounded a tumulus to define the sacred burial ground. At other times, they appear to have been used as temple areas. Going refers to them as the "holy of holies in which the priests perform their rites."[10] Some circles contained stone altars within their confines. One such circle was considered to be a pantheon of pagan gods by St. Patrick, during his travels around Ireland. St. Patrick defined the central stone as "the king idol of Ireland, called Cromm Cruaich: and he was of gold, surrounded by twelve subordinate deities of stone."[11] Cromm Cruaich was worshipped "with rites which involved prostrations, self-mutilations, and human sacrifices, especially the sacrifices of children."[12] These rites were conducted ostensibly to guarantee a bountiful harvest.

England contains probably the most famous circle in the world, the fascinating relic at Stonehenge. Although this structure is still being scrutinized by the scientific community, it is generally considered to be a religious sanctuary containing an astronomical observatory. Another famous prehistoric English monument is located at Avebury on the Salisbury Plain. It consists of a gigantic ditch and circular earthworks containing numerous stone circles, which may identify holy burial places. Fergusson quotes ancient English history as evidence of that intended use: "Many years ago, Mr. Kemble printed a charter of King Athelstan, dated in 939, which describing the boundaries of the manor of Overton, in which Avebury is located, makes use of the following expression: —'then by Collas barrow, as far as the broad road to Hackpen, thence northward up along the Stone-Row, thence to the burying places.'"[13]

Joseph Anderson's study of pagan Scotland gives strength to that theory. Anderson assisted in the excavation of numerous stone circles, and in every one of them he discovered a burial. Early burials, going back into the Stone Age, consisted of stone chambers buried within a tumulus or cairn. With the dawning of the Bronze Age, burial practices changed from inhumation to cremation. Subsequently, the ashes of the deceased were buried in urns beneath barrows of various types. Anderson drew several conclusions from his archaeological studies of the circles: "The burials are placed in an enclosure marked off from the surrounding area by a circular stone-setting, or circle of standing stones.... The circular stone-setting ... has been found to be the external sign by which the burial ground is distinguished from the surrounding area.... Like the cairn, it is thus the visible mark of the spot of the earth to which the remains of the dead have been consigned."[14]

Barrows of one type or another have generally been found to contain burials. Stones were used at one time to outline the shape of the barrow to define the consecrated ground. Anderson, however, noted that the stone circles themselves identified a sacred burial, with or without a barrow. This information would indicate that such fascinating enclosures as those found at Avebury and at Stennis in the Orkney Islands served as holy cemeteries. It is even possible that Stonehenge itself harbors the remains of some prehistoric priest or king. Stone circles endured in Scandinavia over a longer period of time than anywhere else in Europe. Circles were in vogue in Norway and Sweden back in the Bronze Age, yet the Vikings were still using them as late as 800 CE. The Vikings used stone circles during their religious rites involving human sacrifice. The Dom-ring, for instance, was a stone circle with an altar stone in the center. As DuChaillu noted, "There may still be seen the Dom-ring within which men were doomed to be sacrificed."[15] The victim apparently was led into the circle and spread-eagled backwards over the stone, where his back was ceremoniously snapped.

Stone circles were also reported to have been used as battlefield monuments, such as at the battle of Braavalla in Sweden around the year 750 CE. In this case, the circles were incorporated into a cairn burial. The Viking Sagas clearly relate the creation of a battlefield burial. "After the battle, the conqueror, Sigurd Ring, caused a search to be made for the body of his uncle. The body, when found, was washed and placed in the chariot in which Harold had fought, and transported into the interior of a tumulus which Sigurd had caused to be raised."[16] Cairns were particularly popular in Scandinavia and, as with stone circles, they were constructed almost continuously for a period of 3,000 years. Cairns of all shapes and sizes can still be seen throughout Norway, Sweden, and Denmark even today, usually near the coast. Legend has it that celebrated Viking chiefs were entombed in these stone mounds, which were intentionally constructed near the ocean so they could be seen and revered by all passing mariners. These monuments, as well as tumuli, eventually evolved into a ship-shaped grave, more becoming a seafaring people.

The Annals of Ireland also mention the building of large stone tombs on the battlefields of Moytura about 1897 BCE after a battle between the Firlbolgs (Belgae) and the Tuatha De Dananns (Scandinavians). The annals record that on the battlefield of Northern Moytura, "almost every variety of megalithic art can be found. There are stone cairns, with dolmens in their interiors—dolmens standing alone, but which have evidently always been exposed, dolmens with single circles; others with two or three circles of stones around them; and circles without dolmens or anything else in the centres."[17] During the battle of Southern Moytura, the annals note that King Eochy was surprised by three enemy soldiers. The king's servant was killed coming to his rescue, "and as the story goes, was interred with all honours in a cairn close by."[18] Later, in another battle, King Eochy himself was killed with many of his soldiers. "A cairn is still pointed out on a promontory jutting into the bay, which is said to have been erected over the remains of the King."[19]

Anderson had one additional comment regarding the design of chambered mounds in general. "Chambered sepulchral mounds or cairns, with passages leading into them, are found in Denmark and Brittany, but they differ from those in Scotland and Ireland, in being roofed with flat stones of enormous size, and not vaulted."[20] Other sources claim that the most ancient of the Irish tombs, such as Newgrange, are identical with those in Brittany, both in design and size. The vaulted style of Irish tomb is of a later design.

Dolmens were a common mode of interment in Ireland and Brittany, but their popularity was not restricted to these areas alone. Dolmens can be found in many countries. India has dolmens. Persia has dolmens. And North Africa has dolmens. For the purposes of this study, the discussion will be restricted to the dolmens of Western Europe. In reviewing ancient monuments, Fergusson made the observation that "France on the contrary seems to be the native country of the dolmen. They exist there in numbers far beyond anything we can show, and of dimensions exceeding anything we can boast of."[21] Perhaps Brittany developed the dolmen, but Ireland perfected it and used it to such an extent that today, when most people think of dolmens, they think first of Ireland. The design, the symmetry, and the overall graceful beauty of Irish dolmens make them a favorite subject for historians and photographers alike. Macalister was aware of that when he said, "Ireland is preeminently a land of dolmens. There are over 780 dolmens remaining in the country."[22] Dolmens were primarily tombs as Macalister discovered during his comprehensive study of the Irish people. "The use of dolmens began doubtless in the Stone Age, and they cannot be considered apart from the great chambered tumuli which are the most conspicuous of the Irish Bronze Age monuments. That they were places of sepulture is now a commonplace of knowledge."[23]

Now that the origin and development of the stone monuments in the Old World has been reviewed, it is time to survey the American scene in search of similar megalithic structures, and to attempt to determine if they have a common origin. The first American monument to be studied is the dolmen, of which there are numerous examples scattered around the northeast. Perhaps the most imposing dolmen in North America is located in North Salem, New York. It stands next to a barn, alongside a quiet country road, an impressive curiosity that is generally ignored by most of the local inhabitants. A sign positioned in front of the magnificent stone table by the North Salem Historical Society used to refer to it as an accidental formation resulting from the last Ice Age, about 10,000 years ago. Now however, the official position has changed. Since questioning minds around the country are considering the possibility that the dolmen could have been constructed by visiting European mariners, the North Salem town fathers prefer to say that the artifact is of unknown origin. The enormous capstone on the monument weighs 90 tons, and is delicately balanced on five small legs. It has all the appearances of great antiquity, and brings to mind the many megalithic tombs that populate the Irish countryside (see illustration). Today it stands alone, exposed to the elements. Some time in the distant past, it may have been enclosed by a tumuli as so many European dolmens are, but that is only conjecture. Other dolmens can be found in such localities as Kinnelon, New Jersey, Lynn, Massachusetts, and Bartlett, New Hampshire. Salvatore Trento, in *The Search For Lost America*, recorded an impressive inventory of dolmens that are still standing throughout Northeast America. His book also includes a survey of other types of stone structures, such as dry wall chambers, menhirs, and circles. That the dolmens closely resemble the European monuments is undeniable. But whether they were both built by the same people is unknown. At present, there is no evidence that can be used to properly identify the architects of these memorials, or to pinpoint their date of construction.

Cairns are also found in great numbers in the New World. Some of the best examples of cairns can be found in the western Massachusetts town of Washington. A dozen or more well-constructed cairns are spaced

## 10. Ancient Stone Monuments of America

The dolmen pictured is located in North Salem, New York, and has a capstone weighing 90 tons.

This 4,000-year-old dolmen still stands in Brennanstown, County Dublin (courtesy the Commissioners of Public Works, Ireland).

along the east side of October Mountain near the summit, in conjunction with a winding stone wall complex. The cairns are built of small stones carefully piled on top of a massive base stone. These particular units measure about eight feet in diameter at the base, and stand about six or seven feet high. The significance of the nearby stone wall complex is unknown, although Trento found that most of the cairn fields in the New York–New England area are located near similar stone wall systems. Some scientists claim these structures are the result of colonial field clearings, but the evidence does not support the theory. In many cases, the land is not conducive to either pasturage or agriculture, so there would be no reason to clear it of small stones, unless the colonists did it just to beautify their property, which is unlikely. There is some evidence that the cairns were actually ancient burial sites.

Archaeologist Frank Glynn excavated two cairns along the Connecticut River several years ago and discovered the remains of an ancient burial. Ashes, stone implements, and pieces of pottery were unearthed during his work. The style of the artifacts placed their age back into the Woodland period, from 1000 BCE to 700 CE. Glynn was uncertain whether the pottery was of American origin or European origin, and to date other archaeologists have refrained from classifying it. About 25 years ago, a Massachusetts state archaeologist partially excavated one of the cairns at the Washington site. Again, ashes were found, indicating this might also have been a burial site. As far as is known, no radiocarbon dating has ever been done on the ashes. It is interesting to note that an Indian burial ground of the historic period is located only one mile from the cairn field. As far as the identity of the architects of these cairns is concerned, the American Indian or his ancestors are a distinct possibility. The Washington cairns do not resemble the cairns in Europe. In fact, they most nearly resemble the cairns shown in the Smithsonian Institution's 12th Annual Report, which were discovered in an ancient burial mound in North Carolina, a vestige of the mysterious mound building period dating back 1500–2000 years.

There are a number of other Indian traditions that relate to cairns. C.C. Jones closely studied the burial practices of the Cherokee Indians of Tennessee. The Cherokee Indians, as a people, were very respectful of their dead. The body of a deceased person was carefully prepared for burial. First it was placed on a scaffold until the skin had been consumed and the bones had dried. Once this decomposition process was complete, the body was wrapped in white deer skins and was buried in the earth with the proper amount of mourning and lamentation by family and friends. Members of the tribe who died in another territory were still brought home for burial wherever possible. The place where they died was subsequently memorialized by the construction of a cairn. According to Jones, "Piles of stones were heaped up to commemorate the spots where [they fell] ... and to these rude monuments each passer-by added a stone in token of his appreciation of the valor and brave deeds of the deceased."[24]

In Great Barrington, Massachusetts, the local peaks were named Monument Mountain by the first colonists, in recognition of a sizeable cairn that once stood imposingly on the south side of the summit. The cairn, since destroyed, was reported to have consisted of ten cartloads of stone. "This pile, which was some 6 or 8 feet in diameter, circular at its base, and raised in the form of an obtuse cone, was of aboriginal origin, and was in existence before the white settlers occupied the valley," according to Taylor.[25] There are many stories regarding the origin of the cairn, although the one that is generally accepted is the Indian tradition that it marked the grave of an Indian maiden who jumped to her death from that spot upon learning of the death of her lover.

The last significant stone structure to be discussed in this chapter is the menhir, or standing stone. Menhirs by the hundreds cover the landscape of Northeast America, primarily on or near the mountaintops. Early scientists explained these as colonial road markers, but the evidence does not fit the theory. In the locations where most of these menhirs stand, there are no roads, either colonial or modern, only wilderness; wild, untamed, and in some cases, inaccessible. Many of the menhirs appear to be identical in design and size. Europe has some menhirs of much greater stature, some in the Orkneys and Brittany towering 20 feet in the air. Most American menhirs are seven feet high or smaller. European menhirs are also occasionally engraved, the most frequently used scripts being ogam and runic. To date, no scripts have been authenticated on any American menhirs, although some of them were reported to have an ogam inscription.

Warren Dexter, one of the intrepid explorers of our rugged countryside, photographed what appears to be an effigy menhir in central Vermont several years ago. This particular stone, now recumbent, appears incomplete, as if the artist was interrupted in the midst of his work. A hauntingly similar menhir, ornately carved in the likeness of a person or deity, is located in Clochar, Ireland. This menhir, standing in a Christian churchyard, is supposedly a carryover from pagan days.

As with cairns, it is impossible to ignore the American Indian when discussing menhirs. These structures were utilized as graveposts by the Sioux and Western Chippewa Indians. The burial practices of these tribes were similar to those of the Cherokees. Once the body was interred, a grave post of cedar was placed at the head. Schoolcraft noted that the grave posts contained "the symbolic representative figures which record, if it be a warrior, his totem; the symbol of his family, or surname ... [and his battle achievements] ... two facts from which his reputation is to be essentially derived."[26] Although these grave posts were made of wood in the historic period, it is possible that, in the prehistoric period, when the ancestors of the Indian were more settled, the grave markers were made of stone. Even today, modern man continues the practice of marking burial places with menhirs. The millions of gravestones that decorate our cemeteries attest to that fact.

Possible ancient habitation sites are another important part of the puzzle. Robert E. Stone, the owner of America's Stonehenge, feels there is an ancient campsite adjacent to the North Salem complex, and he has conducted numerous excavations in the fields and woodlands surrounding the stone village in an effort to unearth the living quarters of these ancient settlers. Salvatore Trento stated that members of his MARC team observed what could have been ancient habitation sites during their survey of the New York–New England area. As of this date, there has been no followup by any scientific organization. At some point the scientific community will have to get more involved if the megalith builders are to be identified.

Indian tradition, as previously noted, invariably stated that the stone chambers and other stone structures were already built when their forefathers first settled the land. They used the structures, but they didn't know who constructed them. This tradition existed in many tribes, including the Mohawks, Creeks, Cherokees, and Algonquians, and was reported by eighteenth and nineteenth century historians Thomas Jefferson, C.C. Jones, W.L. Stone, C. Atwater, H. Schoolcraft, and others.

## Summary

- Civilization reached Western Europe around 4000 BCE, with settled communities being established in Brittany on the west coast of France.
- With civilization came an increase in two of the world's great forces, religion and worship of the dead. In a relatively short period of time, these forces culminated in the construction of gigantic megalithic monuments. These structures were built for a variety of reasons, but all with the same two objectives: to worship the gods and to bury the dead.
- The types of megalithic structures built in Western Europe included dry wall chambers, dolmens, menhirs, cairns, and stone circles.

- From 4000 BCE to 2000 BCE the cult of the megaliths spread southward into the Iberian Peninsula, northward as far as Scandinavia, and westward to Ireland on the fringe of the great ocean.
- Today, in the twenty-first century, megalithic monuments of possible extreme antiquity are being discovered all along the northeastern seaboard of the United States, the closest approach from Western Europe.
- The American Indians or their ancestors may be involved with some of the monuments, such as the cairns, but many Indian traditions claim they did not build the structures, and they don't know who did.

## Conclusions

- Considerably more evidence is required before the strange stone monuments of America can be ascribed to early European travelers to our shores. This study has identified some things that these stone monuments are not:
  1. They are not generally colonial field-clearing piles.
  2. They are not colonial road markers or boundary markers.
  3. They are not (all) natural remnants of the last Ice Age.

  What they are, however, is still a mystery. They are man made. They are well designed. And they required a tremendous amount of human labor to erect. But who built them, and why, has yet to be determined.

- In order to conclusively identify the architects of the stone ruins as being from the Old World, one of two things probably must occur:
  1. A dolmen or other tomb must be discovered with an undisturbed burial beneath it. And the occupant of that tomb must prove to be a Celt, a Phoenician, or some other early mariner from across the Atlantic.
  OR
  2. An undisturbed habitation site must be located near the stone ruins. The site must contain irrefutable proof of early non–American occupation, such as weapons or household articles recovered in situ.
- Taken in context with the stone chambers, the monuments may form a pattern. Some chambers have been radiocarbon dated to 1500 BCE, but as yet there is no proof of a connection between these chambers and the monuments.

# 11

# *Inscriptions: Ancient Messages or Modern Frauds?*

## Conventional Thinking

All alleged ancient inscriptions in America are either forgeries, modern intrusions, Indian pictographs, arrow or spear sharpening marks, plow marks, or natural weathering of the stone.

## Discussion

The magnificent stone chambers of Northeast America give evidence of great antiquity, with radiocarbon dates extending as far back as 1500 BCE. The multitude of stone monuments along the eastern seaboard of the United States are intriguing duplicates of the megaliths of Brittany, Ireland, and Scandinavia, although no definite dates can be assigned to the construction of the American stones at this time. But by far the most impressive evidence of the intrusion of transatlantic peoples into ancient America may lie in their own words, chiseled out of stone, in ancient languages such as Celtic, Phoenician, and Libyan. There are literally thousands of intelligent messages engraved in stone all the way from Canada to Brazil, and blanketing our vast country from the Atlantic coast to the Pacific. The engravings seem to tell us of expeditionary voyages to our shores from such far-off lands as Egypt, Phoenicia, and the Iberian Peninsula. These voyages may have begun as long ago as 1700 BCE, and may have continued intermittently right up to the time that Christopher Columbus introduced America to the modern world.

Most scientists have brushed aside all reported ancient inscriptions, arguing that the artifacts are either modern forgeries, Indian pictographs, or weathering anomalies. Some scientists have called for a thorough exam-

## 11. Inscriptions

## Development of the Alphabets

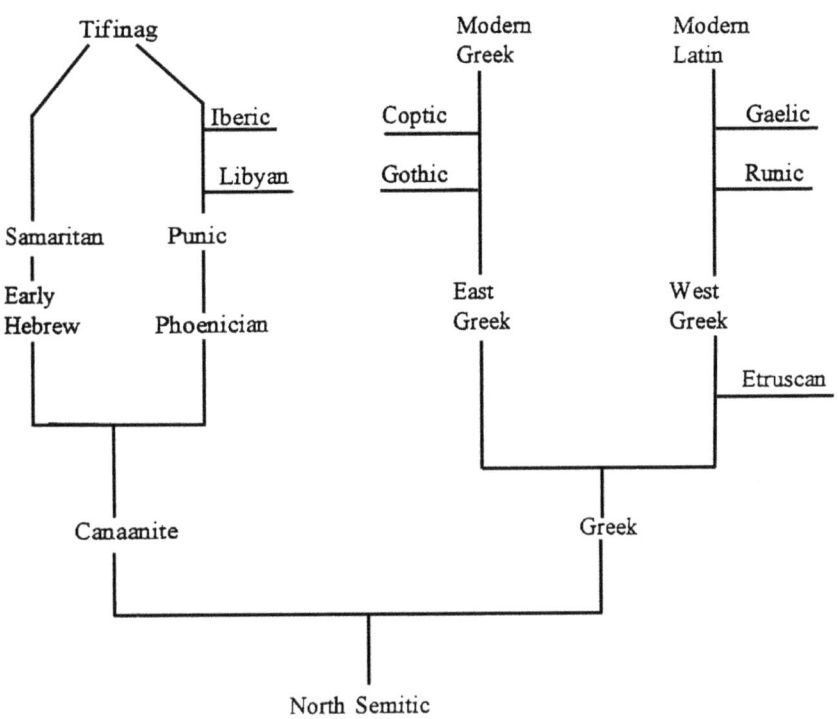

## Invention of the Alphabet

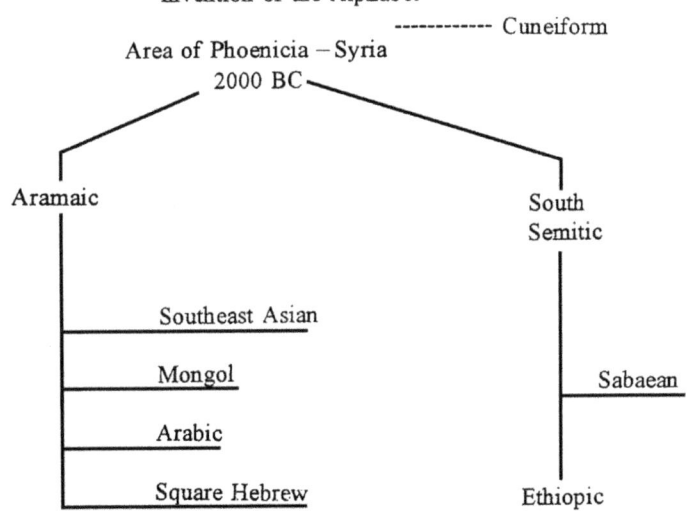

ination of reported ancient inscriptions, but to date their pleas have fallen on deaf ears. Perhaps a review of the evolution of ancient alphabets will permit the interested parties to appreciate the wealth of information that awaits them. The invention of the alphabet supposedly occurred somewhere in the Near East in the vicinity of Phoenicia just as the second millennium BCE dawned (see illustration). It may have occurred even earlier than 2000 BCE, for if history tells us anything, it is that man's conception of time is much too narrow. In almost every area of history and anthropology, the milestones that measure man's progress on this earth continue to be pushed back further and further into the dim recesses of time with each new discovery. For example, as recently as 1945, the history books stated that the first man to cross over the Bering Strait land bridge from Asia to America arrived in this country about 8,000 years ago. We now know that that date is in error — perhaps by 30,000 years or more.

The spread of the alphabet around the world was similar to the spread of civilization, and the spread of the megaliths. Within a few short years it was used by almost all civilized countries of the world. And, as usual, each country adapted the alphabet to their own mode of making characters and signs, to their own writing materials, and to their own language. Gradually, new alphabets developed from the nucleus of the old. The world's oldest known example of writing was discovered on a limestone tablet in the Mesopotamian city of Kish. It was a pre-alphabetic form of picture writing dating back to 3500 BCE. Egypt followed the early example of Sumer and adopted a form of picture writing called hieroglyphics, or sacred carvings, around 3000 BCE. The invention of alphabetic writing along the Levantine coast, some 1500 years later, resulted from the need to keep an accurate accounting of goods and materials in the world's first centers of civilization. This simplified method of written communication made writing accessible to many more people by reducing the number of individual characters from over 600 to less than 30. It is generally believed that almost every alphabet in the world, past and present, developed from this common source.

Initially, the alphabet contained only consonants, no vowels. And the direction of writing varied; the first row of letters went from right to left, the second row went from left to right, and so on. Sometime around 1000 BCE the North Semitic alphabet split into two groups, the Canaanite group and the Greek group. The Greek stem, which became the European branch of the alphabet, standardized the writing direction. Henceforth, writing always proceeded from left to right. Also, vowels were added to the alphabet. This alphabet spread across Europe like wildfire, being slightly modified by each succeeding culture. First the Etruscans adopted the alphabet around 900 BCE. Of course, they had to remodel it to fit their society. Next it was altered by the Scandinavians to produce the runic characters. Then it was changed by the Celtic people to provide the ogam letters needed for their wood engraving. According to scholars, the ogam alphabet was not developed until the fourth century CE; however, there is a reference to writing in the Irish Annals that indicates otherwise. Under the year 724 BCE, there is a reference to poets who chided and scolded their kings in "their rhymes and Writtings."[1]

The Canaanite branch of the North Semitic alphabet continued as before, the direction of the writing varying from right to left and back again, and the alphabet continuing to be vowel-less. The Canaanite branch was the nucleus of the Phoenician, the Punic, the Libyan, and the Iberic, the alphabets that are of interest to this study.

The next illustration compares several of the alphabets that grew out of their mother alphabet from the Levant. The Greek characters are part of the European branch of the alphabet, while the Phoenician and Hebrew letters belong to the Canaanite branch. A careful examination of these three alphabets reveals the marked similarity of letters that existed from one alphabet to another. This resemblance has caused considerable confusion in the attempted decipherment of ancient inscriptions, and has resulted in at least one inscription, the Grave Creek Tablet, being declared a forgery after a renowned philologist stated erroneously that the inscription consisted of characters from no less than six different alphabets. Later it will be shown that the Grave Creek Tablet is made up of a single alphabet: Iberic.

One of the problems that scholars have had in translating and authenticating ancient American inscriptions is the crudeness of many of the engravings. Scholars, of course, are used to reading ancient scripts that were written in the proper and official language of the time, by court historians, royal scribes, and official clerks. But on a ship making a dangerous transoceanic crossing 2,000 years ago, space was a precious commodity. Each man had to be capable of contributing to the operation of the vessel, and scribes were a luxury that the ship's captain could not afford. As a result of these facts of ancient life, many of the inscriptions were carved roughly in a rock by a semiliterate European mariner using poor grammar.

A second problem that scholars have with American inscriptions is the apparent hodgepodge of alphabets and languages that comprise many of the carvings. This incongruity is becoming more understandable to modern epigraphers, and was actually not an incongruity at all. It was a common occurrence, not only in ancient times, but throughout the

| | PHŒNICIAN FORMS. | EARLY GREEK FORMS. | EARLY HEBREW FORMS. | LATER HEBREW. |
|---|---|---|---|---|
| A | ✶ ✶ ⊦ | △ △ ◁ | ✶ ✶ ✕ | א |
| B | 9 9 9 | B ß | 9 9  y | ב |
| G | ⌐ 1 ┐ | 1 ⌐ ∧ | 1 ┐ | ג |
| D | △ ◠ 9 | ▷ △ ▷ | △ ◠ ⌐ | ד |
| H | ∃ ⋺ ⋺ | ⋲ ⋲ E | ⋲ ⋺ | ה |
| W | 7 7 7 | F C | ⌐ ⌐ ⌐ | ו |
| Z | Z ζ N | ∫ I Z | | ז |
| H | ⊟ ⊞ ⊟ | ⊟ ⊞ | ⊟ ◇ ⊡ | ח |
| T | ⊗ ⊘ ⊘ | ⊕ ⊗ ⊙ | | ט |
| Y | ⊓ ⊓ N | ⌇ ⌇ S | ∾ Z | י |
| K | ⌾ 9 У | Ӿ Ӿ K | У | כ |
| L | ⌐ L ⌐ | ⌐ ⌐ L | L ⌐ | ל |
| M | Ψ Ψ ɯ | ⌐ M M | Ɯ | מ |
| N | ⌐ ⌐ У | ⌐ N N | ⌐ У | נ |
| S | ⌐ ⌐ ⌇ | Ȝ | | ס |
| ( | O ⊙ ∪ | O ◇ ▢ | O ◇ ▽ | ע |
| P | ⌐ ⌐ ) | ⌐ Γ Γ | ⌐ | פ |
| S | ⌇ ⌇ ⌇ | | ⌇ ⌇ | צ |
| Q | Ꝑ Ꝑ Ꝑ | Ϙ ϙ | Ꝑ Ꝑ | ק |
| R | ⌐ 9 9 | ⌐ 9 P | 9 ⌐ | ר |
| SH–S | Ш Ш W | ⋀ ⋀ | W ω | ש |
| T | ✢ ✢ ✢ | T T | ✢ ✕ | ת |

Early forms of the Semitic alphabet (table from G. Rawlinson's *History of Phoenicia*).

medieval period as well, as shown by the Norwegian-Swedish mixture on the Kensington Stone. This supposed hodgepodge of scripts and grammar was the result of the international flavor of the ship's crew, men from all parts of the known world sharing a common adventure. The rock-carving Celtic mariner not only carved his message crudely and with poor grammar, but he probably wrote it in the Celtic language using the Iberic alphabet. Many of the American inscriptions that will be examined are in the Iberic alphabet. Iberia was the foremost melting pot of the ancient Western world. Over a period of 2,000 years, an amalgamation of races and cultures gravitated to the Iberian Peninsula, making it their home. These diverse peoples lived together, worked together, and went on long, expeditionary voyages together. Celts from the Danubian Plains worked alongside Phoenicians from Tyre, Egyptians from the banks of the Red Sea, and Libyans from the shores of North Africa. They all traded their goods with visiting Northmen from Sweden and Norway, and with Berbers from the coast of Morocco.

Numerous maritime expeditions were assembled at ports all along the Iberian Peninsula, from Tarshish to Cadiz. Crews were signed on with promises of sharing in the immense wealth that existed in countries just beyond the horizon. Most of the ships that sailed from the Iberian coast carried truly international crews. In addition to the aforementioned nationalities, the ships' companies could also include Nubians from the Upper Nile, as well as Greeks, Persians, and Jews. Ships departed from Iberian ports daily, bound for the far reaches of the known world. Whether that world included America is not yet known. But it is known that ancient ships were capable of making extended ocean crossings, and that their navigational techniques were adequate for guiding them to predetermined locations. In chapter 2, it was learned that there are many favorable sea routes to the Americas from both Europe and Africa. The adventure was possible. In fact, as will be seen in a later chapter, Dennis Stanford, chairman of the anthropology department of the Smithsonian Institution, has suggested that mariners from the Iberian Peninsula may have crossed the Atlantic Ocean to America as long ago as 18,000 BCE. And Betty Meggers, a research archaeologist at the Smithsonian Institution, was quoted as saying "Ancient man saw the ocean as a superhighway and not as a barrier."[2]

## The Brazilian Inscriptions

Brazil apparently contains as many ancient inscriptions as the United States, inscriptions numbering in the thousands. Unfortunately, most of these carvings lie hidden in deep caves within nearly impenetrable rain forests along the Amazon River, their messages perhaps lost forever. There was a time, over 100 years ago, when many of these inscriptions were meticulously copied into a weatherbeaten notebook by a dedicated scientist and explorer named Francisco Pinto. Pinto spent several years bravely and patiently hacking his way through the thick Amazon foliage, battling the hazards of the jungle, including insects, snakes, and hostile natives, to explore the numerous caves along the river basin. In the process of these explorations, he recorded over 250 inscriptions. He subsequently sent his notebook to the director of history and geography who, in the year 1872, authenticated the inscriptions as Phoenician. Almost 40 years later, in 1911, a German philologist was invited to Brazil to inspect the legends, and he too authenticated them. Here the story ends abruptly, however. Sometime during the past 70 years, the valuable notebook was lost or misplaced.

In 1880, eight years after Pinto's discoveries, a French scientist named Ernest Ronan retrieved other engravings from the Brazilian jungles. He reported one message as "Thirty of us reached this land in four ships after a dangerous journey of many weeks. We have spent the last 16 years on the mountain accumulating much gold, copper, and jewels." The message was signed by the leader of the group, a man named Eklton. Another Brazilian, Don Bernardo da Silva Ramos, was perhaps the most tragic figure to become involved with the Brazilian scientific community. Ramos accidentally came across an inscription carved into a high cliff near Rio de Janeiro in 1899. A local scholar[3] declared the writing to be Phoenician, and the message to read, "I, Etbaal, came to this land from Tyre. We are thirsty and tired. Baal save us."[4] Other Brazilian scholars identified Etbaal as a king of Tyre from 887 to 856 BCE. Eventually however, the scholars declared the marks were not man-made after all, but were the natural result of weathering. Ramos, enraged by their decision, disappeared into the treacherous jungles of the Amazon, determined to exonerate himself. He spent the next 20 years wandering through the underbrush of the Amazon basin during which time he photographed and recorded over 2,500 inscriptions. Joyfully, he published the results of his exhaustive research in 1939, hoping to gain the acceptance and recognition of the academic world at last. But such was not the case. His publication was ignored by the scientific community and he himself was looked upon as a pitiful eccentric. He died several years later, broken and disillusioned.

Perhaps the most famous of all Brazilian inscriptions is the notorious Paraiba inscription. The inscription, carved into a large stone, was unearthed on the ranch of Joachim Alves da Costa in the year 1872. A copy of the inscription was immediately sent to Dr. Ladislau Netto, director of the National Museum in Rio de Janeiro, for study. Dr. Netto, after many weeks of intensive research, declared the inscription to be Phoenician, with the following message: "Hiram, our king, sent us from Sidon in the 19th year of his reign (534 BCE). We sailed from the port of Ezion-geber with nine other ships. After two years at sea, the hand of God separated us from our brothers, and carried us to this island. There are only 15 of us left, 12 men and 3 women."[5] Other Brazilian scholars however, did not share Netto's opinion of the inscription, and they soon declared the legend to be spurious. Many years passed before a world-renowned scholar and philologist, Dr. Cyrus Gordon, was called upon to study the inscription in 1967. Dr. Gordon was a specialist in Near Eastern languages, both ancient and modern, and he spent more than 40 years of his life in the American university system. He studied the Paraiba inscription, eventually discovering a cryptogram within the inscribed message, proving to his own satisfaction that the inscription was authentic. Still, in spite of verification by someone of Cyrus Gordon's stature, the scientific community continues to ignore the Paraiba inscription.

## The American Evidence

The science of epigraphy has grown by leaps and bounds in America over the past 20 years. Many people have contributed to this resurgence, but two in particular deserve special credit for leading the assault. First and foremost is Barry Fell, whose book *America BC* shook the scientific community to its very foundations. *America BC* created a new awareness of this country's ancient beginnings, not only at the university level, but right down to the man on the street. Dr. Fell enjoyed a long, distinguished academic career at Harvard University before his retirement to devote his full time to his first love, epigraphy. Fell was a student of ancient languages for more than 40 years, after his introduction to Celtic language and literature at Edinburgh. During the 1980s he became a world recognized expert in the identification and decipherment of ancient alphabets, including ogam, Iberic, Libyan, and Phoenician.

If Barry Fell was the "inside" person in American epigraphy, then Gloria Farley is most certainly the "outside" person. Ms. Farley, a native of Oklahoma, has spent more than 40 years in the field, scouring the Mississippi River and its tributaries in search of traces of ancient explorers. Her many journeys along the banks of the Arkansas and Cimarron Rivers, and her dangerous ascents of the cliffs that embrace these rivers, have earned her the title of First Lady of Epigraphy. Gloria Farley has discovered, photographed, and recorded hundreds of inscriptions covering a span of 2,000 years of recorded history.

Wherever there are friendly coastlines or navigable waterways, there are inscriptions: messages of discovery, hope, despair, and suffering, left on rocks and cliff walls by intrepid mariners from beyond the sunrise. The following study will include inscriptions from across the entire continent, from New Mexico to West Virginia.

## *The Bat Creek Stone*

Cyrus Thomas, and his crew of excavators from the Smithsonian Institution's Department of Ethnology, worked extensively in Tennessee in the mid 1880s, conducting professional archaeological excavations on one ancient mound after another. One day in the summer of 1885, Thomas' crew chanced upon a cluster of three mounds at the confluence of Bat Creek and the Little Tennessee River, about two miles below Morgantown in Loudon County. Excavation commenced immediately on mound no. 3, a small, oval hill, measuring only 28 feet in diameter and 5 feet high. Thomas summarized the work in his report to John Wesley Powell:

> Some large sassafras trees were standing on it, and the owner, Mr. Tipton, stated that he had cut trees from it forty years ago, and that it had been covered by a cluster of trees and grapevines as long ago as the oldest settler in the locality could recollect. At the time the excavation was made, there was an old rotten stump yet on top, the roots of which ran down to the skeletons.... Nothing of interest was discovered until the bottom was reached, where nine skeletons were found lying on the original surface of the ground, surrounded by dark colored earth.... No relics were found with any but No. 1, immediately under the skull and jawbones of which were found two copper bracelets, an engraved stone, a small drilled fossil, a copper bead, a bone implement, and some small pieces of polished wood.... The engraved stone lay partially under the back part of the skull and was struck by the steel prod used in probing.... The engraved characters on it are beyond question letters of the Cherokee alphabet said to have been invented by George Guess (or Sequoyah), a half breed Cherokee about 1821.[6]

Sequoyah was fascinated by the written language, as were many Indians, who considered it to be a form of magic. Sequoyah, a proud man, felt that this magic should not be reserved for the white man alone. He decided to develop a unique Cherokee syllabary, something that would enhance the Indian's self image. The tribal chiefs thought he was crazy to think he could control the "talking leaves" as writing was called. For several years, Sequoyah isolated himself from society and concentrated all his efforts on producing an Indian alphabet. His home fell into disrepair, his crops died from lack of attention, and his wife and children worried that he had become deranged. But Sequoyah had a mission, and he devoted all his time to it. Finally, he produced an alphabet containing 86 characters, one character for each syllable in the Cherokee language. The year was 1821.

The Bat Creek Stone was displayed by the Smithsonian Institution in Washington, D.C., until 1964, when Henriette Mertz, a Chicago lawyer and author, discovered that the stone was actually being shown upside down. When placed in its correct position, the stone was discovered to contain Semitic characters. Cyrus Gordon, taking advantage of Mertz's astounding discovery, quickly identified the stone as being written in the Canaanite (or Hebrew) alphabet of the first century CE. The first five characters from the left translate to D W H Y L, which, when read from right to left says "Judaea" or perhaps "For the Judaeans," hard evidence that Tennessee had a Jewish community almost 2,000 years ago. The small mark to the right of the five characters is a word divider, establishing the fact that the five characters are a separate and complete word. The word divider is an important clue to establishing the authenticity of the stone because it was not known until well into the twentieth century. When the characters on this stone are compared with a Hebrew coin struck between 66 and 70 CE, during the first Jewish revolt against Rome, it is apparent that the characters reading "Judaea" on the stone strongly resemble the characters on the coin (see illustration).

J. Huston McCulloch of Ohio State University did a detailed study of the Bat Creek grave articles for the fall 1988 issue of *The Tennessee Anthropologist*. His study revealed that the brass bracelets could be of ancient Mediterranean manufacture. If they were, their high zinc content matched what was used during the period of 45 BCE to 200 CE and, more than likely, they were produced prior to 100 CE. More importantly, McCulloch, through the Institute for the Study of American Cultures, financed testing of the wood fragments found in the grave. The samples, prepared by the Smithsonian's Conservation Laboratory, gave a radiocarbon date from 32 CE to 769 CE, proving conclusively that the burial and its contents were not only precolonial but prior to 769 CE. McCulloch theorized that, since the stone appeared to have had one letter broken off, it might have been a family heirloom that was passed down from father to son over a period of decades or even centuries. It was finally buried with its owner sometime between 66 CE and 769 CE. The bracelets point toward a burial date between 66 CE and 200 CE.

## The Grave Creek Tablet

The Grave Creek Flats are a fertile plain located 12 miles south of Wheeling, West Virginia, in the present day town of Moundsville. The plain is adjoined by the Great Grave Creek on the north and the Little Grave Creek on the south, both of which flow into the Ohio River, a quarter of a mile away. As Schoolcraft noted, "Grave Creek Flats appears to

The Bat Creek Stone in its correct position.  Coin of Judaea 66–70 CE.

Comparison of Letters

| Bat Creek Stone | Judaea Coin, 66–70 CE | Semitic Alphabet |
|---|---|---|
| ⟨ | ⟨ | ⟨ |
| X | X | X |
| ⊒ | ⊒ | ⊒ |
| ∿ | ∿ | ∿ |
| ⌐ | ⌐ | ⌐ |
| 𐤔 | 𐤔, 𐤔 | 𐤔 or 𐤘 |
| P | P | P |

The Secret of the Bat Creek Stone Revealed (reproduced with permission of the Department of Anthropology, Smithsonian Institution).

have been the site of an ancient Indian town of importance. Seven mounds, or their remains, still existed upon these flats in 1844, although the plough and the spade had done much to obliterate the smaller ones. There were also traces of a large circular work, embracing a part of the public road."[7] The circular work, actually an octagonally shaped earthwork, was part of a large complex of geometrically shaped structures, avenues, and mounds that were obviously a major Adena ceremonial center. The mounds and earthworks were connected to each other by large, walled avenues; and one causeway, 20 feet wide, snaked its way from the largest burial mound, known as the Mammoth Mound, or Grave Creek Mound, to the banks of the Ohio River.

When the first settlers arrived at the Flats around 1770, the earthworks had long been deserted. Many of them were falling down, while others were concealed by a dense growth of brush and trees. Joseph Tomlinson, recognized as Moundsville's first settler, bought a nice piece of property on the Flats and settled down to a pioneer's life of hunting and farming. One day, shortly after building a cabin for his family, Tomlinson was tracking a wounded deer through a thicket when he suddenly found himself standing at the foot of an enormous artificial mound, some 70 feet high. The conical mound was 295 feet in diameter at the base, and its flat top measured 60 feet in diameter and was surrounded by a three-foot parapet. Word of this imposing structure, and rumors of buried treasure, spread through the countryside. Considerable pressure was brought to bear on Tomlinson to excavate the mound, but he steadfastly refused to allow the mound to be vandalized, considering it sacred.

Following his death almost 70 years later, his son Jesse decided it was time to solve the mystery of the burial mound once and for all. Before any digging actually began, the mound was cleared of its heavy growth of brush and trees. The trees gave some indication of the relative age of the mound, as reported by Schoolcraft. "The cortical layers, counted in the mature and heavy forest trees, which covered the summit of this structure, denoted the period of its completion to have been at, or soon after, the close of the twelfth century ... but there was no proof elicited to contradict the impression that it had not been commenced centuries earlier."[8] Subsequent study by the scientific community placed the age of the commencement of the mound at approximately 200 BCE.

The first shovel dug into the ancient soil on March 19, 1838, as Abelard Tomlinson, Jesse's nephew, supervised the long awaited excavation. A horizontal tunnel, ten feet high, was started on the north side of the mound, and proceeded into the interior. As Tomlinson's report described it, "At the distance of one hundred and eleven feet, ... we came to a vault, which had been excavated before the mound was commenced, eight feet by twelve feet, and seven in depth. Along each side and across the ends, upright timbers had been placed, which supported timbers thrown across the vault as a ceiling. These timbers were covered with loose unhewn stone, common to the neighborhood."[9] The burial chamber contained two skeletons, one male and one female. The only treasure that accompanied the remains were 650 shell beads and a stone atlatl, or spear thrower.

Following the location of this vault, a vertical prod located a second vault 36 feet above the first. The second vault was similar in design to the first, indicating it was constructed by the same people. The size of the tomb was somewhat larger, with a length of 18 feet, a width of 8 feet, and a depth of 8 feet. The single male skeleton found there was accompanied by a wealth of articles, including 1,700 ivory beads, 500 seashell beads, a stone gorget or ornamental collar, 5 copper bracelets, and a small inscribed oval stone, 2 inches long by 1.5 inches wide, and .75 inches thick. According to Schoolcraft's study,

> It was evident that the lowermost of the two vaults discovered, was of vastly the most ancient era. It appeared conclusively, that the structure was the result of comparatively trivial sepulchral labors, during an immense period; one age and tribe having added to another the results of its easily accomplished and slowly accumulating toils. It appeared that a mound-like, natural hillock, had been selected as the place of the first interment. By the original surface-line of the sod, disclosed by the lower gallery, it was further shown that the first interment was in a vault six feet below the sod line, over which the earth was heaped — probably by carrying it up in leather bags, from the surrounding plain. The personage interred — from his ornaments, and the attention bestowed in excavating a square vault, lined with timber and covered with stones — was a patriarch or ruler of rank.[10]

One interesting feature of the Grave Creek Mound that is not generally known, is that a covered passageway extended through the original mound connecting the outside with the lower tomb. This indicates that the burial chamber was kept accessible for some time after its construction. Perhaps it was built before the king died, similar to the practice in ancient Egypt. Or maybe the king was buried first, and the tomb was left open until his wife died and could be buried with him. In any case, it is an uncommon type of construction for an Adena burial mound. Modern excavations, designed to increase the size of the lower chamber for spectator viewing, uncovered ten more skeletons in the surrounding earth. This was a typical Adena burial practice. A central burial vault containing the remains of a person of high rank was encircled by numerous earth burials, perhaps servants or slaves.

## 11. Inscriptions

The most important feature of this mound however, was the discovery of the inscribed stone in the upper chamber (see illustration). The stone is the primary reason that the Grave Creek Mound has attained such worldwide renown. It contains three lines of engraved characters that appear to be an ancient alphabetic script. Needless to say, the Adena had no alphabet, and left no written records. The stone was discovered on June 16, 1838, by Abelard Tomlinson, his brother-in-law Thomas Biggs, and Dr. James Clemens. Colonel James E. Wharton, who was outside the mound, witnessed the events"

> Abelard Tomlinson came up and handed Dr. Clemens the inscribed stone ... there was some talk about it, but no doubt of its being a genuine find ... I examined it closely. It was a hard, dark gray sandstone, the letters mostly Phoenician, and I believe I was the only one present who had ever seen that alphabet; ... they were clear, deep, and carefully cut, the stone oval, the edges neatly beveled all round on both sides. There were in the cut creases, particles of sand that partially adhered to it, and on one side a blotch of sand of some size that adhered so as to require scraping to remove. The stone was of its natural color, not smooth or greasy feeling as it would have been if it had been handled; the edges of the letters were rounded off, not sharp as they would have been if recently cut. These facts forbid any doubt of its being genuine.[11]

Schoolcraft visited Grave Creek in 1838 and studied the stone in minute detail. His comments on the relic bear repeating: "It is in the Celtiberic character, but has not been deciphered.... With regard to the inscription, it may be said, if genuine, to be intrusive, and of foreign origin.... This curious relic appears to reveal, in the unknown past, evidences of European intrusion into the continent, of which no vestiges have, thus

"Tumulus in honor of Tadach. His wife caused this engraved stone to be inscribed" (courtesy the Delf Norona Museum).

far, been discovered. Copies of the inscription have been transmitted to London, Paris, Copenhagen, and Lisbon. Mr. Rafn, with considerable confidence, pronounces it to be Celtiberic; but no interpretation has, however, been attempted."[12]

For a period of ten years after the opening of the mound, the stone was studied by interested scholars as an authentic artifact from an Adena burial. Samuel G. Morton, unfortunately, laid the groundwork for the debacle that followed, beginning in the late 1840s and early '50s. Morton published a book called *Crania Americana*, in which he dealt with the characteristics of the human skull. In particular, he compared the skulls of the American Indian with the skulls of the mysterious Mound Builders. Morton was not interested in the Grave Creek Tablet, or with any inscribed stone for that matter, since it had no direct relationship to his work. As a result, he did not include the discovery of the tablet in his book. Within a couple of years, E.G. Squier, American archaeologist and author, made a formal declaration that the Grave Creek Tablet must be a fraud since Morton did not consider it worthy of mention. Squier himself had never laid eyes on the stone, let alone examined it. Other prominent archaeologists soon followed Squier's lead in denouncing the inscribed tablet. Finally, in 1872, even Colonel Charles Whittlesey, one of the leaders in the scientific community, jumped on the bandwagon and declared that the Grave Creek Tablet was not a bona fide ancient artifact at all, but a modern fraud. Whittlesey also discounted the stone based on the results of Schoolcraft's study. As MacLean reported, "Colonel Whittlesey quotes Mr. Schoolcraft as having made the following analysis of the twenty two separate characters of this stone: 'Four Greek; four Etruscan; five North Runic; six ancient Gaelic; seven Old Erse; ten Phoenician; sixteen Old British.'"[13]

Cyrus Thomas put the last nail in the Grave Creek coffin with his remarks to Powell at the Smithsonian Institution:

> Another objection to the Indian origin of these ancient monuments is based upon certain inscribed tablets bearing supposed letters or hieroglyphs, which are claimed to have been found in mounds. For example, the "tablet of the Grave Creek Mound," over which Schoolcraft exercised all his linguistic knowledge, and after corresponding with Prof. Page of Copenhagen, and M. Jonnard of Paris, arrived at the conclusion that, though mainly Celtiberic, the twenty-two alphabetic characters include four corresponding with ancient Greek letters, four with Etruscan, five with old northern runes, six with ancient Gaelic, seven with old Erse, ten with Phoenician, fourteen with Anglo-Saxon, and sixteen with Celtiberic. Prof. Jonnard, after a laborious investigation, pronounced the inscription Libyan, and Mr. W.B. Hodgson, Numidian. The folly of relying on such relics, as this Grave Creek Tablet, as evidence of a written language, is apparent from the above conclusions.

That Schoolcraft and the other savants mentioned could have believed the inscription to be alphabetic, and a genuine mound builder's relic, and yet made up of several alphabets, would be inconceivable but for the undeniable evidence. This simple fact ought to be sufficient to cast it aside as unworthy of consideration.[14]

It is inconceivable that supposedly great minds can be guilty of such spurious thinking, but such a condition is a matter of record. Unfortunately, when such spurious thinking does occur, it can have negative ramifications for decades, even centuries. The facts relating to the discovery should set the record straight as far as the authenticity of this stone is concerned:

- Human testimony by reliable witnesses present during the excavation of the mound confirmed the inscribed tablet to be an authentic artifact of the burial.
- In 1838, almost nothing was known of the various ancient Semitic alphabets. Today we know that many similarities exist from one alphabet to another. We also know that the Grave Creek Tablet is composed of only one alphabet, Iberic, a fact that was not known in 1838.
- Morton's failure to include the discovery in his book is irrelevant.
- MacLean brought to light one more fact that was ignored by the scholars: "Schoolcraft tells us that in one of the minor mounds at Grave Creek, there was found a curious device; also, a circular stone without inscription but identical in material with the inscription stone."[15]

MacLean did a thorough analysis of the entire problem of the Grave Creek Tablet and put the validity of the discovery in perspective. "I have carefully gone over the whole of this evidence, both pro and con, and have no hesitancy in declaring that if the authenticity of the 'Grave Creek Tablet' has not been established, then no reliance can be placed upon human testimony."[16] The evidence to date supports the authenticity of the tablet. In the late 1970s, Barry Fell confirmed the alphabet as being Iberic, and offered the first translation of the inscription. Donal Buchanan subsequently modified the translation slightly as reported in the Early Sites Research Society Bulletin.

> Tumulus in honor of Tadach
> His wife caused this engraved
> tile to be inscribed.[17]

Three other identical tablets have been found in Tennessee and West Virginia, indicating the Grave Creek Tablet may have been a generalized funerary offering rather than a specific burial stone for a particular individual.

## The Braxton Tablet, the Ohio County Stone, and the Morristown Tablet

The Braxton Tablet was discovered in or near Triplett Creek in Braxton County, West Virginia, in the year 1931. The finder, Mr. Ord Blaine Wilson, didn't realize the significance of the 4⅜-inch stone when he first saw it, but he did find it interesting enough to keep. For ten years, the Braxton Tablet served as a handy decorative stone in Mr. Wilson's office. If he needed a doorstop, it was a doorstop. If he needed a paperweight, it suddenly turned into a paperweight. Eventually, the stone came to the attention of the director of archives and history for the State of West Virginia who, realizing the potential importance of the stone, convinced Mr. Wilson to donate it to the State Museum in Charleston, where it now resides.

The Ohio County Stone was discovered in West Virginia in January 1956 by Robert Dunnell. Details of the discovery, beyond this, are unknown. The Moundsville *Daily Echo* carried an article on the find on July 17, 1956, along with an illustration of the tablet. Donal Buchanan recognized the inscription as being Iberic, and also realized it was similar to the Grave Creek Stone. The translation submitted by Buchanan verifies the fact that the Ohio County Stone was also a memorial tablet.

One other similar engraved tablet has come to light in recent years: the Morristown Tablet. This tablet was reported in the ESRS *Bulletin* by Donal Buchanan:

> The author knows little of the provenance of this artifact beyond the fact that it was presumably discovered in or near Morristown, Tennessee, perhaps on the banks of the Holston River where it has widened due to the construction of the Cherokee Dam. There is a Cherokee reservation in the vicinity. The tablet was brought to the attention of the Early Sites Research Society by Dr. Paul Cheesman of Brigham Young University.... On first seeing the Morristown Tablet, one is immediately struck by its similarity to the Grave Creek Tablet.... The Morristown Tablet is oval shaped and measures approximately two and three-quarters inches in length by about one and seven-eighths inches in width. Its thickness could not be judged from the photo, but it appears to be thin and flat. The type of stone is unknown to the author. It seems to have a gray, slate-like appearance. The symbols may have been scratched in with a thin metal tool — perhaps the point of a knife. While some symbols are well formed, a number of them are rather sloppily carved. The Grave Creek Stone, as described by Henry Schoolcraft in 1845, was a "compact, hard piece of dark or neutral sandstone, of an elliptical form, but not made with geometrical accuracy. It measures one inch and three fourths in length, by one inch and a half in breadth. Its thickness is two-tenths of an inch. Its hardness is sufficient to resist the scratch of a knife."[18]

Buchanan compared the inscription on the Morristown Tablet with that on the Grave Creek Stone, and found them to be essentially identical, and to have the same translation. Buchanan's study of the Morristown Tablet led to the conclusion that it is an authentic and original engraved stone. And Donal left us with one last thought for reflection: "The finding of the Morristown Tablet in close proximity to a Cherokee reservation, plus the fact that several (but not all) of the symbols are either exact duplicates or close approximations of known characters of the Cherokee alphabet, suggests that perhaps these inscriptions (as well as the Ohio County inscription formerly published by the author), should be re-examined. It is possible that we are dealing with a variant—and early—form of the Cherokee alphabet."[19]

The contribution of the American Indian to this complicated puzzle has to be studied closely, but it is unlikely that these inscriptions, taken as a whole, are early variants of the Cherokee alphabet. The mounds, and at least one tablet, the Grave Creek Tablet, predate the documented invention of the Cherokee alphabet by at least 600 years—unless the Cherokee are descendants of early European visitors to this continent, and had knowledge of the Iberic alphabet from ancient times.

## *The Bourne Stone*

Chapter 4 presented an inscribed stone that was found on the western end of Cape Cod, Massachusetts. It was at first called the Aptuxcet Stone, and was originally thought to be of Viking origin, as were most ancient artifacts that were unearthed in New England between 1840 and 1960. The stone is now known as the Bourne Stone, and its origin goes back well beyond the Viking Age (see illustration). Bourne, Massachusetts, is located on the north side of the Cape Cod Canal. For many years, prior to the European colonization of America, Bourne was the home of the Wampanoag Indians, a member of the renowned Algonquian Confederation. The Wampanoag, under their great leader Massasoit, were a friendly people, primarily hunters and fishermen, who enjoyed the finer things in life like singing and dancing. They also thrilled to the challenge of athletic events and games of chance, such as soccer, wrestling, and dice.

The first English settlers arrived in the area in 1632 from the Plymouth Plantation. They were interested in establishing a trade route that would connect the Plymouth Plantation with the lucrative Dutch market in and around the settlement of New Amsterdam. The most straightforward route from Plymouth to New Amsterdam was to go by boat from Plymouth to the Scusset River on Cape Cod Bay, then to proceed up the Scusset River to a portage, and from there to the Manomet River, and on

The author examining the Bourne Stone.

to Buzzards Bay, where boats could be launched for the port of New Amsterdam. Realizing the advantages of trade with the Dutch, the English built the Aptuxcet Trading Post at the mouth of the Manomet River in 1627. Trade was brisk at Aptuxcet, not only with the Dutch and English but also with the Indians, who participated in the challenging world of barter.

The trading post attracted other English settlers from Plymouth, and soon a thriving village covered the landscape. With the village came the inevitable missionaries determined to save the souls of the heathen Indians. Richard Bourne and Thomas Tupper organized a church in 1637 and converted over 900 Indians to Christianity. In 1675 the Indians were granted permission to build their own church, a wooden structure that was completed in 1684. About 40 years later, the church was moved to Mashpee, where it still stands, open to the public. During the relocation, the stone that had been used as the doorstep was turned over, and inscribed characters were discovered on the underside. People considered these carvings to be a curiosity, a conversation piece, but nothing of great importance. Over the next 200 years, the stone served as a doorstep at the house of an Indian named Andrew Jackson. In 1930, the Jackson house was sold, and the inscribed stone was given to the Bourne Historical Society, which has displayed it at the Aptuxcet Trading Post ever since.

The authenticity of the Bourne Stone is not in question. Its history is easily traceable back to the early colonial days more than 300 years ago, when it resided in Indian territory. The granite stone, which is native to the area, weighs approximately 300 pounds and measures over five feet long, almost two feet high, and seven inches thick. Barry Fell was able to identify the characters as Iberic, and provided the following translation to the Early Sites Research Society:

> A proclamation of annexation.
> Do not deface.
> By this Hanno takes possession.[20]

## Mill River Stone

> Cease trespassing.
> Anyone treading (here) is desecrating
> a burial place.[21]

So said the warning carved deeply into the rock standing next to the Mill River in South Weymouth, Massachusetts. The noteworthy thing about this warning is that it was written in an ancient Iberic alphabet dating back to around 400 BCE. Whittall was informed about this stone by Gertrude Johnson in 1975, and subsequently located the stone lying in a marshy area not far from the Atlantic Ocean:

> The inscribed stone is located on a knoll that projects out into the surrounding marshy area just east of where the Mill River flows from a large pond down to the sea. It is probable that the area around the knoll was once covered by water. The stone was set originally on two large stones nearby and anyone traveling on foot to the point or by water would have noticed the inscription. The markings are carved into a slab of granite 6 feet long by 18 inches wide by 9 inches deep. Some of the markings are quite deep; whereas others are eroded to the point of being barely visible. It looked like someone had recently "freshened" the first four characters in the first line. The rock had been quarried from a larger boulder nearby, and though there were no signs of drill marks, the stone had been neatly dressed. During the summer, I took Dr. Barry Fell, President of the Epigraphic Society, and Peter Farfall, to examine the inscription. Dr. Fell agreed with Gertrude's opinion that the inscription was Iberian, and he felt that with some study, he could give a translation. We then photographed the inscription and made latex peels to be studied later."[22]

There is a sad footnote to this particular artifact. Whittall announced in the summer of 1984 that someone had taken a hammer to the stone, vandalizing it beyond recognition. All that remains now is Jim's fine photograph, Barry Fell's translation, and the haunting curiosity created by the stone's cryptic message.

## The Yarmouth Stone

The Yarmouth Stone was first discussed in chapter 4. The stone was originally considered to be of Viking origin, although no satisfactory translation was ever made. As noted, the strange engraved rock was first discovered in a cove at the head of Yarmouth harbor, Nova Scotia, in 1812, by Dr. Richard Fletcher. After spending many years in Dr. Fletcher's front yard, the stone found its way to the Yarmouth County Historical Society, then to the Yarmouth County Museum, where it is on display. Scientists from all over the world have studied the stubby, dark gray, 400-pound rock. They generally agree that the stone is authentic, although there is great disagreement over the alphabet and the translation. Eric J. Ruff, curator of the Yarmouth County Museum, recounted the many theories regarding the stone:

> The brochure gives two translations from the Norse, however there are many other translations and theories. Among these is the belief by Yarmouthians that the stone was left by Viking explorers. Our local tourist bureau also believes in this theory and this can be seen by the presence of Leif Erikson Park and Leif Erikson Drive (road to Cape Forchu). Other translations include those from the Japanese, Mycenean, Indian, tree roots, natural erosion, and it is also believed that the inscription was made by the man who found the stone in 1812, Dr. Fletcher. The Scandinavians do not believe the stone to be of Viking origin. Probably the best modern translation comes from Dr. Barry Fell, of Harvard University, author of America B.C., who claims that it is Basque, dates from the 500–150 BCE period, and translates as "The Basque people have subdued this land." He has translated it from the North Iberian alphabet which is a derivative of the Phoenician. The Basque theory seems to be the most plausible one in my view. I can understand how he comes to this translation whereas I cannot understand the Norse translations at all. Another interesting point is that there once existed, in the same area as where the Yarmouth Stone was found, a stone similar to the Yarmouth Stone and has since become lost.[23]

## The Sherbrooke Stones

The first record of the Sherbrooke Stones is contained in a letter from Mr. E.P. McCabe of Ottowa, Canada, to the Reverend J.A. Laporte of East Sherbrooke, dated December 26, 1910. The stones were supposedly found by a farmer in Bromptonville, Quebec, in the early 1700s. This date may be incorrect, the result of a misinterpretation of Mr. McCabe's letter by a recent investigator. But the Sherbrooke Stones were known of at least as far back as 1910, and today they reside in a brightly lit display case in the Museum of the Seminary of Sherbrooke in Quebec, Canada. Information on the display case indicates the stones were discovered in a field near the St. François River by M. Ludger Soucy. M. Soucy's farm was in Bromptonville, five miles north of Sherbrooke. That is all that is known about the early history of these stones. The stones are made of limestone, actually a single limestone rock that was split in half to produce two flat faced stones. Each stone measures about 3 feet long, 1½ feet high, and weighs approximately 400 pounds. There are two rows of characters inscribed on each stone, with some of the characters considerably weathered, indicating their origin may, in fact, be much further back in time than 1910 CE.

As with most of the inscribed stones, there is considerable disagreement over their authenticity. Barry Fell believes the inscription to be an authentic message in the Libyan language, dating to 500 BCE. He provided the following translation: "Thus far, our expedition traveled in the service of Lord Hiram, to conquer land. This is the record of Hanta, who attained the Great River. And these words cut in stone."[24] The Great River could refer to the St. Lawrence River, which is nearby, and into which the St. François River flows. The St. François River is navigable to the area around Bromptonville, making the discovery site plausible. The discovery site of the stones and the translation of the characters on the stones complement each other, strengthening the argument for the authenticity of the stones.

## Gloria Farley's Discoveries

Gloria Farley's career reads like an Indiana Jones adventure story. Her extraordinary book *In Plain Sight*, which was published in 1994, outlines the discovery of several hundred petroglyphs and inscriptions by the intrepid scientist over a period of more than 40 years. It is a book that belongs on the bookshelf of everyone interested in the history of pre–Columbian America. The two inscriptions she provided for this study are both bilingual messages, and both were carved into cliff walls in the Oklahoma Territory. The first inscription, dated to 500 BCE, was cut into a rock on Turkey Mountain, near Tulsa. The inscription is in two languages. The upper segment of the inscription is in the ogam alphabet, and the letters, G — W — N, represent the name of the Celtic explorer, a man named White, or Fair Haired. As Gloria Farley noted, "I knew the minute I saw this inscription on a cliffside by the Arkansas River that it was bilingual of ogam and Iberic, but of course did not know what it said. Dr. Fell translated it.... I also recognized that the Ras inscription was in Numidian (Libyan) and Iberic, when I first saw it in 1975. It was in a cave in southeastern Colorado"[25] (see illustration). The Libyan inscription was identified as the name of Chief Ras by Barry Fell. The name Ras is defined as "watchful" or "wakeful." The

**Bilingual "Ras Inscription" discovered by Gloria Farley (courtesy Gloria Farley).**

North Iberian counterpart has a similar definition. It means "early awake." Chief Ras apparently carved his name in these rugged cliffs along the Cimarron River about 500 BCE.

## Monhegan Inscription

Monhegan Island lies about ten miles off the coast of Maine near the Kennebec River. Monhegan Island was familiar to European mariners at least as far back as 1605, as noted by Whittall:

> During the 17th century Monhegan was a very important fishing station with vessels from Europe crowding the harbor. Historical records indicate that shipping fish to the Spanish coast was one of the major trades. Also, passengers bound for England from Boston would take a coastal packet up to Monhegan where they could take passage to England on a returning vessel. In the 18th century, commerce between Monhegan and Europe died out and the island's importance came to a standstill. In 1855 while roaming about the island of Manana, Dr. Augustus E. Hamlin noticed some markings on an outcrop of ledge which he felt certain was an inscription.... Dr. Hamlin exhibited a cast of the inscription at the Albany meeting of the American Association for the Advancement of Science in 1856, suggesting

it was the work of "some illiterate Scandinavian, whose knowledge of the runic form was imperfect."

During the summer of 1975, with William Nisbet, we traveled out to Monhegan and Manana Islands to examine the inscribed ledge in detail. At that time we made a latex cast of the markings and photographed the inscription as it appears today.... I gave the latex peel to Dr. Barry Fell, President of the Epigraphic Society to cast and study. His research on the inscription and in ancient text from Europe brought to light a new and interesting translation. Dr. Fell, researching other inscriptions in America, had been working with ogam script and all its 71 known variations when he noticed the similarities between the markings on the Manana cast and an ogam script known as Annso (Book of Ballymote, #3) which had been recorded in the 14th century. Working with this script, he came up with the following translation — "Long ships from Phoenicia: Cargo-lots landing-quay."

From previous work by Dr. Fell ... we now know that ogam was used by the Celts in the Iberian Peninsula at a time when they would have had contact with the Phoenicians. This message implies that both Punic seafarers and Celtic explorers had been at Monhegan. From research work we would suggest a time frame of about 400 BCE. Why a message of that nature? The Phoenicians, beyond their well known ability as navigators, were also the merchants of the world in 400 BCE. They dealt in any commodity that would return a profit. As in the 17th century CE, I think that Monhegan was used as a fishing station for export back to the Iberian markets. Ancient Phoenician fishing stations were known on the Iberian Peninsula from Cadiz up the Atlantic coast to Figueira de Foz, an area where extensive salt works were developed by the Phoenicians. As fishing was depleted along the Iberian coast, fishermen looked to new areas. It seems that fishing off the New England coast might have taken place as early as 2000 BCE.... In this case, the fishermen were probably Iberian-Celts who left their cargo for the Phoenician traders at Monhegan. It is possible that they also included furs, which were in high demand in Europe, at the cargo platform. The message near a high point on Manana would be spotted by mariners visiting the island and they would know that they had a trade contact.[26]

## The Davenport Tablets

Three of the most controversial inscribed stones yet discovered in the United States are the infamous Davenport Tablets. The stones, two shale and one limestone, are carefully hidden away in the basement of the Putnam Museum in Davenport, Iowa. The Putnam Museum defends the secrecy surrounding these tablets with the following explanation: "It has been the policy of the Putnam Museum not to circulate photographs of the suspect pipes and tablets. These pieces are not on exhibit and this precludes visitors expecting to see them here. The museum does not take a stand on their authenticity, preferring instead that professional archaeologists discuss the matter."[27]

The history of the Davenport Tablets is interesting. They were found in a group of mounds along the Mississippi River, one mile south of Davenport. About a dozen mounds were excavated in this area between 1874 and 1880, and many interesting artifacts were unearthed during the project. In addition to the tablets, the relics included two stone pipes showing the figure of an elephant, an animal that supposedly had been extinct in that area for thousands of years before the construction of the mounds. The two shale tablets were discovered in mound number three. One tablet contained a picture on both sides: on one side a cremation scene, and on the other side a hunting scene. The second tablet, the smaller of the two, is called the calendar stone because it contains 12 zodiacal signs with three concentric circles.

Cyrus Thomas, in his report of 1894, immediately set out to debunk the discoveries of the tablets and the pipes. He could not comprehend the significance of either discovery. They were different than anything he expected to find, so he believed they must be frauds. Thomas, although making a serious effort to adhere to the philosophy of his superior, John Wesley Powell of the Smithsonian Institution's Bureau of Ethnology, frequently wavered during his attacks on the relics:

> But it is proper to remark that, notwithstanding these seeming doubts at the outset, Dr. Farquharson and all the other members of the society (with possibly one exception), after examination and discussion, settled down into the firm belief in the authenticity and genuineness of the tablets as veritable mound relics, and as entitled to acceptance on the part of archaeologists.... The characters on these tablets render it absolutely certain that they cannot be ascribed to any American tribe or people of ante–Columbian time of whose work and art we possess any knowledge. A few of the inscribed characters and several of the figures can be found in the inscriptions and rock carvings by Indians, but there are others that can not be attributed to them unless after long intercourse with European civilizations.... [The calendar stone] must therefore be post Columbian or have been obtained in some ancient time through contact with people of the eastern hemisphere, as it corresponds with no native American system of which we have any knowledge."[28]

Thomas' concerns centered around the confusing ancient alphabets inscribed on the stones, as well as the drawings of a supposedly extinct animal, the elephant. It is now known that both his concerns were invalid. Scientists of the nineteenth century did not understand ancient alphabets very well, and did not realize that occasionally identical letters could be found in a number of different alphabets. As for the long-trunked animal on the tablets and the pipes, recent archaeological discoveries revealing mastodon bones with spear heads imbedded in them have brought the elephant-like creature out of the world of prehistory and into the historic world.

Barry Fell has studied photographs of the tablets in great detail. He is convinced that the calendar stone is written in three languages:

- The top arc is Egyptian hieroglyphics
- The middle arc is Iberian-Punic
- The bottom arc is Libyan

It may be the American equivalent of the Rosetta Stone.

In view of the facts that have come to light in recent years regarding ancient alphabets and mastodons, it is time for the scientific world to reevaluate these artifacts. Their authenticity is still questionable, but they deserve a thorough review.

## Inscriptions from Colorado, Oklahoma, and New Mexico

It is fairly obvious now, after having reviewed numerous inscriptions around the country, that no one region has a monopoly on these ancient artifacts. If authentic, they are witness to an active exchange of information and technology between Old World cultures and New World cultures going back more than 2,500 years and continuing right up to the colonial period. The southwest was not excluded from this fraternization. With the Mississippi River, the Arkansas River, and the Cimarron River as the ancient equivalent of the modern superhighway, ancient mariners may have blanketed North America from coast to coast. Their messages come not only from Europe and the Near East. They also come from the Far East — Japan, China, and India.

An intrepid band of explorers have been walking the prairies and river banks in southeastern Colorado, New Mexico and Oklahoma for more than 20 years, and have uncovered literally hundreds of inscriptions (as well as other artifacts and evidence of ancient visits) during their long, tedious excursions. Ogam inscriptions, in particular, are prevalent throughout the area, primarily along a 50-mile-long north-south corridor between the Cimarron and Arkansas Rivers in Colorado. A representative sampling of this group of scientists would include Gloria Farley, Rollin Gillespie, Bill McGlone, Phil Leonard, and Jim Guthrie. Many other amateur archaeologists have also contributed to the discoveries. The sites, which are too numerous to discuss individually, include Hicklin Springs, Cliffside, Hanging Rock, Crack Cave, and Anubis Caves. The bulk of the petroglyphs are ogam carvings, indicating that a ceaseless maritime exchange took place between the American southwest and Celtic Europe for a period of at least 400 years. Ogam script, as well as other languages such as Libyan, Iberian, and Semitic, can be found on rock faces, in caves, and on loose stones. Some sites may contain star charts that can be used to date the site. Others appear to be calendar sites used by agricultural communities to identify the change of seasons, a critical determination needed for optimum crop production.

The Anubis caves in the Oklahoma panhandle are perhaps the most famous of the ancient sites in the southwest. These rock shelters, numbering six in total, were first discovered by Gloria Farley in 1978. Cave number two, the most important of the lot, contained numerous drawings, including Anubis, the ancient Egyptian jackal god, and Bel, the ancient Celtic sun god, as well as a number of other gods, animals and inscriptions. Barry Fell, without seeing the site, translated the Libyan script to read, "Enact at sunset the rites of Bel, assembling at that hour in worship." The translation was later verified by actual observation by Farley and others at the time of the equinox sunset. Epigraphers Donal and Ann Buchanan tentatively dated the site to the third or fourth century CE, based on the content of the petroglyph. McGlone, Leonard et al., on the other hand, obtained a cation-ratio (a scientific method for determining the age of rock varnish by measuring the ratio of water-soluble cations to the much less soluble titanium) date from the carving of around the time of Christ. Anubis cave number one is an important astronomical site. Petroglyphs in the cave may be ancient star charts, but that possibility is still being studied. Caves three and four contain ogam inscriptions relating to the sun, and provide additional equinox sightings. In general, it would appear that the visitors to the Anubis caves were mariners from the Iberian Peninsula, since that area was the melting pot of Western Europe at the beginning of the Common Era and even earlier. The people of the peninsula were knowledgeable in many scripts, including ogam, Libyan and Semitic.

David Deal, noted artist, researcher, linguist, and author, has been pursuing the evasive ancient visitors to our country since the early 1980s. He has investigated incursions into North America from all parts of the world, including Mongolia and Israel. One of Deal's most important contributions has been the study of Hidden Mountain, a 500-foot-high hill in central New Mexico, about 35 miles south of Albuquerque. Deal first reported the site in his book *Discovery of Ancient America*, in 1984. Bill McGlone and Phil Leonard also studied Hidden Mountain, with Leonard discovering a petroglyph of the New Mexico sky, carved into a rock. Deal, through some inventive detective work that would have made Sherlock Holmes jealous, subsequently showed the glyph to be a star chart, which he determined by computer analysis to be the record of a solar eclipse dating to 3 PM on September 15, 107 BCE. Deal studied all solar eclipses from 1100 BCE to 700 CE before zeroing in on 107 BCE date.

Deal eventually identified the entire site as an ancient Semitic camp, perhaps occupied for just a few months almost 2,000 years ago. It contains the remains of over 100 small dwellings, a large rectangular enclosure about 100 feet wide by 150 feet long, several inscriptions in ancient Hebrew, an equinox observation site, the star chart petroglyph, and the notorious Decalogue Stone. The large enclosure, built on the summit of the hill, is similar to Middle Eastern Bedouin enclosures that have been used for untold centuries to protect tent sites and animals. The smaller dwellings, measuring 3 by 7 feet, again of Middle Eastern design, were built to house only one or two people each.

The star chart was cut into a horizontal rock on the north side of the summit, while the equinox observation site is located on the east side. The Los Lunas Decalogue Stone is carved into a 100-ton basalt stone at the base of the hill, near the natural entrance to the site (see illustration). The stone, which is written in an ancient Hebrew script, has been known since the early nineteenth century, although it was not identified until 1948 when the head of the Harvard Semitic Museum declared it to be a copy of the Ten Commandments. Patina on the stone proved it was not of modern manufacture, and could be as old as 2,000 years. The script itself appears to date from between 500 BCE to 130 CE, according to Deal. Another Hebrew

The Los Lunas Decalogue Stone (courtesy David Deal).

inscription, carved into a rock on the summit overlooking the Decalogue Stone, reads "Yahweh is our mighty one."

## The Newark, Ohio, Inscribed Stones

Newark, Ohio, is famous in ancient American history as the site of a 2,000-year-old Hopewell ceremonial center. The impressive complex includes an octagonal earthen fort 40 acres in size, with 8 entrances, a 22-acre circular fort, another circular fort of about 26 acres, and a large square stone observatory. The forts all have earthen walls approximately 10 feet high. Wide avenues connect the various enclosures. In 1860, David Wyrick, a surveyor for Licking County, Ohio, unearthed a strange artifact from one of the mounds in the Newark complex. He found it 14 inches below the surface of the earth, in the middle of the ceremonial center. The 4½-inch triangular stone was called the Keystone because of its shape (see illustration). The inscriptions on the four sides of the stone were supplications to God, written in the ancient Square Hebrew alphabet, and dated to the time of construction of the mounds, around the first century CE.

According to J. Huston McCulloch, a professor at Ohio State University and a dedicated student of ancient Ohio history, the Hebrew inscriptions read:

- Qedosh Qedoshim, "Holy of Holies"
- Melek Eretz, "King of the Earth"
- Torath YHWH, "The Law of God"
- Devor YHWH, "The Word of God"[29]

A short five months later, Wyrick made another astounding discovery. Ten miles south of the sacred complex, he dug up a small sandstone box from an ancient Hopewell burial mound. The box contained a small tablet, about five inches long, depicting Moses, and inscribed on all sides with an abbreviated version of the Ten Commandments. Like the Keystone, the Decalogue Stone was written in the ancient Square Hebrew alphabet.

For many years, professional scientists accused Wyrick of perpetrating a hoax to support his alleged theory that the Mound Builder society descended from the Lost Tribes of Israel. Wyrick, however, never advocated such a theory, as far as is known. Bob Alrutz, a professor at Dennison University in Granville, Ohio, rescued the stones from the land of myths and returned them to the land of historical fact. His extensive research on the Newark artifacts during the 1970s uncovered the fact that

## 11. Inscriptions

*Top*: The Newark Decalogue Stone and its box. *Bottom*: The Keystone (reproduced with permission of J. Huston McCulloch).

another stone, similar to the suspect stones, was unearthed by David M. Johnson, a local Newark banker in 1867, in the same area where the Decalogue Stone was found. The Johnson-Bradner Stone, as it was called, was carved with the same alphabet as the other Newark stones. This independent discovery, made by a distinguished local citizen, supported the authenticity of the Wyrick stones.

## The West Virginia Petroglyphs

Petroglyphs were known to exist in West Virginia for many years, particularly in Wyoming, Boone, and Fayette Counties, but until 1982 they were classified as "Indian writing" by scientists. They created little interest among the local citizens, and were generally ignored by the scientific community. Then, in 1982, Robert L. Pyle, during the course of an archaeological survey, visited a sandstone rock shelter in Wyoming County. The shelter contained an extensive rock carving that had been categorized as fourteenth to sixteenth century aboriginal writing by state scientists. Pyle disagreed with that classification. He felt the writing resembled ancient runic script that was much older than 700 years. Feeling the need for more expert opinion, Pyle contacted writer and epigrapher Ida Jane Gallagher, and invited her to visit the site to study the petroglyph. Several months later, in November 1982, Gallagher, Pyle, Tony Shields, and Arnout Hyde, Jr., made their way through the woods, and climbed up to the rock ledge to view the strange carvings. Gallagher immediately recognized them as ogam consaine, an ancient Celtic script that was widely used in Western Europe more than a thousand years ago.

Photographs of the site were quickly mailed to Barry Fell for study. Fell did not disappoint. He confirmed Gallagher's identification of the script as ogam, which he dated to 500–800 CE. Fell also provided the following decipherment: "At the time of sunrise a ray grazes the notch on the left side on Christmas day. A Feast-day of the Church, the first season of the (Christian) year. The season of the Blessed Advent of the Savior. Lord Christ (Salvatoris Domini Christi). Behold, he is born of Mary, a woman."[30] In Fell's opinion, ancient Christian explorers from Western Europe visited West Virginia during the first millennia CE, carved their message of joy into the rock, and celebrated the winter solstice with a sunrise viewing. The event was subsequently confirmed on November 22, 1982, when Ida Jane Gallagher and her team watched with delight as the sun broke through a notch on the rock overhang and illuminated the entire panel.

Robert T. Meyer, professor of Celtic Studies at Catholic University in Washington, D.C., after viewing the inscription, declared it to be an authentic ogam message, dating to the sixth or seventh century CE. He compared the importance of the discovery to that of the Dead Sea Scrolls. In professor Meyer's opinion, Irish monks probably visited West Virginia about 1,500 years ago.

In addition to the Wyoming County adventure, Gallagher and Hyde, accompanied by Claudia Kingsbury, embarked on yet another one, following Jerry and Steve Stone to the Horse Creek Petroglyph in Boone County. After working their way through the mud and brush, the little group reached the rock shelter that housed the inscription. Gallagher recognized it as the same ogam script as that found in Wyoming County. Once again, Barry Fell undertook the decipherment of the script, while excitedly declaring it to be the longest ogam rock inscription in the world. The Horse Creek inscription turned out to be another joyous Christian message praising the birth of Jesus and celebrating Christmas. Fell also identified other Christian messages at the site to be written in Libyan (tifinagh) script. One message was in the Libyan tongue while another message was in the Algonquian language. Beard's Fork, in Fayette County, offered another similar ogam carving. It appeared to be contemporary with the Wyoming County and Boone County petroglyphs.

## *Michigan's Soper-Savage Stones*

Michigan's famous Soper-Savage collection of inscribed artifacts now numbers in the neighborhood of 25,000. The first such relic was unearthed by a farmer ploughing his field near the town of Crystal in 1874. Since that time thousands more of the mysterious items have been discovered by workers around the state. Businessman Dan E. Soper and the Reverend Dean Savage, a Roman Catholic priest from Detroit, began to acquire the artifacts early in the twentieth century. The collection eventually ended up at Notre Dame University, then was loaned to the Morman Church archives in Salt Lake City, where it now resides. The vast collection consists primarily of inscribed plates, but also includes a few other items such as pipes, bowls, and dishes. The most unique item in the collection is an assortment of movable stone type, similar to that invented by Johann Gutenberg in the fifteenth century. According to researcher David Allen Deal, the movable type precedes Gutenberg's invention by a thousand years.

Henriette Mertz first brought the artifacts to light in her book, *The Mystic Symbol: Mark of the Michigan Moundbuilders*. Later, David Deal picked up the gauntlet; he has identified many of the mysteries associated with the collection. Most of the information related here was derived from Deal's writings. According to him, the inscribed plates were made by Coptic

Egyptian Christians during the fourth century CE. In fact, the California researcher successfully deciphered one plate as being the record of a solar eclipse on July 27, 352 CE, as viewed from Rowland Township, Isabella County, Michigan. Deal feels the Coptic Christians fled Alexandria, Egypt, sometime after 325 CE, to escape persecution by Rome after the Council of Nicaea. The clay, copper, and stone plates are written in a Coptic cuneiform script that has still not been translated. They are primarily religious in nature, picturing scenes like the Creation, Noah's flood, and the life of Jesus.

David Deal feels strongly that the Soper-Savage artifacts are authentic. He bases his conclusion on a number of things: the enormous size of the collection (25,000-plus items), the wide area over which the artifacts have been discovered (Michigan, Ohio, Canada), and the religious content of the collection which was not known in the 1800s, including the use of the name, Yahuu (a code name for Yahweh), associated with the Coptic religion.

### The Burrows Cave Enigma

Russell Burrows supposedly discovered a cave filled with thousands of ancient artifacts in southern Illinois in 1982. Over the past 20 years, he has revealed almost 4,000 artifacts, many of which have found their way into private collections across the country. The major problem with authenticating the cave and its contents has been the reluctance on the part of Burrows to allow a qualified scientist to visit the cave. In some cases, he has apparently invited scientists to visit the site, then reneged on the promise at the last minute. As McGlone et al. noted, "The existence of Burrows Cave could be validated in a few hours by examination by someone other than Burrows.... Considering the ten years of veiling and maneuvering that have accompanied this affair, it will quite properly be viewed with suspicion by professional scholars until the presence of the cave and its contents has been established."[31]

## Summary

- More than 6,000 curious inscriptions have been discovered in North and South America. They appear to have been written in a variety of ancient languages that date back as far as 900 BCE.
- Over 3,000 inscriptions were recorded in Brazil alone, but none of them have been accepted by the Brazilian scientific community.
- Over 3,000 North American inscriptions have also been ignored by the American scientific community.

- One inscribed stone unearthed at Bat Creek, Tennessee, under the supervision of the Smithsonian Institution, contains alphabetic writing that has been identified as either ancient Hebrew or modern Cherokee.
- An inscribed stone discovered in 1838 at Grave Creek, West Virginia, may be written in the Iberic alphabet, and may be a funerary offering. Three other stones similar to the Grave Creek stone have been discovered in the last 46 years.
- Gloria Farley has recorded hundreds of inscriptions herself, from cliffs along the Mississippi River and its tributaries, as well as from arroyos in Colorado.
- Barry Fell has provided logical translations for many of the inscriptions, as well as providing probable dates of authorship.
- Other stones that may indicate an early European presence in the Americas include the Bourne Stone, the Mill River Stone, the Yarmouth Stone, the Wyoming Petroglyph, the Horse Creek Petroglyph, the Los Lunas Decalogue Stone, and the Newark Decalogue Stone.

## Conclusions

- There are too many apparently authentic ancient inscriptions carved into stones, cave walls, and cliffs, in the United States, to ignore. The stones appear to be in a variety of ancient scripts, including ogam, Hebrew, Phoenician, and Iberic.
- The Bat Creek Stone, excavated under the supervision of the Smithsonian Institution, points strongly to an ancient Jewish presence in Tennessee around 70 CE.
- The Grave Creek Stone, the Bourne Stone, and the Yarmouth Stone may be authentic ancient artifacts that document maritime activity from Europe to North America as long ago as 400 BCE.
- The scientific community needs to initiate a serious research program to study these inscriptions carefully and impartially, and to determine their authenticity.

# 12

# *Ancient Artifacts in North America*

## Conventional Thinking

All ancient artifacts found in North America are either frauds, modern intrusions, or lost souvenirs.

## Discussion

- Two teenage boys stumble upon an isolated cave in Alabama. In the cave, they find ancient Roman relics over 1,800 years old.
- A high school student in Pennsylvania discovers a large inscribed stone in the vicinity of an old stone chamber. The message on the stone identifies the site as an Iberian religious center of 300 BCE.
- An engineer in Virginia finds strange looking pieces of iron scattered around his property. A subsequent study uncovers numerous Roman artifacts including a 1,900-year-old bronze chalice.
- Roman coins are discovered on a beach in Massachusetts in 1977. Ancient Arabic coins are unearthed during road construction at another Massachusetts site in 1787. Hoards of ancient coins are found in other parts of the New World such as Venezuela and the Azores, some of the coins dating back to 300 BCE.

What does all this activity mean? Is it hard evidence that ancient transatlantic travelers once lived within the boundaries of what are now North and South America? Or are these stories all the result of lost souvenirs and frauds? One interesting tale of discovery and frustration was reported by Charles Boland in his book *They All Discovered America*. It concerned an engineer, one James V. Howe by name. It seems that Howe purchased a large tract of land in Virginia in 1943, in hopes of raising beef cattle during his retirement years. As Howe surveyed his 223-acre farmland he frequently noted strange pieces of worked iron lying on the surface of the ground. This was a great puzzle to him because he knew that the historic Indians of the area never worked in iron, yet here on his property was evidence that someone in precolonial times had a working knowledge of iron smelting. Howe carefully mapped the sections of his property where he found iron, then he developed an intricate plan of excavation to study the areas where the activity seemed particularly intense. The dig proved to be especially rewarding as many unusual artifacts were found buried several feet beneath the rich Virginia soil. These artifacts included a bronze chalice, a short sword, a longer curved sword, and assorted knives, chisels, and tools. Subsequent examination identified these items as of Roman manufacture, probably dating to the first century CE.

This was the discovery part of Mr. Howe's adventure. The frustration part followed. Howe first sent the bronze cup to the Smithsonian Institution for study and identification. He hoped to learn the origin of this fascinating item from the reigning professionals. The experts at the Smithsonian, however, pleaded ignorance as to the cup's origin. Howe, undeterred, mailed photographs of the cup, as well as of other artifacts and several inscribed stones, to various academic experts around the country. Again he came up empty. No one was able or willing to identify the material for him. Some of the sites he worked were located a considerable distance from his farm and not on his property and, as fate would have it, they stood in the way of a new federal dam project. Howe frantically lobbied for a more thorough excavation of these sites before the waters inundated them forever, but all went for naught. Not a single scientist showed any interest in pursuing a possible Roman-American connection. As a result, today the dam is a fact, and most of Howe's sites lie buried under many feet of water.

Barry Fell came across another tale of Roman visitations to ancient America, this one in Alabama. In 1942, Gene Andress and Doug Davis, two restless high school students, were out searching for a summer adventure near Gladsden, Alabama. The two boys had gained the friendship of an old Muskogee Indian chief named Tappawingow, who proceeded to enchant them with tales of ancient visitors. "Many moons ago," Tappawingow would say, "more than 1000 years by your calendar, great sailing ships moved up the Coosa River to trade with my ancestors. The visitors brought with them many brightly colored objects of cloth and stone, and they traded these to my people for wood, furs, and metal...."[1]

For many years these great floating houses visited our villages, their bulky sails billowing in the breeze. Then one year, they came no more." The chief told the boys of a cave that was hidden away in the thick underbrush, not far from the Coosa River. According to Indian tradition, the visitors in the big boats often camped in this cave during their trading excursions. Fascinated by these stories, Andress and Davis set out in search of the mysterious cave, dreams of ancient treasure dancing in their heads. Strangely enough, following the chief's directions, the two boys located the cave five miles south of Gladsden. They proceeded to spend the entire summer gleefully digging in and around the cave and, in the process, they collected several large boxes of assorted artifacts, mostly pottery items. Two of the pieces were subsequently identified as a perfume vial and an oil lamp, both originating in ancient Rome over 2,000 years ago.

Many other ancient artifacts have been uncovered accidentally by surprised and curious people while hunting, fishing, clearing land, planting crops, or just taking a stroll in the woods. One such discovery was a stone axe that was found by Samuel R. Gaskill of Pemberton, New Jersey, in 1859. Details of the find are scanty, and the present location of the axe is unknown, but fortunately an illustration of the relic was made for publication in 1861. The drawing showed an Indian-type stone axe; but what was curious about it was that ten apparently alphabetic characters were inscribed around the edge of the axe blade. These characters remained a mystery for over 100 years, until recently when they were deciphered as letters of the Tartessian alphabet. Tartessus was yet another of the important ancient trading centers of the Iberian Peninsula during the millenia before the birth of Christ.

Salvatore Trento reported two other discoveries of decided interest. The first discovery was made near Binghamton, New York, in 1973. A young boy uncovered an unusual metal urn in his front yard following a heavy rainstorm. The urn, apparently authentic, turned out to be of Phoenician-Egyptian origin of about 600 BCE. How it came to its later location near the confluence of the Susquehanna and Chenango Rivers is unknown. Other artifacts of possible Phoenician origin have also been discovered in the area. Perhaps an ancient Phoenician settlement once stood where the city of Binghamton is now located. Or perhaps it was just a souvenir that some tourist lugged back from Egypt and subsequently lost.

Yet another teenager was the center of attraction in the tiny community of Pleasant Mount, Pennsylvania, in 1974. It was he who discovered the inscribed stone near the old stone chamber. James Knapp was exploring the rocks along the Lackawaxen River one day, when he spotted a stone with funny markings on it. He carefully removed the 8 by 12 inch slab and took it home to study. The stone contained several lines of what looked like alphabetic characters, as well as a drawing of the sun apparently rising or setting over a mountain range. For several years the stone quietly decorated the living room floor of the Knapp home, until one day it came to the attention of a MARC (Middletown Archaeological Research Center) investigator. Trento and several associates journeyed to Pleasant Mount in 1977 to investigate the discovery. They searched the surrounding hills near the stone's find site and, surprisingly enough, they uncovered the ruins of an old stone chamber that resembled those found in Vermont. The location looked just like the drawing on the rock that showed the sun over a cleft in the hills. The final piece of the puzzle fell into place when the inscription was identified as Iberic, circa 300–200 BCE. As Trento reported it, "A rough reading of the script yields the following, 'On the Appointed day, the sun sets in the notch opposite the house of worship.'"[2] The chamber is a possible Celtic religious center, but that still needs to be authenticated. Further work, excavation, and scientific study is required before this anecdote can be removed from the realm of myth and added to the world of fact.

Whittall reported on the discovery of two anforetas, or liquid-storage jars, in the Bay of Castine, Maine, in the ESRS *Bulletin* of February 1977. According to the article,

> In July 1971 Norman Bakeman of Castine, Maine was scuba diving in search of old bottles or anything else of value which might have been thrown overboard from a ship. In the Bay of Castine at a depth of about 12 meters, he recovered two curious ceramic storage jars. They rested on the mud bottom about 15 meters apart, one partially buried, the other on the surface. After the recovery of the two jars he left the area. Mr. Bakeman puzzled over both the origin and use of the two jars as he had never seen anything like them before. Persons he showed the jars to couldn't shed any light on their origin. For awhile they were on display at the University of Maine; later, they were packed away and forgotten.[3]

Further research by Whittall led to another article in the ESRS *Bulletin*.

> In August 1977, Early Sites and the Scientific Exploration and Archaeology Society (SEAS) jointly conducted an underwater exploration of the harbor in Castine, Maine. This was the area where the two anforetas were discovered by Mr. Norman Bakeman. A team of 24 persons from various disciplines gathered at Castine and spent a week as a coordinated research group trying to locate any possible wreck. Numerous artifacts were recovered, but none of these dated before 1755. I think it is impossible to date the Castine anforeta storage jars on design alone. Laboratory research might shed some

light on the date of their firing. It is entirely possible they came off the mid–eighteenth century wreck located in the bay, but again their origin could be a lot older. In all probability, the origin of the design is very ancient and came from the coastal area of the southern Iberian Peninsula. It is possible they did exist in the Lusso-Roman period, but the only excavated evidence is from a Moorish site which would date between 700 and 1100 CE. The general opinion is the design originated with the Arab influx into Iberia.[4]

Still other artifacts of ancient vintage have been presented to the public over the years, but all are singular discoveries, unauthenticated and undocumented. These include:

- A Greek oil lamp of 600 BCE excavated at Amoskeag Falls, New Hampshire, in 1948.
- A Byzantine oil lamp, circa 750–800 CE, found in an Indian shell midden at Clinton Harbor, Connecticut, in 1952.
- A Roman spoon supposedly recovered from an ancient burial mound in Tennessee.
- A sword found during the excavation of a foundation for a new railway station in Concord, New Hampshire, in 1870. The sword appears to be ancient but its provenance is still questionable. Barry Fell identified it as a Celtic sword with an Iberic inscription on the blade. Subsequent research by Donal Buchanan indicated the sword may actually be of Roman origin. Buchanan believes the Iberic inscription is a presentation award in the Latin language. His identification and translation appear to be the most logical explanation at this time.
- Finally, an old oil lamp unearthed on Fish Creek, near Knik, Alaska, by Charles Ulanky on June 15, 1913. The lamp is oval shaped, 12.5 inches long, 11 inches wide, and 1.5 inches high. It weighs 21 pounds and contains a seated figure, obviously of Asian descent. As the Alaska Historical Museum in Juneau described the lamp,

> Perhaps the most important exhibit in the museum, from an archaeological standpoint, is the remarkable stone lamp unearthed on fish Creek.... So unique was the specimen when found, that it was first believed to be a hoax. Since then several more, so similar that they might have come from the hands of the same artisan, have been discovered. One came from the same locality on Fish Creek. Another was found in 1919 near Seward. Still another, however less typical, came from Shageluk River some four hundred miles distant. Lately, a very fine specimen was found at Zeto Point, Adak, in the outer Aleutians. These lamps have been the subject of much scholarly conjecture since the very beginning. Some have held them to be Asiatic, others

Indian, still others Eskimo or Aleut. Yet the authorities in each field have denied their relation to any of these cultures.... Considerable evidence supports the assumption that this lamp was originally the altar of a highly developed race of hunting maritime people. From the features of the figure we may reasonably assume that they were Asiatic in race and origin.[5]

The date of manufacture is unknown, but it was found in the same area as a Chinese coin that was tentatively dated to 700 CE by Mr. Ziang-Ling-Chang, consulate general of the Republic Of China in 1924.

As the literature shows, there have been numerous ancient artifacts discovered throughout the United States of America over the last 300 years, but the case for their establishing an ancient transatlantic presence in this country is very weak. In almost every instance, the discovery was singular, the details of the discovery were vague, and no scientists were involved in the subsequent investigation.

There is one area however, that presents more intriguing evidence of ancient maritime activity around the western ocean: coins. Ancient coins have been unearthed in hundreds of locations in North and South America, as well as on several islands in the western Atlantic Ocean. Most of these, to be sure, are also singular finds, but there have been some discoveries that have been made under such conditions as to warrant serious investigation.

The first discovery of interest to the Americas was made on the east coast of Iceland, where several Roman coins were recently unearthed. The coins, dated to the reign of Probus and other late third century CE Roman emperors, indicate that Iceland was visited by mariners from the European continent at least 600 years before the much-publicized Viking colonization. Rome was the foremost world power in 300 CE, but her interest in maritime exploration was minimal. She preferred to travel the well known sea routes between ports, and to trade her wares at well established international markets. One of the major sea powers at that time was, surprisingly enough, Celtic Ireland. Her rugged oceangoing vessels had been visiting ports along the western seaboard of Europe for well over 400 years, from Scandinavia to the Pillars of Heracles, during which time she established a far-flung trading network of her own. In addition to her mercantile enterprises, her military vessels were a thorn in the side of the Roman Eagle, constantly harassing the Roman shipping lanes between the continent and Roman Britain. She also carried out regular hit-and-run raids in England itself in order to obtain treasure as well as much needed slaves. One such raid brought back to Ireland a young man who would later become the patron saint of that island country. He is known to us as St. Patrick.

All things considered, it is unlikely that Roman ships would have ventured 600 miles northwest of Ireland through uncharted waters controlled by marauding bands of Celtic mariners. It is more likely that Celtic seamen discovered Iceland during one of their annual summer fishing expeditions into the North Atlantic, expeditions that had become routine for them over the centuries.

Pytheas, the Greek geographer, apparently knew of the existence of Iceland in 306 BCE. And Plutarch reported its location 300 years later. The Viking Sagas relate that Irish monks had settled Iceland by 795 CE. It now looks as if Irish mariners had been visiting that remote island as early as 270 CE, and perhaps even 600 years prior to that time! Scholars who claim the Irish could not have visited pre–Columbian America because they did not possess oceangoing vessels are obviously not well versed in ancient European history.

Another fascinating coin discovery was made in the Azore Islands in 1749. Following a violent storm in that year, a small container was washed up on the beach at Corvo, the westernmost island of the group. Upon investigation, the container was found to contain a mass of coins that had become stuck together over the centuries. The entire contents of the jar were shipped back to Lisbon, Portugal, for proper cleaning and for study. Much to the amazement of the Portuguese scientists, the nine coins in the mass were not of the expected medieval vintage at all. Instead, they were found to be ancient coins from the city of Carthage in North Africa, and were dated to 320–310 BCE. Here was evidence that the Phoenicians had ventured far out into the Atlantic Ocean over 2,000 years ago, and had set foot on a group of islands located over 900 miles to the west of Portugal. From the location of the discovery on Corvo, it would appear that a Phoenician ship had been wrecked on the coast of that island heading in an easterly direction — toward Europe, not away from it. The prevailing winds in that latitude are westerly, and make it the most popular sailing route from Chesapeake Bay to the European coast, even today. Phoenician mariners almost always sailed with the wind, not against it. They would never have ventured out into the unknown Atlantic Ocean from Portugal into the face of a stiff wind, and they certainly would not have done it over a distance of 900 miles. It looks as if Phoenician mariners had visited America around 300 BCE and were on their way home to Europe with their treasure, when an unexpected disaster struck and their ship was sent to the bottom off the western tip of the Azores.

Venezuela, South America, was the source of an ancient coin find toward the end of the nineteenth century. A crock of coins was discovered on a Venezuelan beach, probably exposed after a storm similar to the one that produced the Azores discovery. The Venezuelan hoard contained hundreds of Roman coins covering the first four centuries of the Christian era. At first glance, it would appear to be a Roman hoard, except that the crock also contained two eighth century Arab coins. Roman coins were still used as barter around the Mediterranean world in the eighth century, so it is not unusual to find such widely disparate coins in the same hoard. The location of this discovery is on the southern route from Europe to America, the same route that Columbus followed in 1492. It is possible that a Moorish ship from Spain or North Africa preceded Columbus along this sea route by 700 years.

Coin hoards are not relegated only to South America and the Atlantic islands. A large hoard of Arabic coins was dug up near Boston more than 200 years ago. In the year 1787, a project was initiated to construct a new road between Cambridge and Malden. During the excavation of the roadbed, workers came across a large jar full of hundreds of strange-looking metal objects. The unusual rectangular pieces were engraved with a series of curved lines and circular patterns. The designs didn't appear to be writing, and they certainly didn't pique the interest of any of the workers. As a result, the construction crew proceeded to distribute the objects to any passerby who might be interested in obtaining a souvenir. That would have been the end of the story except that one passerby happened to be a college professor, and he carefully made a drawing of one of the coins, and documented the discovery of the container. Many years later, the small metal tokens were identified as Arabic coins of the medieval period. The illustration made by the college professor matched coins that were issued in North Africa between 800 and 1100 CE. This could indicate an Arab presence in New England around 1100 CE, but not necessarily. The coins could have been carried here by Vikings during visits to our shores. Certainly Viking treasure hoards discovered in Scandinavia contained many artifacts from the Arab world, including countless numbers of coins. Arab coins were highly valued by the Vikings, for the purity of the metal content as well as the fact that their women coveted them as jewelry. The best guess at present would be that Vikings carried these Arabic coins to our shores around 1100 CE. At the very least, they point to a foreign presence in Massachusetts about that time. We know from chapter 4 that Vikings were exploring the New England shoreline during that period, as evidenced by the Viking coin discovered in an Indian shell midden in Brooklin, Maine. That Viking coin was dated to 1050 CE.

Whittall reported on a multiple coin find in Beverly, Massachusetts. The coins, four in all, were found in 1977 on a beach in that Boston suburb, with a metal detector. The coins represented four Roman Emperors who ruled during the period from 337 to 383 CE. Did a Roman ship visit Boston around 400 CE? And did it run aground in Boston Harbor during the visit? Further archaeological study will be required to answer those questions. Another Roman coin discovery was made in Boston Harbor in 1960, but it appears to be unconnected to the Beverly hoard. This particular coin belonged to Gordian III, who ruled Rome between 238 and 250 CE. It was discovered on Plum Island, but to date no additional evidence has been forthcoming regarding its provenance.

Many other ancient coins have turned up in the soil of North America over the years, hundreds in fact, and some of them present intriguing possibilities. Here is a sampling of these finds:

- A coin of Roman Britain, circa 250 to 300 CE, was found in Champaign, Illinois, in 1885, under four feet of undisturbed clay, during a road project.
- Several ancient Hebrew coins of the Bar Kochba period, 132 to 135 CE, have been discovered in Kentucky and Missouri. They support the theory that the Bat Creek Stone discovery points to a Jewish settlement in that area during the first or second century CE.
- A coin of Antoninus Pius (138–161 CE) was dug up in Fayetteville, Tennessee in 1819. It was five feet below the surface of the ground, and was covered by trees estimated to be 300–400 years old.
- A coin of Constantine The Great was found in an ancient burial mound in Texas. The mound was built more than 1,000 years ago.

## Summary

Hundreds of ancient artifacts, some as old as 2500 years, have been uncovered in the United States during the past 300 years. Ancient coins have also been found in great numbers in North and South America, and on the islands of the western Atlantic Ocean.

## Conclusions

- The ancient artifacts, for the most part, are unsubstantiated, and cannot be used as evidence of ancient transatlantic activity.
- Some ancient coin discoveries, on the other hand, present a strong case for the continuous European, Middle Eastern, and African exploration

of the western Atlantic Ocean and the American seaboard, over a period of 2,300 years. These discoveries, which have been accepted by the scientific community, include:

1. Nine Carthaginian coins of 300 BCE, discovered on the island of Corvo in the Azores.
2. A number of Roman coins of 300 CE discovered on the east coast of Iceland.
3. A Viking coin of 1050 CE unearthed from an Indian shell midden in Brooklin, Maine.

# 13

# Mound Builders and the American Indian: Where Do They Fit In?

## Conventional Thinking

There is no evidence of contact between the American aborigines and ancient transatlantic mariners. The so-called Mound Builders were actually ancestors of the American Indian. Their cultural development was an independent accomplishment, free of outside influences.

## Discussion

This chapter will address the questions of who the Indians were, where they came from, and how long they had been living in America before the coming of the white man. The historic American Indian constructed stone structures, such as cairns and menhirs, that remind scientists of ancient European building technology. Indians built numerous cairns in Northeast America, and many of them served the same purpose as cairns found in Celtic Ireland and Western Europe. Some cairns were formed over a human burials, either inhumated or incinerated, while others were set up as monuments to the memory of a political, religious, or military leader. Menhirs were also popular in ancient Europe and ancient America, and closely paralleled cairns as far as their intended usage was concerned — grave markers, directional markers, and boundary stones.

The American Indian even lived in houses that resembled those of his European neighbors. The Algonquian Indians of the northeast, for instance, resided in beehive huts similar to those used by the ancient Celts. Only the construction materials were different. Both types were oval shaped, both had a small opening on one side plus an overhead smoke vent, and both were approximately the same size, averaging about 12 feet in diameter and 7 or 8 feet high. The Celts generally built their huts with unmortared stone, tightly packed in a corbeled design, and they enclosed the top with a single capstone. The Indians, on the other hand, did not use stone as a primary building material in the northeast, perhaps because they were not a sedentary people. They relocated their villages from one season to the next as the hunting, fishing, and planting dictated. Their homes were built with materials that could be easily disassembled in one location and reassembled again quickly in another.

Some tribes, like the Iroquois, built longhouses similar to those of the Vikings (see illustration). Both types of longhouses had a single entrance on one side, windows set high in the walls along the long side of the building, and oval roofs to shed the rain and snow. The Indian villages, as shown in Scribner's depiction, were even arranged in an orderly fashion like European villages. Houses were built side by side along wide avenues. Gardens were arranged around the outskirts of the village and a town square was located at one end of the village. The similarity between the structures of the Indians and the structures of the Vikings is no longer coincidental. The discovery of L'Anse aux Meadows proved that social contact existed between the daring Scandinavians and the American aborigines in pre-Columbian times.

The connection between the ancient stone chambers of Northeast America and the Indian was noted in chapter 9. Indian tradition tells that their people made considerable use of the chambers, but they did not build them and they don't know who did. In addition to the archaeological evidence of transatlantic intrusion into ancient America, there is other evidence that is outside the scope of this book, evidence that needs to be investigated by anthropologists, ethnologists, and linguists. For instance, many Indian religions contain definite Christian themes, such as the Deluge and the Virgin Birth. Many social customs duplicate those of ancient Western Europe, and word roots shared between many Indian languages and those of ancient Egypt, Libya, and Iberia appear to be more than mere coincidence.

Two thousand years ago, before the historic period, the American Mound Builders established flourishing civilizations in the Eastern United States. The Mound Builder periods covered the following years.

| | |
|---|---|
| Adena | 1000 BCE–200 CE |
| Hopewell | 500 BCE–700 CE |
| Mississippian | 700 CE–1600 CE |

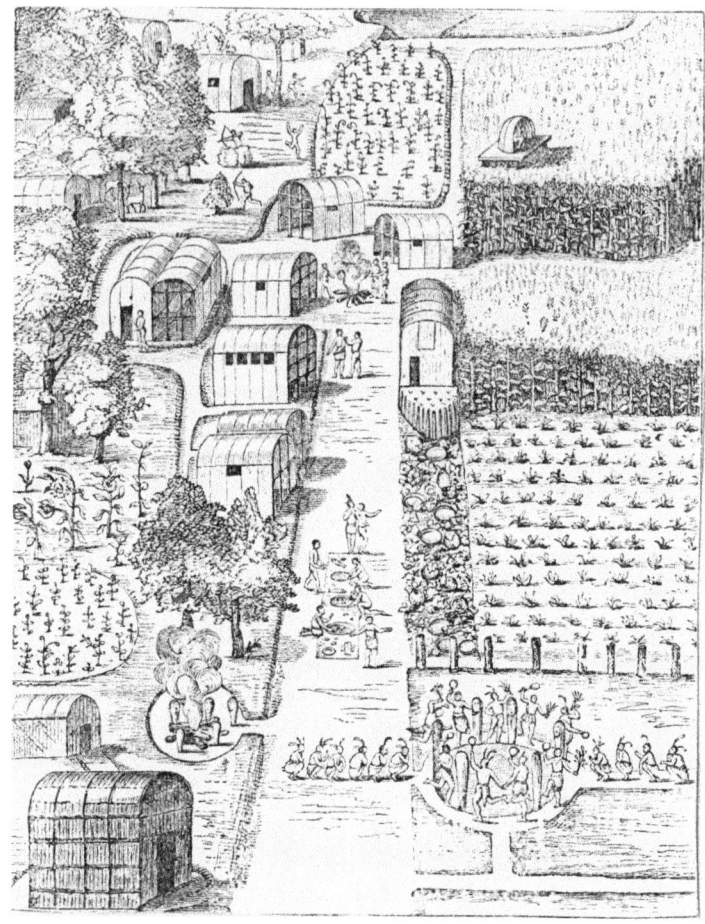

*Top*: A seventeenth century Iroquois village showing their famous long houses. *Bottom*: A depiction of Leif Erikson's booth, or longhouses, in Vinland. Illustrations from *Scribner's Popular History of the United States*.

This study will focus primarily of the Adena and Hopewell cultures. The Mississippian influence apparently originated in Mexico or further south, where it had developed over several millennia.

The first and most obvious similarity between the Mound Builders' culture and that of the ancient Europeans is in the design and construction of the mounds themselves. The United States contains more than 10,000 mounds, most of them constructed during the period 500 BCE to 500 CE. Thomas Jefferson noted that barrows "are to be found all over this country. These are of different sizes, some of them constructed of earth, and some of loose stones."[1] The Indians can be discounted immediately as builders of these monuments. According to Indian tradition itself, the identity of the Mound Builders is unknown. As Jones reported, "The Creeks did not claim that these tumuli were erected by them. They declared that they were here when their ancestors first possessed themselves of the region."[2] Jones also noted, "The Cherokees themselves are as ignorant as we are, by what people or for what purpose these artificial hills were raised … but they have a tradition common with the other nations of Indians, that they found them in much the same condition as they now appear, when their forefathers arrived from the west."[3] And so it went, from one Indian tribe to another. Not a single tribe claimed credit for constructing these monumental barrows. It is obvious, therefore, that the investigation must go back beyond the historic Indians to find the architects of the great mounds. The tumuli at Grave Creek and Miamisburg are strikingly similar to the tumuli located in Westmanland, Sweden, and dating to the Iron Age. The Grave Creek mound was built well back into the prehistoric period, about 200 BCE, based on radiocarbon dating results. This indicates that mound building was in vogue in Europe and America at precisely the same time, and for the same purpose. The interior of the tumuli were also remarkably alike. Some beehive tombs on both sides of the Atlantic were located in mounds, and contained skeletal remains.

Other burial chamber designs were also found in the mounds. In addition to the beehive chambers, some mounds contained souterrains, while other mounds covered rectangular burial chambers similar to the slab roofed stoneworks of New York and New England. Stone coffins or cists were also very popular throughout the Mound Builder country. The construction of these cists closely resemble the European cists (see illustration). The use of cists for burial purposes originated during the Bronze Age in Europe, and continued for several thousand years into the Iron Age. It is a fact that this type of cist was popular in both Europe and America around the time of Christ. Funeral offerings were placed in the tombs alongside the body to accompany the dead person into the next world.

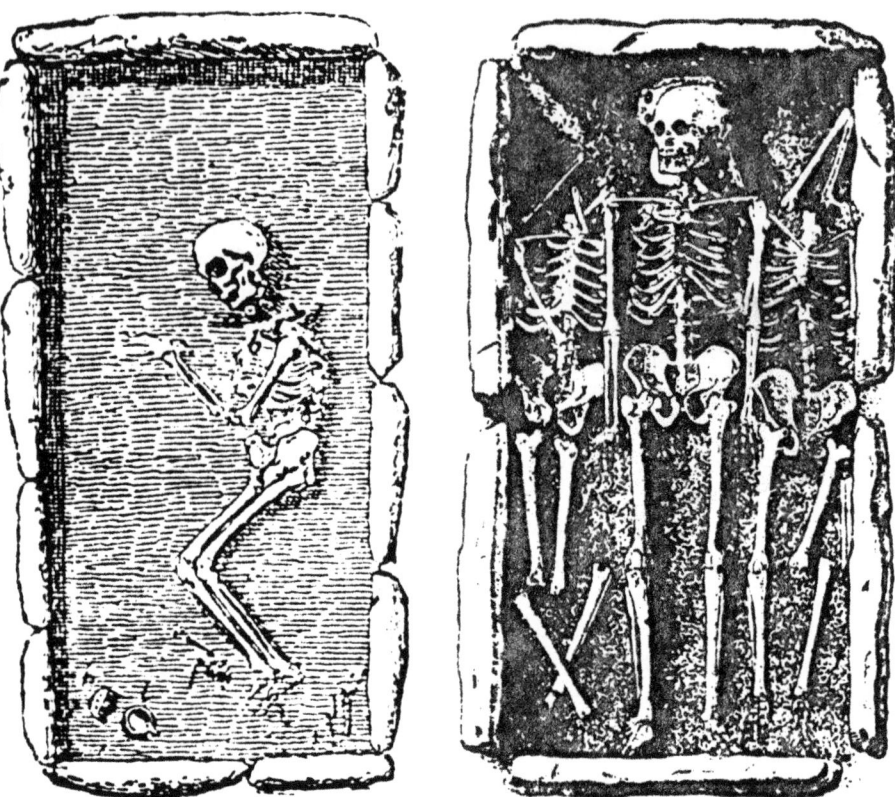

*Left*: An Iron Age cist chamber from Denmark (courtesy *The Viking Age*). *Right*: An ancient American cist found along the Mill Creek. Illinois. (courtesy *Smithsonian Institution 12th Annual Report*).

Ancient Celts were buried with their weapons, jewelry, and tools. So, too, were ancient Mound Builders. And the implements resembled each other in both type and style. There were stone arrowheads, stone axes, atlatls, gorgets, shell and stone beads, hammers, adzes, pottery, and items of bronze or copper.

One last point should be made concerning the Mound Builders, particularly those of the Adena period. In several cases, inscribed stones were discovered in American mounds, some containing messages written in ancient alphabetic scripts like Judaean and Iberic. These stones have been declared to be frauds or modern intrusives by some scholars. Yet one of the distinctive features of the Adena culture, as noted by these same scholars, is their use of inscribed stones. In several mounds, uninscribed stones similar in type and size to inscribed stones have been discovered. Schoolcraft noted the existence of a stone identical to the inscribed Grave Creek tablet. The plain stone was considered to be a genuine relic of the Adena culture, while the inscribed stone was rejected as a forgery. Yet both stones were found under the same circumstances, at the same time, and in the same area. A similar situation exists with regards to the Davenport Tablets. The inscribed stones were cast aside as frauds, but an identical stone, uninscribed, was authenticated as a genuine ancient artifact.

As the evidence shows, there are many similarities between the structures of the American Mound Builders and the ancient inhabitants of Western Europe. It is likely that some type of cultural contact existed between the two groups. Even Thomas Jefferson, in the eighteenth century, was cognizant of the possibility that Europeans had visited our shores in prehistoric times when he wrote, "Discoveries long ago made, were sufficient to show that the passage from Europe to America was always practicable, even to the imperfect navigation of ancient times."[4] Transoceanic contact was a strong possibility during the Mound Builder period. Certainly, the Mound Builders exhibited skills that may have been acquired from outside the North American sphere of influence, and some of the acquired skills may have been subsequently passed along to the American Indian, as vouched for by the Indian himself. But the questions remain. What was the relationship between the American Indian, the Mound Builders, and the ancient European?

Until 75 years or so ago, American scholars believed that the first inhabitants of America crossed over from Asia only 3,000 years ago. Then in 1926, an archaeological project was initiated in Folsom, New Mexico, that would have earthshaking ramifications regarding the beginning of human habitation in North America. That dig unearthed the remains of an ancient bison in conjunction with several man-made weapons, all dating to approximately 8000 BCE, or 7,000 years before the date then accepted by American anthropologists. That discovery was only the tip of the iceberg, anthropologically speaking. The discovery of fluted projectile points in Clovis, New Mexico, and other major discoveries, pushed the advent of American man much further back in time. A site in California was dated to 30,000 BCE, and a Texas site yielded an age of 38,000 BCE. The remains of ancient man were also found together with the bones of prehistoric mammoths who roamed the earth more than 20,000 years ago. It is now generally accepted that ancient man first set foot in North America at least 20,000 years ago. Blood types point to an Asian origin, but the fact that the land bridge from Asia to America came and went with the ice ages points to the intriguing possibility of an ocean voyage.

Recent scientific discoveries have confused the issue even more. In

1940 archaeologists in Nevada discovered a mummy in Spirit Cave, and dated it to the early Common Era. Fifty-four years later, new technology placed the time of the habitation of the site to 8600 BCE. The examination also indicated that the individual was not an American Indian, and more closely resembled the Ainu of Japan. Coincidentally, Betty Meggers, an archaeologist at the Smithsonian Institution, had recovered ancient pottery shards from a site in Validivia, Ecuador, in the 1960s that she theorized originated with the Ainu about 3000 BCE, pointing to transoceanic contact at that early date. Meggers also identified other evidence of early contact, such as the pyramids in Mexico and Asia. According to her, "Ancient man saw the ocean as a superhighway, not as a barrier." A subsequent discovery in Columbia, also identified with the Ainu, pushed the contact period back to 3900 BCE.

In 1977, Tom Dillehay, an archaeologist at the University of Kentucky, excavated a site in Monte Verde, Chile, that presented evidence of human occupation more than 1,500 years before Clovis man entered the United States, thereby destroying the theory that ancient man entered the continents via the Bering land bridge and moved inexorably southward through North America to Central and South America. The new evidence pointed to another tranoceanic voyage, but this time across the South Pacific from Australia or Southeast Asia, based on examination of the human remains.

Another discovery in 1996 also indicated the presence of non–Indian types in America during the ice age. Two men found a skeleton in the Colombia River, near Kennewick, Washington, and a scientific examination of the remains dated the skeleton to 7600 BCE. The skull type and other physical measurements indicated the visitor could have been Polynesian, or Ainu, or even European. More recently, Dennis Stanford, chairman of the anthropology department of the Smithsonian Institution, shocked his colleagues in the late 1990s with his announcement that new evidence from sites in the southeast section of the country indicated that the Clovis culture was predated by a Solutrean culture that originated in the Iberian Peninsula, probably Southern France, as long ago as 18,000 BCE. Stanford stated "It is very clear to me that we are looking at multiple migrations through a very long time period — migrations of many different peoples of many different ethnic origins."[5] He also said, "We are rewriting the textbooks on the First Americans. The peopling of the Americas was never as simple as simple-minded paradigms said. Instead it will tell of an America that beckoned to far flung people long before the Mayflower or the Santa Maria or the Viking ships, of an unknown continent so alluring that men and women endowed with a technology no more sophisticated than sharp rocks braved Siberian tundra and Atlantic ice packs to get here."[6]

## 13. Mound Builders and the American Indian 253

As the ice gradually receded about 10,000 BCE, most of North America became habitable. Grasslands flourished in the south, and thick green forests decorated the northern landscape. A new wave of immigrants entered the continent from both Asia and Europe about this time, and began to settle the country. The first human inhabitants of the Great Lakes–Eastern Canada region, known as Laurentian to present day anthropologists, were characterized by their stocky builds and broad heads. This is in sharp contrast to the immigrants to the south, called Lamoka, who were tall and had narrow heads. The origin of both cultures is now being reevaluated in view of Stanford's recent announcements. Other waves of immigrants found their way into the northeast section of the country over the next several millennia, to join the original Laurentian and Lamoka pioneers. Gradually, a number of distinct cultures evolved, as the various ethnic groups jockeyed for position and power, intermingled, intermarried, fought wars, and generally politicized in the same manner as is done today.

This era, from 8000 BCE to 1000 BCE, is called the Archaic Period. Man was still primarily a hunter-gatherer during this period, but fishing gained greater popularity, and some permanent settlements began to appear in the lowlands along the rivers and coastal regions. One piece of evidence of European intrusion into North America dates to this period, according to Barry Fell. In *Bronze Age America*, Fell announced the exploratory voyage of a Norwegian seafarer named Woden-lithi to the shores of North America almost 3,700 years ago. The physical evidence for Woden-lithi's visit is a gigantic petroglyph that is located in Peterborough, Ontario, Canada. The petroglyph, attributed to Algonquian Indians by Canadian authorities, was interpreted differently by Fell. He claimed that the rock carvings actually contain tifinagh inscriptions of Scandinavian origin. His decipherment told of a Norwegian king, one Woden-lithi, who sailed from his home port of Ringerike, Norway, around the year 1700 BCE, crossed the Atlantic Ocean in the spring of the year, and eventually reached the St. Lawrence River in Canada, near the site of present day Toronto. Woden-lithi spent the next five months in the Peterborough area trading with the natives, establishing a permanent Norwegian settlement, and leaving a detailed record of his visit carved into a 90-foot-long crystalline marble outcrop. In the fall of the year, Woden-lithi bade farewell to the Norwegian colonists, sailed back across the sea to the Oslo Fjord, and disappeared from the pages of history. The rock contains carvings of oceangoing ships that bear an strong resemblance to the ship carvings in Bohuslan, Sweden, that were produced around 1800 BCE and are shown in chapter 3.

As the year 1000 BCE dawned, the Archaic Period drew to a close, and was replaced by the more progressive Eastern Woodland Period, which was characterized by such technological innovations as pottery making, the use of copper and bronze, and the development of agriculture. The knowledge of pottery making adds yet another curious chapter to the history of Northeastern America, and presents another tantalizing bit of evidence in support of the "ancient Europe" theory. Pottery suddenly appeared along the Atlantic seaboard about this time apparently without the aid of any period of development. It was as if the knowledge of pottery manufacture had been imported into the northeast full-blown from some outside source. The two most logical areas capable of providing that knowledge to the Eastern Woodland natives were Mexico and Western Europe. The distinctive cord-marked style, in fact, resembles designs developed by the Bronze Age people of Western Europe. A further strong argument in favor of the introduction of pottery technology from Europe is the fact that the oldest pottery in Eastern America is found along the central Atlantic coast, not to the north, the south, or the west.

During this period, the people known as the Algonquian entered the pages of history. Their origin is still hazy, but it is apparent that these people were the result of a mixture of several stocks. The Algonquian are thought by many to be the result of a union between American aborigines and ancient European colonists. Certainly there is some evidence in support of this theory. The tall, handsome Algonquian warrior bore a striking resemblance to his Celtic counterpart from the Iberian Peninsula. The long-headed Algonquian people were also very light skinned. According to seventeenth and eighteenth century historians, when Algonquians dressed in colonial garb, they were indistinguishable from Europeans.

Their language, even today, contains many European roots, primarily Celtic, Libyan, and Egyptian. Schoolcraft discovered, during his study of the American Indian tribes, that Algonquian tradition claimed their ancestors had reached this land from across the sea. They are the only Indian tribe to claim foreign origin. The Algonquian also believed that other white people had lived in America during the time of their ancestors: they inhabited Florida and had iron tools.

As the Eastern Woodland culture was developing along the Atlantic coast, another culture was blossoming independently along the valley of the Ohio River. This was to become known as the Adena culture. The Adenans were not natives to the area. They were immigrants who appear to have entered the country from the south. They were a broad-headed people who accentuated the shape of their skulls by intentionally deforming them. It is probable that they entered at the mouth of the Mississippi River and worked their way northward until finally settling along the Ohio River.

Their origin is uncertain, but they may have come from central Mexico. The Olmec civilization of the Gulf Coast contained many similarities to the Adena civilization. The Olmec built tombs within earthen mounds at La Venta, Vera Cruz, and other ceremonial centers. It is quite possible that the mound building practice originated south of the United States area, even further south than Mexico. Barnard Shipp commented on similar funeral practices that were observed by a fellow explorer named Bartram.

> In the provinces of Tatabe and Guaca near Antioquia, on the western branch of the river Magdalena, in South America, when one of the chiefs dies, the people mourn him for many days, cut off the hair of his wives, kill those who were most beloved, and raise a tomb the size of a small hill, with an opening towards the rising sun. Within this great tomb, they made a large vault, and here they put the body, wrapped in cloths, and the gold and arms the dead man had used when living. They then take the most beautiful of his wives and some servant-lads, make them drunk with wine made of maize, and bury them alive in the vault, in order that the chief may go down to hell with his companions.[7]

The Olmec were proficient in the construction of geometric earthworks similar to those at Hopeton and Newark. And the Olmec culture was at its zenith during the same period that the Adena culture was flourishing, roughly 1200 BCE to 400 BCE. Silverberg claimed that Olmec mariners crossed the Gulf of Mexico from Vera Cruz to the Mississippi River in large oceangoing canoes. If that is correct, the descendants of the Olmec or Adenans might be found in the historic Indian tribes, particularly the Choctaw, who were called flatheads by the European traders for their practice of artificially flattening or compressing their skulls to give themselves high, lofty foreheads, sloping backwards. The Olmec also deformed their skulls to give them an elongated look.

The Eastern Woodland culture was far superior to its Archaic predecessor, but it was still primitive compared to the more sophisticated Adena culture, which was the most advanced civilization then known in North America. Anthropologists generally concede that the Adena culture was completely unrelated to the Eastern Woodland culture. Such scholars as Spencer, Jennings, et al., noted that only in the Ohio River Valley was such a stage of technical advancement evident. The Adena culture, over the centuries, has been associated with a cult of the dead. The Adenans were often preoccupied with paying homage to deceased members of their tribe and providing them with material goods and slaves to accompany them into the next world. Great earthen mounds were erected over the tombs of the dead, and one generation adding to the moundwork of previous generations. Archaeological studies of Adena mounds showed that the construction of a single mound could encompass a time period of as long as 600 years from start to finish, with periodic burials adding to the size of the mounds. Some Adena mounds, on excavation, have yielded the remains of more than 1,000 skeletons.

As mentioned earlier, stone tablets were a significant part of this culture. So too were tobacco and tubular stone pipes. The tablets and pipes often displayed complicated geometrical designs, even abstract drawings of animals produced by the proficient Adena artisans. The settlers of the Ohio Valley were a sedentary people. They were expert farmers who raised acres of squash and pumpkin. They were adept at hunting and fishing, and gathering wild berries. But they did not travel with the seasons. They built permanent villages and resided in the same location year after year. Gradually the Adena "empire" grew in size. At its peak, it included the valleys of the Scioto and Miami Rivers from Columbus southward to the Ohio. Some minor activity was also evident south of the Ohio, in Kentucky and West Virginia. But, in general, it was a small and close knit society that endured for over a thousand years in an area of approximately 30,000 square miles. It is interesting to note that the Adena apparently were a friendly people who lived at peace with a variety of neighbors over the centuries. No defensive works or fortifications are evident in any Adena centers.

There is other evidence, not discussed yet, that points to cultural contact between the Adena civilization and the peoples of Western Europe. Similarities in the mounds, the tombs, and the cists have already been noted. There are also similarities between the earthworks of the Adena and those of the ancient Europeans, such as the circular earthworks at Hopeton, Ohio, and the earthwork that adorns the impressive hill at Tara, the Court of Kings, in Ireland (see illustration). The Celts constructed many earthworks of this type, not only in Ireland, but all over Western Europe. These Celtic earthworks had diverse uses, such as ceremonial centers and defensive works. The American counterparts were primarily ceremonial. Effigy mounds were also in vogue on both sides of the ocean. American mounds, in the form of turtles, birds, and mammals, often covered several acres. The Great Serpent Mound in Ohio presently runs through the middle of a public golf course. Barnard Shipp, in the nineteenth century, visited and explored a similar mound in Scotland, which he subsequently described in his book: "About three miles from Oban in Scotland, lies a huge serpent shaped mound.... We ... scrambled onto the ridge which forms his backbone, and thence perceived that we were standing on an artificial mound, three hundred feet in length, forming a double curve, like a huge letter S, and wonderfully perfect in anatomical outline."[8]

## 13. Mound Builders and the American Indian 257

Ancient American earthworks constructed by the Adena people at Hopeton, four miles south of Chillicothe, Ohio (courtesy S. D. Peet).

The earthworks constructed by the ancient Celtic people of Ireland. These earthworks are located at the sacred site of Tara (courtesy Bord Failte).

One last similarity between the ancient Americans and the Europeans should be noted. When Schoolcraft visited Grave Creek, in addition to visiting the Great Mound, and inspecting the infamous inscribed stone, he also examined the surrounding territory. He reported on one such excursion into the countryside: "I rode out yesterday three miles back, to the range of high hills which encompass this sub-valley, to see a rude tower of stone standing on an elevated point called Parrs Point, which commands a view of the whole plain, and which appears to have been constructed as a watchtower or lookout, from which to descry an approaching enemy. It is much dilapidated. About six or seven feet of the work is still entire. It is circular, and composed of rough stones laid without mortar or the mark of a hammer. A heavy mass of fallen walls lies around, covering an area of some forty feet in diameter."[9] The original height of the tower can no longer be ascertained, but it must have been moderately high if it was, in fact, an observation tower. Since the tower was unmortared, it was probably less than 30 feet high, according to David Barron, who noted that once a shell-lime mortar mix was discovered, towers could reach 100 feet or more. Similar towers of considerable size were built in Ireland during the early Christian days. And high in the Andes Mountains of South America, round stone towers, called Chullpas, can still be found intact all around Lake Titicaca and the pre-Incan city of Tiahuanaco.

Sometime around 500 BCE, new immigrants began to filter into the Adena territories along the Ohio River Valley. They were a tall, handsome people, with long narrow heads and a fair complexion. Anthropologists suspect these people were of the Algonquian stock, and had left their homelands to the east to begin a new life in a new land for some unknown reason. These people, who are known as the Hopewell Indians, settled peacefully amidst the Adenans, and lived side by side with them for 500 years or more. The Hopewell seem to have observed the Adena way of life very carefully. They adopted those things they admired most about the Adena, then expanded and improved upon them. Over a period of time, the Hopewell culture spread out from a tiny area along the Ohio River to encompass a large expanse of territory. Although a loosely knit amalgamation of tribes or village states, the Hopewell people created North America's greatest trading network. Goods were shipped from one place to another primarily by boat, and every navigable river east of the Rocky Mountains was used as part of this vast liquid highway system. Vessels, mostly canoes of every size and description, traversed the entire length of the great Mississippi, as well as the Arkansas, the Ohio, the Missouri, and the mighty Colorado.

Oceangoing boats even made regular excursions across the formidable

Gulf of Mexico, to exchange goods with the Mayan Indians of the Yucatan Peninsula. Elaborate jewelry and ornaments such as conch shell earrings, obsidian knives, copper bracelets, and beautifully inscribed slate tablets and mica pendants fashioned by the skilled hands of Hopewell artisans, was traded for equally impressive Mayan handiwork such as jade statues, gold jewelry, and colorful textiles. It was an exciting period in American history, as commerce thrived and peace prevailed throughout the land. The Hopewell continued the Adena practice of mound building, although on a smaller scale. Archaeological evidence also revealed that the Hopewell mounds were all completed in one stage. Construction did not continue for centuries, as with Adena mounds. Earthworks were also very much in evidence in Hopewellian America, and in this area the Hopewell far surpassed their Adena brethren. Strangely enough, as the Hopewell culture was reaching its peak, the Adena culture disappeared completely. What happened to the people is still a mystery. Did they peacefully leave their lands in search of greener pastures? Were they forced to leave the country as the result of a war? Or were they slowly and gradually assimilated into the more advanced Hopewell society? No answer is forthcoming, but the Adena were gone as a people by 200 CE, and the Hopewell ruled the land far and wide, from the Rockies to the Atlantic Ocean, and from the Great Lakes to the Gulf of Mexico.

There is still much that is not known about the Hopewell people. What is known is that they were a peaceful people who were industrious and had sophisticated tastes, far beyond those of their numerous Woodland neighbors. They farmed the land, they gathered berries, and they hunted and fished in the vicinity of their permanent villages. They were intelligent, inventive, and adaptive, and they were an extremely religious people who honored their deceased leaders on a magnificent scale. But there is very little evidence to show what type of dwellings they lived in, or what kind of tools or household implements they used. It is very likely that these things were primarily constructed of wood, and have long since perished. Post holes discovered at many Hopewell sites indicate their houses were probably identical to the Algonquian dome-shaped structures (and Celtic beehives) noted previously. Except for the post holes however, and a few axe blades and adzes, the everyday life of the Hopewell family still lies hidden in the dark recesses of mother earth.

Their earthworks are perhaps the most fascinating relics of their society that remain for us to visit, and to ponder over. The earthworks, impressive in size, were a complex of intricate geometric patterns. The intended use of these wondrous engineering feats still has not been determined, but the general opinion is that they were some type of ceremonial center. The size of the geometric complexes could be rather formidable, as related by Caleb Atwater:

> Between the two branches of the Licking River, Racoon Creek, and South Fork, near Newark, in the state of Ohio, are ancient earthworks, which on many accounts are quite as remarkable as any others in North America, or perhaps in any part of the world. These works are of great extent. One structure is a fort containing about forty acres, with its walls, which are generally, I should judge, about ten feet high. Leading into this fort are eight openings or gateways, about fifteen feet in width, in front of which is a small mound of earth, in height and thickness resembling the outer wall. These small mounds are about four feet longer than the gateway is in width. These small mounds of earth were probably intended for the defense of the gates opposite to which they are situated. There is a round fort, consisting of twenty two acres, connected to the first fort by two parallel walls of earth as about the same height, etc., as the others. There is also an observatory, built partly of earth and partly of stone. It commanded a full view of a considerable part, if not all the plain in which these ancient works stand. Under this observatory was a passage, from appearances, and a secret one probably, to the water-course, which once ran near this spot, but has since moved farther off. Another circular fort, containing about twenty six acres, has a wall around it, from twenty five to thirty feet in height. There are also parallel walls of earth, generally five or six yards apart, and four or five feet in height.[10]

It is obvious that, whatever the purpose of these mammoth works, it must have been of primary importance to the Hopewell society. To build such monumental enclosures as these, with different geometrical designs, with wide avenues connecting one enclosure with another, and with walls reaching up to 30 feet in height, required a tremendous amount of manual labor — and there were literally hundreds of these structures adjoining every navigable waterway between the Rocky Mountains and the Atlantic Ocean. Some interesting features of this site should be mentioned. First, the earthworks are similar to the forts built by the Celts in Ireland. Forts were defended enclosures, with high walls, religious structures, and observatories. Souterrains, or underground tunnels used to escape from invading forces, were an integral part of any Celtic fort, as presented in chapter 9. The underground passageway from the Newark observatory to the waterway is a typical Celtic design. If the Hopewell Indians were descendants of the Celts, a fort with a souterrain would have been a natural part of their society.

There is one nineteenth century published work that describes the uses of these earthworks, but the author of that work has generally been regarded as an eccentric. William Pidgeon, an author and explorer of colonial America, wrote a book titled *Traditions of Dee Coo Dah*, in 1858, which dealt primarily with the recollections and tribal traditions of an aged Indian chief named Dee Coo Dah. Perhaps Pidgeon was an eccentric. Perhaps not. In any case, the testimony of Dee Coo Dah should be heard, and should be carefully evaluated. It may have sounded like fantasy in 1842, but in 2004 many of the things he communicated to Pidgeon make sense. Dee Coo Dah claimed to be a descendant of the ancient Mound Builders, probably the Hopewell, although in appearance he was short, dark, and rugged, and his head was broad, more like the Adena. He called his people the Elk nation, and said they were originally a non-Indian race who "came from the north, and once held dominion over all the country east and north from the Mississippi to the great waters."[11] Quoting his great-grandfather's grandfather, Dee Coo Dah declared that the Mississippi Valley was "the primitive residence of their nation, four hundred winters before the birth of his father, which took place 213 winters gone by."[12] The Elk nation, the last of the ancient Americans, was by then (1104 CE) "mingled and amalgamated with the race of the red man from the south."[13] This new red race could have been the forerunners of the Mississippian culture who came from Mexico, Central America, or South America. It was during this period that the Elk nation was broken up into small tribes, through various wars, according to Dee Coo Dah. The old days were forgotten and mound building became less important. Dee Coo Dah's non-Hopewellian physical appearance could have been the result of the intermingling of the Elk nation (Hopewell) with the red men from the south over a period of 700 years. Certainly some of the inhabitants of ancient Mexico were dark, and broad headed.

Regarding the earthworks, Dee Coo Dah stated they were religious and ceremonial centers, and that each geometric enclosure had a specific purpose. For instance, the circle was the residence of the ruling prophet, and his wooden house was located within this enclosure. The square, on the other hand, was a public place where festivals were held, a place for feasting and merrymaking. The Newark earthworks were one of the most important religious centers in the entire Elk nation. As Dee Coo Dah related it, Newark was a "prophets metropolis, or holy seminary of priests or prophets, with its holy circles, festival square, secluded walks, private avenues, sacred residentials, heavenly clusters, and funeral piles." The oral history of the Elk nation also contained considerable information regarding the mounds themselves. There were, according to tradition, two mound builder nations in the distant past. These nations joined each other "at or near the junction of the Missouri and the Mississippi. South from that point, the tumuli gradually partake of the pyramidal form, resembling those found in Mexico, South America, etc." North and east of the junction, the mounds became low conical or flat mounds "resembling those found in the north of Europe."[14]

Pidgeon also visited several countries in Central and South America, in addition to exploring the eastern half of the United States, and he recorded his impressions of the earthen structures in those localities as well as the ones in America. In Venezuela, Pidgeon was specifically interested in the truncated pyramidal mounds, noting that "such structures are found in greater numbers and of larger and more imposing appearance in Central America than elsewhere. They decrease in size and number on coming northward and are scarcely known north of the mouth of the Ohio."[15]

There is a mounting abundance of evidence that links the ancient cultures of Western Europe and those of ancient America. The practices of the Hopewell people only strengthens that connection. Chapters 8 and 9 studied the great stone chambers of Northeast America, their size, shape, construction design, and use; and compared them with their European counterparts. Radiocarbon dates of a number of the chambers put their origin back into the Iron Age, from 200 CE onward. Two radiocarbon dates at America's Stonehenge even went back further in time, to 1600 BCE, but that date might refer to earlier habitation of the site itself and not to the construction of the buildings.

Chapter 10 examined other stone structures, including dolmens, cairns, and menhirs. Again, the evidence pointed across the Atlantic for the location of origin of stone-building technology. It is possible then, that several ancient Old World peoples, such as the Iberian Celts, the Phoenicians, and the Hebrews, planted permanent colonies along the eastern seaboard. During the heyday of the Adena civilization, those colonies may have traded goods with the natives of the Ohio River Valley. The discovery of Old World artifacts in Adena mounds, such as inscribed stones, indicates that this could well have happened. Other evidence has hinted at the possibility that the Algonquian Indians were a mixture of American aborigine and Iberian Celt. These same Algonquians may eventually have migrated from the North Atlantic area to the Ohio River Valley, founding the magnificent Hopewell culture. This scenario is tenuous at best, but it is reinforced by many of the artifacts that have been unearthed from the remnants of Hopewell burial sites. For instance, the beehive hut design, popular in Western Europe, had its counterparts all over the northeast, including at Upton, Massachusetts, Royalton, Vermont, and America's Stonehenge. The same design was used by the Algonquian nation in their house design, and was subsequently used in many Hopewell tombs. Identical souterrain-type chambers were found, one in Vermont, and the other in a Hopewell mound in Minnesota. Both chambers appear to have had their origin in the renowned souterrains of Celtic Ireland, built during the Iron Age.

Even more impressive evidence exists in the dry stone rectangular chambers. Chapter 9 followed the development of those chambers from Ireland and the Iberian Peninsula to New York and New England prior to the Common Era. Subsequently, the design seems to have been transmitted to the Hopewell culture of mid-America, where it was incorporated into numerous burial mounds over the centuries. There is a startling similarity between a Vermont slab roofed chamber and a rectangular burial vault in Missouri. The only difference between the two chambers is that the Vermont structure was originally enclosed by large granite roof slabs while the Missouri example was unroofed.

Burial cists in Hopewellian America closely resembled the burial cists in Western Europe around the time of Christ. The cists may also be used to trace the descendants of the Hopewell Indians in the centuries following the dissolution of the Hopewell empire. At least two historic Indian tribes are known to have buried their dead in cist graves. These tribes, the Delaware and the Shawnee, inhabited territory in Pennsylvania and Ohio that, at one time, had been under the influence of the Hopewell.

There is one other clue that ties the Hopewell culture to the ancient cultures of the European Atlantic seaboard, the cremation rite. Certain burials on both sides of the ocean were preceded by a formal cremation ceremony performed in a specially designed crematory basin. These basins have been discovered in such diverse locations as Newgrange, Ireland, and Illinois. The basin, in both cases, was located within the main burial chamber and, following the completion of the religious services, the chamber was ritually sealed, and a mound was erected over the entire structure. The same sequence of events took place in both Ireland and America, and tombs in both places were of similar design.

During the sixth century CE, new settlers began to infiltrate the Mississippi Valley at its southern extremity. The Hopewell culture was already in a period of decline, having passed through its zenith between 100 BCE and 300 CE. This new race, which was to develop into the Mississippian culture, was more hostile than its Adena and Hopewell predecessors, and it was not adverse to acquiring desirable territory by force of arms, if necessary. Gradually, over the next four centuries, the invaders systematically occupied all the land along the length of the Mississippi River from New Orleans to the Great Lakes. Dee Coo Dah said that his people had been broken up into small tribes through periodic wars, and that by 1100 CE, they had been completely assimilated by the red men from the south. The Mississippians built large ceremonial centers based on the pattern of the ancient Mayan civilization of Mexico and Central America. These centers consisted of expansive open plazas surrounded by numerous large earthen mounds and truncated pyramids (see illustration). These impressive pyramids, or temple mounds, supported the residences of the reigning chieftain, the high priest, and other important personages. Lofty stairways or ramps led up to rectangular, thatched-roof wooden dwellings that graced the flat topped mounds. Other truncated mounds served as foundations for religious edifices where elaborate funeral services were conducted. Following the completion of the services, the dead were interred in conical mounds located adjacent to the temple. Some of the most impressive ceremonial centers of the Mississippian culture were located at Spiro, Oklahoma; Moundville, Alabama; Etowah, Georgia; and Cahokia, Illinois.

This culture was also referred to as the Southern Cult, an obvious reference to their obsession with death. They did emphasize the funeral rite to some extent, similar to their Hopewell and Adena predecessors, but only for the aristocracy. The importance of the veneration of the dead by the Mississippians has been greatly exaggerated. The death of the average peasant was hardly noticed in ancient cultures. His passing was not accompanied by elaborate funeral ceremonies, nor was his grave large or ostentatious. He was normally buried in a simple, open unmarked pit, which was quickly devoured by the encroaching forest. Today only the graves of the rulers and their priests remain to be studied.

Moundville, Alabama, as it appeared around 1200 CE (courtesy Mound State Monument).

## 13. Mound Builders and the American Indian

The characteristics of the Mississippian culture were the omnipresent truncated pyramids, the unique shell tempered pottery, and the intensive cultivation of maize. Cist burials were practiced along the eastern seaboard from Delaware to Georgia during this period, and they continued well into the historic period. In addition to the tribes mentioned previously, the Shawnee and the Delaware (or Lenni Lenape), cist burials were also characteristic of the Choctaw and the Cherokee. The Cherokee and the Shawnee were also adept at decorative shell engraving.

But above all, it was the multi-terraced truncated pyramids that set this culture apart from other American cultures. As with many other structures in North and South America, this particular pyramid design can be traced back across the Atlantic Ocean, in this case to ancient Egypt. The world's oldest known pyramid was built by King Zoser at Sakkara, Egypt, in 2780 BCE. Similar pyramids were constructed in ancient Peru as early as 2500 BCE. In fact, pyramid building continued unabated in the prehistoric civilizations of Peru for more than 3,000 years, a longer period than in Egypt, culminating in the famous Mochica Pyramid of the Sun, constructed around 500 CE. During this same period, a stepped pyramid, called Acapana, was built in Tiahuanaco, Peru, near Lake Titicaca. Acapana had an earthen core and a dressed stone facing. It measured 690 feet square and 50 feet high, and its flat top once supported a large building.

Other stepped pyramids rose from the soil of the Americas over the centuries, including the elegant Mayan structures at Chichén Itzá and Uxmal, as well as the mammoth Mississippian mounds at Cahokia and Jefferson County, Arkansas. Cahokia was by far the most impressive urban center in prehistoric America, covering an area of six square miles. At its apex, around 1050 CE, Cahokia embraced a teeming population of 30,000 bustling inhabitants. Thousands of thatched roof, wattle and daub houses spread across the fertile alluvial plain known as the American Bottoms, adjacent to what is now the city of St. Louis. The central core of the metropolis, containing the religious and ceremonial mounds, was protected by a 15-foot-high wooden stockade. The outlying residents farmed maize, squash, and beans, hunted deer and birds, and fished in Cahokia Creek, which was also the water highway used to transport the plentiful consumer goods to distant markets. During periods of strife, the peasants would seek shelter within the protective walls of the stockade.

The main plaza at Cahokia was surrounded by more than 120 mounds, 40 of which still remain. Monks Mound, standing almost in the shadow of the modern "Gateway to the West" arch in St. Louis, is North America's largest man-made mound. It contains 1 million cubic feet of earth, and was constructed in 14 stages between 900 CE and 1200 CE. Its 16-acre base rises in four terraces to a height of 100 feet. Archaeological studies have shown that a large building once stood on the summit of Monks Mound, a building 48 feet wide, 105 feet long, and 50 feet high. The mound also contained a burial chamber that belonged to a person of high station. When excavated, the male skeleton was reposing on an ornate blanket made from more than 12,000 shell beads. The body was surrounded by hundreds of dazzling artifacts, including many weapons and decorative items. Six male skeletons, probably servants, were laid to rest with their master and, not far away, in a mass grave, the skeletons of 53 females joined their ruler on his journey to the nether world.

Outside the city proper, a fascinating discovery was made a few years ago that showed the high level of scientific achievement attained by these people. Indentations in the earth revealed that the inhabitants of Cahokia had, at one time, used an astronomical calendar, probably to predict the agricultural cycles. Wooden posts had been set up like the pillars of Stonehenge to form a large circle, and one post was erected in the center of the circle to be used as a sighting post. The site, which was called Woodhenge, resembles the ancient stone calendars in America's Stonehenge and in Brittany.

The Mississippian culture flourished between 900 CE and 1200 CE, with some settlements reaching into the colonial period, around 1600 CE. The reason for the demise of the culture is not certain; there may have been several. In the north, the infamous Iroquois Nation rose to prominence in the area of western New York state between 1000 CE and 1300 CE. Eventually this aggressive and hostile confederation attacked the tribes to their west, laying waste the entire territory from New York to the Mississippi River. The Ohio Valley ran red with blood as Iroquois warriors annihilated the entire native population, turning the area into a vast, desolate no-man's land. It remained void of human inhabitants until European colonists repopulated it in the seventeenth century.

The European intrusion into the southeastern section of the United States contributed to the extinction of native cultures in that area. As De Soto and other Spanish conquistadors moved northward from Florida, they systematically destroyed anyone who appeared to be a threat to their authority. Entire Indian tribes became extinct almost overnight. Disease took care of those natives who escaped the Spanish sword. The devastating effects of European-transmitted smallpox on the Indian is well known. Having no natural resistance to this virus, the natives succumbed by the thousands and, over a period of 350 years, approximately 50 percent of the Indian population was wiped out.

Silence settled over the land after the beginning of the sixteenth century. America began to become Europeanized, and the Indian tribes faded

## 13. Mound Builders and the American Indian

back into the bush, away from the evils of civilization. The history of early America came to an abrupt end. The great aboriginal cultures of the Adena, Hopewell, and Mississippian were no more. Mound building ceased, permanent villages disappeared from the countryside, and widespread ancient trade networks fell into disuse.

All evidence of prehistoric visits to America from other continents was quickly forgotten by most people, along with legends of white settlers and the resulting tribes of "white Indians." There are many stories of this type that supposedly prove ancient contact with Europe, and they are intriguing, but the evidence is not solid. Much work remains to be done in this area before the facts can be known one way or the other. A few of the legends are presented here without comment. One of the first "white settler" legends was recorded in Stone's biography of Joseph Brant, or Thayendanegea, who was a Mohawk Indian chief of the Iroquois Nation, and who lived from 1742 to 1807:

> While therefore, every inquiry of the white man concerning these remains in America has ended as it began, leaving the subject of investigation as deep in obscurity as before, the opinion of a man of Brant's information and sagacity, thoroughly conversant as he was, with the traditions of his own people, may not be unacceptable to the curious reader. That opinion, or rather such information as the Chief had derived from the dim light of Indian tradition, has been supplied in the manuscript notes of Mr. Woodruff, already referred to several times in the preceding pages. A few extracts follow: "Among other things relating to the western country," says Mr. Woodruff, "I was curious to learn in the course of my conversations with Captain Brant, what information he could give me respecting the tumuli which are found on or near the margin of the rivers and lakes, from the St. Lawrence to the Mississippi. He stated, in reply, that the subject had long been agitated, but yet remained in some obscurity. A tradition, he said, prevailed among the different nations of Indians throughout the whole extensive range of country, and had been handed down from time immemorial, that in an age long gone by, there came white men from a foreign country, and by consent of the Indians established trading-houses and settlements where these tumuli are found. A friendly intercourse was continued for several years; many of the white men brought their wives, and had children born to them; and additions to their numbers were made yearly from their own country. These circumstances at length gave rise to jealousies among the Indians, and fears began to be entertained in regard to the increasing numbers, wealth, and ulterior views of the newcomers; apprehending that, becoming strong, they might one day seize upon the country as their own. A secret council, composed of the chiefs of all the different nations from the St. Lawrence to the Mississippi, was therefore convoked; the result of which, after long deliberation, was a resolution that on a certain night designated for that purpose, all their white neighbors, men, women, and children, should be exterminated. The most profound secrecy was essential to the

execution of such a purpose; and such was the fidelity of which the fatal determination was kept, that the conspiracy was successful and the device carried completely into effect. Not a soul was left to tell the tale."[16]

An Indian tradition associated with Cahokia confirmed Captain Brant's story. According to the Cahokia legend, white men with blonde hair established trading posts near Cahokia. They brought their wives and raised families. After 100–200 years, the natives, fearing the increased strength of the visitors, massacred them.

MacLean carefully documented another legend about "white Indians" in Eastern America: "The Indian chief, Tobacco, informed Gen. George Rogers Clark of a tradition of a battle at Sandy Island that decided the fall of the ancient inhabitants. The Indian chief, Cornplanter, affirmed that Ohio, Kentucky, and Tennessee had once been inhabited by a white people who were familiar with arts of which the Indian knew nothing and after a series of battles they were exterminated."[17]

The Mandan Indians of the upper Missouri River in North Dakota are the source of one of the most romantic legends of "white Indians" in America. The Mandans supposedly originated in the southeast, somewhere between the Ohio Valley and Florida. Many legends refer to them as Welsh Indians, descendants of the famous Welsh mariner Madoc. The Mandans were driven from their homeland during the seventeenth and eighteenth centuries, eventually settling in North Dakota. In 1832, George Catlin, one of America's foremost artists, visited Mandan country, spending a total of eight years with these fascinating people. Catlin found them to be very gracious and peaceful. He was greatly impressed by their countenance, which appeared to be more European than Indian. Many of the Mandan people were almost white in color, with hazel, gray, and blue eyes. All color of hair was evident except red. Catlin believed that these people were not Indian. They were either a different race or a mixture of Indian with some other race. Unfortunately for the history books, a smallpox epidemic ran rampant through the Mandan nation, and before the end of the nineteenth century, the tribe was completely wiped out.

A complete book could be filled with tales of "white Indians," but these few cases are sufficient to present the type of evidence that exists. The volume of evidence is large, but as of today, none of it has been substantiated.

# Summary

- The first American settlers may have reached this country by boat from the Iberian Peninsula more than 18,000 years ago.

## 13. Mound Builders and the American Indian

- The first people in South America settled in Monte Verde, Chile, about 12,500 BCE, after sailing across the southern route of the Pacific Ocean from Australia or another region of Southeastern Asia.
- Some of the first arrivals from Asia crossed the Bering land bridge about 12,000 years ago.
- Mariners from the Jomon culture in Japan arrived by boat in Valdivia, Ecuador, about 3000 BCE.
- The first civilized American culture east of the Mississippi River was the Eastern Woodland culture, which arose around 1000 BCE.
- During this same period, an even more advanced culture was developing in the Ohio River Valley, the Adena culture. The Adena were a round headed people who may have been immigrants from the south, originating in Mexico or further south.
- The Hopewell Indians succeeded the Adena Indians as the predominant culture in ancient America, around the beginning of the Common Era. The Hopewell were a long headed people who may have been descendants of the Algonquian Indians, who were also long headed. The tall, well muscled Algonquians themselves may have been a mixture of American aboriginal and Western European peoples, possibly Iberian Celts. Algonquian tradition claimed their ancestors came from the east, across the water. They are they only tribe to claim a foreign origin.
- The Algonquians called their tribes living to the east, Abnakis, which means "our white cousins."
- The Adena and Hopewell cultures used many stone structures similar to those erected in Western Europe as early as 1600 BCE.
- The Mississippian culture thrived in the Southeastern United States, from the Ohio River Valley to the mouth of the Mississippi River, from 700 CE until 1700 CE. They may have been immigrants from the Mayan region of the Yucatan Peninsula in Mexico.
- The Adena, Hopewell, and the later Mississippian cultures, all constructed earthen mounds. The Adena built effigy mounds as well as burial mounds and ceremonial mounds. The Hopewell built magnificent earthworks, burial mounds and ceremonial mounds. The Mississippians built primarily truncated temple mounds.
- The historic Indian tribes, such as the Algonquians, the Iroquois, the Creek, the Mohawk, and the Cherokee, claimed their ancestors did not build the mounds, and they didn't know who did build them.

- Some historic Indians have many characteristics in common with the Mound Builders. These include the Shawnee, the Delaware, the Creek, and the Choctaw.

## Conclusions

- The American continent was inhabited as long ago as 20,000 BCE.
- Great civilizations developed in Eastern America as early as 1600 BCE, and continued until the European colonization began in the sixteenth century.
- There is considerable evidence that:

    1. The Adena culture may have been brought to the United States from Mexico or areas further south. The Adena may have had contact with visiting European mariners.
    2. The Hopewell culture may have descended from the Algonquian Indians who, in turn, may have been a mixture of American aborigine and Western European.
    3. The Mississippian culture may have been brought to the United States from the Yucatan region of Mexico.
    4. Some Indian tribes, such as the Mandan, may have been "white Indians," mixtures of American aborigines and European settlers.

    The evidence for these possibilities is still circumstantial. However, there is enough evidence to justify further research into these areas. The American academic community should initiate ethnological and archaeological research programs to uncover the truth about the history of ancient America.

- The many tales of "white Indians" have yet to be substantiated. Perhaps scientific tests, including DNA testing of Mandan skeletons and descendants of Madoc could answer one of those questions: whether or not the Mandan were Welsh Indians.

# 14

## *The Secret of Ancient America*

New evidence continues to surface almost daily, as the search to uncover the secret of ancient America is intensified. Each new discovery strengthens the theory that Europeans and Asians visited ancient America, and that at least one Mound Builder culture originated outside the borders of the United States.

Alejandro von Wuthenau, a specialist in pre–Columbian art at the University of the Americas in Mexico City, made a notable contribution to the history of ancient America in late 1985. Wuthenau had long suspected that ancient voyages to North and South America were a fact, voyages from both Europe and Asia, but until 1985 he lacked definite proof. Then, in October of that year, von Wuthenau was engaged in the scientific excavation of an Olmec tomb in Xochipala, Guerrero, Mexico, when an astounding find came to light. The tomb contained, among other things, the model of an oceangoing ship. The vessel after which the model was constructed appeared to have been about 50 feet long, with a 6-foot-high freeboard, and a prow that towered almost 15 feet in the air. It was equipped with a steering oar on the port side aft, and a large square sail. But what made the vessel particularly fascinating was the fact that the crew of ten oarsmen had distinctly Asian features, possibly Japanese. It proved, according to von Wuthenau, that ancient Japanese mariners had crossed the Pacific Ocean, and had visited the Olmec region of Mexico as early as 500 BCE.

Another piece of the puzzle was slotted neatly into place during a study of the Mississippian culture in the Southeastern United States. In searching out new evidence of the prehistoric Indian tribes of the southeast, archaeologists stumbled upon an important ancient site in the Louisiana bayou country. Near Bayou Macon, scientists found an ancient settlement complete with mounds and burial artifacts. The site, called Poverty Point, at first assumed to be associated with the Mississippian culture, proved to be much older. It was, in fact, dated to 1500 BCE, making it the oldest earthen mound site in North America. Clay figurines found in the excavations had cleft heads similar to those found in jade statues at Olmec sites in Mexico. It would appear from this evidence that Olmec mariners may have crossed the Gulf of Mexico around 1500 BCE and began to push their way inland up the Mississippi River delta. These pioneers may well have traveled as far north as the Ohio River Valley over the next several hundred years, where they subsequently began the development of the Adena culture, around 1000 BCE.

During this same study of Mississippian sites, a unique style of fiber tempered pottery was uncovered along the Atlantic coast, primarily on Stallings Island, Georgia, but also on other sites from South Carolina to Florida. The pottery was found in conjunction with shell rings, earthen enclosures made from various types of seashells. These discoveries pointed to Colombia, South America, as being the source of this revolutionary new pottery technique. If true, this would mean that long ocean voyages from Colombia to the United States were in vogue as early as 2400 BCE. The art of ocean voyaging and open water navigation may be much older than most people think.

So much evidence supporting foreign visits to ancient America has been accumulated in recent years that, at times, it becomes a confusing jumble, and is difficult to assemble in an organized manner. There is evidence of transatlantic visits, not only to North America, but also to Mexico and South America. There is additional evidence of Asiatic visits to Mexico and South America. This study has examined less than a hundred pieces of evidence regarding visits to this continent by ancient mariners. The total weight of evidence would encompass literally thousands of individual artifacts and inscriptions. The evidence in support of ancient visits to the United States is not yet conclusive, but it is substantial and impressive.

For almost a century, from the late 1800s until after 1960, the scientific community has done almost no research to investigate the evidence of pre–Columbian visits to the United States by ancient mariners. During that period, the significant archaeological discoveries regarding the birth of our country were made by people outside the official scientific community — Helge Ingstad, Walter Elliot, Hjalmar Holand, Henriette Mertz, Jim Whittall, Dave Barron, and Gloria Farley, to name a few — ably assisted by independent thinkers like George Carter and Cyrus Gordon. That picture is finally changing, thanks to important contributions by Betty Meggers, Michael Xu, E. James Dixon, Bruce Bradley, Dennis Stanford, and their associates. With a combined effort by both professional and amateur archaeological organizations, that mystery will finally be solved. There are several items that are already generally accepted, by professionals and amateurs alike:

## 14. The Secret of Ancient America

Map identifying important archaeological discoveries relating to ocean voyages of ancient mariners.

- Japanese mariners visited the coast of Ecuador, South America, about 3000 BCE (#8 on the map).
- A cache of Carthaginian coins was discovered on the island of Corvo, in the Azores, in 1749 CE (#3). The coins were dated to 320–310 BCE, indicating that Phoenician mariners were familiar with the Western Atlantic

Ocean at that early date. The location of the coin discovery is on the return route from America to Europe.

- A cache of Roman coins was discovered on the east coast of Iceland (#1). The coins, dating to the third century CE, were most likely carried to Iceland by Irish mariners who controlled the ocean between Iceland and Europe at that time.
- Polynesian mariners colonized the Marquesas Islands and Tahiti around the time of Christ (#6).
- Polynesian mariners colonized Hawaii by 300 CE (#7).
- Easter Island was colonized by Polynesian mariners about 600 CE (#5).
- An inscribed stone, unearthed by agents of the Smithsonian Institution in an ancient burial mound at Bat Creek, Tennessee, contains a legend that the Smithsonian Institution claims is probably a Cherokee script. The Cherokee script, however, was only developed in 1821, and radiocarbon dating places the construction of the mound to between 66 and 769 CE, ruling out that possibility. Many scholars, including Cyrus Gordon, have identified the script as ancient Hebrew, reading "For the Judaeans." The scientific community has authenticated the stone, but has yet to recognize the Hebrew translation.
- Vikings colonized Iceland in 874 CE (#V).
- Vikings colonized Greenland in 985 CE (#V).
- The Vinland map, owned by Yale University, and recently authenticated, is dated to approximately 1440 CE. The map shows the island of Vinland in the Western Atlantic Ocean. It also reports the visit of Bishop Henricus to Vinland in 1117 CE. This map proves that lands in the Western Atlantic Ocean were known to European mariners in Columbus' time.
- Helge Ingstad, a lawyer and amateur archaeologist, discovered a Viking settlement at L'Anse aux Meadows, Newfoundland (#2). The site, which was mistakenly identified as Vinland by academicians, was, in fact, a permanent settlement dating back to 580 CE, according to radiocarbon dating from house hearths. Leif Erikson's Vinland was a temporary settlement in an uninhabited area in the New World, built in 1003 CE.
- A Viking coin was found in an Indian shell midden in Brooklin, Maine (#4). The coin, dated to approximately 1050 CE, establishes a Viking presence within the area of the continental United States.

The evidence outlined above is what has been generally accepted. There are many other pieces of evidence that are almost as compelling,

## 14. The Secret of Ancient America

but that have not been accepted by a majority of people in the scientific community:

- A vast trade network existed between the American Mound Builders and the Mayas in Mexico (#9), as proven by Mayan jade artifacts and colorful textiles found in ancient American mounds.
- The Kensington Stone documents a visit to the interior of the United States in 1362 CE by Viking mariners. Recent evidence regarding linguistics and dates essentially rules out the possibility of fraud.
- The Spirit Pond Rune Stones document Viking explorations in the United States about 1011 CE.
- The Grave Creek Tablet, discovered in situ in an ancient burial mound in 1838 CE, is a memorial tablet written in the Iberian language. The tomb was dated to 200 BCE.
- The model of a Japanese boat discovered by Alejandro von Wuthenau in an Olmec tomb documents a visit to Mexico by Japanese mariners about 500 BCE.
- The Newport Tower is shown on maps of Verrazano, Wood, and Mercator in 1524, 1633, and 1569 respectively, and is described by Englishman Sir Edmund Plowden in 1632. This refutes the claim that the tower was a colonial structure, because Newport wasn't settled until 1639 CE. Recent independent radiocarbon dating on the tower confirms the possibility that the tower may be precolonial.
- Many stone chambers in New England have been radiocarbon dated to 700 CE and earlier.
- Numerous ancient inscriptions give evidence of incursions into our country by foreign mariners more than 1,000 years ago. These include the Bourne Stone, the Yarmouth Stone, the Grave Creek Tablet, and the Bat Creek stone.

As the evidence accumulates, the overall history of the United States will become more cohesive and will exhibit greater continuity. With the evidence that already exists, it is possible to piece together a reasonable chronological scenario of how America was visited from across the oceans, when, and by whom.

40,000–20,000 BCE. The first visitors to the Americas may have entered the continent across the Bering Strait land bridge from Asia, or they may have come by boat, across the Atlantic or Pacific Oceans.

8000 BCE. The Archaic Period begins in North America. The last ice age comes to an end as the great sheets of ice blanketing the northern half of the United States recede, leaving behind land where lush green forests and fertile plains will flourish.

6500 BCE. The country of Ireland is colonized by bold Stone Age mariners from the coast of Brittany.

3900 BCE. Japanese mariners reach the northern coast of Colombia, South America.

3000 BCE. The mammoth tumulus of Newgrange is erected on the east coast of Ireland as a tomb for one of Ireland's ancient kings.

3000 BCE. Japanese mariners reach the coast of Ecuador, South America.

3000 BCE. The Phoenicians begin to develop their maritime expertise along the Levantine coast. Phoenician vessels, occasionally sailing under the flag of Egypt's pharaoh, visit ports in such diverse locations as Crete and India.

2780 BCE. The world's oldest known stepped pyramid is built by King Zoser at Sakkara, Egypt.

2500 BCE. Phoenician vessels explore the eastern coastline of Africa seeking trade relations with any friendly natives they find. Eventually their expeditions carry them around the southern tip of Africa and northwards along the west coast. The cost of these explorations is high, both in ships and in men. Many ships are caught up in the strong currents around the Gulf of Guinea, and are dashed against the rocks or sent to the bottom with all hands. A few are more fortunate. They are carried out to sea by the violent weather conditions and are driven westward across the great ocean to landfalls in South America, Central America, and Mexico. Egyptian, Phoenician, and Libyan adventurers settle in such widely separated locations as Mexico, Peru, Venezuela, and Colombia, where they become highly respected members of the aboriginal societies, teaching the natives such things as architecture, art, mathematics, religion, and astronomy. In many cases, they are recognized as gods by the superstitious inhabitants.

2500 BCE. A stepped pyramid is erected on the coast of Peru by an unknown people.

2400 BCE. Fiber tempered pottery is brought to Stallings Island, Georgia, by voyagers from Colombia, South America.

2000 BCE. Irish objects of bronze and gold are used in Denmark, indicating that ocean voyages and trade relations exist between the two countries.

1800 BCE. Mariners from the Iberian Peninsula, probably Southern

France, cross the Atlantic Ocean to North America, bringing the Solutrean culture to the southeastern section of the United States.

1800 BCE.   Rock carvings in Bohuslan, Sweden, depict large ocean-going vessels with sails, steering oars, and multiple decks.

1700 BCE.   A Scandinavian mariner named Woden-lithi crosses the North Atlantic Ocean and lands at Peterborough, Canada, where he spends six months trading with the natives and establishing a small colony. He leaves a record of his expedition in numerous rock carvings near the Peterborough colony. The carvings depict vessels that are similar to the vessels discovered in Bohuslan, Sweden. Since Norway is not a unified country at this time, but instead a collection of isolated farming communities, transatlantic voyages never become a common occurrence in this area of the world. Perhaps only Woden-lithi and his family knew the northern route to North America, and the secret of that route died with them.

1600 BCE.   Bronze Age people in Brittany build a stone astronomical calendar, as well as giant menhirs, dolmens, and other megalithic monuments.

1600 BCE.   Bronze Age people at America's Stonehenge, New Hampshire, build a stone astronomical calendar, as well as giant menhirs, dolmens, and other megalithic monuments.

1500 BCE.   North America's first earthen mound site is built at Poverty Point, Louisiana, possibly by refugees from the Olmec area of Mexico.

1100 BCE.   Polynesians begin their colonization of the Pacific islands, settling in Tonga and Samoa.

1100 BCE.   Phoenician vessels travel the Mediterranean Sea from one end to the other, and commerce is at an all-time high for the Levantine cities of Tyre and Sidon. The demand for consumer goods is so intense that Phoenician merchants venture farther and farther into unknown waters, finally dispatching their cargo fleets through the Pillars of Heracles and out into the dark, foreboding waters of the Atlantic Ocean.

The city of Gades, as well as several other small settlements, are founded on the Atlantic coast of Spain.

Phoenician traders from the new port of Gades begin to explore the northern reaches of the European coast, as well as the newly discovered British Isles. Some Iberian merchant fleets, carrying mixed crews of Phoenicians, Jews, Egyptians, Libyans, and Iberian Celts, even set sail along the west coast of Africa, erecting small colonies at strategic locations as they go, until they reach the southern settlements that were founded by their Levantine forefathers more than a millennia before.

As might be expected, isolated vessels from these expeditions are periodically blown off course and sent hurtling westward. Not only do some of these ships reach South America, but a few of them reach the coast of North America, the first of many excursions to the New World.

With time, the northern route through Iceland and Greenland is rediscovered, as is the return route home to Spain via the convenient and hospitable Gulf Stream. These discoveries make the New World a vast new source of raw materials for the Eastern Atlantic markets, a source to be kept secret to allow maximum exploitation by the newly formed Iberian Federation.

Iberian ships scour the Atlantic seaboard of North America, all the way from Florida to Maine, and establish permanent colonies up and down the east coast. They also enter many of the navigable waterways of the eastern half of the United States, including the Mississippi, the Arkansas, the Cimarron, and the St. Lawrence, and they leave a record of their explorations carved into the rocky cliffs that adjoin the inland tributaries.

1000 BCE. The Eastern Woodland culture, a natural evolution of American aborigines, begins in the northeastern section of the United States. This is North America's first known civilized society.

1000 BCE. The Adena culture, a more sophisticated culture than the Eastern Woodland culture, begins in the Ohio River Valley. The first Adena settlers may have been immigrants from the Olmec region of Mexico, the same people who settled Poverty Point, Louisiana. The Adena culture is characterized by large earthen burial mounds, engraved stones, and ceremonial earthworks.

There is evidence of contact between the Adena and the ancient inhabitants of Western Europe. The evidence, in addition to the similarity in design and construction of the mounds and earthworks, lies in the engraved stones that have been found in Adena graves, such as those at Bat Creek and Grave Creek.

887 BCE. An inscribed stone, found by Don Bernardo de Silva Ramos in Brazil in 1899, depicts an intentional commercial voyage from the Phoenician city of Tyre to Brazil between 887 and 856 BCE.

825 BCE. The Phoenicians establish the city of Carthage on the north coast of Africa.

534 BCE. Phoenician mariners, under the flag of the Egyptian pharaoh Necho II, circumnavigate Africa for the first time. The expedition lasts three years.

534 BCE. A Phoenician ship, sailing under the authority of King Hiram, leaves Ezion Geber to circumnavigate Africa as part of Necho II's fleet. After two years, the ship is separated from the rest of the fleet and is carried across the Atlantic Ocean to Brazil, where the crew struggles to survive.

## 14. The Secret of Ancient America

The captain carves the tragic story on a rock for posterity. The rock is finally discovered by Joachim Alves da Costa in 1872.

500 BCE. Japanese mariners cross the Pacific Ocean in a large sailing vessel and visit the Olmec Empire, located in the central highlands of Mexico.

500 BCE. The Hopewell Indians move into the Ohio River Valley as neighbors of the Adena. The two peoples live in peace, side by side, for centuries. The Hopewell learn the Adena culture and improve upon it, subsequently developing North America's most advanced society to date.

Many scientists consider the Hopewell Indians to be members of the Algonquin tribe. Other scientists believe the Hopewell are a mixture of American aborigine and Western European stock, possibly Iberian Celt. Hopewell structures closely duplicate those in Western Europe, including dry stone chambers, menhirs, mounds, cists, and earthworks.

500 BCE. Inscribed stones, dated from 500 BCE to 200 BCE, are left all over Northeastern America, as well as along the Arkansas and Cimarron Rivers in Oklahoma, southeast Colorado, and New Mexico. The stones are in a variety of ancient scripts, such as Celtic, Phoenician, Libyan, Hebrew, and Egyptian. This time period corresponds to the period of maximum Punic activity along the Atlantic seaboard of Europe.

450 BCE. The Punic explorer Himilco explores the entire coastline of Western Europe. His ships are becalmed in the Sargasso Sea.

450 BCE. The Punic king Hanno explores the Atlantic coast of Africa. Some Punic settlements already exist when Hanno visits them, verifying that Phoenician mariners had explored this region for many years prior to Hanno's expedition.

450 BCE. A Punic explorer named Hanno leaves an inscribed "annexation" stone at Bourne on Cape Cod, Massachusetts.

350 BCE. Aristotle describes an island in the Atlantic Ocean that has navigable rivers. Some scholars claim this island is England, but England was already well known in 350 BCE. The island may be North or South America.

310 BCE. Carthaginian coins are lost on a beach on the island of Corvo, in the Azores, 1,600 miles due west of the European coast, across open ocean, and on the return route from America to Europe.

306 BCE. A Greek scientist, Pytheas, explores the coast of Western Europe. He describes an island called Ultima Thule. Some scholars identify Ultima Thule as Iceland.

200 BCE. Polynesian mariners cross thousands of miles of open ocean to colonize Tahiti.

200 BCE. An inscribed stone written in an ancient Celtiberic script is buried in an Adena mound at Grave Creek, West Virginia.

146 BCE. Rome defeats Carthage in the third Punic War, razing the city of Carthage to the ground, and ending Phoenician seapower once and for all.

Some scholars believe that colonists from across the Atlantic were left stranded in America after the defeat of the Phoenicians. According to the scholars, these colonists were eventually absorbed into the Indian cultures, but some of their practices were continued and are evident in Indian religion, philosophy, and tradition even today.

As Phoenician seapower wanes in the second century BCE, Celtic seapower is on the rise, particularly from Celtic home ports in Ireland. From 100 BCE onward, Celtic mariners rule the North Atlantic Ocean and all waters to the west of Ireland.

100 BCE. The model of an oceangoing vessel is buried in grave in Broighter, Ireland.

50 BCE. Julius Caesar defeats the Celts in Gaul, destroying Celtic seapower in that area. Despite the defeat of their Continental brethren, Celtic mariners from Ireland continue to harass Roman shipping lanes between the European continent and Britain, and Celtic merchant ships ply their wares at every port along the Atlantic coast, from Norway to Morocco.

40 BCE. The ancient geographer Diodorus describes a large continent off the west coast of Africa, having navigable rivers. The only continents fitting his description are North and South America.

9 CE. The Annals of Ireland report an overseas expedition.

100 CE. Plutarch describes an island in the Atlantic Ocean called Ogygia, and says there is a large continent to the west of it. Many scholars believe Ogygia to be Iceland and the continent to be North America. Certainly the only continents in the Western Atlantic Ocean are the Americas.

100 CE. An inscribed stone written in an ancient Hebrew script is buried in an Adena mound at Bat Creek, Tennessee.

157 CE. A dispute arises over shipping rights in Dublin between the king of Ireland and the son of the king of Spain. The king of Spain's son is killed in the ensuing war, as recorded in the Annals.

240 CE. The Annals report that Cormac sails across the sea with a fleet of ships and conquers Alba (Scotland).

270 CE. Roman coins are left on a beach in Eastern Iceland. It is more than likely that Celtic mariners lost the coins, since the Celts ruled the western seas.

300 CE. Irish mariners use Iceland as a summer fishing base. Within a short period of time they also establish seasonal bases in Greenland.

## 14. The Secret of Ancient America

300 CE.  Polynesian mariners cross 2,400 miles of open ocean from the Marquesas Islands, to colonize Hawaii.

385 CE.  Refugees from Peru, called Long-ears, colonize Easter Island after spending more than 100 days on the open water.

400 CE.  A beehive hut is built at Clochan na Carraige, Ireland.

400 CE.  The Irish build a souterrain in an existing burial mound at Knowth, Ireland.

475 CE.  Rome falls to the Vandals, plunging Europe into anarchy and barbarism. Irish monks keep the flame of Christianity burning brightly throughout the continent during these Dark Ages. Their numerous seafaring pilgrimages frequently reach Europe and Egypt, and even extend as far east as the Holy Land. They visit fellow Christian monks in Alexandria and Jerusalem, establish monasteries, and generally spread the Gospel wherever they travel.

499 CE.  Hoei Shin, a Buddhist monk, sails from China on a missionary voyage to a land called Fu-sang in the eastern ocean. Fu-sang has been identified in many circles as Mexico. Hoei Shin spends several years in Fu-sang trying unsuccessfully to convert the inhabitants to Buddhism.

500 CE.  The Peruvian white god, Kon-Tiki, flees Peru on a raft and sails westward into the uncharted waters of the Pacific Ocean.

500 CE.  The Polynesian god, Tiki, arrives in the Marquesas Islands on a raft after sailing from a desert land to the east.

500 CE.  An underground, dry stone burial chamber is constructed at Carrabeg, Ireland.

500 CE.  Unknown Irish monks cross the Atlantic Ocean to North America after sailing for 40 days and 40 nights. The monks are searching for a quiet, deserted land where they can meditate and pray to their God in peaceful solitude.

520 CE.  The Oracle Chamber is built at America's Stonehenge in New Hampshire.

545 CE.  A souterrain is constructed in Windham, Vermont.

555 CE.  An Irish monk, St. Brendan the Navigator, explores North America in search of other Irish monks.

560 CE.  A tan bark mill is constructed at the Gungywamp, a fortified cashel in Connecticut. The Gungywamp contains stone wall enclosures, stone chambers, and several inscribed stones with Christian Chi-Rho symbols that date to 400–700 CE.

600 CE.  An Irish monk named Cormac explores the Western Atlantic Ocean.

600 CE.  The Inishmurray Clochan is built in Ireland.

600 CE.  Refugees from Mexico or South America cross the Gulf of

Mexico to the Mississippi River delta, and begin to conquer the native inhabitants, including the peaceful Hopewell Indians. This is the beginning of the Mississippian culture.

610 CE. The first house is built at L'Anse aux Meadows, Newfoundland, by an unknown people. It is probable that L'Anse aux Meadows was not Vinland, since the Newfoundland settlement was thriving for 400 years before Leif Erikson ventured forth from his Greenland fjord. There is no evidence that Leif Erikson built his houses in an existing settlement. The settlement was likely built by Irish mariners during one of their frequent visits to North America. The Vikings did live in L'Anse aux Meadows subsequent to 1000 CE, as evidenced by Viking artifacts found there.

700 CE. Several other houses are built at L'Anse aux Meadows between 700 CE and 740 CE, probably by a new influx of Irish immigrants.

710 CE. A beehive hut is constructed at Upton, Massachusetts, according to archaeoastronomical dating techniques.

795 CE. Irish monks maintain a religious community in Iceland.

800 CE. A dry stone chamber is erected at Leacanabuaile, Ireland.

874 CE. Viking mariners colonize Iceland. Irish monks flee before the Vikings arrive.

977 CE. The great Aztec God, Quetzalcoatl, leaves Mexico on a raft and sails eastward into the ocean, promising to return. According to Mexican legend, Quetzalcoatl is a tall white man with dark hair and a long beard, and he wears a flowing white robe.

981 CE. Viking mariners report an Irish settlement on the coast of North America. The settlement is referred to as Greater Ireland by the Vikings.

982 CE. Erik the Red discovers Greenland. The Vikings find evidence of Irish habitation on the island.

1003 CE. Leif Erikson discovers Vinland. Some time later, the Vikings occupy L'Anse aux Meadows.

1012 CE. The Karlsefni expedition to Vinland captures two native boys who tell tales of an Irish colony in Vinland. The Vikings quickly alienate the aborigines, and are constantly defeated in hand-to-hand battles by sheer force of numbers. Without the firearms that Christopher Columbus was later to use with great success against the natives, the Vikings eventually have to give up their thoughts of colonization.

1100 CE. A dry stone, slab roofed chamber is built in Newton, New Hampshire.

1100 CE. Refugees from Augustin, Ecuador, settle on Easter Island and begin to erect gigantic statues.

1100 CE. Viking expeditions to America leave artifacts strewn around the countryside between 1100 CE and 1350 CE. These include weapons found at Lake Nipigon, Canada, the Kensington Stone, the Spirit Pond Runestones, and a Viking coin found in an Indian midden in Brooklin, Maine.

1170 CE.  A Welsh prince named Madoc supposedly makes two voyages to America and establishes a colony near Mobile, Alabama.

1186 CE.  The colonists from the Madoc expedition are defeated by Indians at Sandy Island, near Louisville, Kentucky. Survivors flee up the Missouri River to North Dakota. They intermarry with the Mandan Indians, beginning the legend of the white Indians.

1200 CE.  A European trading community that had lived side by side with the Indians in middle America for more than 200 years is massacred. Men, women, and children are killed by the Indians, who fear the Europeans are becoming a danger to them. The trading settlement may have been near Cahokia, and the European traders may have been Vikings.

1300 CE.  Polynesian mariners called Short-ears reach Easter Island.

1347 CE.  A Greenland ship returning from Markland is blown off course and lands in Iceland. The Greenland Eastern Settlement is harassed by natives.

1354 CE.  Paul Knutson, a Norwegian aristocrat, is commissioned by the king of Norway to lead an expedition to Greenland and Vinland, to locate the colonists. The Knutson expedition returns to Norway in 1364 CE, but whether they located the Vinland settlement is unknown.

1398 CE.  Prince Henry Sinclair of Scotland is reported to have visited North America, probably Newfoundland and Massachusetts. His expedition may have built the Newport Tower.

1410 CE.  The Olafsson expedition makes the last recorded visit to Greenland.

The American continent is devoid of European colonists save for those few who are absorbed into the Indian culture.

1492 CE. Christopher Columbus steps ashore on the tiny island of San Salvador, proudly proclaiming the discovery of America, and claiming title to the lands of the western ocean in the names of King Ferdinand and Queen Isabella of Spain. Columbus didn't know it, but he was just the last of a long line of Mariners to visit the American continent over a period of more than 4,000 years.

As this problem is brought to its final solution, some of the preceding statements will, no doubt, be found to be inaccurate. But it is likely that the overall chronology of events as outlined is essentially correct, and is much closer to the historical facts than the claim that Columbus was the first European to visit the Americas.

The American continent was almost surely visited by European, Middle Eastern, African, and Asian mariners as long ago as 5,000 years, and adventurers from across the oceans continued to visit these shores regularly right up to that fateful day in 1492. The American scientific community, thanks to courageous archaeologists such as Betty Meggers and Dennis Stanford of the Smithsonian Institution, is beginning to investigate the possibility that ancient mariners may have visited this country before Rome was founded. They have taken the first step. And as President John F. Kennedy reminded us, "A journey of a thousand miles must begin with a single step."

# Chapter Notes

## Introduction
1. *Newsweek*, April 26, 1999, p. 56.

## Chapter 1
1. Thomas Jefferson, *Notes on the State of Virginia*, pp. 93–95.

## Chapter 2
1. J.E. Weckler, Jr., *Polynesians: Explorers of the Pacific*, p. 1.
2. Kenneth P. Emory, *National Geographic*, Dec. 1974, p. 739.
3. J.E. Weckler, Jr., *Polynesians: Explorers of the Pacific*, p. 12.
4. David Lewis, *National Geographic*, Dec. 1974, p. 749.
5. Ibid.
6. Ibid.
7. Kenneth P. Emory, p. 739.
8. Thor Heyerdahl, "The Voyage of RA II," *National Geographic*, p. 46.
9. Ibid., p. 46.
10. Ibid., p. 47.
11. Ibid., p. 50.
12. Ibid., p. 70.
13. Timothy Severin, "The Voyage of the Brendan," *National Geographic*, p. 775.
14. Ibid., p. 775.
15. Ibid., p. 777.
16. Ibid., p. 778.

## Chapter 3
1. Howard La Fay, "The Vikings," *National Geographic*, p. 497.
2. Knut Gjerset, *History of the Norwegian People*," p. 20.
3. Ibid., p. 22.
4. Paul B. Du Chaillu, *The Viking Age*, p. 7.
5. Ibid., p. 12.
6. Ibid., p. 13.
7. Edmund F. Slafter, *Voyages of the Northmen to America*, p. 14.
8. Quoted in Howard La Fay, p. 495.
9. Ibid., p. 497.
10. Paul Du Chaillu, p. 141.
11. Ibid., p. 141.
12. Edmund F. Slafter, p. 75.
13. Ibid., p. 75.
14. Ibid., p. 76.
15. Ibid., p. 28.
16. Ibid., pp. 31–33.
17. Ibid., p. 35.
18. Quoted in John Abbott, *The History of Maine*, p. 19.
19. Edmund F. Slafter, p. 14.
20. Quoted in ibid., p. 15.
21. Gary Jennings, "Newfoundland Trusts in the Sea," *National Geographic*, Jan. 1974, pp. 135–136.

## Chapter 4
1. Henry R. Schoolcraft, *History, Condition, and Prospects of the Indian Tribes of the United States*, vol. 1, p. 119 and vol. 6, p. 609.
2. James P. Whittall, Jr., "A Runic Amulet," ESRS *Bulletin*, vol. 3, no.1, p. 1.
3. Ibid., p. 2.
4. Hjalmar Holand, *Westland from Vinland*, p. 101.
5. Philip Ainsworth Means, *Newport Tower*, p. 125.

6. *Collections of the New York Historical Society for the Year 1869*, p. 217.
7. E.D. Fite and A. Freeman, *A Book of Old Maps*.
8. "Re: The Tower of Newport," available at http://Sinclair2.quarterman.org/archive/2000.

# Chapter 5

1. R.D. Archer-Hind, *The Timaeus of Plato*, p. 79.
2. W.S. Blackett, *Researches into the Lost Histories of America*, p. 31.
3. W.S. Hett, *Aristotle: Minor Works*, pp. 271–271.
4. Horace Leonard Jones, *The Geography of Strabo*, vol. 1, 1:3:2.
5. Ibid.
6. Ibid.
7. Ibid., vol. 1, 2:5:14–15.
8. C.H. Oldfather, *Diodorus of Sicily*, vol. 3, 5:19:1–5.
9. Ibid., 5:20:14–15.
10. William W. Goodwin, *Plutarch's Morals*, p. 281.
11. Ibid., p. 283.
12. J.G. Frazer, *Pausanias' Description of Greece'*, p. 33.

# Chapter 6

1. Charles Michael Boland, *They All Discovered America*, pp. 90–92.
2. Edward P. Vining, *An Inglorious Columbus*, pp. 40–42.
3. W.C. Bryant, S.H. Gay, N. Brooks, *Scribners Popular History of the United States*, vol. 1, p. 86.
4. Ibid., pp. 68–69.
5. Ibid., p. 75.
6. Ibid., p. 80.
7. Ibid., p. 81.
8. Clay Perry, *Underground New England*, p. ??.

# Chapter 7

1. Hamilton Child, *Gazeteer and Business Directory of Windham County Vermont*, p. 17.
2. Ibid., p. 17.

3. George Rawlinson, *History of Phoenicia*, p. 281.
4. Ibid., p. 129.
5. Ibid., p. 389.
6. Ibid., p. 550.

# Chapter 8

1. Richard V. Humphrey, *The Mystery Hill Source Book*, p. 117.
2. Ibid., pp. 11–12.
3. Ibid., p. 21.
4. Ibid., p. 44.
5. James P. Whittall Jr., "Structure XI B-North Salem, New Hampshire," ESRS *Bulletin*, p. 23.
6. Ibid., p. 23.
7. Salvatore M. Trento, *The Search for Lost America*, p. 184.
8. James P. Whittall, Jr., "Structure XI B," p. 24.
9. James P. Whittall, Jr., "Excavation Report—Oracle Chamber Drain, New Hampshire," p. 18.
10. James P. Whittall, Jr., "Structure XI B," p. 26.
11. Charles Buxton Going, "The Mysterious Prehistoric Monuments of Brittany," *National Geographic*, July 1923, p. 69.
12. Ibid., p. 69.
13. Ibid., p. 68.

# Chapter 9

1. Alfred Hopkins, *Modern Farm Buildings*, p. 202.
2. Ibid., p. 201.
3. Ibid., p. 202.
4. Ulysses Prentiss Hedrick, *A History of Agriculture in the State of New York*, p. 98.
5. Ibid., p. 189.
6. H.P. Smith, *A History of Addison County Vermont*.
7. Zadock Thompson, *History of Vermont*.
8. Ibid.
9. Ibid., p. 198.
10. Henry Hobart Vail, *Pomfret Vermont*, p. 152.
11. Lewis Cass Aldrich and Frank R. Holmes, *History of Windsor County Vermont*, p. 771.
12. Salvatore Trento, *The Search for Lost America*, p. 51.

13. Ibid., p. 51.
14. Ibid., pp. 51–52.
15. James P. Whittall, Jr., "The Gungywamp Complex — Groton, CT," p. 15.
16. James P. Whittall, Jr., "A Report on the Pearson Stone Chamber, Upton, Massachusetts," p. 29.
17. James P. Whittall, Jr., ESRS Work Report, vol. 3, no. 30.
18. E.B. O'Callaghan, *Documentary History of the State of New York*, p. 1139.
19. Charles Buxton Going, "The Mysterious Prehistoric Monuments of Brittany," *National Geographic*, July 1923, p. 53.
20. Ibid., p. 54.
21. Knut Gjerset, *History of Iceland*, p. 5.
22. W.G. Wood-Martin, *Pagan Ireland*, p. 206.
23. R.A.S. Macalister, *The Archeology of Ireland*.
24. Richard Holt Brash, *The Ecclesiastical Architecture of Ireland*.
25. John Dowden, *The Celtic Church in Scotland*, pp. 294–295.
26. Byron E. Dix and James Mavor Jr., *Possible Astronomical Alignments, Dates, and Origins of the Pearson Stone Chamber*, pp. 11–12.
27. W.G. Wood-Martin, *Pagan Ireland*, p. 204.
28. R.A.S. Macalister, *The Archeology of Ireland*.
29. W.G. Wood-Martin, *Pagan Ireland*, pp. 178–179.
30. David P. Barron and Sharon Mason, *The Greater Gungywamp*.
31. Ibid.

# Chapter 10

1. R.A.S. Macalister, *Ireland in Prehistoric Times*, p. 286.
2. Ibid., p. 308.
3. Ibid., p. 287.
4. Ibid., p. 290.
5. Ibid., pp. 290–291.
6. C.B. Going, *The Mysterious Prehistoric Monuments of Brittany*, p. 53.
7. R.A.S. Macalister, *The Archeology of Ireland*, p. 105.
8. C.B. Going, p. 54.
9. Joseph Anderson, *Scotland in Pagan Times*, p. 119.
10. C.B. Going, p. 68.
11. R.A.S. Macalister, *Ireland in Pre-Celtic Times*, p. 293.
12. Ibid., p. 296.
13. James Fergusson, *Rude Stone Monuments*, pp. 73–74.
14. Joseph Anderson, p. 104, 117.
15. Paul Du Chaillu, *The Viking Age*, pp. 369–370.
16. James Fergusson, p. 282.
17. Ibid., pp. 180–181.
18. Ibid., p. 178.
19. Ibid., p. 179.
20. Joseph Anderson, p. 280.
21. James Fergusson, p. 161.
22. R.A.S. Macalister, *The Archeology of Ireland*, p. 114.
23. Ibid., p. 118.
24. C.C. Jones, *Antiquities of the Southern Indians*, p. 114.
25. Charles J. Taylor, *History of Great Barrington, Mass.*, p. 39.
26. H.R. Schoolcraft, *Condition of the Indian Tribes*, vol. 1, p. 356.

# Chapter 11

1. John O'Donovan, *Annals of the Kingdom of Ireland*, vol. 1, p. 69.
2. "Did Other Sailors Precede Columbus?" Available at abcnews.com, p. 3 of 4.
3. Boland, p. 50. See also Zvi Herman's *Peoples, Seas, and Ships*.
4. Ibid., p. 49.
5. Cyrus Thomas, *Smithsonian Twelfth Annual Report*, pp. 392–393.
6. Gordon, *Riddles in History*, p. 76.
7. Henry R. Schoolcraft, *Condition of the Indian Tribes*, vol. 1, p. 123.
8. Ibid., vol. 4, p. 129.
9. J.W. Foster, *Prehistoric Races of the United States of America*, p. 190.
10. Schoolcraft, vol. 4, p. 129.
11. J.P. MacLean, *The Mound Builders*, p. 97.
12. Schoolcraft, vol. 1, p. 118, 123; vol. 6, p. 610.
13. MacLean, p. 93.
14. John Wesley Powell, *Twelfth Annual Report, Smithsonian Institution*, p. 632.
15. MacLean, p. 105.
16. Ibid., p. 95.
17. Donal Buchanan, ESRS *Bulletin*, vol. 10, no. 1, p. 26.

18. Ibid., pp. 22, 24.
19. Ibid., p. 26
20. James P. Whittall, Jr., ESRS *Bulletin*, vol. 3, no. 2, 1975, p. 6.
21. Whittall, ESRS *Bulletin*, vol. 4, no. 1, 1976, p. 9.
22. Ibid., pp. 8–9.
23. Eric J. Ruff, personal correspondence, 1984.
24. Whittall, ESRS *Bulletin*, vol. 4, no. 1, p. 31.
25. Gloria Farley, personal correspondence, 1984.
26. James P. Whittall, Jr., ESRS *Bulletin*, vol. 4, no. 1, 1976, pp. 1–5.
27. Putnam Museum, personal correspondence, 1983.
28. Cyrus Thomas, pp. 634–635, 641–643.
29. J. Huston McCulloch, *The Newark Decalogue Ohio Stone and Keystone.*
30. Ida Jane Gallagher, *Wonderful West Virginia*, March 1983, p. 8.
31. McGlone et al., *Ancient American Inscriptions: Plow Marks or History?*, p. 60.

## Chapter 12

1. Fell, *Saga America*, pp. 118–119.
2. Salvatore Trento, *The Search for Lost America'*, p. 86.
3. James P. Whittall, Jr., ESRS *Bulletin*, vol. 5, no. 1, 1977, p. 1.
4. James P. Whittall, Jr., ESRS *Bulletin*, vol. 6, no. 1, 1978, p. 5.
5. Edward L. Keithahn, description booklet of the Alaska Historical Museum, pp. 52–53.

## Chapter 13

1. Thomas Jefferson, *Notes on Virginia*, p. 93.
2. C.C. Jones, *Antiquities of the Southern Indians*, p. 161.
3. Ibid., p. 125.
4. Thomas Jefferson, p. 96.
5. Dennis Stanford, *Newsweek*, p. 52.
6. Dennis Stanford, *Newsweek*, p. 57.
7 Barnard Shipp, *The Indians and Antiquities of America*, p. 271.
8. Ibid., pp. 69–70.
9. Schoolcraft quoted in Shipp, pp. 250–251.
10. Atwater quoted in Shipp, p. 238.
11. William Pidgeon, *Traditions of Dee Coo Dah*, p. 161.
12. Ibid., p. 161.
13. Ibid., p. 161.
14. Ibid., pp. 178, 257.
15. Ibid., p. 39.
16. William Leete Stone, *Life of Joseph Brant—Thayendanegea*, pp. 484–486.
17. J.P. MacLean, *The Mound Builders.*

# *Bibliography*

Abbot, John. *The History of Maine*. Boston: B.B. Russell, 1875.
*Academic America Encyclopedia*. Princeton, New Jersey: Arete Pub. Co., 1980.
Airne, C.W. *The Story of Prehistoric and Roman Britain*. Manchester, England: Sankey, Hudson, 1935.
Aldrich, Lewis Cass and Frank R. Holmes. *History of Windsor County Vermont*. Syracuse, New York: D. Mason, 1891.
Allen, John, Ed. *One Hundred Great Lives*. New York: Greystone Press, 1948.
*Ancient American*. Colfax, Wisconsin: Wayne N. May, 1993–1998.
Anderson, J.R.L. *Vinland Voyage*. New York: Funk and Wagnalls, 1967.
Anderson, Joseph. *Scotland in Pagan Times: The Iron Age*. Edinburgh: David Douglas, 1883.
Archer-Hind, R.D. *The Timaeus of Plato*. New York: Macmillan, 1888.
Arnold, Samuel Greene. *History of the State of Rhode Island and Providence Plantations*. New York: D. Appleton, 1859.
Bacon, Edgar Mayhew. *The Hudson River*. New York: G.P. Putnam's Sons, 1903.
Bailey, Paul, ed. *Long Island*. Vol. 1. New York: Lewis Historical Pub. Co., 1949.
Baldwin, James D. *Ancient America*. New York: Harper and Brothers, 1872.
Barber, John Warner. *The History and Antiquities of New England, New York, and New Jersey*. Worcester, Massachusetts.: Dorr, Howland, 1841.
Barron, David. Personal correspondence. 1985–1998.
\_\_\_\_\_, and Sharon Mason. *The Greater Gungywamp*. North Groton, Connecticut: Gungywamp Society, 1990.
Baxter, James Phinney. *Early Voyages to America*. Taunton, Massachusetts: Old Colony Historical Society, 1889.
\_\_\_\_\_.*Miscellaneous Papers*. Portland, Maine, 1906.
Betts, Edwin Morris, ed. *Thomas Jefferson's Farm Book*. Charlottesville: University Press of Virginia, 1976.
Bibby, Geoffrey. *Four Thousand Years Ago*. New York: Alfred E. Knopf, 1961.
Blackett, W.S. *Researches into the Lost Histories of America*. London: Trubner, 1884.
Blake, Robert C., III. *The Younger John Winthrop*. New York: Columbia University Press, 1966.
Blake, William J., Esq. *The History of Putnam County, N.Y.* New York: Baker and Scribner, 1849.
Bogart, Ernest L. *Peacham: The Story of a Vermont Hill Town*. Montpelier: Vermont Historical Society, 1948.
Boland, Charles M. *They All Discovered America*. New York: Doubleday, 1946.

Brash, Richard Holt. *The Ecclesiastical Architecture of Ireland*. London: W.B. Kelly, 1875.
Briard, Jacques. *The Bronze Age in Barbarian Europe*. Translated by Mary Turton. London: Routledge and Kegan Paul, 1976.
Brine, Lindesay. *Travels Amongst American Indians*. London: Sampson Low, Marston, 1894.
Brittain, Alfred. *The History of North America*. Philadelphia: George Barrie and Son, 1903.
Brown, J. Macmillan. *Peoples and Problems of the Pacific*. London: T. Fisher Unwin, 1927.
Bryant, W.C., S.H. Gay, and N. Brooks. *Scribner's Popular History of the United States*. Vol. 1. New York: Charles Scribner's, 1896.
Buchanan, Donal. "The Ohio County Stone Deciphered." *Bulletin of the Early Sites Research Society*, vol. 7, no. 2, Dec. 1979.
\_\_\_\_\_. "Report on the Morristown Tablet." *Bulletin of the Early Sites Research Society*, vol. 10, no. 1, Dec. 1982.
Buck, Peter H. *Vikings of the Pacific*. Chicago: University of Chicago Press, 1972.
Burrows, Russell, and Fred Rydholm. *The Mystery Cave of Many Faces*. Marquette, Michigan: Superior Heartland, 1992.
Bury, R.G. *Plato*. New York: G.P. Putnam's Sons, 1929.
Cahill, Robert Ellis. *New England's Ancient Mysteries*. Salem, Massachusetts: Old Saltbox Publishing, 1993.
\_\_\_\_\_. *New England's Viking and Indian Wars*. Peabody, Massachusetts: Chandler-Smith, 1986.
Canby, Courtland. *A History of Ships and Seafaring*. New York: Hawthorne, 1963.
Carpenter, Rhys. *Beyond the Pillars of Heracles*. New York: Delacorte Press, 1966.
Casson, Lionel. *The Ancient Mariners*. New York: Macmillan, 1959.
Ceram, C.W. *The First American*. New York: New American Library, 1971.
Chapman, Paul H. *The Norse Discovery of America*. Atlanta: One Candle Press, 1981.
\_\_\_\_\_. "Spirit Pond Runestones, Part II." *ESOP, Journal of the Epigraphic Society* (San Francisco), vol. 22 (1994).
Chatterton, E. Kebble. *Ships and Ways of Other Days*. London: Sidgwick and Jackson, 1913.
Child, Hamilton. *Gazetteer and Business Directory of Windham County, Vermont*. Syracuse, New York: Hamilton Child, 1884.
Childe, V. Gordon. *Prehistory of Scotland*. London: Kegan Paul, Trench, Trubner, 1935.
\_\_\_\_\_. *Scotland Before the Scots*. London: Methuen, 1946.
\_\_\_\_\_. *Skara Brae*. London: Kegan Paul, Trench, Trubner, 1931.
Childress, David Hatcher. *Lost Cities of North and Central America*. Stelle, Illinois: Adventures Unlimited Press, 1992.
Clarke, Graham. *Prehistoric England*. New York: Charles Scribner's Sons, 1941.
Clodd, Edward. *The Story of the Alphabet*. New York: McClure Phillips, 1914.
*Collections of the New York Historical Society for the Year 1869*. New York: Trow and South Book Manufacturing Co., 1870.
*Collier's Encyclopedia*. New York: Macmillan Educational, 1983.
Cook, Warren L., ed. *Ancient Vermont*. Rutland, Vermont: Academy Books, 1978.
Cox, Donald W. *Pioneers of Ecology*. Maplewood, New Jersey: Hammond, 1971.
Cunliffe, Barry. *The Celtic World*. New York: McGraw-Hill, 1979.

Cyr, Donald L. ed. *Dragon Treasures*. Santa Barbara, California: Stonehenge Viewpoint, 1989.
Dawson, Henry B. *Westchester County, N.Y.* Morrisania, New York, 1886.
Deacon, Richard. *Madoc and the Discovery of America*. New York: George Braziller, 1966.
\_\_\_\_\_. "Michigan's Ancient Coptic Christian Picture-Library." *Ancient American*, vol. 3, no. 18.
\_\_\_\_\_. "The Mystic Symbol De-Mystified." *Ancient American*, vol. 1, no. 5.
\_\_\_\_\_. "The Ten Commandments and New Mexico's Mountain Citadel." *Ancient American*, vol. 2, no. 9.
Delabarre, Edmund Burke. *The Dighton Rock*. New York: Walter Neale, 1928.
"Did Other Sailors Precede Columbus?" Available at http://www.abcnews.com.
Diringer, David. *The Alphabet*. New York: Philosophical Library, 1948.
Dix, Byron E., and James W. Mavor, Jr. "*Possible Astronomical Alignments, Date and Origins of the Pearson Stone Chamber*." *ESRS Bulletin*, 1980.
Dixon, E. James. "Coastal Navigators." *Discovering Archaeology*, February 2000.
Du Chaillu, Paul B. *The Viking Age*. New York: Charles Scribner's Sons, 1890.
Duff, Thomas A. *Kon-Tiki and Aku-Aku*. New York: Monarch Press, 1966.
Durrett, Reuben T. *Traditions of the Earliest Visits of Foreigners to North America*. Louisville, Kentucky: John P. Morton, 1908.
Early Sites Research Society. Bulletins. Rowley, Massachusetts, 1974–1991.
\_\_\_\_\_. Newsletters. Rowley, Massachusetts, 1983–1998.
Emory, Kenneth P. "The Coming of the Polynesians." *National Geographic*, Dec. 1974.
*Encyclopedia Americana*. New York: Americana, 1977.
*Encyclopaedia Britannica*. Chicago: William Benton, 1973.
Enterline, James Robert. *Viking America*. New York: Doubleday, 1972.
Evans, Estyn. *Prehistoric and Early Christian Ireland*. New York: Barnes and Noble, 1966.
Evans, John G. *Environment of Early Man in the British Isles*. Los Angeles: University of California Press, 1975.
Fell, Barry. *America B.C.* New York: New York Times Book Co., 1977.
\_\_\_\_\_. *Saga America*. New York: Times Books, 1980.
\_\_\_\_\_. *Bronze Age America*. Boston: Little, Brown, 1982.
Fergusson, James. *Rude Stone Monuments*. London: John Murray, 1872.
Finney, Ben R. *Hokule'a: The Way of Tahiti*. New York: Dodd, Mead, 1970.
Fiske, John. *The Discovery of America*. Boston: Houghton Mifflin, 1892.
Fite, E.D., and A. Freeman. *A Book of Old Maps*. Cambridge: Harvard University Press, 1926.
Foster, J.W. *Pre-Historic Races of the United States of America*. Chicago: S.C. Griggs, 1887.
Fowke, Gerard. *Antiquities of Central and Southeastern Missouri*. Washington, D.C.: U.S. Government Printing Office, 1910.
Frazer, J.G., trans. *Pausanias's Description of Greece*. London: Macmillan, 1913.
Furman, Gabriel. *Antiquities of Long Island*. J.W. Bouton, 1875.
Furneaux, Rupert. *Ancient Mysteries*. New York: Ballantine, 1977.
Gabriel, Ralph Henry, ed. *The Pageant of America*. New Haven: Yale University Press, 1925.
Gallagher, Ida Jane. "Assembled Evidence Strengthens Petroglyph Interpretations Case." *Wonderful West Virginia*, June 1986.

\_\_\_\_\_. "Light Dawns on West Virginia History." *Wonderful West Virginia*, March 1983.
Gjerset, Knut. *History of Iceland*. New York: Macmillan, 1925.
\_\_\_\_\_. *History of the Norwegian People*. New York: Macmillan, 1915.
Going, Charles Buxton. "The Mysterious Prehistoric Monuments of Brittany." *National Geographic*, July 1923.
Goodwin, William W. *Plutarch's Morals*. Boston: Little, Brown, 1870.
Gordon, Cyrus. *Before Columbus*. New York: Crown, 1971.
\_\_\_\_\_. *Riddles in History*. New York: Crown, 1974.
Griffin, James B., ed. *Archeology of Eastern United States*. Chicago: University of Chicago Press, 1952.
Hall, Benjamin H. *History of Eastern Vermont*. New York: D. Appleton, 1858.
Harbison, Peter. *The Archeology of Ireland*. New York: Charles Scribner's Sons, 1976.
Harden, Donald B. *The Phoenicians*. London: Thames and Hudson, 1962.
Haugen Einar. *Voyages to Vinland*. New York: Alfred E. Knopf, 1942.
Hedrick, Ulysses Prentiss. *A History of Agriculture in the State of New York*. New York: Hill & Wang, 1933.
Herity, Michael. *Irish Passage Graves*. New York: Barnes and Noble, 1975.
Herman, Zvi. *Peoples, Seas and Ships*. New York: G.P. Putnam's Sons, 1967.
Hett, W.H., trans. *Aristotle: Minor Works*. Cambridge: Harvard University Press, 1936.
Heyerdahl, Thor. *Fatu-Hiva: Back to Nature*. New York: Doubleday, 1974.
\_\_\_\_\_. *Kon-Tiki*. Chicago: Rand McNally, 1950.
\_\_\_\_\_. "Tigris Sails Into the Past." *National Geographic*, Dec. 1978.
\_\_\_\_\_. "The Voyage of RA II." *National Geographic*, 1971.
Holand, Hjalmar. *Explorations in America Before Columbus*. New York: Twayne, 1956.
\_\_\_\_\_. *Westward from Vinland*. New York: Duell Sloan & Pierce, 1970.
Holland, Rupert Sargent. *Historic Ships*. Philadelphia: Macrae Smith, 1926.
Hopkins, Alfred. *Modern Farm Buildings*. New York: Robert M. McBride, 1916.
Hovgaard, William. *The Voyages of the Northmen to America*. Boston: D.B. Updike, Merrymount Press, 1914.
*Hudson-Fulton Celebration*. New York: Trow Press, 1909.
Humphrey, Richard V. *The Mystery Hill Source Book*. Salem, Massachusetts: Teaparty Books, 1979.
Hyde, Arnout Jr. "Petroglyph Case Remains Open." *Wonderful West Virginia*, June 1986.
\_\_\_\_\_. "Wyoming and Boone County Petroglyphs Translated by Ancient Language Expert." *Wonderful West Virginia*, March 1983.
Hyde, Walter Woodburn. *Ancient Greek Mariners*. New York: Oxford University Press, 1947.
Ingstad, Helge. *Westward to Vinland*. New York: St. Martin's Press, 1969.
Irwin, Constance. *Fair Gods and Stone Faces*. New York: St. Martin's Press, 1963.
"Isles of the Pacific." *National Geographic*, Dec. 1974.
Jefferson, Thomas. *Notes on the State of Virginia*. New York: Harper Torchbooks, 1964.
Jennings, Gary. "Newfoundland Trusts in the Sea." *National Geographic*, Jan. 1974.
Jones, Charles C., Jr. *Antiquities of the Southern Indians*. New York: D. Appleton, 1873.
Jones, Horace Leonard, trans. *The Geography of Strabo*. London: William Heinemann, 1917.

Joyce, Thomas H. *Ancient Civilizations of the Andes.*
Kendrick, T.D. *The Druids.* London: Methuen, 1927.
Killanin, Lord and Michael V. Duignan. *The Shell Guide to Ireland.* London: Ebury Press, 1967.
La Fay, Howard. "The Vikings." *National Geographic,* April 1970.
Larsen, Karen. *A History of Norway.* New York: Princeton University Press, 1948.
Leask, Harold G. *Irish Churches and Monastic Buildings.* Dundalk, Ireland: Dundalgan Press, 1955.
Lethbridge, T.C. *Herdsmen and Hermits.* Cambridge: Bowes and Bowes, 1950.
Lewis, David. "Wind, Wave, Star, and Bird." *National Geographic,* December 1974.
Lockyer, Norman. *Stonehenge and Other British Stone Monuments.* London: Macmillan, 1906.
Macalister, R.A.S. *The Archeology of Ireland.* London: Methuen, 1928.
MacCulloch, J.A. *The Religion of the Ancient Celts.* Edinburgh: T and T Clark, 1911.
MacKendrick, Paul. *The Iberian Stones Speak.* New York: Funk and Wagnalls, 1969.
MacLean, J.P. *The Mound Builders.* Cincinnati: Robert Clarke, 1904.
Matthews, Samuel W. "The Phoenicians." *National Geographic,* April 1974.
McCracken, Harold. *George Catlin and the Old Frontier.* New York: 1959.
McCulloch, J. Huston. "The Newark Ohio Decalogue Stone and Keystone." Available at http://www.econ.ohio-state-edu/jhm/arch/decalog.html, January 23, 1998.
_____. "Some Reservations about the Newport Tower C-14 Dates." mcculloch.2@osu.edu, August 2001.
McGlone, William R., Phillip M. Leonard, James L. Guthrie, Rollin W. Gillespie, and James P. Whittall, Jr. *Ancient American Inscriptions: Plow Marks or History?* Independence, Missouri: Early Sites Research Society, 1993.
McNally, Kenneth. *The Islands of Ireland.* New York: W.W. Norton, 1978.
Means, Philip Ainsworth. *Newport Tower.* New York: Henry Holt, 1942.
Morgan, Lewis H. *League of the Iroquois.* New York: Dodd, Mead, 1904.
Morison, Samuel Eliot. *The European Discovery of America.* New York: Oxford University Press, 1971.
Mowat, Farley. *Westviking.* Boston: Little, Brown, 1965.
Nash, Hope. *Royalton Vermont.* Montpelier, Vermont: Royalton Historical Society, 1980.
Neudorfer, Giovanna. *Vermont's Stone Chambers.* Montpelier, Vermont: Vermont Historical Society, 1980.
O'Callaghan, E.B. *The Documentary History of the State of New York.* Albany, New York: Weed Parsons, 1850.
Olcott, Charles S. "The Orkneys and Shetlands—A Mysterious Group of Islands." *National Geographic,* 1921.
Oldfather, C.H., trans. *Diodorus of Sicily.* Cambridge: Harvard University Press, 1939.
Palfrey, John G. *History of New England.* Boston: Little, Brown, 1888.
"Pathfinders." *National Geographic,* Dec. 1974.
Peet, Stephen D. *The Mound Builders.* Chicago: Office of the American Antiquarian, 1903.
*Peoples and Places of the Past.* Washington, D.C.: National Geographic Society, 1983.
Perry, Clay. *Underground New England.* Battleboro, Vermont: Stephen Daye, 1939.
Petrie, W.M. Flinders. *The Formation of the Alphabet.* London: Macmillan, 1912.

Phelps, Charles Shepherd. *Rural Life in Litchfield County*. Connecticut: C.S. Phelps, 1912.
Phillips-Bert, Douglas. *The Building of Boats*. New York: W.W. Norton, 1979.
Pidgeon, William. *Traditions of Dee Coo Dah*. New York: Horace Thayer, 1858.
Piggott, Stuart. *Ancient Europe*. Aldive, 1965.
Pohl, Frederick Jr. *Atlantic Crossings Before Columbus*. New York: W.W. Norton, 1961.
_____. *The Lost Discovery*. New York: W.W. Norton, 1952.
Powell, John Wesley. *Twelfth Annual Report of the Bureau of American Ethnology to the Secretary of the Smithsonian Institution*. Washington, D.C.: U. S. Government Printing Office, 1894.
Rawlinson, George. *History of Phoenicia*. New York: Longmans, Green, 1889.
Renfrew, Colin. *Before Civilization*. New York: Alfred A. Knopf, 1973.
Rhodes, Daniel. *Kilns: Design, Construction, and Operation*, Radnor, Pennsylvania: Chilton, 1968.
Robbins, R.W., and E. Jones. *Hidden America*. New York: Alfred E. Knopf, 1966.
Robinson, Gregory. *Ships That Have Made History*. New York: Kennedy Brothers, 1936.
Roehm, Marjorie Catlin. *The Letters of George Catlin and His Family*. Berkeley: University of California Press, 1966.
Ruttenber, E.M. *History of the Indian Tribes of Hudson's River*. 1872. Reissued, Port Washington, New York: Kennikat Press, 1971.
Rudolph, Wolfgang. *Boats, Rafts, Ships*. New York: Van Nostrand Reinhold, 1974.
Sauer, Carl O. *Northern Mists*. Berkeley: University of California Press, 1968.
Scheltema, J.F. *Monumental Java*. London: Macmillan, 1912.
Schoolcraft, Henry R. *History, Condition, and Prospects of the Indian Tribes of the United States*. Philadelphia: Lippincott Grambo, 1852.
Severin, Timothy. "The Voyage of the 'Brendan.'" *National Geographic*, 1977.
Shetrone, Henry Clyde. *The Mound Builders*. New York: D. Appleton, 1930.
Shipp, Barnard. *The Indian and Antiquities of America*. Philadelphia: Sherman, 1897.
Silverberg, Robert. *Mound Builders of Ancient America*. Greenwich, Connecticut: New York Graphic Society, 1968.
Skelton, R.A., Thomas E. Marston, and George D. Painter. *The Vinland Map and the Tartar Relation*. New Haven: Yale University Press, 1965.
Slafter, Edmund F. *Voyages of the Northmen to America*. Boston: John Wilson & Son, 1877.
Sloane, Eric. *An Age of Barns*. New York: Funk & Wagnalls, 1967.
_____. *American Barns and Covered Bridges*. New York: Wilfred Funk, 1954.
_____. *Diary of an Early American Boy*. Noah Blake, 1805. New York: Wilfred Funk, 1962.
Smith, H.P. *History of Addison County, Vermont*. Syracuse, New York: D. Mason, 1886.
Snow, Dean R. *The Archeology of New England*. New York: Academic Press, 1980.
Squier, E.G. *Antiquities of the State of New York*. Buffalo: Geo. H. Derby, 1851.
Stanford, Dennis, and Bruce Bradley. "The Solutrean Solution." February 2000.
Stefansson, Vilhjalmur. *Great Adventures and Explorations*. New York: Dial Press, 1947.

Stone, Arthur F. *The Vermont of Today.* New York: Lewis Historical, 1929.
Stone, William Leete. *Life of Joseph Brant-Thayendanegea.* New York: George Dearborn, 1838.
*Stonewatch.* Newsletter of the Gungywamp Society, Noank, Conn., 1984–1998.
Stuart, George E. "Who Were 'The Mound Builders?" *National Geographic*, December 1972.
Taylor, Charles J. *History of Great Barrington, Mass.* Town of Great Barrington, Massachusetts, 1928.
Taylor, Isaac. *The Alphabet.* London: Kegan Paul, Trench, 1883.
Thomas, Cyrus. *The Indians of North America in Historic Times.* London: George Barrie & Sons, 1903.
Thompson, Gunnar. *American Discovery.* Seattle, Washington: Argonauts Misty Isles Press, 1994.
Thompson, Zadock. *History of Vermont.* Burlington: Chauncey Goodrich, 1842.
Torr, Cecil. *Ancient Ships.* Chicago: Argonaut, 1964.
Trento, Salvatore M. *The Search for Lost America.* Chicago: Contemporary Books, 1978.
Truettner, William H. *A Natural Man Observed: A Study of Catlins Indian Gallery.* Washington, D.C.: Smithsonian Institution Press, 1979.
*Universal Standard Encyclopedia.* New York: Unicorn, 1955.
Vail, Henry Hobart. *Pomfret, Vermont.* Boston: Cockayne, 1930.
Van Loon, Hendrick Willem. *Ships, and How They Sailed the Seven Seas.* New York: Simon and Schuster, 1935.
Vining, Edward P. *An Inglorious Columbus.* New York: D. Appleton, 1885.
Warrington, John, trans. *Caesar's War Commentaries.* New York: E.P. Dutton, 1958.
Weckler, J.E., Jr. *Polynesians, Explorers of the Pacific.* Washington, D.C.: Smithsonian Institution, 1943.
Whipple, A.B.C. *Tall Ships and Great Captains.* New York: Harper and Brothers, 1960.
Whipple, Chandler. *The Indian and the White Man in Massachusetts and Rhode Island.* Stockbridge, Massachusetts: Berkshire Traveler Press.
Whittall, James P., Jr. "Anforetas Recovered in Maine." *Bulletin of the Early Sites Research Society*, vol. 5 (1977).
\_\_\_\_\_. "Archeological Survey Drystone Chamber WD 16." ESRS *Bulletin*, vol. 7, no. 1 (May 1979).
\_\_\_\_\_. "Drawing—Underground Chamber, Newton, N.H." ESRS *Bulletin*, vol. 7, no. 1 (May 1979).
\_\_\_\_\_. "Excavation Report: Oracle Chamber Drain New Hampshire." ESRS *Bulletin*, vol. 5, no. 1 (Feb. 1977).
\_\_\_\_\_. "The Inscribed Stones of Sherbrooke, Quebec." ESRS *Bulletin*, vol. 4, no. 1 (May 1976).
\_\_\_\_\_. "The Mill River Inscription." ESRS *Bulletin*, May 1976.
\_\_\_\_\_. "The Monhegan Inscription." ESRS *Bulletin*, May 1976.
\_\_\_\_\_. Personal correspondence. 1984–1998.
\_\_\_\_\_. "A Report on the Pearson Stone Chamber, Upton, Massachusetts." ESRS *Bulletin*, vol. 7, no. 1 (May 1979).
\_\_\_\_\_. "A Runic Amulet." ESRS *Bulletin*, vol. 3, no. 1 (Mar. 1975).
\_\_\_\_\_. "Structure XI B—North Salem, N.H." ESRS *Bulletin*, 1977.
*Who's Who.* London: Adam and Charles Black, 1983.
Wilkins, Thurman. *Cherokee Tragedy.* London: Macmillan, 1970.

Willoughby, Charles C. *Antiquities of the New England Indians.* Cambridge, Massachusetts: Peabody Museum of American Archeology and Ethnology, 1935.

Wilson, Daniel. *Prehistoric Annals of Scotland.* London: Macmillan, 1863.

Winlock, H.E. *Models of Daily Life in Ancient Egypt.* Cambridge: Harvard University Press, 1955.

Wood, John Edward. *Sun, Moon, and Standing Stones.* London: Oxford University Press, 1971.

Wood-Martin, W.G. *Pagan Ireland.* London: Longmans, Green, 1895.

# Index

Abbott, John  285, 289
Abnaki Indians  269
Acapana Pyramid, Peru  265
Adam of Bremen  48, 56
Adamnan, Abbot of Iona  177
Adena culture  247, 249–251, 254–259, 261–264, 267, 269, 270, 272, 278, 279
Airne, C.W.  289
Alaska Historical Museum  240
Aldrich, Lewis Cass  286, 289
Alexander the Great  93, 119
Algonquian Confederation  219
Algonquian Indians  61, 200, 233, 246, 247, 253, 254, 258, 259, 262, 269, 270, 279
Allen, Dr. F.J.  81
Allen, John  289
Alrutz, Bob  230
American Association for the Advancement of Science  224
American Ethnological Society  10
America's Stonehenge  141, 145–158, 172, 175, 181, 200, 262, 266, 277, 281, 286, 287
Amyntus II  92
Anderson, Joseph  193, 194, 287, 289
Anderson, J.R.L.  289
Anderson, Magnus  35, 36
Andress, Gene  237, 238
L'Anse aux Meadows  4, 23, 59–64, 140, 247, 274, 282
Antoninus Pius  244
Antony, Marc  67, 96
Anubis Caves  227, 228
Aptuxcet Stone *see* Bourne Stone
Aptuxcet Trading Post  65, 220
Arabic coins  243
Archaic Period  253, 255, 276

Archer-Hind, R.D  286, 289
Aristocles *see* Plato
Aristotle  91–93, 98, 140, 279, 286
Arnold, Gov. Benedict  78, 81
Arnold, Samuel Greene  289
Asbrandson, Bjorn  56
Athelstan, King  193
Attila the Hun  176
Atwater, Caleb  2, 8, 9, 12, 200, 260, 288
Augustus, Caesar  125
Avienus, Rufus Festus  97, 131
Aztec Indians  282

Bacon, Edgar Mayhew  289
Bailey, Paul  289
Bakeman, Norman  239
Baldwin, James, D.  289
Bar Kochba  244
Barber, John Warner  289
Bardson, Ivar  57
Barron, David P.  185, 186, 258, 272, 287, 289
Bartlett, N.H. Dolmen  196
Bartram, Mr.  255
Bat Creek Stone  211, 212, 235, 244, 274, 275, 278, 280
Bath Marine Museum  67
Baxter, James Phinney  289
Beardmore  69
Beard's Fork Petroglyph  233
Belzoni, Giovanni Battista  3
Bethune, Andre J., Emeritus Professor  86
Betts, Edwin Morris,  289
Bibby, Geoffrey  289
Biggs, Thomas  215
Bird, Dr. Junius  150, 151
Bjorndal, Magnus  85

## Index

Black, Adam 296
Black, Charles 296
Blackett, W.S. 286
Blaine, Joseph 85
Blake, Robert C. 289
Blake, William J. 289
Bogart, Ernest L. 290
Bohuslan, Sweden 43, 62, 277
Boland, Charles, M. 85, 236, 286, 287, 290
Boone County Petroglyph 233
Bord Failte 257
Boston College 86
Bourne, Richard 220
Bourne, MA 219
Bourne Historical Society 220
Bourne Stone 65, 219–221, 235, 279
Bradley, Bruce 272
Brant, Joseph 267, 268, 288
Brash, Richard Holt 178, 287, 290
Braxton Tablet 65, 218
*Brendan* (vessel) 31, 38, 39, 285
Brendan the Navigator (saint) 38, 99, 104–108, 113, 114, 121, 139, 140, 281
Brian Boru, King 45
Briard, Jacques 290
Brine, Lindesay 290
Brittain, Alfred 290
Bromptonville, Quebec, Canada 222, 223
Brookhaven Laboratory *see* U.S. Department of Energy
Brooklin, ME 4, 66, 88, 274, 283
Brown, J. Macmillan 290
Bryant, W.C. 102, 111, 286, 290
Buchanan, Ann 228
Buchanan, Donal 68, 217–219, 228, 240, 287, 288, 290
Buck, Peter H. 22, 23, 290
Bureau of Ethnology *see* Smithsonian Institution
Burrows, Russell 234, 290
Burrows Cave 234
Bury, R.G. 290
Byrd, Dr. Junius 151

Cabral, Pedro Alvares 28, 29, 40, 96, 121, 139
Caesar, Gaius Julius 96, 123, 280, 295
Cahill, Robert Ellis 290
Cahill, Thomas 72
Cahokia, IL 264–266, 268

Caligula, Emperor 125
Canaanite script *see* Hebrew script
Canadian Institute, Toronto 170, 171
Canby, Courtland 290
Carpenter, Rhys 290
Carpini, Friar 70
Carter, George 272
Carter, Howard 3
Carthaginian coins 242, 245, 273, 279
Casson, Lionel 290
Catholic University, Washington, D.C. 232
Catlin, George 110, 268, 293, 294
Ceram, C.W. 290
Chan-Chan 30
Chang, Ziang Ling 241
Chapman, Paul H. 48, 58, 60, 62, 63, 68, 69, 84, 140
Charles I, King 82, 88
Chatterton, E. Kebble 290
Cheesman, Dr. Paul 218
Cherokee Indians 109, 110, 198–200, 210, 218, 219, 249, 265, 269
Cherokee script 210, 219, 235, 274
Chichen Itza, Mexico 265
Child, Hamilton 125, 286, 290
Childe, V. Gordon 290
Childress, David Hatcher 290
Chimu culture 30
Choctaw Indians 255, 265, 270
Christ (Jesus) 228, 232, 274
Clark, Gen. George Rogers 268
Clarke, Graham 290
Clemens, Dr. James 215
Cleopatra, Queen 67
Cliffside 227
Clodd, Edward 290
Clovis, NM 251, 252
Coddington, William 83
Cole Harbor Axe 70
Columbus, Christopher 1, 4, 15, 27, 36, 59, 72, 99, 101, 108, 116, 121, 126, 202, 242, 243, 274, 282, 283, 286, 295
Columcille (saint) 185
Connecticut State Historical Society 169
Constantine the Great 134, 244
Cook, Dr. Warren 291
Coptic cuneiform script 234
Cormac 177, 280, 281
Cornplanter (Indian chief) 268
Costa, Joachim Alves da 208, 279
Cox, Donald W. 291

## Index

Crack Cave 227
Creek Indians 200, 249, 269, 270
Cunliffe, Barry 291
Cyr, Donald L. 291

Darius the Great 119
Davenport, IA 225, 226
Davenport Tablets 225, 226, 251
Davis, Doug 237, 238
Davis, Dr. E.H. 2, 10, 11
Dawson, Henry B. 291
Deacon, Richard 291
Deal, David 228–230, 233, 234
Decalogue Stone *see* Newark Holy Stones
Dee Coo Dah 260, 261, 263, 288, 294
Delabarre, Edmund Burke 291
Delaware Indians 263, 265, 270
Delf Norona Museum 215
Demosthenes 91
Dennison University 230
De Soto, Hernando 1, 265
Dexter, Warren W. 199
Dicuil 49, 176, 177
Dighton Rock 64
Dillehay, Tom 252
Diodorus 95, 96, 98, 140, 280, 286
Director of History and Geography, Brazil 208
Diringer, David 291
Division of Ethnology, U.S. National Museum 16
Dix, Byron E. 164, 182, 287, 291
Dixon, E. James 272, 291
Dodd, James E. 69
Dodge, John 185
Dowden, John 178, 179, 287
Drogea 111
Du Chaillu, Paul B. 43, 44, 47, 62, 86, 194, 285, 287, 291
Duff, Thomas A. 291
Duignan, Michael V. 293
Dunnell, Robert 218
Durrett, Reuben T. 291

Early Sites Research Society (ESRS) 67, 68, 82, 86, 113, 171, 217, 221, 239, 291
Eastern Woodland culture 254, 255, 269, 278
Egyptian Hieroglyphics 141, 204, 227, 279
Eklton 208

Elk Nation 261
Elliott, Walter 66, 67, 272
Emmanuel I, King 28
Emory, Kenneth P. 17, 22, 285, 291
Enterline, James Robert 291
Eochy, King 195
Eogan, Dr. George 173
Epigraphic Society 68, 171, 221, 225
Eratosthenes 94
Erik the Red 48–50, 52, 54, 107, 282
Erikson, Freydis 57
Erikson, Leif 38, 48, 52–55, 57, 71, 72, 107, 121, 140, 222, 248, 274, 282
Erikson, Magnus, King 75
Erikson, Thorhild 49
Erikson, Thorstein 54
Erikson, Thorvald 49, 52
Erikson, Thorwald 54, 55, 57
ESRS Bulletin 67, 68, 218, 239, 240, 285, 287, 288, 290, 291, 295, 296
Estotiland 111, 112
Etbaal, King of Tyre 208
Etowah Mound, GA 264
Etruscan script 86, 204, 205, 216
Eudoxus 133
Euphemus 97
Evans, Estyn 291
Evans, John G. 291
Eyulf Soer 49

Fa-Hsien 100
Farfall, Peter 221
Farley, Gloria 73, 209, 223, 224, 227, 228, 235, 272, 288
Farquharson, Dr. 226
Fell, Dr. Barry 70, 152, 157, 170, 209, 217, 221–223, 225–228, 232, 235, 237, 240, 253, 288
Ferdinand, King 283
Fergusson, James 193, 287, 291
Fidelis 177
Finney, Ben R. 30, 34, 139, 291
Fionn-Barr 105
Fiske, Daniel 171, 291
Fite, E.D. 286, 291
*Flateyjarbok* (Flatey Book) 51
Fletcher, Dr. Richard 65, 222
Folgar, Capt. 36
Folsom, NM 251
Foster, J.W. 287, 291
Fowke, Gerard 171, 291
Franklin, Benjamin 169

## Index

Frazer, J.G. 286, 292
Freeman, A. 286, 291
Frode, Ari 48
Furdurstrands 55
Furman, Gabriel 292
Furneaux, Rupert 292
Fu-sang 99, 101–103, 281

Gabriel, Ralph Henry 292
Gaelic script *see* Iberic script
Gallagher, Ida Jane 232, 233, 288, 292
Gallatin, Albert 10
Gaskill, Samuel R. 238
Geological and Geographical Survey of the Territories 13
Gifford, Edward W. 17
Gillespie, Rollin 227, 293
Gjerset, Knut 42, 43, 177, 285, 287, 292
Glooscap 113
Glynn, Frank 113, 151, 152, 198
Godfrey, William 85
Going, Charles Buxton 153, 154, 174, 191, 193, 286, 287, 292
Goodwin, William 113, 148–151, 286, 292
Gordian III 244
Gordon, Dr. Cyrus 67, 75, 76, 209, 211, 272, 274, 287, 292
Goshen, MA, Souterrain 184
Grave Creek, WV 211, 213, 215, 217, 235, 249, 258
Grave Creek Stone (tablet) 65, 202, 211, 213–219, 235, 251, 258, 275, 278, 279
Great Barrington, MA, Cairn 199
Great Ireland (or Greater Ireland) 50, 55, 56, 107, 113, 282
Great Serpent Mound, OH 256
Griffin, James B. 292
Gudlaugson, Gudlief 56
Guess, George 210
Guignes, M. de 101
Gungywamp Complex 141, 171, 185, 186, 281, 287
Gungywamp Society 186
Gunnbjorn 49
Gutenberg, Johann 233
Guthrie, Jim 227, 293
Gutton Owen 108
Gwynedd, David 108
Gwynedd, Edward 108
Gwynedd, Howel 108
Gwynedd, Owen 108

Hall, Benjamin H. 292
Hamlin, Dr. Augustus E. 224
Hanging Rock 227
Hanno, King 97, 121, 131–133, 221, 279
Hanta 223
Harbison, Peter 292
Harden, Donald 292
Harkon Jarl 48
Harold, King 46
Harold Fairhair (Viking chief) 49, 194
Harvard University 222
Hatfield, Fred A. 66
Hatshepsut, Queen 118
Haugen Einar 292
Hauksbok 48
Heavener Runestone 72, 73
Hebrew script 141, 203, 205, 206, 210–212, 228–230, 235, 274, 279, 280
Hedrick, Ulysses Prentiss 168, 286, 292
Heinemeier, Jan 86, 87
Helluland 52
Hencken, Hugh 150
Henricus, Bishop *see* Knuppsen, Eric, Bishop
Henry, John 13
Herity, Michael 292
Herjulf 51
Herjulfsson, Bjarni 46, 48, 50–52, 71, 72
Herman, Zvi 97, 127, 287, 292
Herodotus 90
Hett, W.H. 286, 292
Heyerdahl, Liv 29, 115, 292
Heyerdahl, Thor 3, 29–34, 36–38, 116, 139, 285
Hicklin Springs 227
Hidden Mountain, Los Lunas, NM 228–230
Himilco 121, 131, 132, 279
Hippalos 133, 134
Hiram the Great 129, 134, 209, 223, 278
Hodgson, W. B. 216
Hoei-Shin 99–104, 113, 114, 121, 140, 281
Hokule'a 31, 34, 35, 39
Holand, Hjalmar, R. 75, 76, 272, 285, 292
Holland, Robert Sargent 292
Holmes, Frank R. 286
Holmes, Tommy 34
Honorius 125
Hop (Hoop) 55, 69
Hope, Nash 170
Hopeton, OH 9, 255–257

Hopewell culture  247, 249, 258–264, 267, 269, 270, 279, 282
Hopkins, Alfred  166, 286, 292
Horse Creek Petroglyph  233, 235
Horsford, Cornelia  170
Hovgaard, William  292
Howe, James V.  237
Howland, John  70
Humanitas Americana  104
Humphrey, Richard V.  286, 292
Hyde, Arnout, Jr.  232, 233, 292

Iberic script  141, 157, 170, 202, 203, 205, 207, 216–219, 221–223, 227, 235, 275
Icaria  112
Illinois Wesleyan University  13
Inca Indians  139
Indiana Jones  223
Ingstad, Helge  4, 59, 62, 63, 140, 169, 272, 274, 293
Iroquois Indians  247, 248, 265, 267
Irwin, Constance  293
Isabella, Queen  283
Islendingabok  48
Ithobal  134

Jackson, Andrew  220
Jefferson, Thomas  2, 7, 8, 12, 167, 200, 249, 251, 285, 288, 293
Jefferson County Mound, AR  265
Jennings, Gary  60, 255, 285, 293
Johnson, David M.  232
Johnson, Gertrude  221
Johnson-Bradner Stone  232
Jomard, Prof. M.  216
Jomon culture  4
Jones, C.C.  198–200, 249, 287, 288, 293
Jones, Horace Leonard  286, 293
Jones, Indiana  223
Jones, Inigo  81
Jones, the Rev. Morgan  109
Jonnard, M.  216
Joyce, Thomas H.  293
Jugner, Hogne  86

Kane, Herb Kawainui  19, 30, 34, 139
Karlsefni, Gudrid  55
Karlsefni, Snorri  55
Karlsefni, Thorfinn  54–57, 68, 69, 140, 282
Keelness  54, 55

Keenan (saint)  178
Keithahn, Edward L.  288
Kemble, Mr.  193
Kendrick, T.D.  293
Kennedy, John F.  284
Kennewick Man  4, 252
Kensington Runestone  73–78, 88, 207, 275, 283
Kensington Runestone Museum  see Runestone Museum
Kent Cliffs, NY, Stone Chamber  179
Killanin, Lord  293
Kingsbury, Claudia  233
Kinnelon, NJ, Dolmen  196
Knapp, James  238, 239
Knapp Tablet  238, 239
Knuppsen, Eric, Bishop of Greenland  57, 72, 78, 85, 274
Knutson, Paul  57, 76, 77, 140, 283
Kon  30
Kon-Tiki  3, 30–34, 36, 281, 292
Kormac  see Cormac
Kristni Saga  48
Krossaness  54

La Fay, Howard  45, 285, 293
Lake Nipigon  69, 70, 77, 283
Lamoka  253
Landnamabok  48, 50
L'Anse aux Meadows  4, 23, 59–64, 140, 247, 274, 282
Lapita pottery  17, 18
Laporte, the Rev. J.A.  222
Larsen, Karen  293
LaSalle  1
Latin script  71, 203
Laurentian  253
Leask, Harold G.  293
Le Musée du Séminaire de Sherbrooke  see Museum of the Seminary
Lenni Lenape Indians  see Delaware Indians
Leonard, Phil  227, 228, 293
Le Rouzic, M.  154
Lethbridge, Thomas C.  113, 175, 293
Lewis, David  20, 21, 285, 293
Libyan script  70, 141, 202, 203, 205, 223, 227, 228, 279
Li-Yan-Chen  100, 101
Lloyd, Dr.  109
Lockyer, Norman  293
Longfellow, Henry Wadsworth  65

Los Lunas Decalogue Stone  229, 230, 235
Los Lunas Petroglyph  229
Lovfald, Peer  85
Lynn, MA, Dolmen  196

Macalister, R.A.S.  173, 174, 183, 184, 192, 193, 196, 287, 293
MacCulloch, J.A.  293
Machu Picchu  30
MacKendrick, Paul  293
MacLean, J.P.  216, 217, 268, 287, 288, 293
Madoc, Prince of Wales  99, 108–110, 114, 121, 140, 268, 270, 283
Magnus Erikson, King of Norway  57, 75
Mandan Indians  110, 114, 268, 270, 283
Marcus Aurelius  155
Marietta, OH  9
Markland  52, 55, 60, 61, 283
Marson, Ari  48, 50, 56
Marston, Dr. Thomas E.  71
Mary (mother of Jesus)  232
Mason, Sharon  185, 186, 287
Massasoit  219
Mather, the Rev. Cotton  2, 7, 8, 64, 169
Matthews, Samuel W.  293
Mavor, James W., Jr.  182, 291
May, Wayne N.  289
Mayan culture  103, 107, 111, 113, 259, 263, 265, 269, 275
McCabe, E.P.  222
McCracken Harold  293
McCulloch, Prof. J. Huston  87, 211, 230, 231, 293
McGee, W.J.  171
McGlone, Bill  227, 228, 234, 288, 293
McNally, Kenneth  293
McNeil, Janet  153, 161, 163, 220
McNeil, Michael  25, 26
McNeil, William  163, 220
Means, Philip Ainsworth  81, 85, 285, 293
Meggers, Dr. Betty J.  4, 252, 272, 284
Mela, Pomponius  134
Mercator, Gerald  83, 84, 87, 275
Mernoc  105
Mertz, Henriette  211, 233, 272
Meyer, Prof. Robert T.  232, 233
Miamisburg Mound, OH  9, 249
Micmac Indians  112, 113
Middletown Archaeological Research Center (MARC)  170, 185, 200, 239

Milesius, King  192
Mill River Stone  221, 235
Mississippian culture  247, 249, 263–267, 269–272, 282
Mochica culture  265
Mohawk Indians  200, 267, 269
Monge, Alf  75, 76, 85
Monhegan Inscription  224, 225
Monks Mound, Cahokia, IL  265, 266
Monte Verde, Chile  252, 269
Monument Mountain Cairn  see  Great Barrington Cairn
Morgan, Lewis H.  293
Mormon Church Archives, Salt Lake City, UT  233
Morrison, Samuel Eliot  293
Morristown Tablet  218, 219
Morton, Dr. Samuel G.  216, 217
Mound Builders  11–14, 141, 216, 230, 233, 246, 247, 249–251, 261, 270, 275, 287, 288
Mound State Monument, AL  264
Moundville, AL  264
Moundville *Daily Echo*  218
Moundsville, WV  213
Mowatt, Farley  293
Muscogee Indians  237
Museum of the Seminary, Sherbrooke, Canada  222
Mystery Hill  see  America's Stonehenge

Narragansett Bay Runestone  73
Nash, Hope  293
National Museum, Rio de Janeiro  208
Nebuchadnezzar, King  131
Necho II, Pharaoh  90, 119, 129, 278
Neilsen, Dr. Richard  73, 76
Netto, Dr. Ladislau  208, 209
Neudorfer, Giovanna  159, 160, 165–167, 187, 293
New Amsterdam  219
New England Antiquities Research Association (NEARA)  73, 152, 172, 185
Newark, OH  230, 232, 255, 260, 261
Newark Decalogue Stones  230–232, 235, 288, 293
Newark Keystone  230, 231
Newport, RI  3, 78, 81, 83–88, 275
Newport City Council  86
Newport Historical Society  85
Newport Tower  2, 3, 78–88, 113, 275, 283, 285, 286

Newton, NH, Stone Chamber  172, 282
Nicomachus  92
Nisbet, William  225
North Salem, NY, Dolmen  141, 196, 197
North Salem, NY, Stone Chamber  171, 172, 179
North Salem Historical Society  196
Notre Dame University  233
Numismatic and Antiquarian Society of Philadelphia  65

O'Callaghan, E. B.  172, 287, 293
Oconostota, Chief  109, 110
O'Donovan, John  287
Ogam script  68, 141, 170, 202, 205, 216, 223, 225, 227, 228, 232, 233, 279
Ogygia  96, 280
Ohio County Stone  218, 219
Ohio State University  211
Ohman, Olaf  74–76
Olaf, King  47
Olafsson  283
Olcott, Charles S.  294
Oldfather, C.H.  286, 294
Olmec culture  103, 104, 255, 271, 272, 275, 277, 278, 279
O'Neil of the Nine Hostages  107
Owen, Guttun  108

Page, Prof.  216
Palfrey, John G.  294
Paraiba Inscription  209
Pascal, Pope  72
Patrick, St.  178, 193, 241
Pattee, Jonathon  147, 148, 150, 156
Paul, Saint  105
Pausanius  97, 286, 292
Payto, Sir Edward  81
Pearson, Malcolm  68, 74, 181
Peet, the Rev. Stephen D.  257, 294
Pemberton Axe  238
Penhallow, William  87
Perry, Clay  113, 147, 286, 294
Peterborough Petroglyph, Canada  43, 253, 277
Petrie, W.M. Flinders  294
Phelps, Charles Shepherd  294
Phillips-Bert, Douglas  294
Phoenician script  141, 202, 203, 205, 206, 208, 209, 216, 235, 278, 279
Pidgeon, William  260–262, 288, 294
Piggott, Stuart  294

Pinto, Francisco  208
Plato  91–93, 98, 286
Pliny  178
Plowden, Sir Edmund  82, 88, 275
Plutarch  96–98, 242, 280, 286
Plymouth Plantation  219
Pohl, Frederick, Jr.  82, 83, 112, 113, 294
Polynesian Voyaging Society  34
Poulsen, Dr. Jens  18
Poverty Point, LA  271, 277, 278
Powell, John Wesley  3, 11–14, 210, 226, 287, 294
Probus  241
Ptolemy I  119
Ptolemy II  133
Punic script  see  Phoenician script
Putnam Museum, Davenport, IA  225
Putnam Valley Complex  185
Pyle, Robert L.  232
Pynchon, John  171, 185
Pyramid of the Sun, Peru  265
Pytheas  120–122, 242, 279

Quetzlcoatl  282

RA I  37
RA II  31, 37– 39, 285, 292
Rafn, Prof. Charles Christian  64, 78, 216
Rafn the Duellist  49
Ramos, Don Bernardo da Silva  208, 278
Ramses II  118
Ras, Chief  223, 224
Rawlinson, George  129–131, 134, 206, 286, 294
Renfrew, Colin  294
Rhodes, Daniel  294
Ring, Sigurd  194
*Roald Amundsen*  36
Robbins, R.W.  294
Robinson, Gregory  294
Rocky Nook Axe  70
Roehm, Marjorie Catlin  294
Roman coins  241–245, 280
Roman script  see  Latin script
Ronan, Ernest  208
Royal Academy, London  2, 7, 64
Royal Library, Copenhagen, Denmark  76
Royal Ontario Museum  69, 70
Royal Society, Denmark  64, 78

Royalton Chamber, Vermont *see* South Royalton
Rudolph, Wolfgang 294
Ruff, Eric J. 222, 288
Runestone Museum, Kensington, MN 73, 76
Runic script 65, 67, 68–70, 72–77, 85, 86, 88, 141, 203, 216, 222, 275
Rutenber, E.M. 294
Rydholm, Fred 290

Sandy Island 268, 283
Sauer, Carl O. 294
Savage, the Rev. Dean 233
Scheltema, J.F. 294
Schliemann, Heinrich 3
Schoolcraft, Henry Rowe 2, 10, 64, 169, 200, 211, 214–217, 250, 254, 258, 285, 287, 288, 294
Scientific Exploration and Archaeology Society (SEAS) 239
Scribners History 247, 248, 286
Semitic script *see* Hebrew script
Septimius Severus 134
Sequoyah *see* Guess, George
Seti I, Pharaoh 3
Severin, Dorothy 38
Severin, Timothy 38–40, 139, 285, 294
Sevier, Gov. John 109
Shawnee Indians 263, 265, 270
Sherbrooke Stones 222, 223
Shetrone, Henry Clyde 294
Shields, Tony 232
Shipp, Barnard 255, 256, 288, 294
Shutler, Dr. Richard, Jr. 17
Sigmund 48
Silverberg, Robert 255, 294
Sinclair, Prince Henry 83, 99, 110–114, 121, 140, 283
Sioux Indians 199, 200
Skeleton in Armor 65
Skelton, R.A. 294
Slafter, the Rev. Edmund F. 44, 57, 295
Sloane, Eric 167, 295
Smith, H.P. 168, 286, 295
Smith, Joseph 164
Smithsonian Institution 3, 4, 11, 13, 14, 71, 171, 198, 210–212, 226, 237, 252, 274, 284; 12th annual report 3, 14, 198, 250, 287, 294
Snow, Dean R. 295
Socrates 91

Soer, Eyulf 49
Solomon, King 129
Solutrean culture 252
Soper, Dan E. 233
Soper-Savage Stones, MI 233, 234
Soucy, Ludger 223
South Royalton, VT, Stone Chamber 164, 167, 181, 182, 262
South Woodstock, VT, Stone Chamber 141, 162–164, 166, 167, 179, 180
Spencer, Mr. 255
Spirit Cave Man 252
Spirit Pond Runestones 4, 66–69, 88, 275, 283, 285
Spiro Mound, OK 264
Squier, George 2, 10, 11, 216, 295
Stallings Island, GA 272, 276
Stanford, Dennis 4, 252, 253, 272, 284, 288, 295
Stefansson, Vilhjalmur 295
Stewart, Capt. Isaac 109
Stoddard, Maj. Amos 109
Stone, Arthur F. 295
Stone, Jerry 233
Stone, Robert E. 153, 200
Stone, Steve 233
Stone, William Leete 267, 268, 288, 295
Strabo 93, 94, 98, 286
Straumfjord 55
Stuart, George E. 295
Stuart, Gilbert 84
Sueno, King of Denmark 56

Tacitus 43, 178
Tadach 215, 217
Tappawingow, Chief 237, 238
Taylor, Charles J. 199, 287, 295
Taylor, Isaac 295
Taylor, the Rev. John 172
Thayendanegea *see* Brant, Joseph
Theodosius the Great 125
Thomas, Cyrus 3, 13, 14, 210, 216, 226, 287, 288, 295
Thompson, Gunnar 295
Thompson, Zadock 168, 286, 295
Thorgest 49
Thurid 56
Tiberius Caesar 133
Tifinagh script *see* Libyan script
*Tigris* (vessel) 31, 116, 292
Tiki 30, 281
Tipton, Mr. 210

Tobacco, Chief 268
Tomlinson, Abelard 213–215
Tomlinson, Jesse 213
Tomlinson, Joseph 213
Torr, Cecil 295
Trento, Salvatore 97, 160, 164, 170, 185, 196, 198, 200, 238, 239, 286, 288, 295
Truettner, William H. 295
Tupper, Thomas 220
Turkey Mountain, Oklahoma inscriptions 223
Tuscarora Indians 109
Tutankhamen, pharaoh 3
Tyrker 53

Ulanky, Charles 240
Ulpian 134
Ultima Thule 121, 279
Ungava Bay 61, 62, 77
U.S. Department of Energy, Brookhaven Laboratory 72
United States War Department 31
University College, Dublin 173
University of California at Davis 71, 72
University of Kentucky 252
University of Maine 239
Upton, MA, Beehive Stone Chamber 141, 161, 162, 164, 171, 173, 177, 182, 262, 282, 287
Uvaege 55
Uxmal, Mexico 265

Vail, Henry Hobart 168, 286, 295
Valdivia 4, 252, 269
Van Loon, Hendrick Willem 295
Vathelldi 55
Vermont Division for Historic Preservation 165
Vermont Historical Society 168
Verrazano, Giovanni 83, 87, 275
*Viking* (vessel) 31, 36
Viking coin 66, 88, 140, 243, 245, 274, 283
Viking Ship Museum, Roskilde, Denmark 47
Vincent of Beauvais 71
Vining, Edward P. 101, 103, 286, 295
Vinland 53–63, 68–72, 75–78, 140, 274, 282
Vinland map 70–72, 74, 87, 274
Viscelius, Gary 151

Wampanoag Indians 219
Warrington, John 295
Washburn, Wilcomb E. 71
Washington County, MS 9
Washington, MA, Cairn 196, 198
Webster, MA, Stone Chamber 164, 180, 181, 183, 184
Weckler, J.E., Jr. 16, 285, 295
West Virginia Department of Culture and History 218
West Virginia State Museum 218
Western Chippewa Indians 199, 200
Westford Knight 113, 114
Wharton, Col. James E. 215
Whipple, A.B.C. 295
Whipple, Chandler 295
White (name inscribed on Turkey Mountain) 223
White Indians 109, 110, 267, 268, 270, 283
White Man's Land *see* Great Ireland
Whittall, James P. II 67, 68, 83, 86, 113, 151, 152, 171, 172, 186, 221, 224, 225, 239, 240, 243, 244, 272, 285–288, 293, 295
Whittlesey, Col. Charles 216
Wilkins, Thurman 296
William the Conqueror 46
Williams, Prof. Henrik 76
Williams, John 171
Willoughby, Charles C. 296
Wilson, Daniel 296
Wilson, Ord Blaine 218
Windham County, VT, Souterrain 172, 184, 281
Winlock, H.E. 296
Winnebago Indians 12
Winthrop, John, Jr. 171, 185
Witten, Lawrence 70, 71
Woden-Lithi 253, 277
Wood, John Edward 296
Wood, William 83, 84, 87, 275
Wood-Martin, W.G. 177, 178, 185, 287, 296
Woodruff, Mr. 267
Wuthenau, Alejandro von 104, 271, 275
Wyoming County Petroglyph 232, 233, 235
Wyrick, David 230

Xu, Michael 272

Yale University Library 71, 274
Yarmouth County Historical Society 222
Yarmouth County Museum 65, 222
Yarmouth Stone 65, 66, 222, 235, 275

Zeno, Antonio 99, 107, 110–112, 114, 140
Zeno, Nicolo 99, 107, 110–112, 114
Zoser, King 265, 276

www.ingramcontent.com/pod-product-compliance
Ingram Content Group UK Ltd.
Pitfield, Milton Keynes, MK11 3LW, UK
UKHW041925140426
5217IPUK00014B/313